Episcopal Church

The Hymnal Revised and Enlarged

Being the Preliminary Report of the Committee on the Hymnal...

Episcopal Church

The Hymnal Revised and Enlarged
Being the Preliminary Report of the Committee on the Hymnal...

ISBN/EAN: 9783337100506

Printed in Europe, USA, Canada, Australia, Japan

Cover: Foto ©ninafisch / pixelio.de

More available books at **www.hansebooks.com**

THE HYMNAL

REVISED AND ENLARGED

BEING THE PRELIMINARY REPORT OF THE
COMMITTEE ON THE HYMNAL, APPOINTED
BY THE GENERAL CONVENTION OF 1886

NEW YORK
JAMES POTT & CO., PUBLISHERS
1889

PREFACE.

The Committee on the Hymnal has been occupied for nearly two years and a half in the discharge of the duty intrusted to it by the General Convention. It is not prepared, nor is it yet required by the resolution under which it was appointed, to publish its full report, with the final shape in which the Hymnal may be recommended to the Convention. But the work has so far progressed that it has been decided to print the results at present reached, in order that the Church may have abundant time for a careful examination of them.

In its task of selection and arrangement, the Committee had it in view:

To make a distinction between hymns for common and hymns for special use, placing the latter in an Appendix, yet with continuous numbering, so that they may be available at any and all times;

To make larger provision than heretofore for Holy Days and for special events;

To secure a number of hymns appropriate to the later portions of the longer festival seasons;

To place as many as possible of the hymns for the various seasons under the heading of "General," where they can be readily found by means of the first-line references, and yet where they will more naturally come into use throughout the year;

To group together, as far as possible, the hymns placed under that heading, according to their thought, and to arrange them generally after the plan of the book itself;

To use plural pronouns wherever it was possible;

To separate slightly between the fourth and fifth lines of eight-line hymns so as to facilitate the use of single tunes; also, to secure an even number of verses in four-line hymns, so that double tunes might be available when preferred;

To print Amens only when following a petition or an ascription of praise.

An Index of Subjects has been provided as well as references by first lines.

Thanks are due and rendered for permission to use Hymns from other selections.

Committee.
W. C. Doane, D.D., Bp. of Albany, *Chairman,*
B. H. Paddock, D.D., Bp. of Massachusetts,
F. Courtney, D.D.,
Samuel Benedict, D.D.,
A. Z. Gray, D.D.,
H. W. Nelson, Jr., *Secretary,*
Henry Coppée,
James S. Biddle,
W. K. Ackerman.

CONTENTS.

I. DAILY PRAYER

	HYMNS
Morning	1– 9
Evening	10– 26
The Lord's Day	27– 38

II. THE CHRISTIAN YEAR.

Advent	39– 52
Christmas	53– 63
Epiphany	64– 75
Septuagesima, etc.	76– 81
Lent	82– 88
Holy Week	89–102
Easter Even	103–106
Eastertide	107–121
Ascensiontide	122–127
Whitsuntide	128–131
Trinity Sunday	132–137
St. Andrew	138, 139
St. Thomas	140, 141
St. Stephen	142, 143
St. John Evangelist	144, 145
The Holy Innocents	146–148
The Circumcision	149, 150
The Conversion of St. Paul	151, 152
The Purification	153–156
St. Matthias	157
The Annunciation	158, 159
St. Mark	160
St. Philip and St. James	161, 162
St. Barnabas	163, 164
The Nativity of St. John Baptist	165, 166
St. Peter	167, 168
St. James	169, 170

	HYMNS
The Transfiguration	171–173
St. Bartholomew	174
St. Matthew	175
St. Michael and All Angels	176–178
St. Luke	179, 180
St. Simon and St. Jude	181, 182
General for Saints' Days	183
All Saints	184–191
Ember Days	192–198
Rogation Days	199–203
Thanksgiving Day	204–210

III. THE CHURCH.

Holy Communion	211–228
Holy Baptism	229–234
Confirmation	235–244
Holy Matrimony	245–247
Burial of the Dead	248–255
Ordination	256–259
Institution of Ministers	260

IV. THE HOLY SCRIPTURES... 261–264

V. SPECIAL OCCASIONS.

Laying of a Corner-Stone	265–268
Consecration of Churches	269–271
Restoration of a Church	272
Missions, at Home	273
Missions Abroad	274–284
For the Jews	285–287
Charities	288–292
Almsgiving	293–297
National Festivals and Fasts	298–303

	HYMNS		HYMNS
THE OLD YEAR	304–306	IX. LITANIES	552–563
THE NEW YEAR	307, 308		
FOR THOSE AT SEA	309–314	X. APPENDIX.	
FOR TRAVELERS BY LAND OR SEA	315	CHILDREN'S SERVICES	564–611
		PAROCHIAL MISSIONS	612–645
VI. THE CHRISTIAN LIFE	316–357	LAY HELPERS	646–649
		DEDICATION OF PLACES AND THINGS	650–652
VII. GENERAL	358–538		
		THE SICK AND AFFLICTED	653–662
VIII. PROCESSIONALS	539–551	HOME AND PERSONAL USE	663–688

HYMNS.

I. Daily Prayer.

MORNING.

1   L. M.

1 New every morning is the love
Our wakening and uprising prove;
Through sleep and darkness safely brought,
Restored to life, and power, and thought.

2 New mercies, each returning day,
Hover around us while we pray:
New perils past, new sins forgiven,
New thoughts of God, new hopes of heaven.

3 If on our daily course our mind
Be set to hallow all we find,
New treasures still, of countless price,
God will provide for sacrifice.

4 Old friends, old scenes, will lovelier be,
As more of heaven in each we see;
Some softening gleam of love and prayer
Shall dawn on every cross and care.

5 The trivial round, the common task,
Will furnish all we need to ask;
Room to deny ourselves, a road
To bring us daily nearer God.

6 Only, O Lord, in Thy dear love,
Fit us for perfect rest above;
And help us, this and every day,
To live more nearly as we pray.
    Amen.

2   L. M.
Part I.

1 Awake, my soul, and with the sun
Thy daily stage of duty run;
Shake off dull sloth, and early rise
To pay thy morning sacrifice.

2 Redeem thy misspent time that's past,
And live this day as if thy last;
Improve thy talent with due care;
For the great day thyself prepare.

3 Wake, and lift up thyself, my heart,
And with the angels bear thy part,
Who all night long, unwearied, sing
High praise to the eternal King.

4 Praise God, from Whom all blessings flow;
Praise Him, all creatures here below;
Praise Him above, ye heavenly host;
Praise Father, Son, and Holy Ghost.
    Amen.

Part II.

1 All praise to Thee, Who safe hast kept,
And hast refreshed me while I slept:
Grant, Lord, when I from death shall wake,
I may of endless light partake.

2 Lord, I my vows to Thee renew;
Scatter my sins as morning dew;
Guard my first springs of thought and will,
And with Thyself my spirit fill.

3 Direct, control, suggest, this day,
All I design, or do, or say;
That all my powers, with all their might,
In Thy sole glory may unite.

4 Praise God, from Whom all blessings flow;
Praise Him, all creatures here below;
Praise Him above, ye heavenly host;
Praise Father, Son, and Holy Ghost.
    Amen.

3   L. M.

1 O Jesus, Lord of heavenly grace,
Thou brightness of Thy Father's face,
Thou fountain of eternal light,
Whose beams disperse the shades of night.

2 Come, holy Sun of heavenly love,
Shower down Thy radiance from above;
And to our inward hearts convey
The Holy Spirit's cloudless ray.

3 May faith, deep-rooted in the soul,
Subdue our flesh, our minds control;
May guile depart, and discord cease,
And all within be joy and peace.

4 So gladly let us pass the day,
  With thoughts as pure as morning ray,
  Our faith as strong as midday light,
  Our souls undimmed by shades of night.

5 O Christ, with each returning morn,
  Thine image to our hearts be borne;
  O may we ever clearly see
  Our Saviour and our God in Thee.
               Amen.

4   5.5.10.5.5.10.

1 Framer of the light,
    Who from out the night
  The dawn of joyous day again dost bring,
    On our darkened eyes,
    Bid Thy bright beams rise;
  Of endless glory teach us, Lord, to sing.

2 By Thy mercy still
    Spared our place to fill,
  O Father, be it ours Thy name to bless;
    Sheltered by Thy power,
    In each fleeting hour,
  Thy children guide to paths of holiness.

3 Raised from death-like sleep,
    Ever may we keep
  Alive within us thoughts of that great day!
    Grant the ready mind,
    Give us grace to find,
  The strait gate unto life—the narrow way.

4 Onward to the goal
    Lead each striving soul,
  Upheld by strength divine Thy grace supplies;
    While it still is day,
    May we win our way
  Towards the mark and our high calling's
               prize. Amen.

5   P.M.

1 Come, my soul, thou must be waking,
    Now is breaking
  O'er the earth another day:
  Come, to Him who made this splendor
    See thou render
  All thy feeble strength can pay.

2 Gladly hail the sun returning:
    Ready burning
  Be the incense of thy powers:
  For the night is safely ended;
    God hath tended
  With His care thy helpless hours.

3 Think that He thy ways beholdeth,
    He unfoldeth
  Every fault that lurks within;
  He the hidden shame glossed over
    Can discover,
  And discern each deed of sin.

4 Mayest thou on life's last morrow,
    Free from sorrow,
  Pass away in slumber sweet;
  And, released from death's dark sadness,
    Rise in gladness,
  That far brighter Sun to greet.

5 Only God's free gifts abuse not,
    Light refuse not,
  But His Spirit's voice obey;
  Thou with Him shalt dwell, beholding
    Light enfolding
  All things in unclouded day.

6   L. M.

1 Now that the daylight fills the sky,
  We lift our hearts to God on high,
  That He, in all we do or say,
  Would keep us free from harm to-day;

2 Would guard our tongue in every word,
  Lest sounds of angry strife be heard;
  From all ill sights would turn our eyes,
  And close our ears from vanities:

3 Would keep our inmost conscience pure;
  Our souls from folly would secure;
  Would bid us check the pride of sense
  With due and holy abstinence.

4 So we, when this new day is gone,
  And night in turn is drawing on,
  With conscience by the world unstained,
  Shall praise His Name for victory gained.

DAILY PRAYER—EVENING.

7   7s.

1 Every morning mercies new
Fall as fresh as morning dew;
Every morning let us pay
Tribute with the early day;
For Thy mercies, Lord, are sure;
Thy compassion doth endure.

2 Still the greatness of Thy love
Daily doth our sins remove;
Daily, far as east from west,
Lifts the burden from the breast;
Gives unbought, to those who pray,
Strength to stand in evil day.

3 Let our prayers each morn prevail,
That these gifts may never fail;
And, as we confess the sin
And the tempter's power within,
Feed us with the Bread of Life;
Fit us for our daily strife.

4 As the morning light returns,
As the sun with splendor burns,
Teach us still to turn to Thee,
Ever blessèd Trinity,
With our hands our hearts to raise,
In unfailing prayer and praise. Amen.

8   7s.

1 As the sun doth daily rise,
Brightening all the morning skies,
So to Thee with one accord
Lift we up our hearts, O Lord.

2 Thou, by Whom all things are fed,
Give us for the day our bread;
Strength unto our souls afford
From the Bread of heaven, O Lord.

3 Be our guard in sin and strife;
Be the leader of our life;
While we daily search Thy Word,
Wisdom true impart, O Lord.

4 When the sun withdraws his light,
When we seek our rest at night,
Thou, by sleepless hosts adored,
Hear the prayer of faith, O Lord.

5 When the hours are dark and drear,
When the tempter lurketh near,
By Thy strengthening grace outpoured
Save the tempted ones, O Lord. Amen.

9   [FRIDAY.]   L.M.

1 O Jesus, crucified for man,
O Lamb, all glorious on Thy throne,
Teach Thou our wondering souls to scan
The mystery of Thy love unknown.

2 We pray Thee, grant us strength to take
Our daily cross, whate'er it be,
And gladly for Thine own dear sake
In paths of pain to follow Thee.

3 As on our daily way we go,
Through light or shade, in calm or strife,
Oh! may we bear Thy marks below
In conquered sin and chastened life.

4 And week by week this day we ask
That holy memories of Thy cross
May sanctify each common task,
And turn to gain each earthly loss.

5 Grant us, dear Lord, our cross to bear
Till at Thy feet we lay it down,
Win through Thy blood our pardon there,
And through the cross attain the crown.
                         Amen.

Also the following:

404 Holy, holy, holy, Lord God almighty.
360 Shine on our souls, eternal God.
359 Creator of mankind.
444 Christ, Whose glory fills the skies.
664 My Father, for another night.

EVENING.

10   10,6,10,6.

1 O brightness of the immortal Father's face,
Most holy, heavenly, blest,
Lord Jesus Christ, in Whom His truth and grace
Are visibly expressed:

2 The sun is sinking now, and one by one
The lamps of evening shine;
We hymn the eternal Father, and the Son,
And Holy Ghost divine.

3 Worthy art Thou at all times to receive
Our hallowed praises, Lord;
O Son of God, be Thou, in Whom we live,
Through all the world adored. Amen.

3

DAILY PRAYER—EVENING.

11 L.M.

1 All praise to Thee, my God, this night,
  For all the blessings of the light;
  Keep me, O keep me, King of kings,
  Beneath Thine own almighty wings.

2 Forgive me, Lord, for Thy dear Son,
  The ill that I this day have done;
  That with the world, myself, and Thee;
  I, ere I sleep, at peace may be.

3 Teach me to live, that I may dread
  The grave as little as my bed;
  Teach me to die, that so I may
  Rise glorious at the awful day.

4 O may my soul on Thee repose,
  And may sweet sleep mine eyelids close;
  Sleep that shall me more vigorous make
  To serve my God when I awake.

5 When in the night I sleepless lie,
  My soul with heavenly thoughts supply;
  Let no ill dreams disturb my rest,
  No powers of darkness me molest.

6 On, when shall I, in endless day,
  Forever chase dark sleep away,
  And hymns divine with angels sing,
  All praise to Thee, eternal King?

7 Praise God, from Whom all blessings flow;
  Praise Him, all creatures here below;
  Praise Him above, ye heavenly host:
  Praise Father, Son, and Holy Ghost.

12 7.7.7.5.

1 Holy Father, cheer our way
  With Thy love's perpetual ray:
  Grant us every closing day
  Light at evening-time.

2 Holy Saviour, calm our fears
  When earth's brightness disappears:
  Grant us in our later years
  Light at evening-time.

3 Holy Spirit, be Thou nigh
  When in mortal pains we lie;
  Grant us, as we come to die,
  Light at evening-time.

4 Holy, blessed Trinity,
  Darkness is not dark to Thee:
  Those Thou keepest always see
  Light at evening-time.

13 8.8.8.4.

1 The radiant morn hath passed away,
  And spent too soon her golden store;
  The shadows of departing day
  Creep on once more.

2 Our life is but an autumn day,
  Its glorious noon how quickly past;
  Lead us, O Christ, Thou living Way,
  Safe home at last.

3 Oh, by Thy soul-inspiring grace
  Uplift our hearts to realms on high;
  Help us to look to that bright place
  Beyond the sky;

4 Where light, and life, and joy, and peace
  In undivided empire reign,
  And thronging angels never cease
  Their deathless strain;

5 Where saints are clothed in spotless white,
  And evening shadows never fall,
  Where Thou, eternal Light of Light,
  Art Lord of all. Amen.

14 L.M.

1 Sun of my soul, Thou Saviour dear,
  It is not night if Thou be near;
  Oh, may no earth-born cloud arise
  To hide Thee from Thy servant's eyes.

2 When the soft dews of kindly sleep
  My weary eyelids gently steep,
  Be my last thought, how sweet to rest
  For ever on my Saviour's breast.

3 Abide with me from morn till eve,
  For without Thee I cannot live;
  Abide with me when night is nigh,
  For without Thee I dare not die.

4 If some poor wandering child of Thine
  Have spurn'd to-day the voice divine,
  Now, Lord, the gracious work begin;
  Let him no more lie down in sin.

5 Watch by the sick; enrich the poor
  With blessings from Thy boundless store;
  Be every mourner's sleep to-night,
  Like infant's slumbers, pure and light.

6 Come near and bless us when we wake,
  Ere through the world our way we take,
  Till in the ocean of Thy love
  We lose ourselves in heaven above. Amen.

15   10s.

1 Abide with me: fast falls the eventide;
   The darkness deepens ; Lord, with me abide:
   When other helpers fail, and comforts flee,
   Help of the helpless, oh, abide with me.

2 Swift to its close ebbs out life's little day;
   Earth's joys grow dim, its glories pass away;
   Change and decay in all around I see;
   O Thou Who changest not, abide with me.

3 I need Thy presence every passing hour;
   What but Thy grace can foil the tempter's power?
   Who, like Thyself, my guide and stay can be?
   Through cloud and sunshine, Lord, abide with me.

4 I fear no foe, with Thee at hand to bless:
   Ills have no weight, and tears no bitterness.
   Where is death's sting ? where, grave, thy victory?
   I triumph still, if Thou abide with me.

5 Hold Thou Thy cross before my closing eyes;
   Shine through the gloom, and point me to the skies;
   Heaven's morning breaks, and earth's vain shadows flee;
   In life, in death, O Lord, abide with me.
                     Amen.

16   L. M.

1 At even, when the sun did set,
   The sick, O Lord, around Thee lay;
   Oh, in what divers pains they met!
   Oh, with what joy they went away!

2 Once more 'tis eventide, and we
   Oppressed with various ills draw near;
   What if Thy form we cannot see?
   We know and feel that Thou art here.

3 O Saviour, Christ, our woes dispel;
   For some are sick, and some are sad,
   And some have never loved Thee well,
   And some have lost the love they had;

4 And some are pressed with worldly care;
   And some are tried with sinful doubt;
   And some such grievous passions tear
   That only Thou canst cast them out;

5 And some have found the world is vain.
   Yet from the world they break not free;
   And some have friends who give them pain,
   Yet have not sought a friend in Thee.

6 And none, O Lord, have perfect rest,
   For none are wholly free from sin;
   And they who fain would serve Thee best
   Are conscious most of wrong within.

7 O Saviour, Christ, Thou too art man;
   Thou hast been troubled, tempted, tried;
   Thy kind but searching glance can scan
   The very wounds that shame would hide;

8 Thy touch has still its ancient power;
   No word from Thee can fruitless fall;
   Hear, in this solemn evening hour,
   And in Thy mercy heal us all.   Amen.

17   C. M.

1 The shadows of the evening hours
   Fall from the darkening sky,
   Upon the fragrance of the flowers
   The dews of evening lie;

2 Before Thy throne, O Lord of heaven,
   We kneel at close of day;
   Look on Thy children from on high,
   And hear us while we pray.

3 The sorrows of Thy servants, Lord,
   O do not Thou despise,
   But let the incense of our prayers
   Before Thy mercy rise.

4 The brightness of the coming night
   Upon the darkness rolls;
   With hopes of future glory chase
   The shadows on our souls.

5 Slowly the rays of daylight fade;
   So fade within our hearts
   The hopes in earthly love and joy,
   That one by one depart;

6 Slowly the bright stars, one by one,
   Within the heavens shine:
   Give us, O Lord, fresh hopes in heaven,
   And trust in things divine.

DAILY PRAYER—EVENING.

7 Let peace, O Lord! Thy peace, O God!
Upon our souls descend,
From midnight fears, and perils, Thou
Our trembling hearts defend:

8 Give us a respite from our toil,
Calm and subdue our woes;
Through the long day we labor, Lord,
O give us now repose. Amen.

18   8s.

1 Sweet Saviour, bless us ere we go;
Thy word into our minds instil;
And make our lukewarm hearts to glow
With lowly love and fervent will.
Through life's long day and death's dark night,
O gentle Jesus, be our light.

2 The day is gone, its hours have run,
And Thou hast taken count of all,
The scanty triumphs grace hath won,
The broken vow, the frequent fall.
Through life's long day and death's dark night,
O gentle Jesus, be our light.

3 Grant us, dear Lord, from evil ways
True absolution and release;
And bless us, more than in past days,
With purity and inward peace.
Through life's long day and death's dark night,
O gentle Jesus, be our light.

4 Labor is sweet, for Thou hast toiled;
And care is light, for Thou hast cared;
Let not our works by strife be soiled,
Nor by deceit our hearts ensnared.
Through life's long day and death's dark night,
O gentle Jesus, be our light.

5 For all we love, the poor, the sad,
The sinful, unto Thee we call;
O let Thy mercy make us glad;
Thou art our Saviour, and our all.
Through life's long day and death's dark night,
O gentle Jesus, be our light.

6 Sweet Saviour, bless us; night is come;
Through night and darkness near us be;
Good angels watch about our home,
And we are one day nearer Thee.
Through life's long day and death's dark night,
O gentle Jesus, be our light. Amen.

19   7s.

1 Softly now the light of day
Fades upon my sight away;
Free from care, from labor free,
Lord, I would commune with Thee:

2 Thou, Whose all-pervading eye
Naught escapes, without, within,
Pardon each infirmity,
Open fault, and secret sin.

3 Soon, for me, the light of day
Shall for ever pass away;
Then, from sin and sorrow free,
Take me, Lord, to dwell with Thee:

4 Thou, Who, sinless, yet hast known
All of man's infirmity;
Then, from Thine eternal throne,
Jesus, look with pitying eye. Amen.

20   8.7.

1 Saviour, breathe an evening blessing,
Ere repose our spirits seal;
Sin and want we come confessing;
Thou canst save and Thou canst heal.

2 Though the night be dark and dreary,
Darkness cannot hide from Thee;
Thou art He who, never weary,
Watchest where Thy people be.

3 Though destruction walk around us,
Though the arrows past us fly,
Angel-guards from Thee surround us;
We are safe, if Thou art nigh.

4 Should swift death this night o'ertake us,
And our couch become our tomb,
May the morn in heaven awake us,
Clad in light and deathless bloom.

DAILY PRAYER—EVENING.

5 Father, to Thy holy keeping
　Humbly we ourselves resign;
　Saviour, Who hast slept our sleeping,
　Make our slumbers pure as Thine;

6 Blessed Spirit, brooding o'er us,
　Chase the darkness of our night,
　Till the perfect day before us
　Breaks in everlasting light. Amen.

21　　　　　　　　6.4.6.6.

1 The sun is sinking fast,
　The daylight dies;
　Let love awake, and pay
　Her evening sacrifice.

2 As Christ upon the cross
　His head inclined,
　And to his Father's hands
　His parting soul resigned;

3 So now herself my soul
　Would wholly give
　Into His sacred charge,
　In Whom all spirits live;

4 So now beneath His eye
　Would calmly rest,
　Without a wish or thought
　Abiding in the breast;

5 Save that His will be done,
　Whate'er betide;
　Dead to herself, and dead
　In Him to all beside.

6 Thus would I live: yet now
　Not I, but He,
　In all His power and love,
　Henceforth alive in me.

7 One sacred Trinity,
　One Lord divine,
　May I be ever His,
　And He for ever mine. Amen.

22　　　　　　　7.6.7.6.8.8.

1 The day is past and over:
　All thanks, O Lord, to Thee:
　We pray Thee that offenceless
　The hours of dark may be.
　O Jesus, keep us in Thy sight,
　And save us through the coming night.

2 The joys of day are over:
　We lift our hearts to Thee;
　And call on Thee that sinless
　The hours of gloom may be.
　O Jesus, make their darkness light,
　And save us through the coming night.

3 The toils of day are over;
　We raise the hymn to Thee,
　And ask that free from peril
　The hours of fear may be:
　O Jesus, keep us in Thy sight,
　And guard us through the coming night.

4 Be thou our souls' preserver,
　For Thou alone dost know
　How many are the perils
　Through which we have to go.
　O loving Jesus, hear our call,
　And guard and save us from them all.
　　　　　　　　　　　Amen.

23　　　　　　8.4.8.4.8.8.8.4.

1 God, that madest earth and heaven,
　　Darkness and light;
　Who the day for toil hast given,
　　For rest the night:
　May Thine angel-guards defend us,
　Slumber sweet Thy mercy send us,
　Holy dreams and hopes attend us,
　　This livelong night.

2 Guard us waking, guard us sleeping,
　　And, when we die,
　May we in Thy mighty keeping,
　　All peaceful lie:
　When the last dread trump shall wake us,
　Do not Thou, our God, forsake us,
　But to reign in glory take us
　　With Thee on high. Amen.

24　　　　　　　　　　S.M.

1 Our day of praise is done;
　　The evening shadows fall:
　But pass not from us with the sun,
　　True Light that lightenest all.

7

THE LORD'S DAY.

2 Around the throne on high,
   Where night can never be,
The white-robed harpers of the sky
   Bring ceaseless hymns to Thee.

3 Too faint our anthems here;
   Too soon of praise we tire:
But oh, the strains how full and clear
   Of that eternal choir!

4 Yet, Lord, to Thy dear will
   If Thou attune the heart,
We in Thine angels' music still
   May bear our lower part.

5 'Tis Thine each soul to calm,
   Each wayward thought reclaim,
And make our life a daily psalm
   Of glory to Thy Name.

6 A little while, and then
   Shall come the glorious end;
And songs of angels and of men
   In perfect praise shall blend.

25   10s.

1 The day is gently sinking to a close,
Fainter and yet more faint the sunlight
   glows:
O brightness of thy Father's glory, Thou
Eternal Light of Light, be with us now:
Where Thou art present darkness cannot be;
Midnight is glorious noon, O Lord, with
   Thee.

2 Our changeful lives are ebbing to an end;
Onward to darkness and to death we tend:
O conqueror of the grave, be Thou our guide,
Be Thou our light in death's dark eventide:
Then in our mortal hour will be no gloom,
No sting in death, no terror in the tomb.

3 Thou, Who in darkness walking didst appear
Upon the waves, and Thy disciples cheer,
Come, Lord, in lonesome days, when storms
   assail,
And earthly hopes and human succors fail:
When all is dark may we behold Thee nigh,
And hear Thy voice—"Fear not, for it is I."

4 The weary world is mouldering to decay,
Its glories wane, its pageants fade away;
In that last sunset when the stars shall fall,
May we arise awakened by Thy call,
With Thee, O Lord, for ever to abide
In that blest day which has no eventide.
   Amen.

26   6.5.

1 Now the day is over,
   Night is drawing nigh;
Shadows of the evening
   Steal across the sky;

2 Jesus, grant the weary
   Calm and sweet repose;
With Thy tenderest blessing
   May our eyelids close.

3 Grant to little children
   Visions bright of Thee;
Guard the sailors tossing
   On the deep, blue sea.

4 Comfort every sufferer
   Watching late in pain;
Those who plan some evil
   From their sins restrain.

5 Through the long night-watches
   May Thine angels spread
Their white wings above me,
   Watching round my bed.

6 When the morning wakens,
   Then may I arise
Pure, and fresh, and sinless
   In Thy holy eyes. Amen.

Also the following:

667 Tarry with me, O my Saviour.
668 Inspirer and hearer of prayer.
669 Great God, to Thee, my evening song.

The Lord's Day.

27   7s.

1 On this day, the first of days,
   God the Father's Name we praise;
Who, creation's Lord and Spring,
   Did the world from darkness bring.

THE LORD'S DAY.

2 On this day the eternal Son
Over death His triumph won;
On this day the Spirit came
With His gifts of living flame.

3 Oh that fervent love to-day
May in every heart have sway,
Teaching us to praise aright
God, the source of life and light.

4 Father, Who didst fashion me
Image of Thyself to be,
Fill me with Thy love divine,
Let my every thought be Thine.

5 Holy Jesus, may I be
Dead and buried here with Thee;
And, by love inflamed, arise
Unto Thee a sacrifice.

6 Thou, Who dost all gifts impart,
Shine, sweet Spirit, in my heart:
Best of gifts, Thyself bestow;
Make me burn Thy love to know.

7 God, the blessèd Three in One,
Dwell within my heart alone;
Thou dost give Thyself to me;
May I give myself to Thee. Amen.

28 L. M.

1 This day, by Thy creative word
First o'er the earth the light was poured;
O Lord, this day upon us shine,
And fill our souls with light divine.

2 This day the Lord, for sinners slain,
In might victorious rose again;
O Jesus, may we raisèd be
From death of sin to life in Thee.

3 This day the Holy Spirit came,
With fiery tongues of cloven flame:
O Spirit, fill our hearts this day
With grace to hear, and grace to pray.

4 O day of light and life and grace,
From earthly toils sweet resting-place!
Thy hallowed hours, best gift of love,
We give again to God above.

29 14s.

1 As Thou didst rest, O Father, o'er nature's
finished birth,
As Thou didst in Thy work rejoice, and bless
the new-born earth,
So give us now that Sabbath-rest, which
makes Thy children free,
Free for the work of love to man, of thankfulness to Thee.

2 But in Thy worship, Father, O lift our souls
above,
By holy word, by prayer and hymn, by eucharistic love;
Till e'en the dull cold work of earth, the
earth which Christ hath trod,
Shall be itself a silent prayer, to raise us up
to God.

3 So lead us on to heaven, where in Thy presence blest,
"The wicked cease from troubling, and the
weary are at rest;"
Where faith is lost in vision, where love hath
no alloy,
And through eternity there flows the deepening stream of joy.

4 To Thee, Who giv'st us freedom, our Father
and our King;
To Thee, the risen Lord of life, our ran-
somed spirits sing;
Thou fill'st the Church in earth and heaven,
O Holy Ghost :—to Thee
In warfare's toil, in victory's rest, eternal
glory be. Amen.

30 L. M.

1 Thou glorious Sun of Righteousness,
On this day risen to set no more,
Shine on us now to heal and bless,
With brighter beams than e'er before.

2 Shine on Thy work of grace within,
On each celestial blossom there:
Destroy each bitter root of sin,
And make Thy garden fresh and fair.

3 Shine on Thy pure, eternal word,
Its mysteries to our souls reveal;
And whether read, remembered, heard,
O let it quicken, strengthen, heal.

THE LORD'S DAY.

4 Shine on the temples of Thy grace:
   Thy priests in righteousness be clad ;
   Unveil the brightness of Thy face ;
   And make Thy chosen people glad.

5 Shine on all those for whom we mourn,
   Who know not yet Thy healing ray :
   Quicken their souls and bid them turn
   To Thee, "the Life, the Truth, the Way."

6 Shine, till Thy glorious beams shall chase
   The blinding film from every eye ;
   Till every earthly dwelling-place
   Shall hail the Dayspring from on high.

7 Shine on, shine on, eternal Sun !
   Pour richer floods of life and light,
   Till that bright Sabbath be begun—
   That glorious day which knows no night.

31   7.6.

1 O day of rest and gladness,
   O day of joy and light,
   O balm of care and sadness,
   Most beautiful, most bright ;
   On thee, the high and lowly,
   Through ages joined in tune,
   Sing, holy, holy, holy,
   To the great God Triune.

2 On thee, at the creation,
   The light first had its birth ;
   On thee for our salvation
   Christ rose from depths of earth ;
   On thee our Lord victorious
   The Spirit sent from heaven ;
   And thus on thee most glorious
   A triple light was given.

3 Thou art a port protected
   From storms that round us rise ;
   A garden intersected
   With streams of Paradise ;
   Thou art a cooling fountain
   In life's dry, dreary sand ;
   From thee, like Pisgah's mountain,
   We view our promised land.

4 To-day on weary nations
   The heavenly manna falls :
   To holy convocations
   The silver trumpet calls ;
   Where gospel light is glowing
   With pure and radiant beams :
   And living water flowing
   With soul-refreshing streams.

5 New graces ever gaining
   From this our day of rest,
   We reach the rest remaining
   To spirits of the blest ;
   To Holy Ghost be praises,
   To Father, and to Son ;
   The Church her voice upraises
   To Thee, blest Three in One.   Amen.

32   C.M.

1 With joy we hail the sacred day,
   Which God hath called His own ;
   With joy the summons we obey,
   To worship at His throne.

2 Thy chosen temple, Lord, how fair!
   As here Thy servants throng
   To breathe the humble, fervent prayer,
   And pour the grateful song.

3 Spirit of grace! Oh deign to dwell
   Within Thy Church below :
   Make her in holiness excel,
   With pure devotion glow.

4 Let peace within her walls be found ;
   Let all her sons unite,
   To spread with holy zeal around
   Her clear and shining light.

5 Great God, we hail the sacred day
   Which Thou hast called Thine own :
   With joy the summons we obey
   To worship at Thy throne.

33   S.M.

1 Welcome, sweet day of rest,
   That saw the Lord arise ;
   Welcome to this reviving breast,
   And these rejoicing eyes.

THE LORD'S DAY.

2 The King Himself comes near
  And feasts His saints to-day;
  Here may we seek and see Him here,
  And love, and praise, and pray.

3 One day of prayer and praise
  His sacred courts within,
  Is sweeter than ten thousand days
  Of pleasurable sin.

4 My willing soul would stay
  In such a frame as this,
  And wait to hail the brighter day
  Of everlasting bliss.

34 S.M.

1 This is the day of light:
  Let there be light to-day;
  O Day-spring, rise upon our night,
  And chase its gloom away.

2 This is the day of rest:
  Our failing strength renew;
  On weary brain and troubled breast
  Shed Thou Thy freshening dew.

3 This is the day of peace:
  Thy peace our spirits fill;
  Bid Thou the blasts of discord cease,
  The waves of strife be still.

4 This is the day of prayer:
  Let earth to heaven draw near;
  Lift up our hearts to seek Thee there;
  Come down to meet us here.

5 This is the first of days:
  Send forth Thy quickening breath,
  And wake dead souls to love and praise,
  O vanquisher of death! Amen.

35 C.M.

1 And now the wants are told, that brought
    Thy children to Thy knee;
  Here lingering still, we ask for naught,
    But simply worship Thee.

2 The hope of heaven's eternal days
    Absorbs not all the heart
  That gives Thee glory, love, and praise,
    For being what Thou art.

3 For Thou art God, the one, the same,
    O'er all things high and bright;
  And round us, when we speak Thy name,
    There spreads a heaven of light.

4 O wondrous peace, in thought to dwell
    On excellence divine;
  To know that naught in man can tell
    How fair Thy beauties shine.

5 O Thou, above all blessing blest,
    O'er thanks exalted far,
  Thy very greatness is a rest
    To mortals as we are;

6 For when we feel the praise of Thee
    A task beyond our powers,
  We say, "A perfect God is He,
    And He is fully ours."

36 10s.

1 Saviour, again to Thy dear Name we raise
  With one accord our parting hymn of praise;
  Once more we bless Thee ere our worship cease,
  Then, lowly kneeling, wait Thy word of peace.

2 Grant us Thy peace upon our homeward way;
  With Thee began, with Thee shall end the day;
  Guard Thou the lips from sin, the hearts from shame,
  That in this house have called upon Thy Name.

3 Grant us Thy peace, Lord, thro' the coming night,
  Turn Thou for us its darkness into light;
  From harm and danger keep Thy children free,
  For dark and light are both alike to Thee.

4 Grant us Thy peace throughout our earthly life,
  Our balm in sorrow, and our stay in strife;
  Then, when Thy voice shall bid our conflict cease,
  Call us, O Lord, to Thine eternal peace.
    Amen.

37   L. M.

1 Almighty Father, bless the word,
    Which through Thy grace we now have
      heard ;
    O may the precious seed take root,
    Spring up, and bear abundant fruit.

2 We praise Thee for the means of grace,
    Thus in Thy courts to seek Thy face :
    Grant, Lord, that we who worship here
    May all, at last, in heaven appear.
                              Amen.

38   8. 7. 8. 7. 4. 7.

1 Lord, dismiss us with Thy blessing;
    Fill our hearts with joy and peace;
    Let us each, Thy love possessing,
    Triumph in redeeming grace:
        O refresh us,
    Traveling through this wilderness.

2 Thanks we give and adoration
    For Thy gospel's joyful sound:
    May the fruits of Thy salvation
    In our hearts and lives abound:
        Ever faithful
    To the truth may we be found.

3 So that when Thy love shall call us,
    Saviour, from the world away,
    Fear of death shall not appal us,
    Glad Thy summons to obey.
        May we ever
    Reign with Thee in endless day.
                              Amen.

Also the following:
497 Lord of the worlds above.

II. The Christian Year.
ADVENT.

39   6. 5.

1 Hark! the voice eternal,
    Robed in majesty,
    Calling into being
      Earth and sea and sky;
    Hark! in countless numbers
    All the angel-throng
    Hail creation's morning
      With one burst of song.
    High in regal glory,
      'Mid eternal light,
    Reign, O King immortal,
      Holy, infinite.

2 Bright the world and glorious,
    Calm both earth and sea,
    Noble in its grandeur
      Stood man's purity;
    Came the great transgression,
    Came the saddening fall,
    Death and desolation
      Breathing over all.
    Still in regal glory,
      'Mid eternal light,
    Reigned the King immortal,
      Holy, infinite.

3 Long the nations waited,
    Through the troubled night,
    Looking, longing, yearning
      For the promised light.
    Prophets saw the morning
      Breaking far away,
    Minstrels sang the splendor
      Of that opening day.
    Whilst in regal glory,
      'Mid eternal light,
    Reigned the King immortal,
      Holy, infinite.

4 Brightly dawned the Advent
    Of the new-born King,
    Joyously the watchers
      Heard the angels sing.
    Sadly closed the evening
    Of His hallowed life,
    As the noontide darkness
      Veiled the last dread strife.
    Lo! again in glory,
      'Mid eternal light,
    Reigns the King immortal,
      Holy, infinite.

5 Lo! again He cometh,
    Robed in clouds of light,
    As the Judge eternal,
      Armed with power and might.
    Nations to His footstool
      Gathered then shall be;
    Earth shall yield her treasures,
      And her dead, the sea.
    Till the trumpet soundeth,
      'Mid eternal light
    Reign, Thou King immortal,
      Holy, infinite.

6 Jesus! Lord and Master,
    Prophet, Priest and King,
    To Thy feet triumphant
      Hallowed praise we bring.

Thine the pain and weeping,
    Thine the victory;
Power, and praise, and honor,
    Be, O Lord, to Thee.
High in regal glory,
    'Mid eternal light,
Reign, O King immortal,
    Holy, infinite. Amen.
[This hymn may be sung with or without the refrain, as a Processional or not, as desired.]

40   8.7.

1 Hark! a thrilling voice is sounding;
    "Christ is nigh," it seems to say;
"Cast away the dreams of darkness,
    O ye children of the day!"

2 Wakened by the solemn warning,
    Let the earth-bound soul arise;
Christ, her Sun, all ill dispelling,
    Shines upon the morning skies.

3 Lo! the Lamb, so long expected,
    Comes with pardon down from heaven;
Let us haste, with tears of sorrow,
    One and all to be forgiven;

4 That when next He comes with glory,
    And the world is wrapped in fear,
With His mercy He may shield us,
    And with words of love draw near.

41   8.7.8.7.4.7.

1 Lo, He comes with clouds descending,
    Once for our salvation slain;
Thousand angel-hosts attending
    Swell the triumph of His train:
        Alleluia!
    Christ, the Lord, returns to reign.

2 Every eye shall now behold Him,
    Robed in dreadful majesty;
Those who set at naught and sold Him,
    Pierced, and nailed Him to the tree,
        Deeply wailing,
    Shall the true Messiah see.

3 Now redemption, long expected,
    See in solemn pomp appear:
All His saints, by men rejected,
    Now shall meet Him in the air:
        Alleluia!
    See the day of God appear.

4 Yea, Amen; let all adore Thee,
    High on Thine eternal throne;
Saviour, take the power and glory;
    Claim the kingdom for Thine own:
        Alleluia!
    Thou shalt reign, and Thou alone.
                                    Amen.

42   8s.

1 Come, quickly come, dread Judge of all;
    For, awful though Thine Advent be.
All shadows from the truth will fall,
    And falsehood die, in sight of Thee:
Come, quickly come: for doubt and fear
Like clouds dissolve when Thou art near.

2 Come, quickly come, great King of all;
    Reign all around us, and within;
Let sin no more our souls enthral,
    Let pain and sorrow die with sin;
Come, quickly come: for Thou alone
Canst make Thy scattered people one.

3 Come, quickly come, true Life of all;
    The curse of death is on the ground;
On every home his shadows fall,
    On every heart his mark is found:
Come, quickly come: for grief and pain
Can never cloud Thy glorious reign.

4 Come, quickly come, sure Light of all,
    For gloomy night broods o'er our way:
And fainting souls begin to fall
    With weary watching for the day:
Come, quickly come: for round Thy throne
No eye is blind, no night is known. Amen.

43   8.7.8.7.8.8.7.

1 Great God, what do I see and hear!
    The end of things created!
The Judge of mankind doth appear
    On clouds of glory seated!
The trumpet sounds; the graves restore
The dead which they contained before;
    Prepare, my soul, to meet Him!

2 The dead in Christ shall first arise
    At the last trumpet's sounding,
Caught up to meet Him in the skies,
    With joy their Lord surrounding:
No gloomy fears their souls dismay,
His presence sheds eternal day
    On those prepared to meet Him

3 But sinners, filled with guilty fears,
  Behold His wrath prevailing;
  For they shall rise, and find their tears
  And sighs are unavailing:
  The day of grace is past and gone;
  Trembling, they stand before the throne,
  All unprepared to meet Him.

4 Great God, to Thee my spirit clings,
  Thy boundless love declaring,
  One wondrous sight my comfort brings,—
  The Judge my nature wearing.
  Beneath His cross I view the day
  When heaven and earth shall pass away,
  And thus prepare to meet Him.

44   8s.

1 Day of wrath! oh day of mourning!
  See fulfilled the prophets' warning,
  Heaven and earth in ashes burning!

2 Oh, what fear man's bosom rendeth,
  When from heaven the Judge descendeth,
  On whose sentence all dependeth.

3 Wondrous sound the trumpet flingeth;
  Through earth's sepulchers it ringeth;
  All before the throne it bringeth.

4 Death is struck, and nature quaking,
  All creation is awaking,
  To its Judge an answer making.

5 Lo! the book exactly worded,
  Wherein all hath been recorded;
  Thence shall judgment be awarded.

6 When the Judge His seat attaineth,
  And each hidden deed arraigneth,
  Nothing unavenged remaineth.

7 What shall I, frail man, be pleading?
  Who for me be interceding,
  When the just are mercy needing?

8 King of majesty tremendous,
  Who dost free salvation send us,
  Fount of pity! then befriend us!

9 Think, good Jesus, my salvation
  Cost Thy wondrous incarnation;
  Leave me not to reprobation!

10 Faint and weary Thou hast sought me,
   On the cross of suffering bought me.
   Shall such grace be vainly brought me?

11 Righteous Judge! for sin's pollution
   Grant Thy gift of absolution,
   Ere that day of retribution.

12 Guilty, now I pour my moaning,
   All my shame with anguish owning;
   Spare, O God, Thy suppliant groaning!

13 Thou the sinful woman saved'st;
   Thou the dying thief forgavest;
   And to me a hope vouchsafest.

14 Worthless are my prayers and sighing,
   Yet, good Lord, in grace complying,
   Rescue me from fires undying!

15 With Thy favored sheep O place me!
   Nor among the goats abase me;
   But to Thy right hand upraise me.

16 While the wicked are confounded,
   Doomed to flames of woe unbounded,
   Call me, with Thy saints surrounded.

17 Bow my heart in meek submission,
   Strewn with ashes of contrition;
   Help me in my lost condition.

18 Day of sorrows, day of weeping,
   When, in dust no longer sleeping,
   Man awakes in Thy dread keeping!

19 To the rest Thou didst prepare him,
   By Thy cross, O Christ, upbear him;
   Spare, O God, in mercy spare him.

   Lord, all-pitying, Jesus blest,
   Grant us Thine eternal rest. Amen.

45   L. M.

1 On Jordan's bank the Baptist's cry
  Announces that the Lord is nigh;
  Awake, and hearken, for he brings
  Glad tidings of the King of kings.

2 Then cleansed be every Christian breast,
  And furnished for so great a guest;
  Yea, let us each our hearts prepare
  For Christ to come and enter there.

THE CHRISTIAN YEAR—ADVENT.

3 For Thou art our salvation, Lord,
Our refuge and our great reward;
Without Thy grace we waste away,
Like flowers that wither and decay.

4 To heal the sick stretch out Thine hand,
And bid the fallen sinner stand;
Shine forth, and let Thy light restore
Earth's own true loveliness once more.

5 All praise, eternal Son, to Thee,
Whose Advent doth Thy people free;
Whom with the Father we adore,
And Holy Ghost for evermore. Amen.

46 7.6.

1 Rejoice, rejoice, believers!
And let your lights appear;
The evening is advancing,
And darker night is near.
The Bridegroom is arising,
And soon He will draw nigh;
Up! pray, and watch, and wrestle!
At midnight comes the cry.

2 See that your lamps are burning;
Replenish them with oil;
Look now for your salvation,
The end of sin and toil.
The watchers on the mountain
Proclaim the Bridegroom near,
Go meet Him as He cometh,
With alleluias clear.

3 O wise and holy virgins,
Now raise your voices higher,
Till, in your jubilations
Ye meet the angel choir.
The marriage-feast is waiting,
The gates wide open stand;
Up, up, ye heirs of glory!
The Bridegroom is at hand.

4 Our hope and expectation,
O Jesus, now appear;
Arise, thou Sun so longed for,
O'er this benighted sphere!
With hearts and hands uplifted,
We plead, O Lord, to see
The day of earth's redemption,
And ever be with Thee! Amen.

47 8.7.8.7.4.7

1 Christ is coming! let creation
From her groans and travail cease:
Let the glorious proclamation
Hope restore and faith increase:
Christ is coming!
Come, Thou blessed Prince of Peace.

2 Earth can now but tell the story
Of Thy bitter cross and pain:
She shall yet behold Thy glory,
When Thou comest back to reign:
Christ is coming!
Let each heart repeat the strain.

3 Long Thine exiles have been pining,
Far from rest, and home, and Thee;
But in heavenly vestures shining,
Soon they shall Thy glory see:
Christ is coming!
Haste the joyous jubilee.

4 With that blessed hope before us,
Let no harp remain unstrung;
Let the mighty Advent-chorus
Onward roll from tongue to tongue:
Christ is coming!
Yea, Lord Jesus, quickly come!

48 8s.

1 O come, O come, Emmanuel,
And ransom captive Israel;
That mourns in lonely exile here,
Until the Son of God appear.
Rejoice! Rejoice! Emmanuel
Shall come to thee, O Israel!

2 O come, Thou Rod of Jesse, free
Thine own from Satan's tyranny;
From depths of hell Thy people save,
And give them victory o'er the grave.
Rejoice! Rejoice! Emmanuel
Shall come to thee, O Israel!

3 O come, Thou Day spring, come and cheer
Our spirits by Thine Advent here;
Disperse the gloomy clouds of night,
And death's dark shadows put to flight.
Rejoice! Rejoice! Emmanuel
Shall come to thee, O Israel!

THE CHRISTIAN YEAR—ADVENT.

4 O come, Thou Key of David, come,
   And open wide our heavenly home ;
   Make safe the way that leads on high,
   And close the path to misery.
     Rejoice! Rejoice! Emmanuel
     Shall come to thee, O Israel!

5 O come, O come, Thou Lord of might!
   Who to Thy tribes, on Sinai's height,
   In ancient times didst give the law,
   In cloud, and majesty, and awe.
     Rejoice! Rejoice! Emmanuel
     Shall come to thee, O Israel!

49   S.M.

1 Come, Lord, and tarry not!
   Bring the long-looked-for day!
   Oh, why these years of waiting here,
   These ages of delay?

2 Come, for Thy saints still wait ;
   Daily ascends their sigh ;
   The Spirit and the Bride say, Come!
   Dost thou not hear the cry?

3 Come, for creation groans,
   Impatient of Thy stay,
   Worn out with these long years of ill,
   These ages of delay.

4 Come, and make all things new,
   Build up this ruined earth,
   Restore our faded paradise,—
   Creation's second birth.

5 Come, and begin Thy reign
   Of everlasting peace ;
   Come, take the kingdom to Thyself,
   Great King of Righteousness! Amen.

50   6.6.8.6.6.8.6.6.

1 The Church has waited long
   Her absent Lord to see ;
   And still in loneliness she waits ;—
   A friendless stranger she.
   Age after age has gone,
   Sun after sun has set,
   And still in garb of widowhood
   She weeps a mourner yet.
     Come, then, Lord Jesus, come!

2 Saint after saint on earth
   Has lived, and loved, and died;
   And as they left us one by one,
   We laid them side by side ;
   We laid them down to sleep,
   But not in hope forlorn ;
   We laid them but to rest, and wake
   Upon the glorious morn.
     Come, then, Lord Jesus, come!

3 We long to hear Thy voice,
   To see Thee face to face,
   To share Thy crown and glory then,
   As now we share Thy grace.
   Should not the loving Bride
   The absent Bridegroom mourn?
   Should she not wear the signs of grief,
   Until her Lord return?
     Come, then, Lord Jesus, come!

4 The whole creation groans,
   And waits to hear that voice,
   That shall restore her comeliness,
   And make her wastes rejoice.
   Come, Lord, and wipe away
   The curse, the sin, the stain,
   And make this blighted world of ours
   Thine own fair world again.
     Come, then, Lord Jesus, come!
               Amen.

51   C.M.

1 Hark! the glad sound! the Saviour comes,
   The Saviour promised long :
   Let every heart prepare a throne,
   And every voice a song.

2 He comes the prisoners to release
   In Satan's bondage held :
   The gates of brass before Him burst,
   The iron fetters yield.

3 He comes from thickest films of vice
   To clear the mental ray,
   And on the eyes oppressed with night
   To pour celestial day.

4 He comes the broken heart to bind,
   The bleeding soul to cure:
   And with the treasures of His grace
   To enrich the humble poor.

THE CHRISTIAN YEAR—CHRISTMAS.

5 Our glad hosannas, Prince of Peace,
    Thy welcome shall proclaim;
And heaven's eternal arches ring
    With Thy beloved Name.

52   8.7.8.7.4.7.

1 O'er the distant mountains breaking
    Comes the reddening dawn of day;
Rise, my soul, from sleep awaking,
    Rise, and sing, and watch, and pray;
        'Tis thy Saviour,
    On His bright returning way.

2 O Thou long-expected! weary
    Waits my anxious soul for Thee,
Life is dark, and earth is dreary,
    Where Thy light I do not see;
        O my Saviour,
    When wilt Thou return to me?

3 Nearer is my soul's salvation,
    Spent the night, the day at hand;
Keep me in my lowly station,
    Watching for Thee, till I stand,
        O my Saviour,
    In Thy bright, Thy promised land.

4 With my lamp well trimmed and burning,
    Swift to hear and slow to roam,
Watching for Thy glad returning
    To restore me to my home.
        Come my Saviour,
    Thou hast promised; quickly come.
                                Amen.

Also the following:
423 The world is very evil.
424 Brief life is here our portion.
442 O heavenly Word, eternal Light.
363 Jesus came,—the heavens adoring.
563 Jesus, Life of those who die.
362 Thou art coming, O my Saviour.

CHRISTMAS.
53   P.M.
1 O come, all ye faithful,
    Joyful and triumphant;
O come ye, O come ye, to Bethlehem;
    Come and behold Him
    Born, the King of angels:
O come, let us adore Him,
O come, let us adore Him,
O come, let us adore Him, Christ the Lord.

2 God of God,
    Light of Light,
Lo! He abhors not the Virgin's womb;
    Very God,
    Begotten, not created:
O come, let us adore Him, etc.

3 Sing, choirs of angels,
    Sing, in exultation,
Sing, all ye citizens of heaven above,
    Glory to God
    In the highest;
O come, let us adore Him, etc.

4 Yea, Lord, we greet Thee,
    Born this happy morning;
Jesus, to Thee be glory given;
    Word of the Father,
    Now in flesh appearing;
O come, let us adore Him,
O come, let us adore Him,
O come, let us adore Him, Christ the Lord.

54   7s.

1 Hark! the herald angels sing
Glory to the new-born King;
Peace on earth, and mercy mild,
God and sinners reconciled!

2 Joyful, all ye nations, rise,
Join the triumph of the skies;
With the angelic host proclaim,
Christ is born in Bethlehem!

3 Christ, by highest heaven adored;
Christ, the everlasting Lord;
Late in time behold Him come,
Offspring of the Virgin's womb:

4 Veiled in flesh the Godhead see;
Hail the incarnate Deity,
Pleased as man with men to dwell;
Jesus, our Emmanuel!

5 Hail, the heavenly Prince of Peace!
Hail, the Sun of Righteousness!
Light and life to all He brings,
Risen with healing in His wings.

6 Mild He lays His glory by,
Born that man no more may die,
Born to raise the sons of earth,
Born to give them second birth.

THE CHRISTIAN YEAR—CHRISTMAS.

55 7s.

1 Sing, oh, sing, this blessed morn,
  Unto us a Child is born,
  Unto us a Son is given,
  God Himself comes down from heaven;
  Sing, oh, sing, this blessed morn,
  Jesus Christ to-day is born.

2 God of God, and Light of Light,
  Comes with mercies infinite,
  Joining in a wondrous plan
  Heaven to earth, and God to man.
  Sing, oh, sing, etc.

3 God with us, Emmanuel,
  Deigns for ever now to dwell;
  He on Adam's fallen race
  Sheds the fulness of His grace.
  Sing, oh, sing, etc.

4 God comes down that man may rise,
  Lifted by Him to the skies;
  Christ is Son of Man that we
  Sons of God in Him may be.
  Sing, oh, sing, etc.

5 Oh, renew us, Lord, we pray,
  With Thy Spirit day by day,
  That we ever one may be
  With the Father and with Thee.
  Sing, oh, sing, etc.

56 8.7.8.7.8.7.7.

1 Of the Father sole-begotten,
  Ere the worlds began to be,
  He the Alpha and Omega,
  He the source, the ending He,
  Of the things that are, that have been,
  And that future years shall see.
  Evermore and evermore!

2 O that ever-blessèd birthday,
  When the Virgin, full of grace,
  By the Holy Ghost conceiving,
  Bare the Saviour of our race;
  And that Child, the world's Redeemer,
  First displayed His sacred face,
  Evermore and evermore!

3 Praise Him, O ye heaven of heavens!
  Praise Him, angels in the height!
  Every power and every virtue
  Sing the praise of God aright;
  Let no tongue of man be silent,
  Let each heart and voice unite.
  Evermore and evermore!

4 Thee let age, and Thee let manhood,
  Thee let choirs of infants sing;
  Thee the matrons and the virgins,
  And the children answering:
  Let their guileless song re-echo,
  And their heart its praises bring,
  Evermore and evermore!

5 Laud and honor to the Father!
  Laud and honor to the Son!
  Laud and honor to the Spirit!
  Ever Three and ever One:
  Consubstantial, co-eternal,
  While unending ages run,
  Evermore and evermore! Amen.

57 C.M.

1 While shepherds watched their flocks by night,
  All seated on the ground,
  The angel of the Lord came down,
  And glory shone around.

2 "Fear not," said he, for mighty dread
  Had seized their troubled mind;
  "Glad tidings of great joy I bring
  To you, and all mankind.

3 "To you, in David's town, this day
  Is born of David's line,
  The Saviour, who is Christ the Lord;
  And this shall be the sign:

4 "The heavenly Babe you there shall find,
  To human view displayed,
  All meanly wrapt in swathing bands,
  And in a manger laid."

5 Thus spake the seraph; and forthwith
  Appeared a shining throng
  Of angels, praising God, who thus
  Addressed their joyful song:

6 "All glory be to God on high,
  And to the earth be peace;
  Good-will henceforth from heaven to men
  Begin, and never cease." Amen.

58 P.M.

1 Shout the glad tidings, exultingly sing;
  Jerusalem triumphs, Messiah is king;
  Sion, the marvelous story be telling,
  The Son of the Highest, how lowly His birth!
  The brightest archangel in glory excelling,
  He stoops to redeem thee, He reigns upon earth:
  Shout the glad tidings, etc.

THE CHRISTIAN YEAR—CHRISTMAS.

2 Tell how He cometh; from nation to nation
   The heart-cheering news let the earth echo round:
   How free to the faithful He offers salvation,
   How His people with joy everlasting are crowned:
   Shout the glad tidings, etc.

3 Mortals, your homage be gratefully bringing,
   And sweet let the gladsome hosanna arise:
   Ye angels, the full alleluia be singing;
   One chorus resound through the earth and the skies:
   Shout the glad tidings, etc.

59   P.M.

1 O little town of Bethlehem!
   How still we see thee lie;
   Above thy deep and dreamless sleep
   The silent stars go by;
   Yet in thy dark streets shineth
   The everlasting Light;
   The hopes and fears of all the years
   Are met in thee to-night.

2 For Christ is born of Mary,
   And gathered all above,
   While mortals sleep, the angels keep
   Their watch of wondering love.
   O morning stars, together
   Proclaim the holy birth!
   And praises sing to God the King,
   And peace to men on earth.

3 How silently, how silently,
   The wondrous gift is given!
   So God imparts to human hearts
   The blessings of His heaven.
   No ear may hear His coming,
   But in this world of sin,
   Where meek souls will receive Him still,
   The dear Christ enters in.

4 O holy Child of Bethlehem!
   Descend to us, we pray;
   Cast out our sin, and enter in.
   Be born in us to-day.

   We hear the Christmas angels
   The great glad tidings tell;
   O come to us, abide with us,
   Our Lord Emmanuel!! Amen.

60   8.7.8.7.4.7.

1 Angels, from the realms of glory,
   Wing your flight o'er all the earth;
   Ye who sang creation's story,
   Now proclaim Messiah's birth:
      Come and worship,
   Worship Christ, the new-born King.

2 Shepherds in the field abiding,
   Watching o'er your flocks by night;
   God with man is now residing,
   Yonder shines the infant-light:
      Come and worship,
   Worship Christ, the new-born King.

3 Sages, leave your contemplations;
   Brighter visions beam afar:
   Seek the great Desire of nations,
   Ye have seen His natal star:
      Come and worship,
   Worship Christ, the new-born King.

4 Saints before the altar bending,
   Watching long in hope and fear,
   Suddenly the Lord, descending,
   In His temple shall appear:
      Come and worship,
   Worship Christ, the new-born King.

61   8.7.

1 Hark! what mean those holy voices
   Sweetly sounding through the skies?
   Lo! the angelic host rejoices,
   Heavenly alleluias rise.

2 Listen to the wondrous story,
   Which they chant in hymns of joy—
   "Glory in the highest, glory!
   Glory be to God most high!

3 "Peace on earth, good-will from heaven,
   Reaching far as man is found;
   Souls redeemed and sins forgiven,
   Loud our golden harps shall sound.

4 "Christ is born; the great Anointed!
   Heaven and earth His praises sing!
   O receive whom God appointed
   For your Prophet, Priest, and King!

5 "Hasten, mortals, to adore Him;
   Learn His name to magnify,
   Till in heaven ye sing before Him,
   Glory be to God most high!"

62 8.7.

1 Hail! Thou long-expected Jesus,
  Born to set Thy people free;
  From our fears and sins release us;
  Let us find our rest in Thee.

2 Israel's strength and consolation,
  Hope of all the earth Thou art;
  Long desired of every nation,
  Joy of every waiting heart.

3 Born Thy people to deliver,
  Born a child, yet God our King,
  Born to reign in us for ever,
  Now Thy gracious kingdom bring.

4 By Thine own eternal Spirit,
  Rule in all our hearts alone:
  By Thine all-sufficient merit,
  Raise us to Thy glorious throne.
      Amen.

63 C.M.

1 To hail Thy rising, Sun of life,
  The gathering nations come;
  Joyous as when the reapers bear
  Their harvest treasures home.

2 For Thou our burden hast removed;
  The oppressor's reign is broke;
  Thy fiery conflict with the foe
  Has burst his cruel yoke.

3 To us the promised Child is born;
  To us the Son is given;
  Him shall the tribes of earth obey,
  And all the hosts of heaven.

4 His name shall be the Prince of Peace,
  For evermore adored;
  The Wonderful, the Counsellor,
  The mighty God and Lord.

5 His power increasing still shall spread,
  His reign no end shall know:
  Justice shall guard His throne above,
  And peace abound below.

      Also the following:
364 Thou didst leave Thy throne and Thy
     kingly crown.
371 Once in royal David's city.

64 EPIPHANY. 6.5.

1 From the eastern mountains
    Pressing on they come,
  Wise men in their wisdom
    To His humble home;
  Stirred by deep devotion,
    Hasting from afar,
  Ever journeying onward,
    Guided by a star.
  Light of Light that shineth
    Ere the worlds began,
  Draw Thou near, and lighten
    Every heart of man.

2 There their Lord and Saviour
    Meek and lowly lay,
  Wondrous Light that led them
    Onward on their way,
  Ever now to lighten
    Nations from afar,
  As they journey homeward
    By that guiding Star.
      Light of Light, etc.

3 Thou Who in a manger
    Once hast lowly lain,
  Who dost now in glory
    O'er all kingdoms reign,
  Gather in the heathen,
    Who in lands afar
  Ne'er have seen the brightness
    Of Thy guiding Star.
      Light of Light, etc.

4 Gather in the outcasts,
    All who have gone astray,
  Throw Thy radiance o'er them,
    Guide them on their way,
  Those who never knew Thee,
    Those who have wandered far,
  Lead them by the brightness
    Of Thy guiding Star.
      Light of Light, etc.

5 Onward through the darkness
    Of the lonely night,
  Shining still before them
    With Thy kindly light,
  Guide them, Jew and Gentile,
    Homeward from afar,
  Young and old together,
    By Thy guiding Star:—
      Light of Light, etc.

65   8.7.

1. Earth has many a noble city;
Bethlehem, thou dost all excel :
Out of thee the Lord from heaven
Came to rule His Israel.

2. Fairer than the sun at morning
Was the star that told His birth,
To the world its God announcing
Seen in fleshly form on earth.

3. Eastern sages at His cradle
Make oblations rich and rare;
See them give, in deep devotion,
Gold, and frankincense, and myrrh.

4. Sacred gifts of mystic meaning :
Incense doth their God disclose,
Gold the King of kings proclaimeth,
Myrrh His sepulchre foreshows.

5. Jesus, Whom the Gentiles worshipped
At Thy glad Epiphany,
Unto Thee, with God the Father
And the Spirit, glory be. Amen.

6. Until every nation,
Whether bond or free,
'Neath Thy starlit banner,
Jesus, follows Thee
O'er the distant mountains
To that heavenly home,
Where nor sin nor sorrow
Evermore shall come.
Light of Light that shineth
Ere the worlds began,
Draw Thou near, and lighten
Every heart of man. Amen.

[This hymn may be sung, either with or without the refrain, as a Processional, or not, as desired.]

66   C.M.

1. O Thou, Who by a star didst guide
The wise men on their way,
Until it came and stood beside
The place where Jesus lay;

2. Although by stars Thou dost not lead
Thy servants now below,
Thy Holy Spirit, when they need,
Will show them how to go.

3. As yet we know Thee but in part;
But still we trust Thy word,
That blessed are the pure in heart,
For they shall see the Lord.

4. O Saviour! give us, then, Thy grace,
To make us pure in heart ;
That we may see Thee face to face
Hereafter, as Thou art. Amen.

67   L.M.

1. When from the East the wise men came,
Led by the Star of Bethlehem,
The gifts they brought to Jesus were
Of gold and frankincense and myrrh.

2. Bright gold of Ophir, passing fine,
Proclaims a King of royal line;
For David's son in David's town,
Is born the heir of David's crown.

3. The incense-clouds, with fragrance rare,
The presence of a God declare;
Lo! kings in adoration fall,
For Mary's Son is Lord of all.

4. The myrrh, with bitter taste, foreshows
A life of sorrows, wounds and woes;—
The deadly cup, that overran
With anguish for the Son of Man.

5. Our gold upon Thine altar lies;
Our prayers to Thee, as incense, rise;
Accept as myrrh our tears and sighs :
O King, O God, O Sacrifice!

68   P.M.

1. Brightest and best of the sons of the morning,
Dawn on our darkness, and lend us Thine aid ;
Star of the East, the horizon adorning,
Guide where our infant Redeemer is laid.

2. Cold on His cradle the dew-drops are shining,
Low lies His head with the beasts of the stall;
Angels adore Him in slumber reclining,
Maker and Monarch and Saviour of all.

3 Shall we not yield Him, in costly devotion,
  Odors of Edom, and offerings divine,
  Gems of the mountain, and pearls of the
    ocean,
  Myrrh from the forest, and gold from the
    mine?

4 Vainly we offer each ample oblation,
  Vainly with gifts would His favor secure;
  Richer by far is the heart's adoration,
  Dearer to God are the prayers of the poor.

5 Brightest and best of the sons of the morn-
    ing,
  Dawn on our darkness, and lend us Thine
    aid;
  Star of the East, the horizon adorning,
  Guide where our infant Redeemer is laid.

69   8. 7.

1 Hail, Thou source of every blessing!
  Sovereign Father of mankind!
  Gentiles now, Thy truth possessing,
  In Thy courts admission find.

2 Grateful now we bow before Thee,
  In thy Church obtain a place,
  Now by faith behold Thy glory,
  Praise Thy truth, adore Thy grace.

3 Once far off, but now invited,
  We approach Thy sacred throne;
  In Thy covenant united,
  Reconciled, redeemed, made one.

4 Now revealed to eastern sages,
  See the Star of mercy shine,
  Mystery hid in former ages,
  Mystery great of love divine.

5 Hail, Thou manifested Saviour!
  Gentiles now their offerings bring,
  In Thy temples seek Thy favor,
  Jesus Christ, our Lord and King.

6 May we, body, soul, and spirit,
  Live devoted to Thy praise,
  Glorious realms of bliss inherit,
  Grateful anthems ever raise! Amen.

70   7s.

1 As with gladness men of old
  Did the guiding star behold ;
  As with joy they hailed its light,
  Leading onward, beaming bright;
  So, most gracious Lord, may we
  Evermore be led to Thee.

2 As with joyful steps they sped
  To that lowly manger-bed;
  There to bend the knee before
  Him whom heaven and earth adore;
  So may we with willing feet
  Ever seek the mercy-seat.

3 As they offered gifts most rare
  At that manger rude and bare;
  So may we with holy joy,
  Pure and free from sin's alloy,
  All our costliest treasures bring,
  Christ! to Thee our heavenly King.

4 Holy Jesus! every day
  Keep us in the narrow way;
  And, when earthly things are past,
  Bring our ransomed souls at last
  Where they need no star to guide,
  Where no clouds Thy glory hide.

5 In the heavenly country bright,
  Need they no created light;
  Thou its Light, its Joy, its Crown,
  Thou its Sun which goes not down,
  There for ever may we sing
  Alleluias to our King. Amen.

71   7s.

1 Songs of thankfulness and praise,
  Jesus, Lord, to Thee we raise,
  Manifested by the star
  To the sages from afar;
  Branch of royal David's stem
  In Thy birth at Bethlehem;
  Anthems be to Thee addressed,
  God in Man made manifest.

2 Manifest at Jordan's stream,
  Prophet, Priest, and King supreme;
  And at Cana, wedding-guest,
  In Thy Godhead manifest ;
  Manifest in power divine,
  Changing water into wine;
  Anthems be to Thee addressed,
  God in Man made manifest.

THE CHRISTIAN YEAR—EPIPHANY.

3 Manifest in making whole
  Palsied limbs and fainting soul;
  Manifest in valiant fight,
  Quelling all the devil's might;
  Manifest in gracious will,
  Ever bringing good from ill;
  Anthems be to Thee addressed,
  God in Man made manifest.

4 Sun and moon shall darkened be,
  Stars shall fall, the heavens shall flee;
  Christ will then like lightning shine,
  All will see His glorious sign;
  All will then the trumpet hear;
  All will see the Judge appear;
  Thou by all wilt be confessed,
  God in Man made manifest.

5 Grant us grace to see Thee, Lord,
  Present in Thy holy word;
  May we imitate Thee now,
  And be pure, as pure art Thou;
  That we like to Thee may be
  At Thy great Epiphany;
  And may praise Thee, ever blest,
  God in Man made manifest. Amen.

72   S. M.

1 Within the Father's house
  The Son hath found His home;
  And to His temple suddenly
  The Lord of Life hath come.

2 The doctors of the law
  Gaze on the wondrous child,
  And marvel at His gracious words
  Of wisdom undefiled.

3 Yet not to them is given
  The mighty truth to know,
  To lift the earthly veil which hides
  Incarnate God below.

4 The secret of the Lord
  Escapes each human eye,
  And faithful pondering hearts await
  The full Epiphany.

5 Lord, visit Thou our souls
  And teach us by Thy grace
  Each dim revealing of Thyself
  With loving awe to trace;

6 Till from our darkened sight
  The cloud shall pass away,
  And on the cleansèd soul shall burst
  The everlasting day;

7 Till we behold Thy face,
  And know, as we are known,
  Thee, Father, Son and Holy Ghost,
  Co-equal Three in One. Amen.

73   S. M.

1 All praise to Thee, O Lord,
  Who by Thy mighty power
  Didst manifest Thy glory forth
  In Cana's marriage hour.

2 Thou spakest: it is done;
  Obedient to Thy word,
  The water reddening into wine
  Proclaims the present Lord.

3 Blest were the eyes which saw
  That wondrous mystery,
  The great beginning of Thy works,
  That kindled faith in Thee.

4 And blessèd they who know
  Thine unseen presence true,
  When in the kingdom of Thy grace
  Thou makest all things new.

5 For by Thy loving hand
  Thy people still are fed;
  Thou art the Cup of blessing, Lord,
  And Thou the heavenly Bread.

6 Oh, may that grace be ours,
  In Thee for aye to live,
  And drink of those refreshing streams,
  Which Thou alone canst give;

7 So, led from strength to strength,
  Grant us, O Lord, to see
  The marriage supper of the Lamb,
  Thy great Epiphany. Amen.

74   S. M.

1 Fierce raged the storm of wind,
  The surging waves ran high,
  Failed Thy disciples' hearts with fear,
  Though Thou, their Lord, wast nigh.

2 But at the stern rebuke
 Of Thy almighty word,
The wind was hushed, the billows ceased,
 And owned Thee God and Lord.

3 So, now, when depths of sin
 Our souls with terrors fill,
Arise, and be our helper, Lord,
 And speak Thy "Peace, be still."

4 When death's dark sea we cross,
 Be with us in Thy power,
Nor let the water-floods prevail
 In that dread trial-hour.

5 And, when amid the signs,
 Which speak Thine Advent near,
The roaring of the sea and waves
 Fills faithless hearts with fear;

6 May we all undismayed
 The raging tempest see,
Lift up our heads and hail with joy
 Thy great Epiphany.

75 S. M.

1 Not by Thy mighty hand,
 Thy wondrous works alone,
But by the marvels of Thy Word,
 Thy glory, Lord, is known.

2 Forth from the eternal gates,
 Thine everlasting home,
To sow the seed of truth below,
 Thou didst vouchsafe to come.

3 And still from age to age,
 Thou, gracious Lord, hast been
The bearer forth of goodly seed,
 The sower still unseen.

4 And Thou wilt come again,
 And heaven beneath Thee bow,
To reap the harvest Thou hast sown,
 Sower and reaper Thou.

5 Watch, Lord, Thy harvest-field,
 With Thine unsleeping eye,
The children of the kingdom keep
 To Thy Epiphany;

6 That, when in Thy great day
 The tares shall severed be,
We may be surely gathered in
 With all Thy saints to Thee.

Also the following:

369 O One with God the Father.
370 Joy to the world, the Lord is come.
371 Hail to the Lord's anointed.
372 God of mercy, God of grace,
573 Saw you never in the twilight.

SEPTUAGESIMA, Etc.

76 8, 7.

1 Alleluia, song of sweetness,
 Voice of joy that cannot die;
Alleluia is the anthem
 Ever dear to choirs on high;
In the house of God abiding,
 Thus they sing eternally.

2 Alleluia thou resoundest,
 True Jerusalem and free;
Alleluia joyful mother,
 All thy children sing with thee;
But by Babylon's sad waters
 Mourning exiles now are we.

3 Alleluia cannot always
 Be our song while here below;
Alleluia our transgressions
 Make us for a while forego:
For the solemn time is coming
 When our tears for sin must flow.

4 Therefore in our hymns we pray Thee,
 Grant us blessèd Trinity,
At the last to keep Thine Easter
 In our home beyond the sky;
There to Thee forever singing
 Alleluia joyfully. Amen.

77 7. 6. 7. 6. 8. 6. 8. 6.

1 In exile here we wander
 In heaven is our abode,—
 The city of the angels,
 The city of our God.
And here we toil, and strive, and fight,
 With sin and woe opprest;
There God will give the sons of light
 Eternal joy and rest.

2 Through many sore temptations,
    By many sorrows torn,
    We strive to win the glory;
    Our many falls we mourn.
But faith holds out the vision bright
    Of our eternal home;
And hope assures that realm of light,
    When we have overcome.

3 Jesus, our joy and gladness.
    To Thee for aid we flee:
    Give tears of true contrition;
    Our souls from guilt set free:—
And we shall see that gladsome day,
    Where, bathed in joy divine,
Among Thy saints, and bright as they,
    We shall forever shine.

4 There we, as children dwelling,
    Who here as exiles groan,
    God's praises shall be telling
    Before His glorious throne;
There in our endless home shall rest
    From strife and sorrow free,
And join the anthem of the blest,
    For ever, Lord, to Thee.

78   S.M.

1 Lord of the hearts of men,
    Thou hast vouchsafed to bless,
    From age to age, Thy chosen saints
    With fruits of holiness.

2 Here faith, and hope and love
    Reign in sweet bond allied;
    There, when this little day is o'er,
    Shall love alone abide

3 Here, bearing the good seed,
    'Mid cares and tears we come;
    There, with rejoicing hearts, we bring
    Our harvest-treasures home.

4 O give us mighty Lord,
    The fruits Thyself dost love:
    Soon shalt Thou from Thy judgment seat
    Crown Thine own gifts above.

79   7.7.7.5.

1 Gracious Spirit, Holy Ghost,
    Taught by Thee we covet most
    Of Thy gifts at Pentecost
    Holy, heavenly love.

2 Love is kind, and suffers long,
    Love is meek, and thinks no wrong.
    Love than death itself more strong;
    Therefore, give us love.

3 Prophecy will fade away,
    Melting in the light of day;
    Love will ever with us stay ;
    Therefore, give us love.

4 Faith will vanish into sight ;
    Hope be emptied in delight ;
    Love in heaven will shine more bright ;
    Therefore, give us love.

5 Faith and hope and love we see
    Joining hand in hand agree.
    But the greatest of the three,
    And the best, is love.

6 From the overshadowing
    Of Thy gold and silver wing,
    Shed on us, who to Thee sing,
    Holy, heavenly love. Amen.

80   8.7.8.7.7.7.

1 Blessèd Saviour, Thou hast taught us,
    Taught us in Thy Word divine.
    That our doings are but nothing
    If they be not linked with Thine;
    If we be not bound to Thee
    With the bond of charity.

2 Though with tongues of men and angels.
    Soaring may our voices rise:
    Though we have the gift of knowledge,
    Understanding mysteries;
    All will still as nothing be,
    If we have not charity.

3 Though with faith, that even mountains
    At our word we may remove,
    Though our bodies to be burned
    Yield we,—and possess not love,
    We have nothing—till we be
    Bound with bonds of charity.

4 Bind us with the bond that bindeth
    Human hearts to God above.
    Bind us with the bond uniting
    Rich and poor with heavenly love.
    With the bond that binds to Thee,
    Never failing charity.

THE CHRISTIAN YEAR—LENT.

81 8.5.8.5.

1 Thou, Who on that wondrous journey
  Sett'st Thy face to die,
  By Thy holy, meek example
  Teach us charity!

2 Thou, Who that dread cup of suffering
  Didst not put from Thee;
  O most loving of the loving,
  Give us charity!

3 Thou, Who reignest, bright in glory,
  On God's throne on high,
  Oh, that we may share Thy triumph,
  Grant us charity!

4 Send us faith, that trusts Thy promise;
  Hope, with upward eye;
  But more blest than both, and greater,
  Send us charity! Amen.

LENT.

82 8s.

1 Bowed down with sorrow, sin, and shame,
  In faith, O Lord, we come to Thee,
  That Thou wilt by Thine own dear Name
  From sin and sorrow set us free;
  That Thou, in this Thy mercy's day,
  Wilt hear, and wash our sins away.

2 In wondrous love Thou cam'st as man,
  For man to suffer and to die,
  To live on earth a little span,
  To teach us how to live thereby;
  We come for strength, Thou Strength of
      God,
  To tread the path that Thou hast trod.

3 Thou cam'st to this poor earth and there
  Wast tempted; and, though Lord of all,
  Didst poverty and hunger bear,
  Yet ne'er didst yield to Satan's thrall;
  O give us grace, Thou Grace divine,
  To sanctify our fast by Thine.

4 Thou, Lord, hast known the bitter throe,
  The saddened heart, the falling tear,
  The lowest deep of human woe,
  With none to aid, and none to cheer:
  Then pity take, and pitying, prove
  The wealth of Thy redeeming love.

5 Thine, Lord, the life that paid the cost
  For all the lives Thou cam'st to save;
  And Thine the life that bought the lost
  From all the terrors of the grave:
  Thou Lord of life, Thou Life divine,
  Give us the life that lives in Thine.

6 Thou on the bitter cross didst bear
  For us the burden all alone,
  And on the cross Thou hast died,—and there
  True life o'er death the victory won;
  Victorious Lord, to Thee we cry,
  Give us o'er death the victory.

7 Mould Thou the weak and wayward will,
  And every hallowed thought supply;
  And may Thy Holy Spirit fill
  Our spirits with all purity;
  That these frail bodies, Lord, may be
  Fit habitations, meet for Thee.

8 O grant that when this Lent is past
  We still may live the life divine,
  Thrice hallowed here while life shall last;
  And then e'en death shall own us Thine!
  O death! where then shall be thy sting?
  O grave! where then thy triumphing?

83 C.M.

1 Lord! Who throughout these forty days,
  For us didst fast and pray,
  Teach us with Thee to mourn our sins,
  And close by Thee to stay.

2 As Thou with Satan didst contend,
  And didst the victory win,
  Oh, give us strength in Thee to fight,
  In Thee to conquer sin.

3 As Thou didst hunger bear and thirst,
  So teach us, gracious Lord,
  To die to self, and chiefly live
  By Thy most holy Word.

4 And through these days of penitence,
  And through Thy Passion-tide,
  Yea, evermore, in life and death,
  Jesus! with us abide.

5 Abide with us, that so, this life
  Of suffering overpast,
  An Easter of unending joy
  We may attain at last! Amen.

84   L.M.

1 Awhile in spirit, Lord, to Thee
Into the desert would we flee;
Awhile upon the barren steep
Our fast with Thee in spirit keep;

2 Awhile from Thy temptation learn
False Satan's wileful lures to spurn,
And in our hearts to feel and own
"Man liveth not by bread alone."

3 O Thou once tempted like as we,
Thou knowest our infirmity;
Be Thou our helper in the strife,
Be Thou our true, our inward life.

4 And while at Thy command we pray,
"Give us our bread from day to day,"
May we with Thee, O Christ, be fed,
Thou Word of God, Thou living Bread.
Amen.

85   8, 8, 6, 8, 8, 6.

1 O Thou Who dost to man accord,
His highest prize, his best reward,
Thou hope of all our race;
Jesus, to Thee we now draw near,
Our earnest supplications hear,
Who humbly seek Thy face.

2 With self accusing voice within
Our conscience tells of many a sin
In thought, and word, and deed;
O cleanse that conscience from all stain,
The penitent restore again,
From every burden freed.

3 If Thou reject us, who shall give
Our fainting spirits strength to live?
'Tis Thine alone to spare;
With cleansèd hearts to pray aright,
And find acceptance in Thy sight,
Be this our lowly prayer.

4 'Tis Thou hast blessed this solemn fast;
So may its days by us be passed
In self-control severe,
That, when our Easter morn we hail,
Its mystic feast we may not fail
To keep with conscience clear.

5 O Blessèd Trinity, bestow
Thy pardoning grace on us below,
And shield us evermore;
Until, within Thy courts above,
We see Thy face, and sing Thy love,
And with Thy saints adore. Amen.

86   7s.

1 Saviour! when in dust to Thee
Low we bow the adoring knee,
When, repentant, to the skies
Scarce we lift our weeping eyes,
Oh! by all Thy pains and woe
Suffered once for man below;
Bending from Thy throne on high,
Hear our solemn litany!

2 By Thy helpless infant years,
By Thy life of want and tears,
By Thy days of sore distress
In the savage wilderness,
By the dread mysterious hour
Of the insulting tempter's power;
Turn, O turn a favoring eye,
Hear our solemn litany!

3 By the sacred griefs that wept
O'er the grave where Lazarus slept;
By the boding tears that flowed
Over Salem's loved abode;
By the anguished sigh that told
Treachery lurked within Thy fold;
From Thy seat above the sky,
Hear our solemn litany!

4 By the burden Thou didst bear,
By Thine agony of prayer,
By the cross, the nail, the thorn,
Piercing spear, and torturing scorn;
By the gloom that veiled the skies
O'er the dreadful sacrifice;
Listen to our humble cry,
Hear our solemn litany!

5 By Thy deep expiring groan;
By the sad sepulchral stone;
By the vault, whose dark abode
Held in vain the rising God;
Oh! from earth to heaven restored,
Mighty, re-ascended Lord,
Listen, listen to the cry
Of our solemn litany! Amen.

87   L.M.

1 With broken heart and contrite sigh
A trembling sinner, Lord, I cry;
Thy pardoning grace is rich and free:
O God, be merciful to me.

2 I smite upon my troubled breast,
   With deep and conscious guilt oppressed ;
   Christ and His cross my only plea ;
   O God, be merciful to me.

3 Far off I stand with tearful eyes,
   Nor dare uplift them to the skies ;
   But Thou dost all my anguish see :
   O God, be merciful to me.

4 Nor alms, nor deeds that I have done,
   Can for a single sin atone ;
   To Calvary alone I flee :
   O God, be merciful to me.

5 And when, redeemed from sin and hell,
   With all the ransomed throng I dwell,
   My raptured song shall ever be,
   God has been merciful to me.

Also the following:

316 O Thou that hear'st when sinners cry.
317 O Jesus, Saviour of the lost.
319 Weary of earth and laden with my sin.
322 O Thou the contrite sinner's friend.
325 In the hour of trial.
375 Sinful, sighing to be blest.
376 Out of the deep I call.
377 Jesus, Lord of life and glory.
378 Have mercy, Lord, on me.
379 Lord when we bend before Thy throne.
380 Heal me. O my Saviour, heal.
381 Son of Man, to Thee I cry.
382 O Jesus, Thou art standing.
383 Lord I beseech Thee, on this day.
405 God my Father hear me, pray.
557 Pity on us, heavenly Father. Litany.
558 Son of God, for man decreed. "
559 God the Father, God the Son. "
560 Father hear Thy children's call. "
614 When at Thy footstool, Lord, I bend.
624 Thy life was given for me.

88   P.M.

1 Lord, in this Thy mercy's day,
   Ere from us it pass away,
   On our knees we fall and pray.

2 Holy Jesus, grant us tears,
   Fill us with heart-searching fears,
   Ere the hour of doom appears.

3 Lord, on us Thy Spirit pour,
   Kneeling lowly at Thy door,
   Ere it close for evermore.

4 By Thy night of agony,
   By Thy supplicating cry,
   By Thy willingness to die,

5 By Thy tears of bitter woe
   For Jerusalem below,
   Let us not thy love forego.

6 Judge and Saviour of our race,
   When we see Thee face to face,
   Grant us 'neath Thy wings a place.

7 On Thy love we rest alone,
   And that love shall then be known
   By the pardoned round Thy throne.

89   HOLY WEEK.   7.6.

1 All glory, laud, and honor.
   To Thee, Redeemer, King!
   To whom the lips of children
   Made sweet hosannas ring.

2 Thou art the King of Israel,
   Thou David's royal Son.
   Who in the Lord's name comest,
   The King and blessèd One.
                            All glory, etc.

3 The company of angels
   Are praising Thee on high ;
   And mortal men, and all things
   Created, make reply.
                            All glory, etc.

4 The people of the Hebrews
   With palms before Thee went :
   Our praise and prayer and anthems
   Before Thee we present.
                            All glory, etc.

5 To Thee before Thy passion
   They sang their hymns of praise:
   To Thee, now high exalted
   Our melody we raise.
                            All glory, etc.

THE CHRISTIAN YEAR—HOLY WEEK.

6 Thou didst accept their praises;
  Accept the prayers we bring,
  Who in all good delightest,
  Thou good and gracious King.
    All glory, etc.

90   L. M.

1 Ride on! ride on in majesty!
  Hark! all the tribes hosanna cry;
  O Saviour meek, pursue Thy road
  With palms and scattered garments strowed.

2 Ride on! ride on in majesty!
  In lowly pomp ride on to die:
  O Christ, Thy triumphs now begin
  O'er captive death and conquered sin.

3 Ride on! ride on in majesty!
  The wingèd armies of the sky
  Look down with sad and wondering eyes
  Upon the approaching sacrifice.

4 Ride on! ride on in majesty!
  Thy last and fiercest strife is nigh;
  The Father on His sapphire throne
  Awaits His own anointed Son.

5 Ride on! ride on in majesty!
  In lowly pomp ride on to die:
  Bow Thy meek head to mortal pain,
  Then take, O God, Thy power, and reign.
    Amen.

91   L. M.

1 The royal banners forward go;
  The cross shines forth in mystic glow;
  Where He in flesh, our flesh Who made,
  Our sentence bore, our ransom paid.

2 Where deep for us the spear was dyed,
  Life's torrent rushing from His side,
  To wash us in that precious flood
  Where mingled water flowed, and blood.

3 Fulfilled is all that David told
  In true prophetic song of old:
  Amidst the nations God, saith he,
  Hath reigned and triumphed from the tree.

4 O tree of beauty, tree of light:
  O tree with royal purple dight!
  Elect on whose triumphal breast
  Those holy limbs should find their rest;

5 On whose dear arms, so widely flung,
  The weight of this world's ransom hung:
  The price of human kind to pay,
  And spoil the spoiler of his prey.

6 To Thee, Eternal Three in One,
  Let homage meet by all be done:
  Whom by the cross Thou dost restore,
  Preserve and govern evermore. Amen.

92   C. M.

1 O Thou, Who through this holy week
    Didst suffer for us all;
  The sick to heal, the lost to seek,
    To raise up them that fall:

2 We cannot understand the woe
    Thy love was pleased to bear;
  O Lamb of God, we only know
    That all our hopes are there.

3 Thy feet the path of suffering trod,
    Thy hand the victory won;
  What shall we render to our God
    For all that He hath done?

4 To God, the Blessèd Three in One,
    All praise and glory be;
  Crown, Lord, Thy servants who have won
    The victory through Thee. Amen.

93   8.7.8.7.8.8.7.

1 O sinner, lift the eye of faith,
    To true repentance turning;
  Bethink thee of the curse of sin,
    Its awful guilt discerning:
  Upon the crucified one look,
  And thou shalt read, as in a book,
    What well is worth thy learning.

2 Look on His head, that bleeding head,
    With crown of thorns surrounded;
  Look on his sacred hands and feet
    Which piercing nails have wounded:
  See every limb with scourges rent·
  On Him, the just, the innocent,
    What malice hath abounded!

3 'Tis not alone those limbs are racked,
    But friends too are forsaking;
  And, more than all, for thankless man
    That tender heart is aching;
  Oh, fearful was the pain and scorn,
  By Jesus, Son of Mary, borne,
    Their peace for sinners making.

29

4 None ever knew such pain before,
   Such infinite affliction,
 None ever felt a grief like His
   In that dread crucifixion ;
 For us He bare those bitter throes,
 For us those agonizing woes,
   In oft-renewed infliction.

5 O sinner, mark, and ponder well
   Sin's awful condemnation;
 Think what a sacrifice it cost
   To purchase thy salvation ;
 Had Jesus never bled and died,
 Then what could thee and all betide
   But uttermost damnation?

6 Lord, give us grace to flee from sin,
   And Satan's wiles ensnaring,
 And from those everlasting flames
   For evil ones preparing.
 Jesus, we thank Thee, and entreat
 To rest forever at Thy feet,
   Thy heavenly glory sharing.   Amen.

94   L. M.

1 Lord Jesus! when we stand afar,
   And gaze upon Thy holy cross,
 In love of Thee, and scorn of self,
   O may we count the world as loss!

2 When we behold Thy bleeding wounds,
   And the rough way that Thou hast trod,
 Make us to hate the load of sin
   That lay so heavy on our God.

3 O holy Lord, uplifted high,
   With outstretched arms, in mortal woe
 Embracing in Thy wondrous love
   The sinful world that lies below;

4 Give us an ever-living faith
   To gaze beyond the things we see;
 And in the mystery of Thy death
   Draw us and all men unto Thee.   Amen.

95   7s.

1 See the destined day arise!
   See, a willing sacrifice,
 Jesus, to redeem our loss,
 Hangs upon the shameful cross!

2 Jesus, who but Thou had borne,
   Lifted on that tree of scorn,
 Every pang and bitter throe,
 Finishing Thy life of woe?

3 Who but Thou had dared to drain
   Steeped in gall the cup of pain,
 And with tender body bear
 Thorns, and nails, and piercing spear?

4 Thence the cleansing water flowed,
   Mingled from Thy side with blood;
 Sign to all attesting eyes
 Of the finished sacrifice.

5 Holy Jesus, grant us grace
   In that sacrifice to place
 All our trust for life renewed,
 Pardoned sin and promised good.   Amen.

96   L. M.

1 We sing the praise of Him who died,
   Of Him who died upon the cross:
 The sinner's hope let men deride :
   For this we count the world but loss.

2 Inscribed upon the cross we see
   In shining letters, God is love :
 He bears our sins upon the tree ;
   He brings us mercy from above.

3 The cross—it takes our guilt away;
   It holds the fainting spirit up;
 It cheers with hope the gloomy day,
   And sweetens every bitter cup.

4 It makes the coward spirit brave,
   And nerves the feeble arm for fight ;
 It takes its terror from the grave,
   And gilds the bed of death with light.

5 The balm of life, the cure of woe,
   The measure and the pledge of love,
 The sinner's refuge here below,
   The angels' theme in heaven above

97   L. M.

1 When I survey the wondrous cross
   On which the Prince of glory died,
 My richest gain I count but loss,
   And pour contempt on all my pride.

2 Forbid it, Lord, that I should boast,
   Save in the death of Christ, my God;
 All the vain things that charm me most,
   I sacrifice them to His blood.

THE CHRISTIAN YEAR—HOLY WEEK.

3 See, from His head, His hands, His feet,
  Sorrow and love flow mingled down!
  Did e'er such love and sorrow meet?
  Or thorns compose so rich a crown?

4 Were the whole realm of nature mine,
  That were a tribute far too small;
  Love so amazing, so divine,
  Demands my soul, my life, my all.

98   C. M.
1 This day the wondrous mystery
  Is set before our eyes,
  Of Jesus stretched upon the cross
  In dying agonies.

2 O deed of love! the Prince becomes
  A victim for the slave ;
  The sinner an acquittal finds,
  The innocent a grave.

3 O Blessèd Jesus, valiant chief,
  We hail the triumph won
  O'er sin, the world, and hell, and death,
  By Thee, the incarnate Son!

4 Be Thine the banner under which
  From this time forth we fight
  Against the depth of Satan's guile,
  And all the powers of night.

5 So, dead to our old life, may we
  A better life begin;
  And through Thy cross, O Christ, at length
  A heavenly crown attain.

99   7. 6.
1 O Sacred head, surrounded
  By crown of piercing thorn!
  O bleeding head, so wounded,
  Reviled and put to scorn!

  Death's pallid hue comes o'er Thee,
  The glow of life decays,
  Yet angel-hosts adore Thee,
  And tremble as they gaze.

2 I see Thy strength and vigor,
  All fading in the strife,
  And death with cruel rigor,
  Bereaving Thee of life;

  O agony and dying!
  O love to sinners free!
  Jesus, all grace supplying,
  O turn Thy face on me.

3 In this, Thy bitter passion,
  Good Shepherd, think of me
  With Thy most sweet compassion,
  Unworthy though I be :

  Beneath Thy cross abiding
  For ever would I rest,
  In Thy dear love confiding,
  And with Thy presence blest.

4 Be near when I am dying,
  O show Thy cross to me:
  And to my succor flying,
  Come, Lord, and set me free.

  These eyes, new faith receiving,
  From Jesus shall not move ;
  For he, who dies believing,
  Dies safely through Thy love.

100   8.8.7.8.8.7.
1 At the cross her station keeping
  Stood the mournful Mother weeping,
  Where He hung, the dying Lord ;
  For her soul of joy bereavèd,
  Bowed with anguish deeply grievèd,
  Felt the sharp and piercing sword.

2 Oh, how sad and sore distressèd
  Now was she, that Mother blessèd
  Of the sole-begotten One;
  Deep the woe of her affliction,
  When she saw the crucifixion
  Of her ever-glorious Son.

3 Who, on Christ's dear Mother gazing,
  Pierced by anguish so amazing,
  Born of woman, would not weep?
  Who, on Christ's dear Mother thinking,
  Such a cup of sorrow drinking,
  Would not share her sorrows deep?

4 For His people's sins chastisèd,
  She beheld her Son despisèd,
  Scourged, and crowned with thorns entwined ;
  Saw Him then from judgment taken,
  And in death by all forsaken,
  Till His Spirit He resigned.

THE CHRISTIAN YEAR—EASTER EVEN.

5 Jesus, may her deep devotion
  Stir in me the same emotion,
  Fount of love, Redeemer kind,
  That my heart fresh ardor gaining,
  And a purer love attaining,
  May with Thee acceptance find. Amen.

101　　　　　　　　8.7.

1 Sweet the moments, rich in blessing,
  Which before the cross we spend ;
  Life and health and peace possessing
  Through the sinner's dying friend.

2 Kneel we here, in wonder, viewing
  Mercy poured in streams of blood ;
  Precious drops, for pardon suing,
  Make and plead our peace with God.

3 Truly blessèd is the station,
  Low before His cross to lie,
  While we see divine compassion
  Beaming in His dying eye.

4 Here we find our hope of heaven,
  While upon the Lamb we gaze ;
  Loving much, and much forgiven,
  Let our hearts o'erflow with praise.

5 Lord, in loving contemplation
  Fix our hearts and eyes on Thee,
  Till we taste Thy full salvation,
  And Thine unveiled glories see.

6 For Thy sorrows we adore Thee,
  For the griefs that wrought our peace ;
  Gracious Saviour, we implore Thee,
  In our hearts Thy love increase. Amen.

102　　　　　　　　L M.

1 O come and mourn with me awhile ;
  And tarry here the cross beside ;
  O come, together let us mourn ;
  Jesus, our Lord, is crucified.

2 Have we no tears to shed for Him,
  While soldiers scoff and Jews deride?
  Ah ! look how patiently He hangs ;
  Jesus, our Lord, is crucified.

3 Seven times He spake, seven words of love ;
  And all three hours His silence cried
  For mercy on the souls of men ;
  Jesus, our Lord, is crucified.

4 O love of God ! O sin of man!
  In this dread act your strength is tried ;
  And victory remains with love ;
  For Thou, our Lord, art crucified !

Also the following:
384 Glory be to Jesus.
385 There is a green hill far away.
386 O Jesus, we adore Thee.
387 O Jesus, Lord most merciful.
388 Christ, the life of all the living.
561 Jesus, Who for us didst bear.
562 Jesus, in Thy dying woes.

EASTER EVEN.

103　　　　　　　　7s.

1 Resting from His work to-day
  In the tomb the Saviour lay ;
  Still He slept, from head to feet
  Shrouded in the winding sheet,
  Lying in the rock alone,
  Hidden by the sealèd stone.

2 Late at even there was seen
  Watching long the Magdalene ;
  Early, ere the break of day,
  Sorrowful she took her way
  To the holy garden glade,
  Where her buried Lord was laid.

3 So with Thee, till life shall end,
  I would solemn vigil spend ;
  Let me hew Thee, Lord, a shrine
  In this rocky heart of mine,
  Where in pure embalmèd cell
  None but Thou may ever dwell.

4 Myrrh and spices will I bring,
  True affection's offering ;
  Close the door from sight and sound
  Of the busy world around ;
  And in patient watch remain
  Till my Lord appear again.

104　　　　　　　　8.7.

1 It is finished ! Blessèd Jesus,
  Thou hast breathed Thy latest sigh,
  Teaching us, the sons of Adam,
  How the Son of God can die.

2 Lifeless lies the broken body,
　Hidden in its rocky bed.
　Laid aside like folded garment ;
　Where is now the Spirit fled?

3 In the gloomy realms of darkness
　Shines a light unknown before,
　For the Lord of dead and living
　Enters at the open door.

4 See ! He comes a willing victim,
　Unresisting hither led ;
　Passing from the cross of sorrow
　To the mansions of the dead.

5 Lo! the heavenly light around Him
　As He draws His people near ;
　All amazed they stand, rejoicing
　At the gracious words they hear.

6 For Himself proclaims the story
　Of His own incarnate life,
　And the death He died to save us,
　Victor in that awful strife.

7 Patriarch and priest and prophet
　Gather round Him as He stands,
　In adoring faith and gladness,
　Hearing of the piercèd hands.

8 Oh, the bliss to which He calls them
　Ransomed by His precious blood,
　From the gloomy realm of darkness
　To the Paradise of God!

9 There in lowliest joy and wonder
　Stands the robber at His side,
　Reaping now the blessèd promise
　Spoken by the Crucified.

10 Jesus, Lord of dead and living,
　Let Thy mercy rest on me ;
　Grant me too, when life is finished,
　Rest in Paradise with Thee.　Amen.

105　　　　4.4.7.7.6.

1 So rest, our Rest!
　Thou ever blest!
　Thy grave with sinners making ;
　By Thy precious death, from sin
　Our dead souls awaking.

2 Here hast Thou lain
　After much pain,
　Life of our life, reposing ;
　Round Thee now a rock-hewn grave,
　Rock of Ages, closing.

3 Breath of all breath!
　We know, from death
　Thou wilt our dust awaken ;
　Wherefore should we dread the grave,
　Or our faith be shaken?

4 The body dies,
　(Naught else), and lies
　In dust until victorious
　From the grave, it shall arise
　Beautiful and glorious.

5 Meantime we will,
　Our Saviour, still
　Deep in our bosoms lay Thee,
　Musing on Thy death ; in death
　Be with us, we pray Thee.　Amen.

106　　　　　　C. M.

1 The grave itself a garden is,
　Where loveliest flowers abound ;
　Since Christ, our never-fading life,
　Sprang from that holy ground.

2 O give us grace to die to sin,
　That we, O Lord, may have
　A holy, happy rest in Thee,
　A sabbath in the grave.

3 Thou, Lord, baptized in Thine own blood,
　And buried in the grave,
　Didst raise Thyself to endless life,
　Omnipotent to save.

4 Baptized into Thy death we died,
　And buried were with Thee,
　That we might live with Thee to God,
　And ever blest might be.

5 Lord, through the grave and gate of death
　May we, with Thee, arise
　To an eternal Easter-day
　Of glory in the skies!　Amen.

EASTERTIDE.

107 11s.

1 "Welcome, happy morning!" age to age
shall say:
Hell to-day is vanquished, heaven is won to-
day!
Lo! the dead is living, God for evermore!
Him, their true Creator, all His works adore!
" Welcome, happy morning!" age to age
shall say.

2 Earth her joy confesses, clothing her for
spring.
All fresh gifts returned with her returning
King :
Bloom in every meadow, leaves on every
bough,
Speak His sorrow ended, hail His triumph
now.
Hell to-day is vanquished, heaven is won to-
day.

3 Months in due succession, days of lengthen-
ing light,
Hours and passing moments praise Thee in
their flight ;
Brightness of the morning, sky and fields
and sea,
Vanquisher of darkness, bring their praise
to Thee!
" Welcome, happy morning!" age to age
shall say.

4 Maker and Redeemer, life and health of all,
Thou from heaven beholding human nature's
fall,
Of the Father's Godhead true and only Son,
Manhood to deliver, manhood didst put on.
Hell to-day is vanquished, heaven is won to-
day.

5 Thou, of life the author, death didst un-
dergo,
Tread the path of darkness, saving strength
to show;
Come then, true and faithful, now fulfill Thy
word:
'Tis Thine own third morning, rise O buried
Lord!
" Welcome, happy morning!" age to age
shall say.

6 Loose the souls long prisoned, bound with
Satan's chain;
All that now is fallen raise to life again:
Shew Thy face in brightness, bid the nations
see,
Bring again our daylight ; day returns with
Thee!
Hell to-day is vanquished, heaven is won to-
day!
[Both the first and second lines of verse 1 may be
sung as a refrain after each verse, if desired.]

108 7.6.

1 Come, ye faithful, raise the strain
  Of triumphant gladness ;
God hath brought His Israel
  Into joy from sadness;
Loosed from Pharaoh's bitter yoke
  Jacob's sons and daughters;
Led them with unmoistened foot
  Through the Red Sea waters.

2 'Tis the spring of souls to-day;
  Christ hath burst His prison,
And from three days' sleep in death
  As a sun hath risen ;
All the winter of our sins,
  Long and dark, is flying
From His light, to Whom we give
  Laud and praise undying.

3 Now the Queen of seasons, bright
  With the day of splendor.
With the royal feast of feasts,
  Comes its joy to render ;
Comes to glad Jerusalem,
  Who with true affection
Welcomes in unwearied strains
  Jesu's resurrection.

4 Alleluia now we cry
  To our King immortal,
Who triumphant burst the bars
  Of the tomb's dark portal ;
Alleluia, with the Son
  God the Father praising ;
Alleluia yet again
  To the Spirit raising. Amen.

109 7s.

1 Christ the Lord is risen to-day,
Sons of men and angels say :
Raise your joys and triumphs high,
Sing, ye heavens and earth reply.

2 Love's redeeming work is done,
Fought the fight, the victory won:
Jesu's agony is o'er,
Darkness veils the earth no more.

3 Vain the stone, the watch, the seal,
Christ hath burst the gates of hell;
Death in vain forbids Him rise,
Christ hath opened Paradise.

4 Soar we now where Christ hath led,
Following our exalted Head;
Made like Him, like Him we rise;
Ours the cross, the grave, the skies.

110　　　　　　　　　　　7s.

1 Jesus Christ is risen to-day,
Our triumphant holy day,
Who did once upon the cross
Suffer to redeem our loss.
　　　Alleluia!

2 Hymns of praise then let us sing
Unto Christ, our heavenly King,
Who endured the cross and grave,
Sinners to redeem and save.
　　　Alleluia!

3 But the pains which He endured
Our salvation have procured;
Now above the sky He's King,
Where the angels ever sing,
　　　Alleluia!

111　　　8.7.8.7.7.5.7.5.8.7.8.7.

1 Christ is risen! Christ is risen!
He hath burst His bonds in twain;
Christ is risen! Christ is risen!
Alleluia! swell the strain!
　For our gain He suffered loss
　By divine decree;
　He hath died upon the cross,
　But our God is He.
Christ is risen! Christ is risen!
He hath burst His bonds in twain;
Christ is risen! Christ is risen!
Alleluia! swell the strain!

2 See the chains of death are broken;
Earth below and heaven above
Joy in each amazing token
Of His rising, Lord of love;
　He for evermore shall reign
　By the Father's side,
　Till He comes to earth again,
　Comes to claim His bride.
Christ is risen! etc.

3 Glorious angels downward thronging
Hail the Lord of all the skies;
Heaven, with joy and holy longing
For the Word incarnate, cries,
　"Christ is risen! Earth, rejoice!
　Gleam, ye starry train!
　All creation, find a voice;
　He o'er all shall reign."
Christ is risen! Christ is risen!
He hath burst His bonds in twain;
Christ is risen! Christ is risen,
O'er the universe to reign.

112　　　　　　　　　　　7s.

1 Christ the Lord is risen again;
Christ hath broken every chain;
Hark, angelic voices cry,
Singing evermore on high,
　　　Alleluia!

2 He Who gave for us His life,
Who for us endured the strife,
Is our Paschal Lamb to-day;
We too sing for joy, and say
　　　Alleluia!

3 He Who bore all pain and loss
Comfortless upon the cross,
Lives in glory now on high,
Pleads for us and hears our cry;
　　　Alleluia!

4 He Who slumbered in the grave
Is exalted now to save;
Now through Christendom it rings
That the Lamb is King of kings.
　　　Alleluia!

5 Now He bids us tell abroad
How the lost may be restored,
How the penitent forgiven,
How we too may enter heaven.
　　　Alleluia!

6 Thou, our Paschal Lamb indeed,
Christ, Thy ransomed people feed;
Take our sins and guilt away,
Let us sing by night and day
               Alleluia.

113   7.6.

1 The day of resurrection!
Earth, tell it out abroad;
The Passover of gladness,
The Passover of God.

From death to life eternal,
From this world to the sky,
Our Christ hath brought us over
With hymns of victory.

2 Our hearts be pure from evil,
That we may see aright
The Lord in rays eternal
Of resurrection-light:

And, listening to His accents,
May hear so calm and plain
His own "All hail," and bearing
May raise the victor strain.

3 Now let the heavens be joyful,
Let earth her song begin,
Let the round world keep triumph,
And all that is therein:

Invisible and visible
Their notes let all things blend,
For Christ the Lord is risen,
Our joy that hath no end.

114   8.7.8.7.7.7.

1 He is risen, He is risen;
Tell it out with joyful voice;
He has burst His three days' prison;
Let the whole wide earth rejoice:
Death is conquered, man is free,
Christ has won the victory.

2 Come, ye sad and fearful-hearted,
With glad smile and radiant brow;
Lent's long shadows have departed;
All His woes are over now,
And the passion that He bore:
Sin and pain can vex no more.

3 Come, with high and holy gladness
Chant our Lord's triumphal lay;
Not one touch of twilight sadness
Dims yon glorious morning ray
Breaking o'er the purple cast;
Brighter far our Easter feast.

4 He is risen, He is risen:
He hath opened heaven's gate:
We are free from sin's dark prison,
Risen to a holier state.
Soon a brighter Easter beam
On our longing eyes shall stream.

115   7s.

1 At the Lamb's high feast we sing
Praise to our victorious King,
Who hath washed us in the tide
Flowing from His pierced side;

Praise we Him, Whose love divine
Gives His sacred blood for wine,
Gives His body for the feast,
Christ the victim, Christ the priest.

2 Where the Paschal blood is poured,
Death's dark angel sheathes his sword;
Israel's hosts triumphant go
Through the wave that drowns the foe.

Praise we Christ, Whose blood was shed,
Paschal victim, Paschal bread;
With sincerity and love
Eat we manna from above.

3 Mighty victim from the sky!
Hell's fierce powers beneath Thee lie;
Thou hast conquered in the fight,
Thou hast brought us life and light:

Now no more can death appal,
Now no more the grave enthral;
Thou hast opened Paradise,
And in Thee Thy saints shall rise.

4 Easter triumph, Easter joy,
Sin alone can this destroy;
From sin's power do Thou set free
Souls new-born, O Lord, in Thee.

Hymns of glory and of praise,
Risen Lord, to Thee we raise;
Holy Father, praise to Thee,
With the Spirit, ever be. Amen.

THE CHRISTIAN YEAR—EASTERTIDE.

116 P.M.

1 The foe behind, the deep before,
 Our hosts have dared and passed the sea:
 And Pharaoh's warriors strew the shore,
 And Israel's ransomed tribes are free.

2 Lift up, lift up your voices now!
 The whole wide world rejoices now!
 The Lord hath triumphed gloriously :
 The Lord shall reign victoriously!

3 Happy morrow,
 Turning sorrow
 Into peace and mirth!
 Bondage ending,
 Love descending
 O'er the earth!

4 Seals assuring,
 Guards securing,
 Watch His earthly prison :
 Seals are shattered,
 Guards are scattered,
 Christ hath risen!

5 No longer must the mourners weep,
 Nor call departed Christians dead :
 For death is hallowed into sleep,
 And every grave becomes a bed.

6 Now once more
 Eden's door
 Opened stands to mortal eyes ;
 For Christ hath risen, and man shall rise!

7 Now at last,
 Old things past,
 Hope, and joy, and peace begin :
 For Christ hath won, and man shall win!

8 It is not exile, rest on high:
 It is not sadness, peace from strife :
 To fall asleep is not to die :
 To dwell with Christ is better life.

9 Where our banner leads us,
 We may safely go :
 Where our chief precedes us,
 We may face the foe.

10 His right arm is o'er us,
 He our guide will be :
 Christ hath gone before us, .
 Christians follow ye!

117 P.M.

1 The strife is o'er, the battle done !
 The victory of life is won ;
 The song of triumph has begun,
 Alleluia !

2 The powers of death have done their worst.
 But Christ their legions hath dispersed:
 Let shout of holy joy outburst,
 Alleluia!

3 The three sad days are quickly sped ;
 He rises glorious from the dead:
 All glory to our risen Head!
 Alleluia!

4 He closed the yawning gates of hell,
 The bars from heaven's high portals fell ;
 Let hymns of praise His triumphs tell!
 Alleluia!

5 Lord! by the stripes which wounded Thee,
 From death's dread sting Thy servants free,
 That we may live, and sing to Thee,
 Alleluia! Amen.

118 7.8.

1 Jesus lives! thy threatening woe,
 Death, no longer need appal us:
 Jesus lives! by this we know
 Thou, O grave, canst not enthral us.
 Alleluia!

2 Jesus lives! henceforth is death
 But the gate of life immortal ;
 This shall calm our trembling breath,
 When we pass its gloomy portal.
 Alleluia!

3 Jesus lives! for us He died;
 Then, alone to Jesus living,
 Pure in heart may we abide,
 Glory to our Saviour giving.
 Alleluia!

4 Jesus lives! our hearts know well
 Naught from us His love shall sever;
 Life, nor death, nor powers of hell
 Tear us from His keeping ever.
 Alleluia!

5 Jesus lives! to Him the throne
 Over all the world is given ;
 May we go where He has gone,
 Rest and reign with Him in heaven.
 Alleluia!

119
8.7.

1 Alleluia! Alleluia!
  Hearts and voices heaven-ward raise;
  Sing to God a hymn of gladness,
  Sing to God a hymn of praise:
  He, Who on the cross a victim
  For the world's salvation bled,
  Jesus Christ, the King of glory,
  Now is risen from the dead.

2 Now the iron bars are broken,
  Christ from death to life is born,
  Glorious life, and life immortal,
  On this holy Easter morn:
  Christ has triumphed and we conquer
  By His mighty enterprise,
  We with Him to life eternal
  By His resurrection rise.

3 Christ is risen, Christ, the first-fruits
  Of the holy harvest-field,
  Which will all its full abundance
  At His second coming yield:
  Then the golden ears of harvest
  Will their heads before Him wave,
  Ripened by His glorious sunshine
  From the furrows of the grave.

4 Christ is risen, we are risen!
  Shed upon us heavenly grace,
  Rain and dew and gleams of glory
  From the brightness of Thy face:
  That, with hearts in heaven dwelling,
  We on earth may fruitful be,
  And by angel-hands be gathered,
  And be ever, Lord, with Thee.

5 Alleluia! Alleluia!
  Glory be to God on high,
  To the Father, and the Saviour
  Who has won the victory;
  Glory to the Holy Spirit,
  Fount of love and sanctity;
  Alleluia! Alleluia!
  To the Triune Majesty. Amen.

120
8.7.

1 Sing, with all the sons of glory,
  Sing the resurrection-song!
  Death and sorrow, earth's dark story,
  To the "former days" belong.

  Even now the dawn is breaking,
  Soon the night of time shall cease,
  And, in God's own likeness waking,
  Man shall know eternal peace.

2 Oh, what glory, far exceeding
  All that eye has yet perceived!
  Holiest hearts, for ages pleading,
  Never that full joy conceived.
  God has promised, Christ prepares it,
  There on high our welcome waits;
  Every humble spirit shares it,
  Christ has passed the eternal gates.

3 "Life eternal!" heaven rejoices,
  Jesus lives Who once was dead;
  Join, O man, the deathless voices,
  Child of God, lift up thy head.
  Patriarchs from distant ages,
  Saints all longing for their heaven,
  Prophets, psalmists, seers, and sages,
  All await the glory given.

4 "Life eternal!" Oh, what wonders
  Crowd on faith—what joy unknown,
  When, amidst earth's closing thunders,
  Saints shall stand before the throne!
  Oh! to enter that bright portal,
  See that glowing firmament,
  Know, with Thee, O God immortal,
  "Jesus Christ, Whom Thou hast sent!"

121
8.7.

1 Hark! ten thousand voices sounding
  Far and wide throughout the sky;
  'Tis the voice of joy abounding,
  Jesus lives, no more to die!

2 Jesus lives, His conflict over,
  Lives to claim His great reward;
  Angels round the victor hover,
  Crowding to behold their Lord.

3 Yonder throne for Him erected
  Now becomes the victor's seat;
  Lo, the Man on earth rejected,
  Angels worship at His feet!

4 All the powers of heaven adore Him,
  All obey His sovereign word;
  Day and night they cry before Him,
  "Holy, Holy, Holy Lord!"

Also the following:
251 On the resurrection morning.
889 To Him, Who for our sins was slain.
390 Glory, glory everlasting.
392 Christ, above all glory seated.
420 Those eternal bowers.
458 Alleluia! sing to Jesus.
459 Jesus, our risen King.
468 Come, let us sing the song of songs.
474 Rejoice, the Lord is King.
541 Come ye faithful, raise the anthem.

122
ASCENSIONTIDE. 8.7.

1 See the conqueror mounts in triumph;
  See the King in royal state,
Riding on the clouds His chariot
  To His heavenly palace gate!

Hark! the choirs of angel voices
  Joyful alleluias sing,
And the portals high are lifted
  To receive their heavenly King.

2 Who is this that comes in glory,
  With the trump of jubilee?
Lord of battles, God of armies,
  He hath gained the victory!

He Who on the cross did suffer,
  He Who from the grave arose,
He has vanquished sin and Satan,
  He by death has spoiled His foes.

3 While He raised His hands in blessing,
  He was parted from His friends;
While their eager eyes behold Him,
  He upon the clouds ascends;

He Who walked with God and pleased Him,
  Preaching truth and doom to come,
He, our Enoch, is translated,
  To His everlasting home.

4 Now our heavenly Aaron enters,
  With His blood, within the veil;
Joshua now is come to Canaan,
  And the kings before Him quail;

Now He plants the tribes of Israel
  In their promised resting-place;
Now our great Elijah offers
  Double portion of His grace.

5 Thou hast raised our human nature
  On the clouds to God's right hand:
There we sit in heavenly places,
  There with Thee in glory stand.

Jesus reigns, adored by angels;
  Man with God is on the throne;
Mighty Lord, in Thine ascension,
  We by faith behold our own.

123
7s.

1 Hail the day that sees Him rise
  To His throne above the skies;
Christ, the Lamb for sinners given,
Enters now the highest heaven.
    Alleluia!

2 There for Him high triumph waits;
  Lift your heads, eternal gates:
He hath conquered death and sin;
Take the King of glory in.
    Alleluia!

3 Lo! the heaven its Lord receives,
  Yet He loves the earth He leaves;
Though returning to His throne,
Still He calls mankind His own.
    Alleluia!

4 See! He lifts His hands above;
  See! He shews the prints of love;
Hark! His gracious lips bestow
Blessings on His church below.
    Alleluia!

5 Still for us He intercedes,
  His prevailing death He pleads,
Near Himself prepares our place,
He the first-fruits of our race.
    Alleluia!

6 Lord, though parted from our sight
  Far above the starry height,
Grant our hearts may thither rise,
Seeking Thee above the skies.
    Alleluia!
    Amen.

[The Alleluia may be sung at the end of each line if desired.]

124 L.M.

1 O King eternal, King most high,
  Who for lost man didst freely die,
  Thy warfare with the grave is done,
  Thy last and greatest glory won.

2 Ascending by the starry road
  This day Thou wentest home to God;
  Henceforth upon the throne divine
  The powers of heaven and earth are Thine.

3 The triple frame of earth and heaven
  And things beneath to Thee is given,
  And every tongue confesseth Thee,
  And at Thy Name bows every knee.

4 Be Thou our joy on earth, O Lord,
  Be Thou in heaven our great reward;
  Earth's joys to Thee are nothing worth,
  The joy and crown of heaven and earth.

5 We pray Thee to unloose the chain
  That binds us to a world of pain,
  And draw our hearts by cords of grace
  To Thy celestial dwelling place:

6 So at Thy last most dread return
  When skies in wrathful glory burn,
  Our sins wiped out for evermore.
  Thou shalt our forfeit crowns restore.

125 8.7.

1 Christ our King to heaven ascendeth,
  Past the blue sky's utmost bound;
  Christ our King to heaven ascendeth,
  Clouds of angels close Him round.

  Alleluia, alleluia,
  Alleluia loud they cry:
  Christ our King to heaven ascendeth,
  Glory be to God on high!

2 Our High-Priest to heaven ascendeth,
  Lo! the Lamb, as it were slain!
  Our High-Priest to heaven ascendeth,
  On God's throne He lives again;

  Pleads His sacrifice of wonder,
  Claims the fruit of all His pain:
  Our High-Priest to heaven ascendeth,
  Peace on earth, good-will to men!

3 Christ our Lord to heaven ascendeth,
  Cloven tongues of fire appear,
  Christ our Lord to heaven ascendeth,
  Lo! the rushing wind is here!

  Mighty armies forth with banners
  Conquering and to conquer go:
  Christ our Lord to heaven ascendeth,
  He shall reign o'er all below.

4 Christ now reigns, the King of glory,
  All His foes before Him fall;
  Christ now reigns, the King of glory,
  He alone is all in all.

  King of kings shall men behold Him,
  Lord of lords for evermore;
  Christ now reigns, the King of glory,
  Bow before Him, and adore!

126 L.M.

1 O Saviour, Who for man hast trod
  The winepress of the wrath of God,
  Ascend, and claim again on high
  Thy glory, left for us to die.

2 A radiant cloud is now Thy seat,
  And earth lies stretched beneath Thy feet;
  Ten thousand thousands round Thee sing,
  And share the triumph of their King.

3 The angel-host enraptured waits:
  "Lift up your heads, eternal gates!"
  O God and Man! the Father's throne
  Is now for evermore Thine own.

4 Our great High Priest and Shepherd, Thou
  Within the veil art entered now,
  To offer there Thy precious blood
  Once poured on earth, a cleansing flood.

5 And thence the Church, Thy chosen bride,
  With countless gifts of grace supplied,
  Through all her members draws from Thee
  Her hidden life of sanctity.

6 O Christ, our Lord, of Thy dear care
  Thy lowly members heaven-ward bear;
  Be ours with Thee to suffer pain,
  With Thee for evermore to reign. Amen.

THE CHRISTIAN YEAR—WHITSUNTIDE.

127 L.M.

1 Our Lord is risen from the dead;
  Our Captain is gone up on high;
  The powers of hell are captive led,
  Dragged to the portals of the sky.

2 There His triumphal chariot waits,
  And angels chant the solemn lay:
  " Lift up your heads, ye heavenly gates,"
  Ye everlasting doors, give way.

3 Loose all your bars of massy light,
  And wide unfold the radiant scene;
  He claims those mansions as His right;
  Receive the King of glory in.

4 Who is the King of glory, who?
  The Lord that all His foes o'ercame,
  The world, sin, death, and hell o'erthrew;
  And Jesus is the Conqueror's name.

5 Lo! His triumphal chariot waits,
  And angels chant the solemn lay:
  " Lift up your heads, ye heavenly gates,"
  Ye everlasting doors, give way.

6 Who is the King of glory, who?
  The Lord, of boundless power possessed
  The King of saints and angels too,
  God over all, for ever blessed.

Also the following:

391 Triumphant Lord, Thy work is done.
392 Christ above all glory seated.
393 The Head that once was crowned with thorns.
394 Thou art gone up on high.
395 Crown Him with many crowns.
459 Jesus, our risen King.
469 All hail the power of Jesus' name.
473 Lift up your heads, ye mighty gates.
474 Rejoice, the Lord is King.
575 Golden harps are sounding.

WHITSUNTIDE.

128 6.5.

1 Hear us, Thou that broodedst
  O'er the watery deep,
  Waking all creation
  From its primal sleep;
  Holy Spirit, breathing
  Breath of life divine,
  Breathe into our spirits,
  Blending them with Thine.
  Light and Life immortal!
  Hear us as we raise
  Hearts, as well as voices,
  Mingling prayer and praise.

2 When the sun ariseth
  In a cloudless sky,
  May we feel Thy presence,
  Holy Spirit, nigh;
  Shed Thy radiance o'er us,
  Keep it cloudless still.
  Through the day before us,
  Perfecting Thy will.
  Light and Life immortal! etc

3 When the fight is fiercest
  In the noontide heat,
  Bear us, Holy Spirit,
  To our Saviour's feet;
  There to find a refuge
  Till our work is done,
  There to fight the battle,
  Till the battle's won.
  Light and Life immortal! etc

4 If the day be falling
  Sadly as it goes,
  Slowly in its sadness
  Sinking to its close,
  May Thy love in mercy
  Kindling, ere it die,
  Cast a ray of glory
  O'er our evening sky.
  Light and Life immortal! etc.

5 Morning, noon, and evening,
  Whensoe'er it be,
  Grant us, gracious Spirit,
  Quickening life in Thee;
  Life, that gives us, living,
  Life of heavenly love,
  Life, that brings us, dying,
  Life from heaven above.
  Light and Life immortal!
  Hear us as we raise
  Hearts, as well as voices,
  Mingling prayer and praise.
                      Amen

This hymn may be sung, with or without the refrain,
as a Processional or not, as desired.

THE CHRISTIAN YEAR—TRINITY SUNDAY.

129 8.8.6.

1 To Thee, O Comforter divine,
For all Thy grace and power benign,
Sing we Alleluia!

2 To Thee, Whose faithful love had place
In God's great covenant of grace,
Sing we Alleluia!

3 To Thee, Whose faithful voice doth win
The wandering from the ways of sin,
Sing we Alleluia!

4 To Thee, Whose faithful power doth heal,
Enlighten, sanctify, and seal,
Sing we Alleluia!

5 To Thee, Whose faithful truth is shown
By every promise made our own,
Sing we Alleluia!

6 To Thee, our Teacher and our Friend,
Our faithful Leader to the end,
Sing we Alleluia!

7 To Thee, by Jesus Christ sent down,
Of all His gifts the sum and crown,
Sing we Alleluia!

8 To Thee, Who art with God the Son,
And God the Father ever One,
Sing we Alleluia! Amen.

130 7.7.7.5.

1 Come to our poor nature's night
With Thy blessèd inward light,
Holy Ghost the infinite,
Comforter divine.

2 We are sinful, cleanse us, Lord,
Sick and faint, Thy strength afford,
Lost, until by Thee restored,
Comforter divine.

3 Orphan are our souls and poor,
Give us from Thy heavenly store
Faith, love, joy for evermore,
Comforter divine.

4 Like the dew Thy peace distil:
Guide, subdue our wayward will,
Things of Christ unfolding still,
Comforter divine.

5 Gentle, awful, holy guest,
Make Thy temple in each breast;
There Thy presence be confessed,
Comforter divine.

6 With us, for us, intercede,
And with voiceless groanings plead
Our unutterable need,
Comforter divine.

7 In us, "Abba, Father," cry;
Earnest of the bliss on high,
Seal of immortality,
Comforter divine.

8 Search for us the depths of God!
Upwards, by the starry road,
Bear us to Thy high abode,
Comforter divine. Amen.

131 L.M.

1 Spirit of mercy, truth, and love,
O shed Thine influence from above;
And still from age to age convey
The wonders of this sacred day.

2 In every clime, by every tongue,
Be God's surpassing glory sung:
Let all the listening earth be taught
The deeds our great Redeemer wrought.

3 Unfailing Comfort, heavenly Guide,
Still o'er Thy holy Church preside;
Still let mankind Thy blessings prove;
Spirit of mercy, truth, and love.   Amen

Also the following:

259 Come, Holy Ghost, our souls inspire.
396 Our blest Redeemer, ere He breathed.
397 Come, Holy Spirit, come.
398 Come, Thou Holy Spirit, come.
402 Spirit divine, attend our prayers.
400 Come, Holy Ghost, Creator blest.
401 Creator Spirit, by Whose aid.
399 Come, gracious Spirit, heavenly Dove.
552 Holy Spirit, heavenly Dove.

TRINITY SUNDAY.

132 8s.

1 All glory to the Father be,
Who made the earth and sky and sea,
Gave life to every living thing,
Created man their earthly king;
Then gave His Son for man to die;
Thee, Father, God, we glorify!

THE CHRISTIAN YEAR—TRINITY SUNDAY.

2 All glory to the Son, Who came
Clothed in our flesh and mortal frame;
Who bare our sins, vouchsafed to give
Himself to die that we might live;
All-perfect God and Man in One,
Be praise to Thee, incarnate Son!

3 All glory to the Holy Ghost,
Who on the day of Pentecost
From heaven to earth in mercy came,
Descending as in tongues of flame;
The promised Comforter and Guide,
Through Whom our souls are sanctified.

4 Three Persons, but One God! Whose grace
Has formed and saves our human race;
With joyful hearts and lips to Thee,
We sing this mighty mystery;
Thy Holy Name we magnify,
O Trinity in Unity.

133   L.M.

1 O Holy, holy, holy Lord,
Bright in Thy deeds and in Thy Name,
For ever be Thy Name adored,
Thy glories let the world proclaim.

2 O Jesus, Lamb once crucified
To take our load of sins away,
Thine be the hymn that rolls its tide
Along the realms of upper day.

3 O Holy Spirit from above,
In streams of light and glory given,
Thou source of ecstacy and love,
Thy praises ring through earth and heaven.

4 O God Triune, to Thee we owe
Our every thought, our every song;
And ever may Thy praises flow
From saint and seraph's burning tongue.
Amen.

134   8s.

1 O God of life, Whose power benign
Doth o'er the world in mercy shine,
Accept our praise, for we are Thine.

2 O Father, uncreated Lord,
Be Thou in every land adored,
Be Thou by all with faith implored.

3 O Son of God, for sinners slain,
We bless Thee, Lord, Whose dying pain
For us did endless life regain.

4 O Holy Ghost, Whose guardian care
Doth us for heavenly joys prepare,
May we in Thy communion share.

5 O Holy Blessèd Trinity,
With faith we sinners bow to Thee;
In us, O God, exalted be. Amen.

135   L.M.

1 Father of heaven, Whose love profound
A ransom for our souls hath found,
Before Thy throne we sinners bend:
To us Thy pardoning love extend.

2 Almighty Son, incarnate Word,
Our Prophet, Priest, Redeemer, Lord,
Before Thy throne we sinners bend;
To us Thy saving grace extend.

3 Eternal Spirit, by Whose breath
The soul is raised from sin and death,
Before Thy throne we sinners bend;
To us Thy quickening power extend.

4 Jehovah, Father, Spirit, Son!
Mysterious Godhead, Three in One!
Before Thy throne we sinners bend;
Grace, pardon, life, to us extend.
Amen.

136   7.8.7.8.7.7.

1 Hark! the loud celestial hymn,
Angel choirs above are raising:
Cherubim and seraphim
In unceasing chorus praising,
Fill the heavens with sweet accord;
Holy, holy, holy Lord!

2 Lo! the apostolic train
Join Thy sacred Name to hallow!
Prophets swell the loud refrain,
And the white-robed martyrs follow;
And from morn to set of sun,
Through the church the song goes on.

3 Holy Father, holy Son,
Holy Spirit, Three we name Thee;
While in essence only One,
Undivided God, we claim Thee;
And, adoring bend the knee,
While we own the mystery.

4 Spare Thy people, Lord, we pray,
By a thousand snares surrounded:
Keep us without sin to-day,
Never let us be confounded.
Lo! I put my trust in Thee;
Never, Lord, abandon me. Amen.

OTHER FEASTS AND FASTS.

137   8.7.8.7.8.8.7.

1 Sound aloud Jehovah's praises,
   Tell abroad the awful Name;
Heaven the ceaseless anthem raises,
   Let the earth her God proclaim:
God, the hope of every nation,
God, the source of consolation,
   Holy, blessèd Trinity!

2 This the Name from ancient ages
   Hidden in its dazzling light;
This the Name that kings and sages
   Prayed and strove to know aright,
Through God's wondrous incarnation
Now revealed the world's salvation,
   Ever blessèd Trinity!

3 Into this great Name and holy,
   We all tribes and tongues baptize;
Thus the Highest owns the lowly,
   Homeward, heavenward, bids them rise;
Gathers them from every nation,
Bids them join in adoration
   Of the blessèd Trinity!

4 In this Name the heart rejoices,
   Pouring forth its secret prayer;
In this Name we lift our voices,
   And our common faith declare;
Offering humble supplication,
Thanks, and praise, and veneration
   To the blessèd Trinity!

Also the following :

405 God my Father, hear me pray.
403 Praises to Him Whose love has given.
404 Holy, holy, holy, Lord God almighty.
409 Three in One, and One in Three.
406 Holy, holy, holy Lord.
408 Come thou almighty King.
576 Great Creator, Lord of all.

Other Feasts and Fasts.

ST. ANDREW.

138   8.7.

1 Jesus calls us; o'er the tumult
   Of our life's wild, restless sea,
Day by day His sweet voice soundeth,
   Saying, "Christian, follow Me;"

44

2 As of old, Saint Andrew heard it
   By the Galilean lake,
Turned from home, and toil, and kindred,
   Leaving all for His dear sake.

3 Jesus calls us from the worship
   Of the vain world's golden store;
From each idol that would keep us,
   Saying, "Christian, love Me more."

4 In our joys and in our sorrows,
   Days of toil and hours of ease,
Still He calls, in cares and pleasures,
   "That we love Him more than these."

5 Jesus calls us ; by Thy mercies,
   Saviour, make us hear Thy call.
Give our hearts to Thine obedience,
   Serve and love Thee best of all. Amen.

139   8.7.

1 King of saints, O Lord incarnate,
   In Thy saints Thy praise we sing,
As to-day, with glad thanksgiving,
   Hymns of grateful love we bring.
Of the thronèd Twelve, Saint Andrew
First received, and heard, Thy call :
Thine the wondrous grace that made him
Gentlest, meekest, of them all.

2 Thee, true Lamb of God, beholding,
   (As the Baptist testified,)
He obeys Thy gracious bidding
   In Thy dwelling to abide :
Finding there the true Messiah,
   Whom his faith so long had sought,
There with joy his brother Simon
   To his Saviour's feet he brought.

3 From the Galilean waters
   At Thy word he follows Thee,
Fisher's net and craft exchanging
   For the Apostle's dignity ;
Strengthened by Thy Whitsun largess,
   Armed with the Spirit's sword,
Forth he goes to preach the gospel,
   Herald of the incarnate Word.

4 Grant that we, Thy call obeying,
   May like Andrew follow Thee,
Here in gentle love and suffering
   To a blest eternity;
Sharers of Thy cross, and with him
   Sharers of Thy crown above,
See the vision of Thy beauty,
   Taste the sweetness of Thy love. Amen.

OTHER FEASTS AND FASTS.

ST. THOMAS.
140 C.M.

1 O Thou, Who didst, with love untold,
  Thy doubting servant chide,
  And bad'st the eye of sense behold
  Thy wounded hands and side;

2 Grant us, like him, with heartfelt awe,
  To own Thee God and Lord,
  And from his hour of darkness draw
  A fuller faith's reward.

3 And while that wondrous record now
  Of unbelief we hear,
  Oh, let us only lowlier bow
  In self-distrusting fear;

4 And pray that we may never dare
  Thy loving heart to grieve;
  But at the last their blessing share
  Who see not, yet believe! Amen.

141 L.M.

1 How oft, O Lord, Thy face hath shone
  On doubting souls whose wills were true!
  Thou Christ of Cephas and of John,
  Thou art the Christ of Thomas too.

2 He loved Thee well, and calmly said,
  "Come, let us go, and die with Him:"
  Yet when Thine Easter-news was spread,
  'Mid all its light his eyes were dim.

3 His brethren's word he would not take,
  But craved to touch those hands of Thine:
  The bruisèd reed Thou didst not break;
  He saw, and hailed his Lord divine.

4 He saw Thee risen; at once he rose
  To full belief's unclouded height;
  And still through his confession flows
  To Christian souls Thy life and light.

5 O Saviour, make Thy presence known
  To all who doubt Thy Word and Thee;
  And teach them in that Word alone
  To find the truth that sets them free.

6 And we who know how true Thou art,
  And Thee as God and Lord adore,
  Give us, we pray, a loyal heart,
  To trust and love Thee more and more.
  Amen.

Also the following:
528 We walk by faith and not by sight.

ST. STEPHEN.
142 7s.

1 Jesus, Lord, Thy praise we sing,
  Thou the martyr's Crown and King,
  Who dost raise above the skies
  All who earth and sin despise:
  Hear us now, and as we tell
  How Thy martyr Stephen fell,
  Grant the prayer Thy servants pray,
  Wash our stain of guilt away.

2 'Twas Thy Spirit from above
  Filled his heart with strength and love;
  First to own his Lord in death,
  First to gain the crown of faith;
  Gazing upward to the skies,
  With his parting breath he cries,
  Jesus, Lord, my soul receive,
  Jesus, Lord, my foes forgive.

3 Lord, for him Thy name we bless,
  Grant to us like holiness;
  May we ever live to Thee,
  And in death have victory:
  Then through ages all along,
  This shall be our endless song,
  Praise the Father and the Son,
  And the Spirit, Three in One. Amen.

143 L.M

1 O Son of Man, Thyself once crossed
  By every suffering here below,
  Who taught'st Thy noble martyr-host
  To follow in Thy path of woe:

2 O Son of God, whose glory cast
  Its light upon Thy champion's face,
  Revealing to his eyes at last
  The marvels of the holiest place:

3 Be ours the faith that sees Thee stand
  Beside the throne of God on high,
  To succor with Thy strong right hand
  Thy soldiers when to Thee they cry

4 Be ours the hope, resigned and meek,
  That trusts the spirit to Thy care,
  That longs Thy face in heaven to seek,
  And dwell with Thee in glory there.

5 Be ours the love, divine and free,
  Which asks forgiveness for our foes;
  Which draws, in life, its life from Thee,
  And, dying, finds in Thee repose.
  Amen

OTHER FEASTS AND FASTS.

ST. JOHN EVANGELIST.
144 L.M.

1 O Thou, who gav'st Thy servant grace
On Thee the living Rock to rest,
To look on Thine unveilèd face,
And lean on Thy protecting breast ;

2 Grant us, O King of mercy, still
To feel Thy presence from above,
And in Thy word and in Thy will
To hear Thy voice and know Thy love ;

3 And when the toils of life are done,
And nature waits Thy just decree,
To find our rest beneath Thy throne,
And look in certain hope to Thee.

4 To Thee, O Jesus, Light of Light,
Whom as their King the saints adore,
Thou strength and refuge in the fight,
Be laud and glory evermore. Amen.

145 S.M.

1 An exile for the faith
Of his incarnate Lord,
Beyond the stars, beyond all space,
His soul in vision soared :

2 There saw in glory Him
Who liveth, and was dead,
There Judah's Lion, and the Lamb
That for our ransom bled:

3 There of the Kingdom learned
The mysteries sublime ;
How, sown in martyrs' blood, the faith
Should spread from clime to clime.

4 Lord, give us grace, like him,
In Thee to live and die ;
To spurn the fleeting things of earth,
And seek for joys on high. Amen.

THE HOLY INNOCENTS.
146 L.M.

1 Oh, who are they so pure and bright,
Before the throne arrayed in white ?
They stand, serene and calmly fair,
As conscious of high welcome there.

2 That starry crown around their brow,
It tells their sacred glory now ;
Blest virgin-souls who, 'faultless,' come
From font of grace, or martyrdom.

3 'And in their mouth is found no guile,'
Christ's ' Holy Innocents,' whose smile
Shines purer, from their knowing not
Upon their souls sin's conscious blot.

4 These, these are they, the undefiled,
The child-like saint, the saint-like child,
Marked with Christ's cross or earth's dark frown,
But wearing there that starry crown.

5 O help us, Saviour, by Thy grace
Near Thee to win that heavenly place ;
Now following where Thy footsteps trod
' Blameless and harmless sons of God.'
Amen.

147 7s.

1 Lord, to Thee glad songs of praise
For Thine Innocents we raise,
Firstlings of Thy martyr band,
Slain by Herod's cruel hand.

2 First to follow Thee, the Lamb,
Triumphing with crown and palm,
Death shall never touch them more,
Pain and grief for them are o'er.

3 Infant martyrs round Thy throne,
Thou dost keep them for Thine own ;
Thy blest steps they follow still,
Praise Thy Name, and work Thy will.

4 With their anthems, Lord, we sing,
"Glory to the new-born King,
Glory to the Father, Son,
Holy Spirit, Three in One." Amen.

148 S.M.

1 Glory to Thee, O Lord,
Who, from this world of sin,
By cruel Herod's ruthless sword
Those precious ones didst win.

2 Baptized in their own blood,
Earth's untried perils o'er,
They passed unconsciously the flood,
And safely gained the shore.

3 Glory to Thee for all
　The ransomed infant band,
　Who since that hour have heard Thy call,
　And reached the quiet land.

4 Oh, that our hearts within,
　Like theirs, were pure and bright;
　Oh, that as free from deeds of sin
　We shrank not from Thy sight.

5 Lord, help us every hour
　Thy cleansing grace to claim;
　In life to glorify Thy power,
　In death to praise Thy Name.　Amen.

THE CIRCUMCISION.
149　　　　　　　　　　　　　L.M.

1 O blessèd day, when first was poured
　The blood of our redeeming Lord!
　O blessèd day, when first began
　His sufferings for sinful man!

2 Scarce born to this our world of woe
　His precious blood begins to flow;
　The foretaste of a deadly strife,
　The prelude of a loving life.

3 From heaven descending to fulfil
　The bidding of His Father's will,
　Thus early He the victim lies,
　The Lamb marked out for sacrifice.

4 For love of us His woes begin;
　The Sinless suffers for our sin;
　The Law's great Maker for our aid
　Obedient to the Law is made.

5 The wound He through the Law endures
　Our freedom from that Law secures;
　Henceforth a holier law prevails,
　The law of love which never fails.

6 Lord, circumcise our hearts, we pray,
　And take what is not Thine away;
　Thy Name, Thy likeness may they bear;
　Oh, stamp Thy holy image there.
　　　　　　　　　　　　Amen.

150　　　　　　　　　　　　　7s.

1 Jesus! Name of wondrous love!
　Name all other names above!
　Unto which must every knee
　Bow in deep humility.

2 Jesus! Name decreed of old:
　To the maiden mother told,
　Kneeling in her lowly cell,
　By the angel Gabriel.

3 Jesus! Name of priceless worth
　To the fallen sons of earth,
　For the promise that it gave,
　"Jesus shall His people save."

4 Jesus! Name of mercy mild,
　Given to the holy Child,
　When the cup of human woe
　First He tasted here below.

5 Jesus! only Name that's given
　Under all the mighty heaven,
　Whereby man, to sin enslaved,
　Bursts his fetters, and is saved.

6 Jesus! Name of wondrous love!
　Human Name of God above;
　Pleading only this we flee,
　Helpless, O our God, to Thee.

　　　Also the following:

　365 To the Name of our salvation.
　366 Conquering kings their titles take.
　367 There is a Name I love to hear.

THE CONVERSION OF ST. PAUL.
151　　　　　　　　　　　　　L.M.

1 To Thee, O God, we Gentiles pay
　Our thanks, on our Apostle's day:
　Whose doctrine, like the thunder, sounds
　Throughout the wide world's farthest bounds.

2 O bliss of Paul, beyond all thought!
　To Paradise, yet living, caught,
　He hears the heavenly mysteries there,
　Which mortal tongue cannot declare.

3 The Word's blest seed around he flings;
　And straight a mighty harvest springs;
　And fruits of holy deeds supply
　God's everlasting granary.

4 The lamp his holy lore displays
　Hath filled the world with glorious rays;
　And doubt and error are o'erthrown,
　That truth may reign, and reign alone.

152 7.6.

1 We sing the glorious conquest
   Before Damascus' gate,
   When Saul, the Church's spoiler,
   Came breathing threats and hate;
   The ravening wolf rushed forward
   Full early to the prey;
   But lo! the Shepherd met him,
   And bound him fast to-day.

2 Oh, glory most excelling
   That smote across his path!
   Oh, light that pierced and blinded
   The zealot in his wrath!
   Oh, voice that spake within him
   The calm reproving word!
   Oh, love that sought and held him
   The bondman of his Lord!

3 O Wisdom, ordering all things
   In order strong and sweet,
   What nobler spoil was ever
   Cast at the Victor's feet?
   What wiser master-builder
   E'er wrought at Thine employ
   Than he, till now so furious
   Thy building to destroy?

4 Lord, teach Thy Church the lesson,
   Still in her darkest hour
   Of weakness and of danger
   To trust Thy hidden power;
   Thy grace by ways mysterious
   The wrath of man can bind,
   And in Thy boldest foeman
   Thy chosen saint can find.

THE PURIFICATION.

153 8.7.

1 In His temple now behold Him,
   See the long-expected Lord!
   Ancient prophets had foretold Him;
   God hath now fulfilled His word.
   Now to praise Him, His redeemed
   Shall break forth with one accord.

2 In the arms of her who bore Him,
   Virgin pure, behold Him lie,
   While His agèd saints adore Him,
   Ere in perfect faith they die:
   Alleluia! Alleluia!
   Lo, the incarnate God most high!

3 Jesus, by Thy Presentation,
   Thou, Who didst for us endure,
   Make us see Thy great salvation,
   Seal us with Thy promise sure;
   And present us in Thy glory
   To Thy Father cleansed and pure.

4 Prince and Author of salvation,
   Be Thy boundless love our theme!
   Jesus, praise to Thee be given
   By the world Thou didst redeem,
   With the Father and the Spirit,
   Lord of majesty supreme! Amen.

154 6.6.6.6.8.8.

1 Rejoice ye sons of men!
   Your brightest praises yield!
   The everlasting Son
   See in the flesh revealed!
   The world's Redeemer comes to-day
   His own redemption's price to pay!

2 Lo! Simeon's saintly arms
   The holy burden bear;
   He sees with raptured eye
   His true salvation there.
   The weary waiting now is past:
   The long-expected comes at last.

3 The agèd saint's embrace
   The blessèd mother saw,
   And on his words so strange
   She mused with silent awe.
   What conflict for her Child is stored?
   And what for her this piercing sword?

4 O Saviour, in Thy courts
   We all our sins confess:
   But Thou didst once for us
   Fulfil all righteousness.
   Impure, unclean, oh, may we be
   Presented pure and clean in Thee!

5 And when, O God made Man,
   Upon our waiting eye,
   In glorious might revealed,
   Salvation draweth nigh;
   In that great day Thy servants bless,
   And be "the Lord our Righteousness"!
   Amen.

OTHER FEASTS AND FASTS.

155 S.M.

1 Behold a humble train
  The courts of God draw near;
  A virgin mother and her babe
  Before the Lord appear.

2 O wondrous, blessèd sight!
  To faithful eyes made known,
  That lowly babe—the mighty God,
  The Prince of Peace, they own.

3 And now this temple shines
  With glory far more bright
  Than e'er the former temple saw,
  E'en at its greatest height.

4 The cloud indeed was there,
  The symbol of the Lord;
  But here the Lord Himself appears,
  The true, incarnate Word.

5 Blest Saviour, come once more
  With power and grace divine:
  Our hearts Thy living temples make,
  Wholly and ever Thine. Amen.

156 6s.

1 Hail to the Lord Who comes,
  Comes to His temple gate;
  Not with His angel host,
  Not in His kingly state:
  No shouts proclaim Him nigh,
  No crowds His coming wait.

2 But, borne upon the shrine
  Of Mary's gentle breast,
  Watched by her duteous love,
  In her fond arms at rest:
  Thus to His Father's house
  He comes, the heavenly Guest.

3 Hail to the great First-born
  Whose ransom-price they pay!
  The Son, before all worlds;
  The Child of man, to-day;
  That He might ransom us
  Who still in bondage lay.

4 O Light of all the earth,
  Thy children wait for Thee!
  Come to Thy temples here,
  That we, from sin set free,
  Before Thy Father's face
  May all presented be! Amen.

ST. MATTHIAS.

157 7s.

1 Bishop of the souls of men,
  When the foeman's step is nigh,
  When the wolf lays wait by night
  For the lambs continually,
  Watch, O Lord, about us keep,
  Guard us, Shepherd of the sheep.

2 When the hireling flees away,
  Caring only for his gold,
  And the gate unguarded stands
  At the entrance to the fold,
  Stand, O Lord, Thy flock before,
  Thou the Guardian, Thou the Door.

3 Lord, Whose guiding finger ruled
  In the casting of the lot,
  That Thy Church might fill the throne
  Of the lost Iscariot,
  In our trouble ever thus
  Stand, good Master, nigh to us.

4 When the saints their order take
  In the New Jerusalem,
  And Matthias stands elect,
  Give us part and lot with him,
  Where in Thine own dwelling-place
  We may witness face to face.

THE ANNUNCIATION.

158 8.7.

1 The angel sped on wings of light,
  With wondrous tidings laden;
  He came from heaven's unclouded height
  To greet a lowly maiden.

2 For God upon her low estate
  Had looked with royal favor;
  And all earth's kindreds celebrate
  The mighty gift He gave her.

3 Oh, awful bliss! that from her womb
  Should spring the Uncreated,
  The great and holy One, for Whom
  The world so long had waited.

4 O Son divine! we fain would trace
   Thy mother's steps so lowly,
   Her joys and woes, her saintly grace,
   Her life so calm and holy.

5 But lo! as all too near we press,
   A veil the scene enfoldeth!
   No tongue may sing its loveliness,
   No eye its peace beholdeth!

6 And as we read with kindling eye
   This day's all-gracious story,
   The blessèd mother passeth by,
   And Thine is all the glory!

159   S. M.

1 Praise we the Lord this day,
   This day so long foretold,
   Whose promise shone with cheering ray
   On waiting saints of old.

2 The prophet gave the sign
   For faithful men to read;
   A virgin born of David's line,
   Shall bear the promised Seed.

3 Ask not how this should be,
   But worship and adore,
   Like her whom heaven's majesty
   Came down to shadow o'er.

4 Meekly she bowed her head
   To hear the gracious word,
   Mary, the pure and lowly maid,
   The favored of the Lord.

5 Blessèd shall be her name
   In all the Church on earth,
   Through whom that wondrous mercy came,
   The incarnate Saviour's birth.

ST. MARK.
160   7. 6.

1 We praise Thy grace, O Saviour,
   That beareth with us long,
   And ever out of weakness
   Thy servants maketh strong.

2 The saint, who left his comrades,
   And turned back from the fight,
   Behold at last victorious
   In Thy prevailing might!

3 From Thee, Lord, came the courage,
   Once more to front the host;
   Thy strength, most mighty Saviour,
   In weakness shineth most.

4 Thy love Thy saint hath numbered
   Among the blessèd Four,
   And all the world rejoiceth
   To learn his Gospel-lore.

5 O Lord, our human weakness
   With pitying eye behold;
   Uplift the fainting spirit,
   And make the coward bold.

6 O Jesus, glorious Victor
   O'er all the hosts of sin,
   In us Thy strength make perfect,
   In us the victory win. Amen.

ST. PHILIP AND ST. JAMES.
161   L. M.

1 There is one way, and only one,
   Out of our gloom, and sin, and care,
   To that fair land where shines no sun
   Because the face of God is there.

2 There is one truth, the truth of God,
   That Christ came down from heaven to show,
   One life that His redeeming blood
   Has won for all His saints below.

3 The lore from Philip once concealed,
   To us is fully known in Christ;
   In Him the Father is revealed,
   And all our longing is sufficed.

4 And still unwavering faith holds sure
   The words that James wrote sternly down;
   Except we labor and endure,
   We cannot win the heavenly crown.

5 O Way divine, through gloom and strife,
   Bring us Thy Father's face to see;
   O heavenly Truth, O precious Life,
   At last, at last, to rest in Thee.

OTHER FEASTS AND FASTS.

162 C.M.

1 Blest be, O Lord, the grace of love
   Shed on our hearts by Thee;
   Which makes to us another's soul
   Dear as our own to be.

2 "Follow thou Me," the heavenly Guide
   Jesus to Philip said;
   He followed Christ, and on the way,
   To heaven he others led.

3 The heart that loves and leads to Thee,
   Is nurtured by Thy grace;
   And in the apostolic band
   Now Philip finds a place.

4 To-day with Thine own brother, Lord,
   Philip is linked in love;
   A brother to that brother joined
   By graces from above.

5 Not by the ties of flesh and blood
   Thy kinsmen, Lord, are we;
   But fellowship in holy love
   Is brotherhood to Thee.

6 Oh, bring us to that holy place,
   That heavenly home above,
   Where brethren shall united be,
   And every word be love. Amen.

Also the following:
530 Thou art the Way, to Thee alone.

ST. BARNABAS.

163 11.10.11.10.

1 O Son of God, our Captain of salvation,
   Thyself by suffering schooled to human grief,
   We bless Thee for Thy sons of consolation,
   Who follow in the steps of Thee their Chief;

2 Those whom Thy Spirit's dread vocation severs
   To lead the vanguard of Thy conquering host;
   Whose toilsome years are spent in brave endeavors
   To bear Thy saving Name from coast to coast;

3 Those whose bright faith makes feeble hearts grow stronger,
   And sends fresh warriors to the great campaign,
   Bids the lone convert feel estranged no longer,
   And wins the sundered to be one again;

4 And all true helpers, patient, kind, and skillful,
   Who shed Thy light across our darkened earth,
   Counsel the doubting, and restrain the willful,
   Soothe the sick bed, and share the children's mirth.

5 Such was Thy Levite, strong in self oblation
   To cast his all at Thine Apostles' feet;
   He whose new name, through every Christian nation,
   From age to age our thankful strains repeat.

6 Thus, Lord, Thy Barnabas in memory keeping,
   Still be Thy Church's watchword, "Comfort ye;"
   Till in our Father's house shall end our weeping,
   And all our wants be satisfied in Thee.

164 7.6.

1 The son of Consolation!
   Of Levi's priestly line,
   Filled with the Holy Spirit
   And fervent faith divine,
   With lowly self-oblation,
   For Christ an offering meet,
   He laid his earthly riches
   At the Apostles' feet.

2 The son of Consolation!
   Oh, name of soothing balm!
   It fell on sick and weary
   Like breath of heaven's own calm!
   And the blest son of Comfort
   With fearless, loving hand
   The Gentiles' great Apostle
   Led to the faithful band.

OTHER FEASTS AND FASTS.

3 The son of Consolation!
  Drawn near unto his Lord,
He won the martyr's glory,
  And passed to his reward.
With him is faith now ended,
  For ever lost in sight,
But love, made perfect, fills him
  With praise, and joy, and light.

4 The son of Consolation!
  Lord, hear our humble prayer
That each of us Thy children
  Such blesséd name may bear!
That we, sweet comfort shedding
  O'er homes of pain and woe,
Midst sickness and in prisons,
  May seek Thee here below.

5 The sons of Consolation!
  Oh, what their bliss will be,
When Christ the King shall tell them
  "Ye did it unto Me"!
The merciful and loving
  The Lord of life shall own,
And as His priceless jewels
  Shall set them round His throne.

THE NATIVITY OF ST. JOHN BAPTIST.
165 L. M.

1 When Christ the Lord would come on earth,
  His messenger before Him went;
The greatest born of mortal birth,
  And charged with words of deep intent.

2 The least of all that here attend
  Hath honor greater far than he;
He was the Bridegroom's joyful friend,
  His Body and His Spouse are we:

3 A higher race, the sons of light,
  Of water and the Spirit born;
He the last star of parting night,
  And we the children of the morn!

4 And, as he boldly spake Thy word,
  And joyed to hear the Bridegroom's voice,
Thus may Thy pastors teach, O Lord;
  And thus Thy hearing Church rejoice.
      Amen.

166 S. M.

1 The heavenly King must come
    His desert realm to see;
  Must leave His own eternal home,
    And all His majesty.

2 And lo! before Him sent
    His herald, who must cry
  And never spare, "Repent, repent;
    Your King, your God, is nigh!"

3 He, when his work is done,
    Must see his light decay,
  Must hail with joy the brighter Sun,
    The glorious King of day.

4 O Lord, O King, O Sun,
    Whose messenger he came,
  Baptize us all, most holy One,
    In Thy refining flame.

5 Give us Thy grace, that we
    All evil may forsake,
  May boldly speak the truth for Thee,
    The lowest place may take.

6 So, when Thou com'st again,
    Thy realm redeemed to see,
  Thy steps shall find 'mid hearts of men
    A way made straight for Thee.

ST. PETER.
167 6.6.6.6.8.8.

1 "Thou art the Christ, O Lord,
    The Son of God most high!"
  For ever be adored
    That Name in earth and sky,
  In which, though mortal strength may fail,
  The saints of God at last prevail!

2 Oh, surely he was blest
    With blessedness unpriced,
  Who, taught of God, confessed
    The Godhead in the Christ!
  For of Thy Church, Lord, Thou didst own
  Thy saint a true foundation-stone.

3 Thrice fallen, thrice restored!
    The bitter lesson learnt,
  That heart for Thee, O Lord,
    With triple ardor burnt.
  The cross he took, he laid not down
  Until he grasped the martyr's crown.

4 Oh, bright triumphant faith!
  Oh, courage void of fears!
  Oh, love, most strong in death!
  Oh, penitential tears!
  By these, Lord, keep us lest we fall,
  And make us go where Thou shalt call.
      Amen.

168   9.8.

1 O Rock of ages, one Foundation,
  On which the living Church doth rest,—
  The Church, whose walls are strong salvation,
  Whose gates are praise,—Thy Name be blest!

2 Son of the living God! Oh, call us
  Once and again to follow Thee!
  And give us strength, whate'er befal us,
  Thy true disciples still to be.

3 When fears appal, and faith is failing,
  Make Thy voice heard o'er wind and wave,
  "Why doubt?" and in Thy love prevailing
  Put forth Thine hand to help and save.

4 And if our coward hearts deny Thee,
  In inmost thought, in deed, or word,
  Let not our hardness still defy Thee,
  But with a look subdue us, Lord.

5 Oh, strengthen Thou our weak endeavor
  Thee in Thy sheep to serve and tend,
  To give ourselves to Thee for ever,
  And find Thee with us to the end!
      Amen.

ST. JAMES.
169   L. M.

1 We praise Thy Name, O Lord most high,
  Redeemer of our souls from death,
  And all Thy mercies magnify,
  In making known Thy saving faith.

2 Thou didst the humble fisher call,
  Beside the shores of Galilee:
  At Thy command he gave up all,
  And left his nets to follow Thee.

3 O happy choice, for earthly toil,
  The strife to rescue souls from sin;
  For treasures that may rust and spoil,
  The crown of heavenly life to win.

4 O favored one, who, ere he knew
  The sharpness of the coming cross,
  Of Thy bright beauty caught the view
  That turns to gain all earthly loss.

5 Thy promise is fulfilled, and he
  Dares in thy painful steps to go;
  To drink Thy cup of agony,
  And drain the bitter dregs of woe.

6 Grant, Lord, that hope of seeing Thee
  In bliss, may us with courage nerve,
  The world and all its pomp to flee,
  Our cross to bear and Thee to serve.
      Amen.

170   C. M.

1 For all Thy saints, a noble throng,
  Who fell by fire and sword,
  Who soon were called, or waited long,
  We praise Thy Name, O Lord.

2 For him who left his father's side,
  Nor lingered by the shore,
  When, softer than the weltering tide,
  Thy summons glided o'er;

3 Who stood beside the maiden dead,
  Who climbed the mount with Thee,
  And saw the glory round Thy head,
  One of Thy chosen three;

4 Who knelt beneath the olive shade,
  Who drank Thy cup of pain,
  And passed from Herod's flashing blade
  To see Thy face again.

5 Lord give us grace, and give us love,
  Like him to leave behind
  Earth's cares and joys, and look above
  With true and earnest mind.

6 So shall we learn to drink Thy cup,
  So meek and firm be found,
  When Thou shalt come to take us up
  Where Thine elect are crowned.

OTHER FEASTS AND FASTS.

THE TRANSFIGURATION.

171 8s.

1 Lord, it is good for us to be
High on the mountain here with Thee;
Where stand revealed to mortal gaze
Those glorious saints of other days;
Who once received on Horeb's height
The eternal laws of truth and right;
Or caught the still small whisper, higher
Than storm, than earthquake, or than fire.

2 Lord, it is good for us to be
Entranced, enwrapt, alone with Thee;
And watch Thy glistering raiment glow
Whiter than Hermon's whitest snow,
The human lineaments that shine
Irradiant with a light divine :
Till we too change from grace to grace,
Gazing on that transfigured face.

3 Lord, it is good for us to be
Here on the holy mount with Thee ;
When darkling in the depths of night,
When dazzled with excess of light,
We bow before the heavenly voice
That bids bewildered souls rejoice,
Though love wax cold, and faith be dim,
"This is My Son; Oh, hear ye Him!"

172 8.7.8.7.8.8.7.

1 With trembling awe the chosen three
The holy mount ascended,
Where, wrapped in blissful ecstasy,
They saw the vision splendid;
Their Lord arrayed in living light,
And on His left hand and His right
By glorious saints attended.

2 O vision bright, too bright to tell,
The joys of heaven unveiling!
How precious on those hearts it fell,
When earthly hopes were failing;
When, saints no more on either side,
Between the thieves the Saviour died,
'Mid hate and scorn and railing!

3 Grant us, dear Lord, some vision brief,
Of future triumph telling,
Gilding with hope our night of grief,
Our clouds of fear dispelling.
If the dim foretaste was so bright,
Oh, what shall be the dazzling light
Of Thy eternal dwelling! Amen.

173 L. M.

1 O wondrous type! O vision fair
Of glory that the Church shall share,
Which Christ upon the mountain shows,
Where brighter than the sun He glows!

2 From age to age the tale declare,
How with the three disciples there,
Where Moses and Elias meet,
The Lord holds converse high and sweet.

3 With shining face and bright array,
Christ deigns to manifest to-day
What glory shall be theirs above,
Who joy in God with perfect love.

4 And faithful hearts are raised on high
By this great vision's mystery ;
For which in joyful strains we raise
The voice of prayer, the hymn of praise.

5 O Father, with the eternal Son,
And Holy Spirit ever One,
Vouchsafe to bring us by Thy grace
To see Thy glory face to face. Amen.

Also the following:
521 Upon the holy mount they stood.

ST. BARTHOLOMEW.

174 8.7.

1. King of saints, to whom the number
Of Thy starry host is known,
Many a name, by man forgotten,
Lives for ever round Thy throne:
Lights, which earth-born mists have darkened,
There are shining full and clear,
Princes in the court of heaven,
Nameless, unremembered here.

2 In the roll of Thine apostles
One there stands, Bartholomew,
He for whom to-day we offer,
Year by year, our praises due :
How he toiled for Thee and suffered
None on earth can now record;
All his saintly life is hidden
In the knowledge of his Lord.

OTHER FEASTS AND FASTS.

3 Noted well, it all is written
In the Lamb's great book of life,
All the faith, and prayer, and patience,
All the toiling, and the strife :
There are told Thy hidden treasures ;
Number us, O Lord, with them,
When Thou makest up the jewels
Of Thy living diadem.

ST. MATTHEW.
175 L. M.
1 Behold, the Master passeth by!
Oh, seest thou not His pleading eye?
With low sad voice He calleth thee,
"Leave this vain world, and follow Me."

2 O soul, bowed down with harrowing care,
Hast thou no thought for heaven to spare?
From earthly toils lift up thine eye;
Behold, the Master passeth by!

3 One heard Him calling long ago,
And straightway left all things below,
Counting his earthly gain as loss
For Jesus and His blessèd cross.

4 That "follow Me" his faithful ear
Seemed every day afresh to hear:
Its echoes stirred his spirit still,
And fired his hope, and nerved his will.

5 God gently calls us every day:
Why should we then our bliss delay?
He calls to heaven and endless light;
Why should we love the dreary night?

6 Praise, Lord, to Thee for Matthew's call,
At which he rose and left his all;
Thou, Lord, e'en now art calling me;
I will leave all, and follow Thee.

ST. MICHAEL AND ALL ANGELS.
176 10s.
1 Stars of the morning, so gloriously bright,
Filled with celestial splendor and light,
These that, where night never followeth day,
Raise the "Thrice Holy" song ever and aye;

2 These are Thy ministers, these dost Thou own,
Lord God of Sabaoth, nearest Thy throne;
These are Thy messengers, these dost Thou send,
Help of the helpless ones! man to defend.

3 These keep the guard amid Salem's dear bowers,
Thrones, Principalities, Virtues, and Powers,
Where, with the living Ones, mystical Four,
Cherubim, Seraphim bow and adore.

4 Still let them succor us ; still let them fight,
Lord of angelic hosts, battling for right ;
Till, where their anthems they ceaselessly pour,
We with the angels may bow and adore.
Amen.

177 S. 7.
1 Where the angel-hosts adore Thee,
Thou, O God, in heaven dost reign ;
At Thy word they rose around Thee,
And Thy word doth them sustain.

2 Thousand times ten thousand, bending
At Thy throne, their homage pay;
Flames of fire in strength excelling,
Swift Thy pleasure to obey.

3 Fashioned in a wondrous order,
Thee they serve, their Lord and King ;
Grant that in our cares and dangers
They may timely succor bring.

4 Praise to Thee who hast created
Earth and heaven with all their host ;
Praise to Thee, O God most mighty,
Father, Son, and Holy Ghost. Amen.

178 D. C. M.
1 Father, before Thy throne of light
The guardian angels bend,
And ever in Thy presence bright
Their psalms adoring blend ;
And casting down each golden crown
Beside the crystal sea,
With voice and lyre, in happy choir
Hymn glory, Lord, to Thee.

OTHER FEASTS AND FASTS.

2 And as the rainbow lustre falls
   Athwart their glowing wings,
While seraph unto seraph calls,
   And each Thy goodness sings;
Oh! may we feel, as low we kneel
   To pray Thee for Thy grace,
That Thou art here for all who fear
   The brightness of Thy face.

3 Here where the angels see us come
   To worship day by day,
Teach us to seek our heavenly home,
   And serve Thee e'en as they;
With them to raise our notes of praise,
   With them Thy love to own;
That boyhood's time and manhood's prime,
   Be Thine, and Thine alone! Amen.

ST. LUKE.

179   C.M.

1 Oh, blest was he, whose earlier skill
   The suffering frame made whole,
Called, Lord, by Thee from deadlier woes
   To heal the dying soul!

2 O true Physician! heal the souls
   That sick and wounded lie;
With wholesome medicine of Thy word
   Oh, heal them lest they die!

3 Lord, to our nature cleaveth still
   The leprosy of sin;
Put forth Thy hand and touch us, Lord,
   And make us clean within.

4 Lo! souls are lying cold and dead
   In palsy's numbing chain;
Speak Thou the word of power, good Lord,
   And bid them live again.

5 The fever burns in guilty breasts,
   Hot passion's wilful fire:
Calm Thou the storm with words of peace,
   And quell each vain desire.

6 O Jesus, healer of all ills,
   To Thee for help we flee;
Our souls, by Thine all-cleansing grace
   From every bond set free. Amen.

180   L.M.

1 What thanks and praise to Thee we owe,
   O Priest and Sacrifice divine,
For Thy dear saint through whom we know
   So many gracious words of Thine:

2 Whom Thou didst choose to tell the tale
   Of all Thy manhood's toils and tears,
And for a moment lift the veil
   That hides Thy boyhood's spotless years.

3 And still the Church through all her days
   Uplifts the strains that never cease,
The blessed Virgin's hymn of praise,
   The aged Simeon's words of peace.

4 O happy saint! whose sacred page,
   So rich in words of truth and love,
Pours on the Church from age to age
   This healing unction from above:

5 The witness of the Saviour's life,
   The great apostle's chosen friend
Through weary years of toil and strife,
   And still found faithful to the end.

6 So grant us, Lord, like him to live,
   Beloved by man, approved by Thee,
Till Thou at last the summons give,
   And we, with him, Thy face shall see.
                                  Amen.

ST. SIMON AND ST. JUDE.

181   8.7.

1 Thou Who sentest Thine apostles
   Two and two before Thy face,
Partners in the night of toiling,
   Heirs together of Thy grace,
Throned at length, their labors ended,
   Each in his appointed place;

2 Praise to Thee for those Thy champions
   Whom our hymns to-day proclaim;
One, whose zeal by Thee enlightened
   Burned anew with nobler flame;
One, the kinsman of Thy childhood,
   Brought at last to know Thy Name.

3 Praise to Thee! Thy fire within them
   Spake in love, and wrought in power;
Seen in mighty signs and wonders
   In Thy Church's morning hour;
Heard in tones of sternest warning
   When the storms began to lower.

OTHER FEASTS AND FASTS.

4 Once again those storms are breaking;
   Hearts are failing, love grows cold;
   Faith is darkened, sin abounding;
   Grievous wolves assail Thy fold:
   Save us, Lord, our one Salvation;
   Save the faith revealed of old.

5 Call the erring by Thy pity;
   Warn the tempted by Thy fear;
   Keep us true to Thine allegiance,
   Counting life itself less dear,
   Standing firmer, holding faster,
   As we see the end draw near:

6 Till, with holy Jude and Simon
   And the thousand faithful more,
   We, the good confession witnessed
   And the lifelong conflict o'er,
   On the sea of fire and crystal
   Stand, and wonder, and adore. Amen.

182   C. M.

1 When Thou, O Lord, didst send the twelve,
   Thy work of grace to do,
   Then joined in holy bands of love
   They went forth two and two.

2 To-day, O Lord, before our eyes
   Two blest apostles stand,
   For ever in Thy holy Church
   United hand in hand.

3 Jude bids us for the holy faith
   With fervent zeal to fight,
   And zeal shines brightly in thy name,
   Simon the Cananite.

4 O Lord, send down into our hearts
   Thy Spirit from above;
   And give us ever fervent zeal
   Tempered with holy love:

5 So may we with Thy brethren, Lord,
   In heavenly glory be!
   For fellowship in holy love
   Is brotherhood to Thee.

6 Glory to Father, and to Son,
   Who clad with zeal and love,
   Sent down the blessèd Comforter,
   The pure and holy Dove.

7 O gracious Spirit, ever brood
   On us with golden wing,
   Give zeal and love, that we Thy praise
   In heaven may alway sing. Amen.

183   GENERAL FOR SAINTS' DAYS.   7. 6.

1 From all Thy saints in warfare, for all Thy
   saints at rest,
   To Thee, O blessèd Jesus, all praises be addressed.
   Thou, Lord, didst win the battle that they
   might conquerors be;
   Their crowns of living glory are lit with rays
   from Thee.

[Insert here the stanza for the special Saint's Day to be celebrated.]

ST. ANDREW.

2 Praise, Lord, for Thine apostle, the first to
   welcome Thee,
   The first to lead his brother the very Christ
   to see.
   With hearts for Thee made ready, watch we
   throughout the year,
   Forward to lead our brethren to own Thine
   Advent near.

ST. THOMAS.

3 All praise for Thine apostle, whose short-
   lived doubtings prove
   Thy perfect twofold nature, the fulness of
   Thy love.
   On all who wait Thy coming shed forth Thy
   peace, O Lord,
   And grant us faith to know Thee, true Man,
   true God, adored.

ST. STEPHEN.

4 Praise for the first of martyrs, who saw Thee
   ready stand
   To aid in midst of torments, to plead at
   God's right hand.
   Share we with him, if summoned by death
   our Lord to own,
   On earth the faithful witness, in heaven the
   martyr crown.

ST. JOHN THE EVANGELIST.

5 Praise for the loved disciple, exile on Patmos' shore;
   Praise for the faithful record he to Thy Godhead bore;
   Praise for the mystic vision, through him to
   us revealed.
   May we, in patience waiting, with Thine
   elect be sealed.

OTHER FEASTS AND FASTS.

THE HOLY INNOCENTS.

6 Praise for Thine infant martyrs, by Thee
  with tenderest love
Called early from the warfare to share the
  rest above.
O Rachel! cease thy weeping: they rest from
  pains and cares.
Lord, grant us hearts as guileless, and
  crowns as bright as theirs.

THE CONVERSION OF ST. PAUL.

7 Praise for the light from heaven, praise for
  the voice of awe,
Praise for the glorious vision the persecutor
  saw.
Thee, Lord, for his conversion, we glorify
  to-day:
So lighten all our darkness with Thy true
  Spirit's ray.

ST. MATTHIAS.

8 Lord, Thine abiding presence directs the
  wondrous choice;
For one in place of Judas the faithful now
  rejoice.
Thy Church from false apostles for evermore defend,
And by Thy parting promise be with her to
  the end.

ST. MARK.

9 For him, O Lord, we praise Thee, the weak
  by grace made strong,
Whose labors and whose Gospel enrich our
  triumph-song.
May we in all our weakness find strength
  from Thee supplied,
And all, as fruitful branches, in Thee, the
  Vine, abide.

ST. PHILIP AND ST. JAMES.

10 All praise for Thine apostle, blessed guide
  to Greek and Jew,
And him surnamed Thy brother; keep us
  Thy brethren true,
And grant us grace to know Thee, the
  Way, the Truth, the Life;
To wrestle with temptations till victors in
  the strife.

ST. BARNABAS.

11 The Son of Consolation, moved by Thy law
  of love,
Forsaking earthly treasures, sought riches
  from above.
As earth now teems with increase, let gifts
  of grace descend,
That Thy true consolations may through
  the world extend.

ST. JOHN BAPTIST.

12 We praise Thee for the Baptist, forerunner
  of the Word,
Our true Elias, making a highway for the
  Lord.
Of prophets last and greatest, he saw Thy
  dawning ray:
Make us the rather blessèd, who love Thy
  glorious day.

ST. PETER.

13 Praise for Thy great apostle, the eager and
  the bold;
Thrice falling, yet repentant, thrice charged
  to keep Thy fold.
Lord, make Thy pastors faithful, to guard
  their flocks from ill,
And grant them dauntless courage, with
  humble, earnest will.

ST. JAMES.

14 For him, O Lord, we praise Thee, who, slain
  by Herod's sword,
Drank of Thy cup of suffering, fulfilling
  thus Thy word.
Curb we all vain impatience to read Thy
  veiled decree,
And count it joy to suffer, if so brought
  nearer Thee.

ST. BARTHOLOMEW.

15 All praise for Thine apostle, the faithful,
  pure, and true,
Whom underneath the fig tree Thine eye
  all-seeing knew.
Like Him may we be guileless, true Israel-
  ites indeed,
That Thy abiding presence our longing
  souls may feed.

OTHER FEASTS AND FASTS.

ST. MATTHEW.

16 Praise, Lord, for him whose Gospel Thy
    human life declared,
  Who, worldly gains forsaking, Thy path of
    suffering shared
  From all unrighteous mammon, oh, give us
    hearts set free,
  That we, whate'er our calling, may rise and
    follow Thee.

ST. LUKE.

17 For that "beloved physician," all praise,
    whose Gospel shows
  The healer of the nations, the sharer of our
    woes.
  Thy wine and oil, O Saviour, on bruised
    hearts deign to pour,
  And with true balm of Gilead anoint us
    evermore.

ST. SIMON AND ST. JUDE.

18 Praise, Lord, for Thine apostles, who sealed
    their faith to-day:
  One love, one zeal impelled them to tread
    the sacred way.
  May we with zeal as earnest the faith of
    Christ maintain,
  And, bound in love as brethren, at length
    Thy rest attain.

GENERAL ENDING.

19 Apostles, prophets, martyrs, and all the
    sacred throng,
  Who wear the spotless raiments, who raise
    the ceaseless song;
  For these, passed on before us, Saviour, we
    Thee adore,
  And, walking in their footsteps, would serve
    Thee more and more.

20 Then praise we God the Father, and praise
    we God the Son,
  And God the Holy Spirit, eternal Three in
    One;
  Till all the ransomed number fall down be-
    fore the throne,
  And honor, power, and glory ascribe to God
    alone. Amen.

ALL SAINTS.

184 8s.

1 The saints of God! Their conflict past,
  And life's long battle won at last,
  No more they need the shield or sword,
  They cast them down before their Lord:
    O happy saints! for ever blest,
    At Jesus' feet how safe your rest!

2 The saints of God! Their wanderings done,
  No more their weary course they run,
  No more they faint, no more they fall,
  No foes oppress, no fears appal:
    O happy saints! for ever blest,
    In that dear home how sweet your rest!

3 The saints of God! Life's voyage o'er,
  Safe landed on that blissful shore,
  No stormy tempests now they dread,
  No roaring billows lift their head:
    O happy saints! for ever blest,
    In that calm haven of your rest!

4 The saints of God their vigil keep
  While yet their mortal bodies sleep,
  Till from the dust they too shall rise
  And soar triumphant to the skies:
    O happy saints! rejoice and sing:
    He quickly comes, your Lord and King!

5 O God of saints! To Thee we cry;
  O Saviour! plead for us on high;
  O Holy Ghost! our guide and friend,
  Grant us Thy grace till life shall end;
    That with all saints our rest may be
    In that bright Paradise with Thee!
                                    Amen.

185 P. M.

1 For all the saints, who from their labors rest,
  Who Thee by faith before the world con-
    fest,
  Thy Name, O Jesus, be for ever blest.
                                    Alleluia.

2 Thou wast their rock, their fortress, and their
    might:
  Thou, Lord, their Captain in the well-fought
    fight;
  Thou, in the darkness drear the Light of
    Light.   Alleluia.

59

3 O may Thy soldiers, faithful, true, and bold,
  Fight as the saints who nobly fought of old,
  And win, with them, the victor's crown of gold.
      Alleluia.

4 O blest communion, fellowship divine!
  We feebly struggle, they in glory shine;
  Yet all are one in Thee, for all are Thine.
      Alleluia.

5 And when the strife is fierce, the warfare long,
  Steals on the ear the distant triumph-song,
  And hearts are brave again, and arms are strong.
      Alleluia.

6 The golden evening brightens in the west;
  Soon, soon to faithful warriors comes the rest;
  Sweet is the calm of Paradise the blest.
      Alleluia.

7 But lo! there breaks a yet more glorious day;
  The saints triumphant rise in bright array;
  The King of glory passes on His way.
      Alleluia.

8 From earth's wide bounds, from ocean's farthest coast,
  Through gates of pearl streams in the countless host,
  Singing to Father, Son, and Holy Ghost,
      Alleluia.

186　　　　　　　　6.4.6.4.

1 Their names are names of kings
    Of heavenly line;
  The pride of earthly things
    They dared resign.

2 They bore the Spirit's sword
    And faith's strong shield;
  They fought for God the Lord
    On many a field.

3 Though hard their earthly lot,
    'Mid hate and scorn,
  In life regarded not,
    In death forlorn;

4 Yet blest that end of woe,
    And those sad days ;
  Only man's blame below;
    Above, God's praise.

5 So did the life of pain
    In glory close ;
  Lord God, may we attain
    Their grand repose. Amen.

187　　　　　　　　L. M.

1 Lo! round the throne, a glorious band,
  The saints in countless myriads stand,
  Of every tongue redeemed to God,
  Arrayed in garments washed in blood.

2 Through tribulation great they came;
  They bore the cross, despised the shame;
  From all their labors now they rest,
  In God's eternal glory blest.

3 They see their Saviour face to face,
  And sing the triumphs of His grace ;
  Him day and night they ceaseless praise,
  To Him the loud thanksgiving raise:

4 "Worthy the Lamb, for sinners slain,
  Through endless years to live and reign;
  Thou hast redeemed us by Thy blood,
  And made us kings and priests to God."

5 Oh, may we tread the sacred road
  That saints and holy martyrs trod;
  Wage to the end the glorious strife,
  And win, like them, a crown of life.
      Amen.

188　　　　　　　　8.7.8.7.7.7.

1 Who are these like stars appearing,
    These, before God's throne who stand?
  Each a pure white robe is wearing ;
    Who are all this glorious band?
      Alleluia! hark they sing,
      Praising loud their heavenly King.

2 These are they who have contended
    For their Saviour's honor long,
  Wrestling on till life was ended,
    Following not the sinful throng;
      These, who well the fight sustained,
      Triumph by the Lamb have gained.

3 Those are they whose hearts were riven,
    Sore with woe and anguish tried,
  Who in prayer full oft have striven
    With the God they glorified:
  Now, their painful conflict o'er,
  God has bid them weep no more.

4 These, like priests, have watched and waited,
    Offering up to Christ their will.
  Soul and body consecrated,
    Day and night they serve Him still.
  Now in God's most holy place,
  Blest they stand before His face.
                                Amen.

189   8.7.

1 Hark! the sound of holy voices,
    Chanting o'er the crystal sea,
  Alleluia, alleluia,
    Alleluia, Lord, to Thee:

  Multitudes which none can number,
    Like the stars in glory stand,
  Clothed in white apparel, holding
    Conquering palms in every hand.

2 Patriarch, and holy prophet,
    Who prepared the way of Christ,
  King, apostle, saint, confessor,
    Martyr and evangelist;

  Saintly maiden, godly matron,
    Widows who have watched to prayer
  Joined in holy concert, singing
    To the Lord of all, are there.

3 Marching with Thy cross, their banner,
    They have triumphed, following
  Thee, the Captain of salvation,
    Thee, their Saviour and their King.

  Gladly, Lord, with Thee they suffered;
    Gladly, Lord, with Thee they died;
  And by death to live immortal
    They were born and glorified.

4 Now they reign in heavenly glory,
    Now they walk in golden light,
  Now they drink, as from a river,
    Holy bliss and infinite:

  Love and peace they taste for ever.
    And all truth and knowledge see
  In the beatific vision
    Of the blessed Trinity.

5 God of God, the One-begotten,
    Light of Light, Emmanuel,
  In Whose Body joined together
    All the saints for ever dwell,

  Pour upon us of Thy fulness,
    That we may for evermore
  God the Father, God the Son, and
    God the Holy Ghost adore. Amen.

190   7s.

1 Who are these in bright array,
  This innumerable throng,
  Round the altar, night and day,
  Tuning their triumphant song?

  "Worthy is the Lamb, once slain,
  Blessing, honor, glory, power,
  Wisdom, riches to obtain,
  New dominion every hour."

2 These through fiery trials trod;
  These from great affliction came;
  Now before the throne of God,
  Sealed with His eternal Name;

  Clad in raiment pure and white,
  Victor palms in every hand,
  Through their great Redeemer's might,
  More than conquerors they stand.

3 Hunger, thirst, disease unknown,
  On immortal fruits they feed;
  Them the Lamb amidst the throne,
  Shall to living fountains lead:

  Joy and gladness banish sighs;
  Perfect love dispels their fears;
  And for ever from their eyes,
  God shall wipe away their tears.

191   S.M.

1 For Thy dear saint, O Lord,
    Who strove in Thee to live,
  Who followed Thee, obeyed, adored,
    Our grateful hymn receive.

2 For Thy dear saint, O Lord,
    Who strove in Thee to die,
  And found in Thee a full reward,
    Accept our thankful cry.

OTHER FEASTS AND FASTS.

3 Thine earthly members fit
   To join Thy saints above,
In one communion ever knit,
   One fellowship of love.

4 Jesus, Thy Name we bless,
   And humbly pray that we
May follow them in holiness,
   Who lived and died for Thee. Amen.

Also the following:
249 God of the living, in Whose eyes.
410 Let saints on earth in concert sing.
411 Soldiers who are Christ's below.
412 Oh what, if we are Christ's.
413 Not to the terrors of the Lord.
415 Ten thousand times ten thousand.
416 O heavenly Jerusalem.
419 Oh, what the joy and the glory must be.
579 God hath two families of love.
580 King of glory, Saviour dear.

EMBER DAYS.
192   8.8.6.8.8.6.

1 Lord of the Church, we humbly pray
   For those who guide us in Thy way,
      And speak Thy holy word;
With love divine their hearts inspire,
And touch their lips with hallowed fire,
      And needful strength afford.

2 Help them to preach the truth of God,
   Redemption through the Saviour's blood;
      Nor let the Spirit cease
On all the Church His gifts to shower;
To them a messenger of power,
      To us, of life and peace.

3 So may they live to Thee alone;
   Then hear the welcome word, "Well done!"
      And take their crown above;
Enter into their Master's joy,
And all eternity employ
      In praise, and bliss, and love. Amen.

193   C.M.

1 Guide Thou, O God, the guardian hands
   Which rule Thy ransomed sheep,
And may they faithful shepherds choose,
   Their Master's flock to keep.

2 We pray Thee, Jesus, Who didst first
   The chosen twelve ordain,
In order due and holy life,
   The Church they ruled sustain.

3 We pray Thee, Jesus, with Thy gifts
   Our pastors still to bless,
With doctrine uncorrupt and pure,
   With zeal and righteousness.

4 We pray Thee, Jesus, that their lips
   May still be clothed with power,
Their hearts with love and strength upheld,
   Sufficient for the hour.

5 O Holy Ghost, Anointer, come;
   Both priest and people fill;
Till all the nations of the earth
   Shall do their Father's will:

6 Then to the Father and the Son,
   And Thee, her songs of praise,
One living undivided Church
   Through endless years shall raise.

194   C.M.

1 The earth, O Lord, is one wide field
   Of all Thy chosen seed;
The crop prepared its fruit to yield;
   The laborers few indeed.

2 We therefore come before Thee now
   With fasting, and with prayer,
Beseeching of Thy love that Thou
   Wouldst send more laborers there.

3 Endue the bishops of Thy flock
   With wisdom and with grace,
Against false doctrine, like a rock
   To set the heart and face.

4 To all Thy priests Thy truth reveal,
   And make Thy judgments clear;
Make Thou Thy deacons full of zeal,
   And humble, and sincere:

5 And give their flocks a lowly mind
   To hear and to obey;
That each and all may mercy find
   At Thine appearing-day. Amen.

OTHER FEASTS AND FASTS.

195 L.M.

1 Lord, pour Thy Spirit from on high,
　And Thine ordained servants bless;
Graces and gifts to each supply,
　And clothe Thy priests with righteousness.

2 Within Thy temple when they stand,
　To teach the truth as taught by Thee,
Saviour, like stars in Thy right hand,
　Let all Thy Church's pastors be.

3 Wisdom, and zeal, and faith impart,
　Firmness and meekness from above,
To bear Thy people in their heart,
　And love the souls whom Thou dost love;

4 To love, and pray, and never faint,
　By day and night strict guard to keep,
To warn the sinner, cheer the saint,
　To feed Thy lambs, and fold Thy sheep.

5 So, when their work is finished here,
　They may in hope their charge resign:
So, when their Master shall appear,
　They may with crowns of glory shine.
　　　　　　　　　　　Amen.

196 8s.

1 Thou who the night in prayer didst spend,
And then Thy twelve apostles send;
And bidd'st us pray the harvest's Lord
To send forth sowers of Thy word,
Hear, and Thy chosen servants bless
With seven-fold gifts of holiness.

2 Oh, may Thy pastors faithful be,
Not laboring for themselves, but Thee;
Give grace to feed with wholesome food
The sheep and lambs bought by Thy blood;
To tend Thy flock, and thus to prove
How dearly they the Shepherd love!

3 Oh, may Thy people faithful be,
And in Thy pastors honor Thee,
And with them work, and for them pray,
And gladly Thee in them obey;
Receive the prophet of the Lord,
And gain the prophet's own reward!

4 So may we, when our work is done,
Together stand before the throne;
And joyful hearts and voices raise
In one united song of praise,
With all the bright celestial host,
To Father, Son, and Holy Ghost.   Amen.

197 S.M.

1 Lord of the harvest, hear
　Thy needy servants' cry;
Answer our faith's effectual prayer,
　And all our wants supply.

2 On Thee we humbly wait,
　Our wants are in Thy view;
The harvest, Lord, is truly great,
　The laborers are few.

3 Anoint and send forth more
　Into Thy Church abroad,
And let them speak Thy word of power,
　As workers with their God.

4 Oh, let them spread Thy Name,
　Their mission fully prove;
Thy universal grace proclaim,
　Thine all-redeeming love.   Amen.

198 S.M.

1 Ye servants of the Lord,
　Each in your office, wait,
Observant of His heavenly word,
　And watchful at His gate.

2 Let all your lamps be bright,
　And trim the golden flame;
Gird up your loins as in His sight,
　For awful is His Name.

3 Watch! 'tis your Lord's command,
　And while we speak He's near;
Mark the first signal of His hand,
　And ready all appear.

4 O happy servant he
　In such a posture found;
He shall his Lord with rapture see,
　And be with honor crowned.

ROGATION DAYS.

199 C.M.

1 Great King of nations, hear our prayer,
　While at Thy feet we fall,
And humbly with united cry
　To Thee for mercy call.

2 The guilt is ours, but grace is Thine,
　Oh, turn us not away;
But hear us from Thy lofty throne,
　And help us when we pray.

63

OTHER FEASTS AND FASTS.

3 Our fathers' sins were manifold,
   And ours no less we own,
   Yet wondrously from age to age
   Thy goodness hath been shown.

4 When dangers, like a stormy sea,
   Beset our country round,
   To Thee we looked, to Thee we cried,
   And help in Thee was found.

5 With one consent we meekly bow
   Beneath Thy chastening hand,
   And, pouring forth confession meet,
   Mourn with our mourning land.

6 With pitying eye behold our need,
   As thus we lift our prayer;
   Correct us with Thy judgments, Lord,
   Then let Thy mercy spare. Amen.

200   C. M.

1 In grief and fear to Thee, O Lord,
   We now for succor fly;
   Thine awful judgments are abroad,
   Oh, shield us lest we die.

2 The fell disease on every side
   Walks forth with tainted breath;
   And pestilence, with rapid stride,
   Bestrews the land with death.

3 Oh, look with pity on the scene
   Of sadness and of dread;
   And let Thine angel stand between
   The living and the dead.

4 With contrite hearts to Thee, our King,
   We turn who oft have strayed;
   Accept the sacrifice we bring,
   And let the plague be stayed. Amen.

201   6.6.6.6.8.8.

1 To Thee our God we fly
   For mercy and for grace;
   Oh, hear our lowly cry,
   And hide not Thou Thy face.
   O Lord, stretch forth Thy mighty hand,
   And guard and bless our fatherland.

2 Arise, O Lord of hosts,
   Be jealous for Thy Name,
   And drive from out our coasts
   The sins that put to shame.
   O Lord, stretch forth Thy mighty hand,
   And guard and bless our fatherland.

3 Thy best gifts from on high
   In rich abundance pour,
   That we may magnify
   And praise Thee more and more.
   O Lord, stretch forth Thy mighty hand,
   And guard and bless our fatherland.

4 The powers ordained by Thee
   With heavenly wisdom bless;
   May they Thy servants be,
   And rule in righteousness.
   O Lord, stretch forth Thy mighty hand,
   And guard and bless our fatherland.

5 The Church of Thy dear Son
   Inflame with love's pure fire,
   Bind her once more in one,
   And life and truth inspire.
   O Lord, stretch forth Thy mighty hand,
   And guard and bless our fatherland.

6 Give peace, Lord, in our time;
   Oh, let no foe draw nigh,
   Nor lawless deed of crime
   Insult Thy Majesty.
   O Lord, stretch forth Thy mighty hand,
   And guard and bless our fatherland. Amen.

202   C. M.

1 Lord, in Thy Name Thy servants plead,
   And Thou hast sworn to hear;
   Thine is the harvest, Thine the seed,
   The fresh and fading year.

2 Our hope, when autumn winds blew wild,
   We trusted, Lord, with Thee:
   And now that spring has on us smiled,
   We wait on Thy decree.

3 The former and the latter rain,
   The summer sun and air,
   The green ear, and the golden grain,
   All Thine, are ours by prayer.

4 Thine too by right, and ours by grace,
   The wondrous growth unseen,
   The hopes that soothe, the fears that brace,
   The love that shines serene.

5 So grant the precious things brought forth
   By sun and moon below,
   That Thee in Thy new heavens and earth
   We never may forego. Amen.

OTHER FEASTS AND FASTS.

203 7s.

1 Christ, by heavenly hosts adored,
Gracious, mighty, sovereign Lord,
God of nations, King of kings,
Head of all created things,
By the Church with joy confest,
God o'er all for ever blest:
Pleading at Thy throne we stand,
Save Thy people, bless our land.

2 On our fields of grass and grain
Send, O Lord, the kindly rain;
O'er our wide and goodly land
Crown the labors of each hand.
Let Thy kind protection be
O'er our commerce on the sea:
Open, Lord, Thy bounteous hand,
Bless Thy people, bless our land.

3 Let our rulers ever be
Men that love and honor Thee;
Let the powers by Thee ordained
Be in righteousness maintained;
In the people's hearts increase
Love of piety and peace:
Thus united we shall stand
One wide, free, and happy land.

THANKSGIVING DAY.
204 8.8.8.8.4.4.8.

1 Lord of the harvest, Thee we hail!
Thine ancient promise doth not fail:
The varying seasons haste their round;
With goodness all our years are crowned;
  Our thanks we pay,
  This holy day;
Oh, let our hearts in tune be found.

2 When spring doth wake the song of mirth,
When summer warms the fruitful earth,
When winter sweeps the naked plain,
Or autumn yields its ripened grain,
  We still do sing
  To Thee our King;
Through all their changes Thou dost reign.

3 But chiefly when Thy liberal hand
Scatters now plenty o'er the land,
When sounds of music fill the air,
As homeward all their treasures bear;
  We too will raise
  Our hymn of praise,
For we Thy common bounties share.

4 Lord of the harvest, all is Thine:
The rains that fall, the suns that shine,
The seed once hidden in the ground,
The skill that makes our fruits abound:
  New every year,
  Thy gifts appear;
New praises from our lips shall sound.

205 7.6.7.6.7.6.7.6.6.6.8.6.

1 We plough the fields, and scatter
  The good seed on the land,
But it is fed and watered
  By God's almighty hand;
He sends the snow in winter,
  The warmth to swell the grain,
The breezes, and the sunshine,
  And soft refreshing rain.
    All good gifts around us
    Are sent from heaven above,
    Then thank the Lord, oh, thank the Lord,
    For all His love.

2 He only is the Maker
  Of all things near and far;
He paints the wayside flower,
  He lights the evening star;
The winds and waves obey Him,
  By Him the birds are fed;
Much more to us, His children,
  He gives our daily bread.
    All good gifts around us, etc.

3 We thank Thee then, O Father,
  For all things bright and good,
The seed-time and the harvest,
  Our life, our health, our food;
Accept the gifts we offer
  For all Thy love imparts,
And what Thou most desirest,
  Our humble, thankful hearts.
    All good gifts around us, etc.

206 8.7.

1 To Thee, O Lord, our hearts we raise
  In hymns of adoration.
To Thee bring sacrifice of praise
  With shouts of exultation:

Bright robes of gold the fields adorn,
  The hills with joy are ringing,
The valleys stand so thick with corn
  That even they are singing.

OTHER FEASTS AND FASTS.

2 And now on this our festal day,
   Thy bounteous hand confessing,
Upon Thine altar, Lord, we lay
The first-fruits of Thy blessing.

By Thee the souls of men are fed
   With gifts of grace supernal.
Thou Who dost give us earthly bread,
   Give us the bread eternal.

3 We bear the burden of the day,
   And often toil seems dreary;
But labor ends with sunset ray,
   And rest comes for the weary.

May we, the angel-reaping o'er,
   Stand at the last accepted,
Christ's golden sheaves for evermore
   To garners bright elected.

4 Oh, blessèd is that land of God,
   Where saints abide for ever;
Where golden fields spread far and broad,
   Where flows the crystal river:

The strains of all its holy throng
   With ours to-day are blending;
Thrice blessèd is that harvest-song
   Which never hath an ending.

207   C. M.
1 Father of mercies, God of love,
   Whose gifts all creatures share,
The rolling seasons as they move
   Proclaim Thy constant care.

2 When in the bosom of the earth
   The sower hid the grain,
Thy goodness marked its secret birth,
   And sent the early rain.

3 The spring's sweet influence, Lord, was Thine,
   The seasons knew Thy call;
Thou mad'st the summer sun to shine,
   The summer dews to fall.

4 Thy gifts of mercy from above
   Matured the swelling grain;
And now the harvest crowns Thy love,
   And plenty fills the plain.

5 Oh, ne'er may our forgetful hearts
   O'erlook Thy bounteous care,
But what our Father's hand imparts
   Still own in praise and prayer. Amen.

208   8s.
1 Lord of the harvest, once again
   We thank Thee for the ripened grain;
For crops safe carried, sent to cheer
   Thy servants through another year;
And for all holy thoughts supplied
   By seed time, and by harvest-tide.

2 The bare dry grain, in autumn sown,
   Its robe of vernal green puts on;
Glad from its wintry grave it springs,
   Fresh garnished by the King of kings;
So, Lord, to those who sleep in Thee
   Shall new and glorious bodies be.

3 Nor vainly of Thy word we ask
   A lesson from the reaper's task;
So shall Thine angels issue forth;
   The tares be burnt; the just of earth,
To wind and storm exposed no more,
   Be gathered to their Father's store.

4 Daily, O Lord, our prayer is said,
   As Thou hast taught, for "daily bread;"
But not alone our bodies feed,
   Supply our fainting spirits' need;
O Bread of life, from day to day,
   Be Thou their comfort, food, and stay.
                              Amen.

209   7s.
1 Praise to God, immortal praise,
   For the love that crowns our days;
Bounteous source of every joy,
   Let Thy praise our tongues employ;
All to Thee, our God, we owe,
   Source whence all our blessings flow.

2 All the plenty summer pours;
   Autumn's rich o'erflowing stores;
Flocks that whiten all the plain;
   Yellow sheaves of ripened grain;
Lord, for these our souls shall raise
   Grateful vows and solemn praise.

3 Peace, prosperity, and health,
   Private bliss, and public wealth,
Knowledge with its gladdening streams,
   Pure religion's holier beams;
Lord, for these our souls shall raise
   Grateful vows and solemn praise.

4 As Thy prospering hand hath blest,
May we give Thee of our best ;
And by deeds of kindly love
For Thy mercies grateful prove;
Singing thus through all our days,
Praise to God, immortal praise.

210 7s.

1 Come, ye thankful people, come,
Raise the song of harvest-home:
All is safely gathered in,
Ere the winter storms begin ;
God, our Maker, doth provide
For our wants to be supplied ;
Come to God's own temple, come,
Raise the song of harvest-home.

2 All the world is God's own field,
Fruit unto His praise to yield ;
Wheat and tares together sown,
Unto joy or sorrow grown:

First the blade, and then the ear,
Then the full corn shall appear:
Lord of harvest, grant that we
Wholesome grain and pure may be.

3 For the Lord our God shall come,
And shall take His harvest home ;
From His field shall in that day
All offences purge away;

Give His angels charge at last
In the fire the tares to cast,
But the fruitful ears to store
In His garner evermore.

4 Even so, Lord, quickly come
To Thy final harvest-home:
Gather Thou Thy people in,
Free from sorrow, free from sin ;

There for ever purified,
In Thy presence to abide :
Come with all Thine angels, come,
Raise the glorious harvest-home. Amen.

Also the following:

477 Sing praise to God Who reigns above.
484 For the beauty of the earth.
487 Now thank we all our God.
496 O Lord of heaven and earth and sea.

III. The Church.

HOLY COMMUNION.

211 10s.

1 Here, O my Lord, I see Thee face to face:
Here faith can touch and handle things unseen;
Here would I grasp with firmer hand Thy grace,
And all my weariness upon Thee lean.

2 Here would I feed upon the bread of God ;
Here drink with Thee the royal wine of heaven;
Here would I lay aside each earthly load,
Here taste afresh the calm of sin forgiven.

3 I have no help but Thine; nor do I need
Another arm save Thine to lean upon ;
It is enough, my Lord, enough indeed ;
My strength is in Thy might, Thy might alone.

4 Mine is the sin, but Thine the righteousness:
Mine is the guilt, but Thine the cleansing blood :
Here is my robe, my refuge, and my peace:
Thy blood, Thy righteousness, O Lord, my God! Amen.

212 10s.

1 Draw nigh and take the body of the Lord,
And drink the holy blood for you outpoured.

2 Saved by that body and that holy blood,
With souls refreshed, we render thanks to God.

3 Salvation's giver, Christ, the only Son,
By His dear cross and blood the victory won.

4 Offered was He for greatest and for least,
Himself the victim, and Himself the priest.

5 Victims were offered by the law of old,
Which in a type this heavenly mystery told.

6 He, Ransomer from death, and Light from shade,
Now gives His holy grace His saints to aid.

7 Approach ye then with faithful hearts sincere,
And take the safeguard of salvation here.

THE CHURCH—HOLY COMMUNION.

8 He, that His saints in this world rules and shields,
To all believers life eternal yields;

9 With heavenly bread makes them that hunger whole,
Gives living waters to the thirsting soul.

10 Alpha and Omega, to Whom shall bow
All nations at the doom, is with us now.

213   C.M.

1 Once, only once, and once for all,
His precious life He gave:
Before the cross our spirits fall,
And own it strong to save.

2 "One offering, single and complete,"
With lips and hearts we say;
But what He never can repeat
He shews forth day by day.

3 For, as the priest of Aaron's line
Within the holiest stood,
And sprinkled all the mercy-shrine
With sacrificial blood ;

4 So He Who once atonement wrought,
Our Priest of endless power,
Presents Himself for those He bought
In that dark noontide hour.

5 His Manhood pleads where now It lives
On heaven's eternal throne,
And where in mystic rite He gives
Its presence to His own.

6 And so we shew Thy death, O Lord,
Till Thou again appear;
And feel, when we approach Thy board,
"We have an altar" here.

214   C.M.

1 O God, unseen yet ever near,
Thy presence may we feel ;
And thus inspired with holy fear,
Before Thine altar kneel.

2 Here may Thy faithful people know
The blessings of Thy love,
The streams that through the desert flow,
The manna from above.

3 We come, obedient to Thy word,
To feast on heavenly food ;
Our meat the body of the Lord,
Our drink His precious blood.

4 Thus may we all Thy word obey,
For we, O God, are Thine ;
And go rejoicing on our way,
Renewed with strength divine.   Amen.

215   10s.

1 Thee we adore, O hidden Saviour, Thee,
Who in Thy sacrament dost deign to be:
Both flesh and spirit at Thy presence fail,
Yet here Thy presence we devoutly hail.

2 O blest memorial of our dying Lord,
Who living bread to men doth here afford!
Oh, may our souls for ever feed on Thee,
And Thou, O Christ, for ever precious be!

3 Fountain of goodness, Jesus, Lord and God,
Cleanse us, unclean, with Thy most cleansing blood ;
Increase our faith and love, that we may know
The hope and peace which from Thy presence flow.

4 O Christ, Whom now beneath a veil we see,
May what we thirst for soon our portion be,
To gaze on Thee unveiled, and see Thy face,
The vision of Thy glory and Thy grace.
                                       Amen.

216   7s.

1 Jesus to Thy table led,
Now let every heart be fed,
With the true and living bread.

2 While in penitence we kneel,
Thy blest presence let us feel,
All Thy wondrous love reveal.

3 While on Thy dear cross we gaze,
Mourning o'er our sinful ways,
Turn our sadness into praise.

4 When we taste the mystic wine,
Of Thine outpoured blood the sign,
Fill our hearts with love divine.

5 Draw us to Thy wounded side,
Whence there flowed the healing tide;
There our sins and sorrows hide.

THE CHURCH—HOLY COMMUNION.

6 From the bonds of sin release;
  Cold and wavering faith increase;
  Lamb of God, grant us Thy peace.

7 Lead us by Thy piercèd hand,
  Till around Thy throne we stand,
  In the bright and better land. Amen.

217 7.7.6.7.7.6.

1 O Bread of Life, from heaven
  To saints and angels given;
    O manna from above!
  The souls that hunger, feed Thou,
  The hearts that seek Thee, lead Thou,
    With Thy sweet, tender love.

2 O fount of grace redeeming,
  O river ever streaming
    From Jesus' holy side!
  Come Thou, Thyself bestowing
  On thirsting souls, and flowing
    Till all are satisfied.

3 Jesus, this feast receiving,
  Thy word of truth believing,
    We Thee unseen adore;
  Grant, when the veil is rended,
  That we, to heaven ascended,
    May see Thee evermore. Amen.

218 10s.

1 O heavenly Father, mindful of the love
  That bought us, once for all, on Calvary's tree,
  And having with us Him that pleads above,
  We here present, we here spread forth to Thee
  That only offering perfect in Thine eyes,
  The one true, pure, immortal sacrifice.

2 Look, Father, look on His anointed face,
  And only look on us as found in Him;
  Look not on our misusings of Thy grace,
  Our prayer so languid, and our faith so dim;
  For lo! between our sins and their reward,
  We set the passion of Thy Son our Lord.

3 And then for those, our dearest and our best,
  By this prevailing presence we appeal;
  Oh, fold them closer to Thy mercy's breast!
  Oh, do Thine utmost for their souls' true weal!

From tainting mischief keep them white and clear,
And crown Thy gifts with strength to persevere.

4 And so we come; Oh, draw us to Thy feet,
  Most patient Saviour, Who canst love us still!
  And by this food, so awful and so sweet,
  Deliver us from every touch of ill;
  In Thine own service make us glad and free,
  And grant us never more to part with Thee. Amen.

219 8.8.7.8.8.7.

1 Come, O Saviour, to Thy table,
  Come, for else we are not able
    True refreshment to receive:
  But if Thou vouchsafe to feed us,
  To this feast of blessing lead us,
    There to taste Thee and believe.

2 In the bread which here is broken,
  In the wine, no empty token
    Of an absent Lord we see,
  Flesh and blood indeed are given,
  When by faith, O Bread of heaven,
    Not by sense, we feed on Thee.

3 Sweet it is, O Christ, to meet Thee,
  In Thy sacrament to greet Thee,
    Thee, our God, as host and friend.
  By Thy presence here prepare us
  For the day when Thou shalt bear us
    To the feast that knows no end. Amen.

220 C.M.

1 I am not worthy, holy Lord,
    That Thou shouldst come to me;
  Speak but the word; one gracious word
    Can set the sinner free.

2 I am not worthy; cold and bare
    The lodging of my soul;
  How canst Thou deign to enter there?
    Lord, speak, and make me whole.

3 I am not worthy; yet, my God,
    How can I say Thee nay;
  Thee, Who didst give Thy flesh and blood
    My ransom-price to pay?

THE CHURCH—HOLY COMMUNION.

4 Oh, come! in this sweet morning hour
   Feed me with food divine;
   And fill with all Thy love and power
   This worthless heart of mine. Amen.

221   L.M.

1 My God, and is Thy table spread,
   And does Thy cup with love o'erflow,
   Thither be all Thy children led,
   And let them Thy sweet mercies know.

2 Hail! sacred feast, which Jesus makes,
   Rich banquet of His flesh and blood:
   Thrice happy he who here partakes
   That sacred stream, that heavenly food.

3 Oh, let Thy table honored be,
   And furnished well with joyful guests:
   And may each soul salvation see,
   That here its holy pledges tastes.

4 Drawn by Thy quickening grace, O Lord,
   In countless numbers let them come;
   And gather from their Father's board
   The bread that lives beyond the tomb.

5 Nor let Thy spreading Gospel rest,
   Till through the world Thy truth has run;
   Till with this bread all men be blest,
   Who see the light or feel the sun. Amen.

222   P.M.

1 Bread of the world, in mercy broken,
   Wine of the soul, in mercy shed,
   By Whom the words of life were spoken,
   And in Whose death our sins are dead;

2 Look on the heart by sorrow broken,
   Look on the tears by sinners shed;
   And be Thy feast to us the token
   That by Thy grace our souls are fed.
           Amen.

223   7s.

1 Bread of heaven, on Thee we feed,
   For Thy flesh is meat indeed:
   Ever may our souls be fed
   With this true and living bread;
   Day by day with strength supplied,
   Through the life of Him Who died.

2 Vine of heaven, Thy blood supplies
   This blest cup of sacrifice;
   Lord, Thy wounds our healing give,
   To Thy cross we look and live;
   Jesus, may we ever be
   Grafted, rooted, built in Thee. Amen.

224   7.6.

1 Thou standest at the altar,
   Thou offerest every prayer;
   In faith's unclouded vision
   We see Thee ever there.

2 Out of Thy hand the incense
   Ascends before the throne.
   Where Thou art interceding,
   Lord Jesus, for Thine own.

3 And through Thy blood accepted,
   With Thee we keep the feast;
   Thou art Thyself the victim,
   Thou art Thyself the priest.

4 We come, O only Saviour,
   On Thee, the Lamb, to feed;
   Thy flesh is bread from heaven,
   Thy blood is drink indeed.

225   P.M.

1 O Holy Jesus, Prince of peace!
   Thy peace be with us gathering round Thy board,
   Where the dread presence of an unseen Lord
   Waits to be gracious, charged with full release
   To every heavy-laden soul
   Which here remembers Thee.

2 Once more, as in that upper room,
   Thou Who didst love Thine own unto the end,
   Thou Whose dear voice to every sorrowing friend
   Spoke the great promise through the deepening gloom,
   Thou bidst us, Master of the feast,
   To-day remember Thee.

3 And e'en as in our hands we take
   This broken bread, this precious cup of love,
   Thy dying testament, which from above
   Thou deignest ever new and fresh to make,
   A fount of grace and life to all;
   We do remember Thee.

THE CHURCH—HOLY BAPTISM.

4 Ours is the bond of love divine,
   Which knits us each to all and all to each,
   That love whose ever-lengthening cords can
      reach
   From the white choir around Thy heavenly
      shrine
   To those who come in faith to-day
      Here to remember Thee.

5 Thy banquet over, as we go,
   Strong in the strength of this celestial meat,
   To tread the path of life with firmer feet,
   To work the works which Thou hast bid us
      do,
   Abide with us, O Lord, that still
      We may remember Thee! Amen.

226 C.M.

1 According to Thy gracious word,
   In meek humility,
   This will I do, my dying Lord,
   I will remember Thee.

2 Thy body, broken for my sake,
   My bread from heaven shall be;
   The cup, Thy precious blood, I take,
   And thus remember Thee.

3 Gethsemane, can I forget?
   Or there Thy conflict see,
   Thine agony and bloody sweat,
   And not remember Thee?

4 When to the cross I turn mine eyes,
   And rest on Calvary,
   O Lamb of God, my sacrifice,
   I must remember Thee.

5 And when these failing lips grow dumb,
   And mind and memory flee,
   When Thou shalt in Thy kingdom come,
   Then, Lord, remember me. Amen.

227 C.M.

1 Shepherd of souls, refresh and bless
   Thy chosen pilgrim flock,
   With manna in the wilderness,
   With water from the rock.

2 Hungry and thirsty, faint and weak,
   As Thou when here below,
   Our souls the joys celestial seek
   Which from Thy sorrows flow.

3 We would not live by bread alone
   But by that word of grace,
   In strength of which we travel on
   To our abiding-place.

4 Be known to us in breaking bread,
   But do not then depart;
   Saviour, abide with us, and spread
   Thy table in our heart.

5 Lord, sup with us in love divine;
   Thy body and Thy blood,
   That living bread, that heavenly wine,
   Be our immortal food. Amen.

228 7s.

1 "Till He come:" Oh, let the words
   Linger on the trembling chords;
   Let the little while between
   In their golden light be seen ;
   Let us think how heaven and home
   Lie beyond that "Till He come."

2 When the weary ones we love
   Enter on their rest above,
   Seems the earth so poor and vast,
   All our life-joy overcast ?
   Hush, be every murmur dumb;
   It is only, "Till He come."

3 Clouds and conflicts round us press;
   Would we have one sorrow less ?
   All the sharpness of the cross,
   All that tells the world is loss,
   Death, and darkness, and the tomb,
   Only whisper, "Till He come."

4 See, the feast of love is spread;
   Drink the wine, and break the bread;
   Sweet memorials: till the Lord
   Call us round His heavenly board;
   Some from earth, from glory some,
   Severed only, "Till He come."

HOLY BAPTISM.

229 10.6.10.6.8.8.4.

1 Father of heaven, Who hast created all
   In wisest love, we pray,
   Look on this child, who at Thy gracious call
   Is entering on life's way!
   Oh, make it Thine, Thy blessing give,
   That to Thy glory it may live,
   Father of heaven!

THE CHURCH—HOLY BAPTISM.

2 O Son of God, atoning Lord, behold
    We bring this child to Thee;
  Take it, O loving Shepherd, to Thy fold,
    For ever Thine to be:
  Defend it through this earthly strife,
  And lead it in the path of life,
    O Son of God!

3 O Holy Ghost, Who broodest o'er the wave,
    Descend upon this child;
  Give it undying life, its spirit lave
    With waters undefiled;
  And make it evermore to be
  A child of God, a home for Thee,
    O Holy Ghost!

4 O Triune God, what Thou hast willed is
    done;
  We speak: but Thine the might;
  This child hath scarce yet seen our earthly
    sun,
  Yet pour on it Thy light
  Of faith, and hope, and joyful love,
  Thou Sun of all below, above,
    O Triune God.   Amen.

230   8.7.

1 Saviour, Who Thy flock art feeding,
  With the shepherd's kindest care,
  All the feeble gently leading,
  While the lambs Thy bosom share;

2 Now, *these* little ones receiving,
  Fold *them* in Thy gracious arm;
  There we know, Thy word believing,
  Only there secure from harm.

3 Never from Thy pasture roving,
  Let *them* be the lion's prey;
  Let Thy tenderness, so loving,
  Keep *them* all life's dangerous way.

4 Then, within Thy fold eternal,
  Let *them* find a resting-place;
  Feed in pastures ever vernal,
  Drink the rivers of Thy grace.   Amen.

231   L.M.

1 God of that glorious gift of grace,
  By which Thy people seek Thy face,
  When in Thy presence we appear,
  Vouchsafe us faith to venture near!

2 Confiding in Thy truth alone,
  Here, on the steps of Jesus' throne,
  We lay the treasure Thou hast given,
  To be received and reared for heaven.

3 Lent to us for a season, we
  Lend *him* for ever, Lord, to Thee;
  Assured that, if to Thee *he* live,
  We gain in what we gladly give.

4 Make *him* and keep *him* Thine own child,
  Meek follower of the Undefiled;
  Possessor here of grace and love;
  Inheritor of heaven above!   Amen.

232   8.7.

1 O God our strength, our hope, our rock,
  Whose promise faileth never,
  Into Thy chosen blood-bought flock,
  Receive this child for ever.

2 Now sealed with Thy thrice holy Name
  In these baptismal waters,
  For *him* a place we humbly claim
  Among Thy sons and daughters.

3 We mark the cross upon *his* brow,
  The symbol of Thy Passion;
  O Christ, vouchsafe *his* earliest vow
  May be *his* life's confession.

4 This banner over *him* unfurled,
  May *he* fight on, subduing
  The flesh, the devil, and the world;
  His strength in Thee renewing.

5 May nothing, Lord, in life or death
  From Thee Thy servant sever;
  Thy soldier true to plighted faith,
  Henceforward, and for ever.   Amen.

233   C.M.

1 In token that thou shalt not fear
    Christ crucified to own,
  We print the cross upon thee here,
    And stamp thee His alone.

2 In token that thou shalt not blush
    To glory in His Name,
  We blazon here upon thy front,
    His glory and His shame.

THE CHURCH—CONFIRMATION.

3 In token that thou too shalt tread
    The path He travelled by,
Endure the cross, despise the shame,
    And sit thee down on high;

4 Thus outwardly and visibly
    We seal thee for His own:
And may the brow that wears His cross
    Hereafter share His crown. Amen.

BAPTISM OF ADULTS.

234   S. M.
1 Stand, soldier of the cross,
    Thy high allegiance claim,
And vow to hold the world but loss
    For thy Redeemer's Name.

2 Arise, and be baptized,
    And wash thy sins away;
Thy league with God be solemnized,
    Thy faith avouched to-day.

3 Thine is our country now,
    Our Lord and Master thine,
Receive imprinted on thy brow
    His Passion's awful sign.

4 No more thine own, but Christ's;
    With all the saints of old,
Apostles, seers, evangelists,
    And martyr throngs enrolled.

5 Oh, bright the conqueror's crown,
    The song of triumph sweet,
When faith casts every trophy down
    At our great Captain's feet.

Also the following:

347 Soldiers of Christ, arise.
349 Go forward, Christian soldier.
352 If thou wouldest life attain.
521 O Lord, our strength in weakness.
624 Thy life was given for me.
639 O holy Saviour, friend unseen.

CONFIRMATION.

235   8s.
1 O God, in Whose all-searching eye
    Thy servants stand, to ratify
The vow baptismal, by them made
When first Thy hand was on them laid;

Bless them, O Holy Father, bless.
Who Thee with heart and voice confess;
May they, acknowledged as Thine own,
Stand evermore before Thy throne.

2 O Christ, Who didst at Pentecost
Send down from heaven the Holy Ghost;
And at Samaria baptize
Those whom Thou didst evangelize;

And then on Thy baptized confer
The best of gifts, the Comforter.
By apostolic hands, and prayer;
Be with us now, as Thou wert there.

3 Arm these Thy soldiers, mighty Lord,
With shield of faith, and Spirit's sword;
Forth to the battle may they go,
And boldly fight against the foe,

With banner of the cross unfurled,
And by it overcome the world;
And so at last receive from Thee
The palm and crown of victory.

4 Come, ever blessèd Spirit, come,
And make Thy servants' hearts Thy home;
May each a living temple be,
Hallowed for ever, Lord, to Thee.

Enrich that temple's holy shrine
With sevenfold gifts of grace divine;
With wisdom, light, and knowledge, bless,
Strength, counsel, fear, and godliness.

5 O Trinity in Unity,
One only God, and Persons Three,
In Whom, through Whom, by Whom, we live,
To Thee we praise and glory give.

Oh, grant us so to use Thy grace
That we may see Thy glorious face,
And ever, with the heavenly host,
Praise Father, Son, and Holy Ghost.
                      Amen.

236   S. M.
1 The cross is on our brow,
    Redemption's awful sign:
Come Thou, O Holy Spirit, now,
    To seal the work divine.

2 Thy sevenfold gifts impart,
    O Comforter most sweet:
Inflame with zeal each lukewarm heart,
    And guide the trembling feet.

3 With Pentecostal force
    Thy presence let us feel ;
  With strength, Who art Thyself its source,
    Inspire us as we kneel.

4 Confirm in us to-day
    The work that Thou hast wrought ;
  Illume the souls with love's pure ray,
    Which Jesus' blood hath bought.

5 The fiend, the flesh, the world,
    We swear to give them fight ;
  Our Monarch's banner floats unfurled ;
    Who fails with that in sight ?

6 Who fails with Jesus Christ
    For leader and for guide ;
  For food, for treasure all unpriced,
    And friend who ne'er denied?

7 The powers of ill allure ;
    Our foes come thick and fast ;
  Oh, keep us steadfast, loving, pure,
    And we shall win at last.

8 No earth-forged arms we bear :
    Strength, weapons, all are Thine :
  Accept each vow and hear each prayer,
    Blest Trinity divine.   Amen.

237   8s.

1 Behold us, Lord, before Thee met,
    Whom each bright angel serves and fears,
  Who on Thy throne rememberest yet
    Thy spotless boyhood's quiet years,
  Whose feet the hills of Nazareth trod,
  Who art true Man and perfect God.

2 To Thee we look, in Thee confide,
    Our help is in Thine own dear Name ;
  For who on Jesus e'er relied
    And found not Jesus still the same ?
  Thus far Thy love our souls hath brought ;
  Oh, stablish well what Thou hast wrought.

3 From Thee was our baptismal grace,
    The holy seed by Thee was sown ;
  And now before our Father's face
    We make the three great vows our own ;
  And ask, in Thine appointed way,
  Confirm us in Thy grace to-day.

4 We need Thee more than tongue can speak,
    'Mid foes that well might cast us down ;
  But thousands, once as young and weak,
    Have fought the fight, and won the crown ;
  We ask the help that bore them through ;
  We trust the Faithful and the True.

5 So bless us with the gift complete
    By hands of Thy chief pastors given,
  That awful presence, kind and sweet,
    Which comes in sevenfold might from heaven ;
  Eternal Christ, to Thee we bow :
  Give us Thy Spirit here and now. Amen.

238   7s.

1 Holy Spirit, Lord of love,
  Thou Who camest from above,
  Gifts of blessing to bestow
  On Thy waiting Church below ;
  Once again in love draw near
  To Thy children gathered here.

2 From their bright baptismal day,
  Through their childhood's onward way,
  Thou hast been their constant guide,
  Watching ever by their side :
  May they now till life shall end,
  Choose and know Thee as their friend.

3 Give them light Thy truth to see,
  Give them life to live for Thee,
  Daily power to conquer sin,
  Patient faith the crown to win ;
  Shield them from temptation's breath,
  Keep them faithful unto death.

4 When the holy vow is made,
  When the hands are on them laid,
  Come, in this most solemn hour,
  With Thy sevenfold gifts of power,
  Come, Thou blessèd Spirit, come,
  Make each heart Thy happy home.
                                Amen.

239   L.M.

1 Draw, Holy Ghost, Thy sevenfold veil
    Between us and the fires of youth ;
  Breathe, Holy Ghost, Thy freshening gale
    Our fevered brow in age to soothe.

2 For ever on our souls be traced
    This blessing from the Saviour's hand,
  A sheltering rock in memory's waste,
    O'ershadowing all the weary land.
                                Amen

THE CHURCH—CONFIRMATION.

240 8.7.

1 Holy Spirit, Lord of glory,
  Look on us Thy flock to-day,
Meekly kneeling at Thy footstool
  For Thy sevenfold gifts we pray;
Guide us all our earthly journey
  In the true and narrow way.

2 Foes on every hand are round us,
  And our hearts are weak and frail;
Gird us with Thy heavenly armor;
  Never let us yield or quail;
Give us victory in the struggle,
  When the hosts of sin assail.

3 Blessèd Jesus, draw Thou near us,
  As before Thy cross we bow;
Help us to be true and faithful,
  Seal our sacramental vow;
We Thy soldiers are, and servants;
  Hear our solemn promise now.

4 Lead us by Thy guiding presence
  Through the waste, with danger rife;
Feed us with the heavenly manna,
  That we faint not in the strife;
Slake our weary spirits' thirsting,
  From the living well of life.

5 Looking ever unto Jesus,
  Leaning on His staff and rod;
May we follow in His footsteps,
  Tread the path that He has trod,
Till we dwell with Him for ever
  In the Paradise of God. Amen.

241 7.6.

1 O gracious Saviour, bless us
  This Confirmation hour,
And send Thy Holy Spirit,
  In all His gifts and power.

2 Send Him to guide with *Wisdom*
  Our footsteps through the world;
Thy banner we have chosen
  Be over us unfurled.

3 When all looks dark and dreary,
  And dim the far-off land,
Then teach us, Holy Spirit,
  Thy ways to *understand*.

4 If doubt should weave around us
  A wily, tangled coil,
Then guide us by Thy *counsel*,
  Its subtilty to foil.

5 When weak, our hearts are shrinking
  From sorrow, pain, or grief,
Give *ghostly strength* to aid us,
  And bring us sweet relief.

6 When many thoughts perplex us
  What mission to fulfil,
Grant *knowledge* to our judgment,
  That we may do Thy will.

7 If earthly joys grow bitter,
  Help us true peace to gain,
And in life's persecution
  True godliness retain.

8 When thoughts that shrink from conscience
  Betray the tempter near,
Oh, then awaken in us
  The voice of *holy fear!*

9 And so defend us, Master,
  With Thy calm, heavenly grace,
Till we are called to worship
  Within Thy dwelling-place;

10 To fall before Thy footstool,
  And sing, all glory be
To Father, Son, and Spirit,
  Thrice Holy Trinity. Amen.

242 7s.

1 Thine for ever: God of love,
  Hear us from Thy throne above;
Thine for ever may we be,
  Here and in eternity.

2 Thine for ever: Lord of life,
  Shield us through our earthly strife:
Thou the Life, the Truth, the Way,
  Guide us to the realms of day.

3 Thine for ever: O how blest
  They who find in Thee their rest!
Saviour, Guardian, heavenly Friend,
  Oh, defend us to the end!

4 Thine for ever: Saviour, keep
  These Thy frail and trembling sheep;
Safe alone beneath Thy care,
  Let us all Thy goodness share.

THE CHURCH—HOLY MATRIMONY.

5 Thine for ever : Thou our guide,
All our wants by Thee supplied,
All our sins by Thee forgiven,
Lead us, Lord, from earth to heaven.
                      Amen.

243   L.M.

1 O happy day, that stays my choice
On Thee, my Saviour and my God
Well may this glowing heart rejoice,
And tell Thy goodness all abroad.

2 Here rest, my oft-divided heart,
Fixed on thy God, thy Saviour, rest;
Who with the world would grieve to part
When called on angels' food to feast ?

3 High Heaven, that heard the solemn vow,
That vow renewed shall daily hear;
Till in life's latest hour I bow,
And bless in death a bond so dear.

244   C.M.

1 My God, accept my heart this day,
And make it always Thine,
That I from Thee no more may stray,
No more from Thee decline.

2 Before the cross of Him who died,
Behold, I prostrate fall ;
Let every sin be crucified,
And Christ be all in all.

3 Anoint me with Thy heavenly grace
And seal me for Thine own;
That I may see Thy glorious face,
And worship near Thy throne.

4 Let every thought, and work, and word,
To Thee be ever given ;
Then life shall be Thy service, Lord,
And death the gate of heaven! Amen.

HOLY MATRIMONY.
245   D.C.M.

1 Lord, Who at Cana's wedding feast
Didst as a guest appear,
Thou dearer far than earthly guest
Vouchsafe Thy presence here;
For holy Thou indeed dost prove
The marriage vow to be,
Proclaiming it a type of love
Between the Church and Thee.

2 The holiest vow that man can make,
The golden thread in life,
The bond that none may dare to break,
That bindeth man and wife;
Which, blessed by Thee, whate'er betides,
No evil shall destroy,
Through care-worn days each care divides,
And doubles every joy.

3 On those who at Thine altar kneel,
O Lord, Thy blessing pour,
That each may wake the other's zeal
To love Thee more and more;
Oh, grant them here in peace to live,
In purity and love,
And, this world leaving, to receive
A crown of life above ! Amen.

246   7.6.

1 O Father all-creating,
Whose wisdom and Whose power
First bound two lives together
In Eden's primal hour;
To-day to these Thy children
Thine earliest gift renew;
A home by Thee made blessèd,
A love by Thee kept true.

2 O Saviour, guest most bounteous
Of old in Galilee,
Vouchsafe to-day Thy presence,
With these who wait on Thee;
Their store of earthly gladness
Transform to heavenly wine,
And teach them, in the tasting,
To know the gift is Thine.

3 O Spirit of the Father
Breathe on them from above,
So searching in Thy pureness,
So tender in Thy love ;
That guarded by Thy presence,
From sin and strife kept free,
Their lives may own Thy guidance,
Their hearts be ruled by Thee.

4 Except Thou build it, Father,
The house is built in vain:
Except Thou, Lord, sustain it.
The joy will turn to pain:
But nought can break the union
Of hearts in Thee made one,
And love, which Thou hast hallowed,
Is endless love begun.

THE CHURCH—BURIAL OF THE DEAD.

247 8s.

1 To Thee, O Father throned on high,
 Our marriage hymn, we duly sing;
Knit Thou the sacred bond we tie,
 And do Thou bless the wedding ring.
Thy love, at first, in Paradise,
 It was that made one flesh of twain;
Work Thou, while here our prayers arise,
 That sacred mystery, again.

2 To Thee, O Jesus, throned beside
 Thy Father's right hand, here we cry;
True Bridegroom of Thy spotless Bride,
 With all Thy human love, draw nigh.
Our human nature, Thy divine
 Has wedded, and in Thee, dear Lord,
As Cana's water turned to wine,
 Its lost godlikeness is restored.

3 O Holy Ghost the Paraclete,
 Thee too we worship, God and Lord,
And honor Thee, with praises meet,
 One with the Father and the Word.
Lord and Life-giver, hear our prayer,
 Come, sanctify and bless, and guide,
Strengthen, and shelter 'neath Thy care,
 The life of bridegroom and of bride.

4 O God Triune, Whom heaven's host
 Adores, with sweet and ceaseless song;
O Father, Son and Holy Ghost,
 To Whom all worship doth belong;
Hear, in these echoes faint and dim
 Of chant and prayer and holy psalm,
Their songs, the heavenly feast who hymn,
 The marriage supper of the Lamb.
  Amen.

BURIAL OF THE DEAD.

248 7s.

1 Blessing, honor, thanks, and praise,
 Pay we, gracious God, to Thee;
Thou in Thine abundant grace
 Givest us the victory.

 True and faithful to Thy word,
  Thou hast glorified Thy Son:
 Jesus Christ, our dying Lord,
  Has for us the victory won.

2 Lo! the prisoner is released!
 Lightened of *his* earthly load,
Where the weary are at rest
 And are gathered unto God.

 Lo! the pain of life is past,
  All *his* warfare now is o'er,
 Death and hell behind are cast,
  Grief and sufferings are no more.

3 Happy are the faithful dead,
 Blessèd who in Jesus die;
They from all their toils are freed
 In God's keeping safely lie.

 These the Spirit hath declared
  Blest, unutterably blest,
 Jesus is their great reward,
  Jesus is their endless rest.

4 Absent from our loving Lord
 We shall not continue long;
Join we then with one accord
 In the new, the joyful song;

 Blessing, honor, thanks, and praise,
  Triune God, we pay to Thee,
 Who in Thine abundant grace
  Givest us the victory! Amen.

249 8s.

1 God of the living, in Whose eyes
 Unveiled Thy whole creation lies;
All souls are Thine: we must not say
 That those are dead who pass away;
From this our world of flesh set free,
 We know them living unto Thee.

2 Released from earthly toil and strife,
 With Thee is hidden still their life;
Thine are their thoughts, their works, their powers,
 All Thine, and yet most truly ours;
For well we know, where'er they be,
 Our dead are living unto Thee.

3 Not spilt like water on the ground,
 Not wrapped in dreamless sleep profound,
Not wandering in unknown despair
 Beyond Thy voice, Thine arm, Thy care;
Not left to lie like fallen tree;
 Not dead, but living unto Thee.

4 Thy word is true, Thy will is just;
 To Thee we leave them, Lord, in trust;
And bless Thee for the love which gave
 Thy Son to fill a human grave,
That none might fear that world to see,
 Where all are living unto Thee.

THE CHURCH—BURIAL OF THE DEAD.

5 O breather into man of breath,
O holder of the keys of death,
O giver of the life within.
Save us from death, the death of sin;
That body, soul, and spirit be
For ever living unto Thee! Amen.

250   7.7.7.7.8.8.

1 Now the laborer's task is o'er;
Now the battle day is past;
Now upon the farther shore
Lands the voyager at last.
Father, in Thy gracious keeping
Leave we now Thy servant sleeping.

2 There the tears of earth are dried;
There its hidden things are clear;
There the work of life is tried
By a juster Judge than here.
Father, in Thy gracious keeping
Leave we now Thy servant sleeping.

3 There the sinful souls, that turn
To the cross their dying eyes,
The dear love of Christ shall learn
At His feet in Paradise.
Father, in Thy gracious keeping
Leave we now Thy servant sleeping.

4 There no more the powers of hell
Can prevail to mar their peace;
Christ the Lord shall guard them well,
He Who died for their release.
Father, in Thy gracious keeping
Leave we now Thy servant sleeping.

5 "Earth to earth, and dust to dust,"
Calmly now the words we say,
Leaving *him* to sleep in trust
Till the resurrection-day.
Father, in Thy gracious keeping
Leave we now Thy servant sleeping.

251   8.7.8.3.

1 On the resurrection morning
Soul and body meet again;
No more sorrow, no more weeping,
No more pain!

2 Here awhile they must be parted,
And the flesh its sabbath keep,
Waiting in a holy stillness,
Wrapt in sleep.

3 For a space the tired body
Lies with feet toward the dawn;
Till there breaks the last and brightest
Easter morn.

4 But the soul in contemplation
Utters earnest prayer and strong;
Breaking at the resurrection
Into song.

5 Soul and body reunited,
Thenceforth nothing shall divide,
Waking up in Christ's own likeness,
Satisfied.

6 Oh, the beauty, oh, the gladness
Of that resurrection-day!
Which shall not, through endless ages,
Pass away!

7 On that happy Easter morning
All the graves their dead restore,
Father, sister, child and mother,
Meet once more.

8 To that brightest of all meetings
Bring us, Jesus Christ, at last;
To Thy cross, through death and judgment,
Holding fast. Amen.

252   L.M.

1 Asleep in Jesus! blessèd sleep!
From which none ever wakes to weep;
A calm and undisturbed repose,
Unbroken by the last of foes.

2 Asleep in Jesus! Oh, how sweet
To be for such a slumber meet;
With holy confidence to sing
That death hath lost its painful sting!

3 Asleep in Jesus! peaceful rest!
Whose waking is supremely blest;
No fear, no woe shall dim that hour
That manifests the Saviour's power.

4 Asleep in Jesus! Oh, for me
May such a blissful refuge be!
Securely shall my ashes lie;
Waiting the summons from on high.

5 Asleep in Jesus! far from thee
Thy kindred and their graves may be;
But there is still a blessèd sleep,
From which none ever wakes to weep.

THE CHURCH—BURIAL OF THE DEAD.

253   11.6.

1 A voice is heard on earth of kinsfolk weeping
   The loss of one they love:
But he is gone where the redeemed are keeping
   A festival above.

2 The mourners throng the way, and from the steeple
   The funeral bell tolls slow:
But on the golden streets, the holy people
   Are passing to and fro:

3 And saying as they meet, rejoice! another,
   Long waited for is come:
The Saviour's heart is glad; a younger brother
   Hath reached the Father's home.

FOR A CHILD.

254   7s.

1 Let no hopeless tears be shed,
Holy is this narrow bed.
   Alleluia.

2 Death eternal life bestows,
Open heaven's portal throws.
   Alleluia.

3 And no peril waits at last
Him who now away hath past.
   Alleluia.

4 Not salvation hardly won,
Not the meed for race well run:
   Alleluia.

5 But the pity of the Lord
Gives His child a full reward;
   Alleluia.

6 Grants the prize without the course,
Crowns, without the battle's force.
   Alleluia.

7 Christ, when this sad life is done,
Join us to Thy little one:
   Alleluia.

8 And in Thine own tender love,
Bring us to the ranks above.
   Alleluia. Amen.

255   L.M.

1 Blessèd art thou, who, passed before
   Hast found through death thy greatest gain;
Whose opening life, so quickly o'er,
   Is hidden where is no more pain.

2 Blessèd art thou, whose childish feet
   Stray where the living waters flow;
For thee no glow of summer heat,
   No chilling touch of winter's snow.

3 Blessèd art thou; no storm can sweep
   Where love so soon hath wafted thee:
We toil in rowing on life's deep;
   But where thou art is "no more sea."

4 The Shepherd hath Himself removed
   The lamb which to His care was given;
For He on earth, Whom children loved,
   Hath called His child from earth to heaven.

5 No cloud is there, no sound of woe,
   But peace unearthly, pure and deep;
We know thou art with Christ; for "so
   He giveth His belovèd sleep." Amen.

Also the following:

105 So rest, our Rest.
106 The grave itself a garden is.
116 The foe behind, the deep before.
118 Jesus lives! Thy threatening woe.
119 Alleluia! Alleluia!
120 Sing, with all the sons of glory.
185 For all the saints, who from their labors rest.
191 For Thy dear saint, O Lord.
321 Rock of ages.
331 My God, my Father, while I stray.
332 Nearer, my God, to Thee.
389 To Him, Who for our sins was slain.
419 Oh, what the joy and the glory must be.
424 Brief life is here our portion.
534 O God, our help in ages past.
535 Soon and for ever.
536 When our heads are bowed with woe.
563 Jesus, life of those who die.
579 God hath two families of love.

ORDINATION.
CONSECRATION OF BISHOPS.

256 7.6.

1 Lord of the living harvest
   That whitens o'er the plain,
Where angels soon shall gather
   Their sheaves of golden grain;

Accept these hands to labor,
   These hearts to trust and love,
And deign with them to hasten
   Thy kingdom from above.

2 As laborers in Thy vineyard
   Still faithful may they be,
Content to bear the burden
   Of weary days for Thee;

To ask no other wages,
   When Thou shalt call them home,
But to have shared the travail
   Which makes Thy kingdom come.

3 Come down, Thou Holy Spirit,
   And fill their souls with light,
Clothe them in spotless raiment,
   In vesture clean and white;

Within Thy sacred temple
   Be with them where they stand,
To guide and teach Thy people
   Throughout our native land.

4 Be with them, God the Father!
   Be with them, God the Son!
And God the Holy Spirit!
   Most blessèd Three in One!

Make them a holy priesthood,
   Thee humbly to adore,
And fill them with Thy fullness
   Both now and evermore! Amen.

257 L. M.

1 Bow down Thine ear, almighty Lord,
And hear Thy Church's suppliant cry
For all who preach Thy saving word,
And wait upon Thy ministry.

2 In mercy, Father, now give heed,
And pour Thy quickening Spirit's breath
On those whom Thou dost call to feed
Thy flock redeemed by Jesus' death.

3 O Saviour, from Thy pierced hand
Shed o'er them all Thy gifts divine:
That those who in Thy presence stand
May do Thy will with love like Thine.

4 Blest Spirit, in their hearts abide,
And give them grace to watch and pray;
That as they seek Thy flock to guide,
Themselves may keep the narrow way.

5 O God, Thy strength and mercy send
To shield them in their strife with sin;
Grant them, enduring to the end,
The crown of life at last to win. Amen.

258 L. M.

1 O Spirit of the living God,
   In all Thy plenitude of grace,
Where'er the foot of man hath trod,
   Descend on our apostate race.

2 Give tongues of fire and hearts of love,
   To preach the reconciling word;
Give power and unction from above,
   Where'er the joyful sound is heard.

3 Be darkness, at Thy coming, light;
   Confusion, order, in Thy path;
Souls without strength inspire with might,
   Bid mercy triumph over wrath.

4 Convert the nations! far and nigh
   The triumphs of the cross record;
The name of Jesus glorify,
   Till every people call Him Lord. Amen.

259 P. M.

1 Come, Holy Ghost, our souls inspire,
   And lighten with celestial fire.

2 Thou the anointing Spirit art,
   Who dost Thy sevenfold gifts impart.

3 Thy blessèd unction from above
   Is comfort, life, and fire of love.

4 Enable with perpetual light
   The dullness of our blinded sight.

5 Anoint and cheer our soiled face
  With the abundance of Thy grace.

6 Keep far our foes, give peace at home;
  Where Thou art guide, no ill can come.

7 Teach us to know the Father, Son,
  And Thee of both to be but One,

8 That, through the ages all along,
  This may be our endless song:

9 Praise to Thy eternal merit,
  Father, Son, and Holy Spirit.   Amen.

Also the following:

520 Come, pure hearts, in sweetest measures.

INSTITUTION OF MINISTERS.

260   7s.

1 Heavenly Shepherd, Thee we pray
  For Thy servant here to-day;
  By the cross upon his brow,
  By his ordination vow,
  By the prayers which we have prayed
  For the Holy Spirit's aid,
  By the deep and fervent love
  Owing to his Lord above,
  Grant him faithful watch to keep,
  Tend Thy lambs, and feed Thy sheep.

2 From the silent power of sin
  Lurking secretly within,
  May the grace that flows from Thee,
  Heavenly Shepherd, set him free;
  By the blessing on him breathed,
  By the charge to him bequeathed,
  Thou the Way, the Truth, the Life,
  Gird him for the sacred strife,
  Aye his faithful watch to keep,
  Tend Thy lambs, and feed Thy sheep.

3 Speed him on his life-long way,
  Speed him whom we speed to-day;
  Thou, the gracious, loving Lord,
  Give him souls for his reward;
  Till he win the promised crown,
  When he lays his burden down
  Humbly at his Saviour's feet,
  Low before the mercy-seat:
  Give him, Lord, Thy grace to keep,
  Tend Thy lambs, and feed Thy sheep.

4 To the blessed Trinity
  Now let praise and glory be,
  In Whose Name we meet to-day
  For our guidance, as we pray,
  That we may, in all we do,
  Pastor, and his flock, be true;
  True to man in heavenly love,
  True to Thee, our God, above,
  Till we, sheep and shepherd, meet,
  Ransomed, at Thy judgment seat.
                                Amen.

IV. The Holy Scriptures.

261   C.M.

1 Lamp of our feet, whereby we trace
  Our path when wont to stray;
  Stream from the fount of heavenly grace,
  Brook by the traveler's way;

2 Bread of our souls, whereon we feed,
  True manna from on high;
  Our guide and chart, wherein we read
  Of realms beyond the sky;

3 Pillar of fire, through watches dark,
  And radiant cloud by day;
  When waves would 'whelm our tossing bark,
  Our anchor and our stay:

4 Word of the everlasting God,
  Will of His glorious Son;
  Without thee how could earth be trod,
  Or heaven itself be won?

5 Lord, grant us all aright to learn
  The wisdom it imparts;
  And to its heavenly teaching turn,
  With simple, childlike hearts.   Amen.

262   6s.

1 Lord, Thy word abideth,
  And our footsteps guideth;
  Who its truth believeth
  Light and joy receiveth.

2 When our foes are near us,
  Then Thy word doth cheer us,
  Word of consolation,
  Message of salvation.

SPECIAL OCCASIONS—LAYING OF A CORNER STONE.

3 When the storms are o'er us,
And dark clouds before us,
Then its light directeth,
And our way protecteth.

4 Who can tell the pleasure,
Who recount the treasure,
By Thy word imparted
To the simple-hearted?

5 Word of mercy, giving
Succor to the living ;
Word of life, supplying
Comfort to the dying!

6 Oh, that we discerning
Its most holy learning,
Lord, may love and fear Thee,
Evermore be near Thee! Amen.

263 C. M.

1 Father of mercies! in Thy word
What endless glory shines!
For ever be Thy Name adored
For these celestial lines.

2 Here the Redeemer's welcome voice
Spreads heavenly peace around ;
And life and everlasting joys
Attend the blissful sound.

3 Oh, may these heavenly pages be
My ever dear delight ;
And still new beauties may I see,
And still increasing light.

4 Divine Instructor, gracious Lord,
Be Thou for ever near ;
Teach me to love Thy sacred word,
And view my Saviour there. Amen.

264 7. 6.

1 O Word of God incarnate,
O wisdom from on high,
O truth unchanged, unchanging,
O light of our dark sky;

We praise Thee for the radiance
That from the hallowed page,
A lantern to our footsteps,
Shines on from age to age.

2 The Church from her dear Master
Received the gift divine,
And still that light she lifteth
O'er all the earth to shine.

It is the golden casket
Where gems of truth are stored,
It is the heaven-drawn picture
Of Christ the living Word.

3 It floateth like a banner
Before God's host unfurled ;
It shineth like a beacon
Above the darkling world ;

It is the chart and compass
That o'er life's surging sea,
Mid mists, and rocks, and quicksands
Still guides, O Christ, to Thee.

4 Oh, make Thy Church, dear Saviour,
A lamp of burnished gold,
To bear before the nations
Thy true light as of old ;

Oh, teach Thy wandering pilgrims
By this, their path to trace,
Till, clouds and darkness ended,
They see Thee face to face. Amen.

Also the following :
75 Not by Thy mighty hand.

V. Special Occasions.

LAYING OF A CORNER STONE.

265 L. M.

1 O Lord of hosts, Whose glory fills
The bounds of the eternal hills,
And yet vouchsafes, in Christian lands,
To dwell in temples made with hands;

2 Grant that all we who here to-day
Rejoicing this foundation lay,
May be in very deed Thine own,
Built on the precious Corner-stone.

3 Endue the creatures with Thy grace,
That shall adorn Thy dwelling-place ;
The beauty of the oak and pine,
The gold and silver, make them Thine.

4 To Thee they all pertain ; to Thee
The treasures of the earth and sea ;
And when we bring them to Thy throne
We but present Thee with Thine own.

SPECIAL OCCASIONS—LAYING OF A CORNER STONE.

5 The minds that guide endue with skill;
  The hands that work preserve from ill;
  That we, who these foundations lay,
  May raise the top-stone in its day.

6 Both now and ever, Lord, protect
  The temple of Thine own elect;
  Be Thou in them, and they in Thee,
  O ever blessèd Trinity! Amen.

266   8.7.

1 In the Name which earth and heaven
    Ever worship, praise, and fear,
  Father, Son, and Holy Spirit,
    Shall a house be builded here:
  Here with prayer its deep foundations,
    In the faith of Christ, we lay,
  Trusting by His help to crown it
    With the top-stone in its day.

2 Here as in their due succession
    Stone on stone the workmen place,
  Thus, we pray, unseen but surely,
    Jesus, build us up in grace;
  Till, within these walls completed,
    We complete in Thee are found;
  And to Thee, the one Foundation,
    Strong and living stones, are bound.

3 Fair shall be Thine earthly temple:
    Here the careless passer-by
  Shall bethink him, in its beauty,
    Of the holier house on high;
  Weary hearts and troubled spirits
    Here shall find a still retreat;
  Sinful souls shall bring their burden
    Here to the Absolver's feet.

4 Yet with truer, nobler beauty,
    Lord, we pray, this house adorn,
  Where Thy Bride, Thy Church redeemed,
    Robes her for her marriage morn;
  Clothed in garments of salvation,
    Rich with gems of heavenly grace,
  Spouse of Christ, arrayed and waiting
    Till she may behold His face.

5 Here in due and solemn order
    May her ceaseless prayer arise;
  Here may strains of holy gladness
    Lift her heart above the skies;
  Here the word of life be spoken,
    Here the child of God be sealed;
  Here the bread of heaven be broken,
    "Till He come" Himself revealed.

6 Praise to Thee, O Master-Builder,
    Maker of the earth and skies;
  Praise to Thee, in Whom Thy temple
    Fitly framed together lies;
  Praise to Thee, eternal Spirit,
    Binding all that lives in one:
  Till our earthly praise be ended,
    And the eternal song begun! Amen.

267   L. M.

1 O Thou, in Whom alone is found
  The strength by which our toil is blest.
  Upon this consecrated ground
  Now bid Thy cloud of glory rest.

2 In Thy great Name we place this stone:
  To Thy great truth these walls we rear:
  Long may they make Thy glory known,
  And long our Saviour triumph here.

3 And while Thy sons, from earth apart,
  Here seek the truth from heaven that sprung,
  Fill with Thy Spirit every heart,
  With living fire touch every tongue.

4 Lord, feed Thy Church with peace and love;
  Let sin and error pass away,
  Till truth's full influence from above
  Rejoice the earth with cloudless day.
                                Amen.

268   L. M.

1 And will the great eternal God
  On earth establish His abode?
  And will He, from His radiant throne.
  Accept our temples for His own?

2 These walls we to Thy honor raise;
  Long may they echo with Thy praise:
  And Thou, descending, fill the place
  With choicest tokens of Thy grace.

3 Here let the great Redeemer reign,
  With all the graces of His train:
  While power divine His word attends,
  To conquer foes, and cheer His friends.

4 And in the great decisive day,
  When God the nations shall survey,
  May it before the world appear
  That souls were born to glory here.
                                Amen.

CONSECRATION OF CHURCHES.

269   C.M.

1 O Thou, Whose own vast temple stands,
   Built over earth and sea,
Accept the walls that human hands
   Have raised to worship Thee.

2 Lord, from Thine inmost glory send,
   Within these courts to bide,
The peace that dwelleth without end
   Serenely by Thy side!

3 May erring minds that worship here
   Be taught the better way;
And they who mourn, and they who fear,
   Be strengthened as they pray.

4 May faith grow firm, and love grow warm,
   And pure devotion rise,
While round these hallowed walls, the storm
   Of earth-born passion dies.   Amen.

270   7.6.

1 Great God of our salvation,
   Be this Thy resting place,
Thy holy habitation,
   Thy mercy-seat of grace.
What time the tempests gather,
   Light, love, peace, praise be here:
The children with their Father:
   God with us: where is fear?

2 Though pilgrim hearts are moaning
   The sin and strife of earth,
The whole creation groaning
   In travail-pangs of birth,
Emmanuel leads us onward:
   His cross is in the van;
The clouds are rifted sunward:
   God with us: what is man?

3 Though more the devil rages
   As nearer draws his hour,
Hid in the Rock of ages
   We bide His wrath and power:
For still the Dove is hovering
   O'er every suppliant saint:
God with us, shadowing, covering;
   Who dares to fail or faint?

4 Praise ye our God for ever,
   In these His courts adored:
Nor death nor hell can sever
   The servant and his Lord.
On, brothers, on; victorious
   The Gospel's trumpet-call;
The Lord of hosts before us:
   God with us, one and all.   Amen.

271   L.M.

1 Jesus! where'er Thy people meet,
There they behold Thy mercy-seat;
Where'er they seek Thee, Thou art found,
And every place is hallowed ground.

2 And since within no walls confined,
Thou dwellest in the humble mind:
Let all within Thy house who come,
Departing, take Thee to their home.

3 Yet everywhere Thou guid'st Thine own
To raise for Thee an earthly throne;
And where Thy Name Thou dost record,
There Thou wilt come and bless them, Lord!

4 [* Behold, at Thy commanding word,
We stretch the curtain and the cord;
Come Thou and fill this wider space,
And bless us with a large increase.]

5 Great Shepherd of Thy chosen few,
Thy former mercies here renew;
And here to wayward hearts proclaim
The sweetness of Thy saving Name!

6 Here may we prove the might of prayer,
To strengthen faith and sweeten care;
To teach our faint desires to rise,
And bring all heaven before our eyes!

7 Here to the babe new-born on earth,
Grant Thou the newer, better birth;
By water and the Holy Ghost
Restoring all that Adam lost.

8 Here to the weary, hungry soul
Give Thou the gift that maketh whole;
The bread that is Christ's flesh, for food,
The wine that is the Saviour's blood.

             * For enlargement of the Church.

9 Lord, we are few, but Thou art near;
   Nor short Thine arm, nor deaf Thine ear;
   Oh, rend the heavens, come quickly down,
   And make a thousand hearts Thine own!
                                    Amen.

   Also the following:

500 Lo! God is here; let us adore.
501 Christ is made the sure foundation.
502 We love the place, O God.

RESTORATION OF A CHURCH.
272   S.7.

1 Lift the strain of high thanksgiving!
   Tread with songs the hallowed way!
   Praise our fathers' God for mercies
   New to us their sons to-day;
   Here they built for Him a dwelling,
   Served Him here in ages past,
   Fixed it for His sure possession,
   Holy ground, while time shall last.

2 When the years had wrought their changes,
   He, our own unchanging God,
   Thought on this His habitation,
   Looked on His decayed abode;
   Heard our prayers, and helped our counsels,
   Blessed the silver and the gold,
   Till once more His house is standing
   Firm and stately as of old.

3 Entering then Thy gates with praises,
   Lord, be ours Thine Israel's prayer:
   'Rise into Thy place of resting,
   Shew Thy promised Presence there!'
   Let the gracious word be spoken
   Here, as once on Sion's height,
   'This shall be My rest for ever,
   This My dwelling of delight.'

4 Fill this latter house with glory
   Greater than the former knew;
   Clothe with righteousness its priesthood,
   Guide us all to reverence true;
   Let Thy Holy One's anointing
   Here its sevenfold blessing shed;
   Spread for us the heavenly banquet,
   Satisfy Thy poor with bread.

5 Praise to Thee, almighty Father,
   Praise to Thee, eternal Son,
   Praise to Thee, all-quickening Spirit,
   Ever blessèd Three in One;

   Threefold Power and Grace and Wisdom,
   Moulding out of sinful clay,
   Living stones for that true temple
   Which shall never know decay. Amen.

MISSIONS:
AT HOME.
273   L.M.

1 Look from Thy sphere of endless day,
   O God of mercy and of might!
   In pity look on those who stray,
   Benighted in this land of light.

2 In peopled vale, in lonely glen,
   In crowded mart, by stream or sea,
   How many of the sons of men
   Hear not the message sent from Thee!

3 Send forth Thy heralds, Lord, to call
   The thoughtless young, the hardened old,
   A scattered, homeless flock, till all
   Be gathered to Thy peaceful fold.

4 Send them Thy mighty word to speak,
   Till faith shall dawn, and doubt depart,
   To awe the bold, to stay the weak,
   And bind and heal the broken heart.

5 Then all these wastes, a dreary scene
   That makes us sadden as we gaze,
   Shall grow with living waters green,
   And lift to heaven the voice of praise.

MISSIONS:
ABROAD.
274   L.M.

1 Fling out the banner! let it float
   Skyward and seaward, high and wide;
   The sun, that lights its shining folds,
   The cross, on which the Saviour died.

2 Fling out the banner! angels bend
   In anxious silence o'er the sign;
   And vainly seek to comprehend
   The wonder of the love divine.

3 Fling out the banner! heathen lands
   Shall see from far the glorious sight,
   And nations, crowding to be born,
   Baptize their spirits in its light.

SPECIAL OCCASIONS—MISSIONS.

4 Fling out the banner! sin-sick souls
   That sink and perish in the strife,
Shall touch in faith its radiant hem,
   And spring immortal into life.

5 Fling out the banner! let it float
   Skyward and seaward, high and wide,
Our glory, only in the cross:
   Our only hope, the Crucified!

6 Fling out the banner! wide and high,
   Seaward and skyward, let it shine:
Nor skill, nor might, nor merit ours;
   We conquer only in that sign.

275   7.6.

1 From Greenland's icy mountains,
   From India's coral strand,
Where Afric's sunny fountains
   Roll down their golden sand;
From many an ancient river,
   From many a palmy plain,
They call us to deliver
   Their land from error's chain.

2 What though the spicy breezes
   Blow soft o'er Ceylon's isle;
Though every prospect pleases,
   And only man is vile:
In vain with lavish kindness
   The gifts of God are strewn;
The heathen in his blindness
   Bows down to wood and stone.

3 Can we, whose souls are lighted
   With wisdom from on high;
Can we to men benighted
   The lamp of life deny?
Salvation, Oh, salvation,
   The joyful sound proclaim,
Till each remotest nation
   Has learnt Messiah's Name.

4 Waft, waft, ye winds, His story,
   And you, ye waters, roll,
Till, like a sea of glory,
   It spreads from pole to pole:
Till o'er our ransomed nature
   The Lamb for sinners slain
Redeemer, King, Creator,
   In bliss returns to reign.

276   6.6.6.6.8.8.

1   Arise, O Lord, and shine
    In all Thy saving might,
    And prosper each design
      To spread Thy glorious light:
   Let healing streams of mercy flow,
   That all the earth Thy truth may know.

2   Oh, bring the nations near,
    That they may sing Thy praise:
    Let all the people hear
    And learn Thy holy ways:
   Reign, mighty God, assert Thy cause,
   And govern by Thy righteous laws.

3   Put forth Thy glorious power:
    The nations then shall see,
    And earth present her store,
      In converts born to Thee:
   God, our own God, His Church shall bless,
   And earth be filled with righteousness.

277   8.7.

1 Lord, her watch Thy Church is keeping,
   When shall earth Thy rule obey?
When shall end the night of weeping?
   When shall break the promised day?
See the whitening harvest languish,
   Waiting still the laborers' toil;
Was it vain—Thy Son's deep anguish?
   Shall the strong retain the spoil?

2 Tidings, sent to every creature,
   Millions yet have never heard:
Can they hear without a preacher?
   Lord almighty, give the word!
Give the word! in every nation
   Let the gospel trumpet sound,
Witnessing a world's salvation,
   To the earth's remotest bound.

3 Then the end! Thy Church completed,
   All Thy chosen gathered in,
With their King in glory seated,
   Satan bound, and banished sin;
Gone for ever parting, weeping,
   Hunger, sorrow, death, and pain:
Lo! her watch Thy Church is keeping;
   Come, Lord Jesus, come to reign!
                        Amen.

SPECIAL OCCASIONS—MISSIONS.

278 8.7.

1 Saviour, sprinkle many nations;
  Fruitful let Thy sorrows be;
By Thy pains and consolations
  Draw the Gentiles unto Thee!

2 Of Thy cross the wondrous story,
  Be it to the nations told ;
Let them see Thee in Thy glory
  And Thy mercy manifold.

3 Far and wide, though all unknowing,
  Pants for Thee each mortal breast,
Human tears for Thee are flowing,
  Human hearts in Thee would rest.

4 Thirsting as for dews of even,
  As the new-mown grass for rain,
Thee they seek as God of heaven,
  Thee as Man for sinners slain.

5 Saviour, lo! the isles are waiting !
  Stretched the hand and strained the sight,
For Thy Spirit, new creating,
  Love's pure flame, and wisdom's light.

6 Give the word, and of the preacher
  Speed the foot and touch the tongue,
Till on earth by every creature
  Glory to the Lamb be sung! Amen.

279 8.7.

1 Lord, a Saviour's love displaying,
  Show the heathen lands Thy way;
Thousands still like sheep are straying
  In the dark and cloudy day.

2 Shades of death are gathering o'er them,
  Lord, they perish from Thy sight !
Let Thine angel go before them ;
  Bring the Gentiles to Thy light.

3 Fetch them home from every nation,
  From the islands of the sea;
By the word of Thy salvation
  Call the wanderers back to Thee.

4 Thou their pasture hast provided,
  Grant the blessing long foretold ;
Let Thy sheep, divinely guided,
  Find at last the one true fold.

280 8.7.8.7.4.7.

1 Souls in heathen darkness lying,
    Where no light has broken through,
  Souls that Jesus bought by dying,
    Whom His soul in travail knew:
      Thousand voices
  Call us, o'er the waters blue.

2 Christians, hearken ! None has taught them
    Of His love so deep and dear ;
  Of the precious price that bought them ;
    Of the nail, the thorn, the spear ;
      Ye who know Him,
  Guide them from their darkness drear.

3 Haste, oh haste, and spread the tidings
    Wide to earth's remotest strand ;
  Let no brother's bitter chidings
    Rise against us, when we stand
      In the judgment,
  From some far, forgotten land.

4 Lo! the hills for harvest whiten,
    All along each distant shore;
  Seaward far the islands brighten ;
    Light of nations ! lead us o'er :
      When we seek them,
  Let Thy Spirit go before. Amen.

281 L. M.

1 Jesus shall reign where'er the sun
  Does his successive journeys run ;
His kingdom stretch from shore to shore,
  Till moons shall wax and wane no more.

2 To Him shall endless prayer be made,
  And praises throng to crown His head ;
His Name like sweet perfume shall rise
  With every morning sacrifice.

3 People and realms of every tongue
  Dwell on His love with sweetest song ;
And infant voices shall proclaim
  Their early blessings on His Name.

4 Blessings abound where'er He reigns ;
  The prisoner leaps to burst his chains,
The weary find eternal rest,
  And all the sons of want are blest.

5 Let every creature rise and bring
  Peculiar honors to our King ;
Angels descend with songs again,
  And earth repeat the loud Amen.

SPECIAL OCCASIONS—MISSIONS.

282 8.7.8.7.4.7.

1 Speed Thy servants, Saviour, speed them;
  Thou art Lord of winds and waves;
  They were bound, but Thou hast freed them;
  Now they go to free the slaves;
    Be Thou with them:
  'Tis Thine arm alone that saves.

2 Friends and home and all forsaking,
  Lord, they go at Thy command,
  As their stay Thy promise taking,
  While they traverse sea and land:
    Oh, be with them!
  Lead them safely by the hand.

3 When they reach the land of strangers,
  And the prospect dark appears,
  Nothing seen but toils and dangers,
  Nothing felt but doubts and fears,
    Be Thou with them;
  Hear their sighs, and count their tears.

4 Where no fruit appears to cheer them,
  And they seem to toil in vain:
  Then in mercy, Lord, draw near them,
  Then their sinking hopes sustain:
    Thus supported,
  Let their zeal revive again.

5 In the midst of opposition,
  Let them trust, O Lord, in Thee;
  When success attends their mission,
  Let Thy servants humbler be;
    Never leave them,
  Till Thy face in heaven they see:

6 There to reap in joy for ever
  Fruit that grows from seed here sown;
  There to be with Him, Who never
  Ceases to preserve His own;
    And with gladness
  Give the praise to Him alone. Amen.

283 6.5.

1 Hark! the swelling breezes,
    Rising from afar,
  Bring the sound of conflict
    From the holy war.
  God is with our armies;
    He the word has given;
  He is watching o'er you,
    Messengers of heaven.

2 Go, thou mighty gospel,
    Conquering on thy way;
  Night upon the mountains
    Changes into day.
  Idols bow before thee,
    Heathen temples fall;
  Soon the world shall own thee,
    Victor over all.

3 O Thou blessèd Saviour,
    Reigning now on high,
  May Thy faithful soldiers
    Find Thee ever nigh.
  Bid their glorious mission
    Spread from sea to sea,
  Till the whole creation
    Worship only Thee. Amen.

284 L.M.

1 Arm of the Lord, awake, awake,
  Put on Thy strength, the nations shake;
  And let the world adoring see
  Triumphs of mercy wrought by Thee.

2 Say to the heathen from Thy throne,
  I am Jehovah, God alone:
  Thy voice their idols shall confound,
  And cast their altars to the ground.

3 Let Sion's time of favor come;
  Oh, bring the tribes of Israel home:
  And let our wondering eyes behold
  Gentiles and Jews in Jesus' fold.

4 Almighty God, Thy grace proclaim
  In every clime, of every name;
  Let adverse powers before Thee fall,
  And crown the Saviour Lord of all.
                                Amen.

Also the following:

371 Hail to the Lord's Anointed.
372 God of mercy, God of grace.
495 From all that dwell below the skies.
512 Thy kingdom come, O God.
513 Thou, Whose almighty Word.
514 Hark, the song of Jubilee.
515 Blow ye the trumpet, blow.
516 Lord of all power and might.
517 O brothers, lift your voices.
648 Christ for the world we sing.

SPECIAL OCCASIONS—CHARITIES.

FOR THE JEWS.

285 7.6.

1 Oh, that the Lord's salvation
  Were out of Sion come,
To heal His ancient nation,
  To lead His outcasts home!

2 How long the holy city
  Shall heathen feet profane?
Return, O Lord, in pity;
  Rebuild her walls again.

3 Let fall Thy rod of terror;
  Thy saving grace impart;
Roll back the veil of error;
  Release the fettered heart.

4 Let Israel, home returning,
  Her lost Messiah see;
Give oil of joy for mourning,
  And bind Thy Church to Thee.
          Amen.

286 C.M.

1 Wake, harp of Sion, wake again,
  Upon Thine ancient hill,
On Jordan's long deserted plain,
  By Kedron's lowly rill.

2 The hymn shall yet in Sion swell,
  That sounds Messiah's praise,
And Thy loved Name, Emmanuel,
  As once in ancient days.

3 For Israel yet shall own her King.
  For her, salvation waits,
And hill and dale shall sweetly sing,
  With praise in all her gates.

4 Oh, hasten, Lord, these promised days,
  When Israel shall rejoice;
And Jew and Gentile join in praise,
  With one united voice!   Amen.

287 L.M.

1 Oh, why should Israel's sons, once blest,
  Still roam the scorning world around;
Disowned of heaven, by man opprest,
  Outcasts from Sion's hallowed ground?

2 O God of Israel, view their race;
  Back to Thy fold the wanderers bring,
Teach them to seek Thy slighted grace,
  To hail in Christ their promised King.

3 The veil of darkness rend in twain,
  Which hides their Shiloh's glorious light;
The severed olive branch again
  To its own parent stock unite.

4 Haste, glorious day, expected long,
  When Jew and Greek one prayer shall raise,
With eager feet one temple throng,
  One God with grateful rapture praise.
              Amen.

CHARITIES.

288 8.8.8.6.

1 O God of mercy, God of might,
  In love and pity infinite,
  Teach us, as ever in Thy sight,
    To live our life to Thee.

2 And Thou, Who cam'st on earth to die,
  That fallen man might live thereby,
  Oh, hear us, for to Thee we cry,
    In hope, O Lord, to Thee.

3 Teach us the lesson Thou hast taught,
  To feel for those Thy blood hath bought,
  That every word, and deed, and thought
    May work a work for Thee.

4 For all are brethren, far and wide,
  Since Thou, O Lord, for all hast died;
  Then teach us, whatsoe'er betide,
    To love them all in Thee.

5 In sickness, sorrow, want, or care,
  Whate'er it be, 'tis ours to share;
  May we, where help is needed, there
    Give help as unto Thee.

6 And may Thy Holy Spirit move
  All those who live, to live in love,
  Till Thou shalt greet in heaven above
    All those who give to Thee.   Amen.

289 L.M.

1 O Thou through suffering perfect made,
  On Whom the bitter cross was laid;
  In hours of sickness, grief, and pain,
  No sufferer turns to Thee in vain.

2 The halt, the maimed, the sick, the blind,
  Sought not in vain Thy tendance kind;
  Now in Thy poor Thyself we see,
  And minister through them to Thee

SPECIAL OCCASIONS—CHARITIES.

3 O loving Saviour, Thou canst cure
The pains and woes Thou didst endure;
For all who need, Physician great,
Thy healing balm we supplicate.

4 But, oh, far more, let each keen pain
And hour of woe be heavenly gain,
Each stroke of Thy chastising rod
Bring back the wanderer nearer God!

5 Oh, heal the bruisèd heart within!
Oh, save our souls all sick with sin!
Give life and health in bounteous store,
That we may praise Thee evermore!
Amen.

290   D.C.M.

1 Thine arm, O Lord, in days of old
Was strong to heal and save;
It triumphed o'er disease and death,
O'er darkness and the grave.

To Thee they went, the blind, the dumb,
The palsied and the lame,
The leper with his tainted life,
The sick with fevered frame.

2 And lo! Thy touch brought life and health,
Gave speech, and strength, and sight;
And youth renewed and frenzy calmed
Owned Thee, the Lord of light.

And now, O Lord, be near to bless,
Almighty as of yore,
In crowded street, by restless couch,
As by Gennesareth's shore.

3 Though love and might no longer heal
By touch, or word, or look;
Though they who do Thy work must read
Thy laws in nature's book;

Yet come to heal the sick man's soul,
Come, cleanse the leprous taint,
Give joy and peace, where all is strife,
And strength, where all is faint.

4 Be Thou our great deliverer still,
Thou Lord of life and death.
Restore and quicken, soothe and bless
With Thine almighty breath.

To hands that work and eyes that see
Give wisdom's heavenly lore,
That whole and sick, and weak and strong,
May praise Thee evermore. Amen.

291   8.7.8.7.7.7.

1 Thou to Whom the sick and dying
Ever came, nor came in vain,
Still with healing words replying
To the wearied cry of pain;
Hear us, Jesus, as we meet,
Suppliants at Thy mercy seat.

2 Every care, and every sorrow,
Be it great, or be it small,
Yesterday, to-day, to-morrow,
When, where'er, it may befall,
Lay we humbly at Thy feet,
Suppliants at Thy mercy seat.

3 Still the weary, sick, and dying
Need a brother's, sister's care;
On Thy higher help relying
May we now their burden share,
Bringing all our offerings meet,
Suppliants at Thy mercy seat.

4 May each child of Thine be willing,
Willing both in hand and heart,
All the law of love fulfilling,
Ever comfort to impart;
Ever bringing offerings meet,
Suppliant to Thy mercy seat.

5 So may sickness, sin, and sadness,
To Thy healing power yield,
Till the sick and sad, in gladness,
Rescued, ransomed, cleansèd, healed,
One in Thee together meet,
Pardoned at Thy judgment seat.
Amen.

292   8s.

1 Father, Who mak'st Thy suffering sons
Thy ministers to stronger ones,
To light love's holy flame within,
Deposing self, abasing sin,
Oh, teach my soul, confiding still,
To suffer or to do Thy will!

2 If in this world of mystery,
Unequal favors fall on me,
While brothers, better far than I,
Are called to languish or to die,
Help me in turn their ills to share,
Their wounds to heal, their load to bear.

SPECIAL OCCASIONS—ALMSGIVING.

3 Blest is their task, 'mid human woe
  Thy gifts on others who bestow;
  For suffering lies at plenty's door,
  And God appeals, when cries the poor.
  His law ordains for all that live,
  What sorrow lacks let mercy give.

4 The day shall come when veils remove,
  And all shall see that God is love.
  Then He Himself all tears shall dry,
  And show of pain the reason why;
  And theirs shall be the great reward
  Who in His poor beheld their Lord.

293   ALMSGIVING.   C. M.

1 Lord, lead the way the Saviour went,
  By lane and cell obscure,
  And let love's treasures still be spent,
  Like His, upon the poor.

2 Like Him through scenes of deep distress,
  Who bore the world's sad weight,
  We, in their crowded loneliness,
  Would seek the desolate.

3 For Thou hast placed us side by side,
  In this wide world of ill,
  And, that Thy followers may be tried,
  The poor are with us still.

4 Mean are all offerings we can make,
  But Thou hast taught us, Lord,
  If given for the Saviour's sake,
  They lose not their reward.

294   8.7.

1 Lord of glory, Who hast bought us
  With Thy life-blood as the price,
  Never grudging for the lost ones
  That tremendous sacrifice;
  And with that hast freely given
  Blessings, countless as the sand,
  To the unthankful and the evil
  With Thine own unsparing hand;

2 Grant us hearts, dear Lord, to yield Thee
  Gladly, freely of Thine own;
  With the sunshine of Thy goodness
  Melt our thankless hearts of stone;
  Till our cold and selfish natures,
  Warmed by Thee, at length believe
  That more happy and more blessèd
  'Tis to give than to receive.

3 Wondrous honor hast Thou given
  To our humblest charity,
  In Thine own mysterious sentence,
  "Ye have done it unto Me."
  Can it be, O gracious Master,
  Thou dost deign for alms to sue,
  Saying by Thy poor and needy,
  "Give as I have given to you?"

4 Yes: the sorrow and the suffering,
  Which on every hand we see,
  Channels are for tithes and offerings
  Due by solemn right to Thee;
  Right of which we may not rob Thee,
  Debt we may not choose but pay,
  Lest that face of love and pity
  Turn from us another day.

5 Lord of glory, Who hast bought us
  With Thy life-blood as the price,
  Never grudging for the lost ones
  That tremendous sacrifice.
  Give us faith, to trust Thee boldly,
  Hope, to stay our souls on Thee;
  But oh, best of all Thy graces,
  Give us Thine own charity.   Amen.

295   S. M.

1 We give Thee but Thine own,
  Whate'er the gift may be:
  All that we have is Thine alone,
  A trust, O Lord, from Thee.

2 May we Thy bounties thus
  As stewards true receive,
  And gladly, as Thou blessest us,
  To Thee our first-fruits give.

3 Oh, hearts are bruised and dead,
  And homes are bare and cold,
  And lambs for whom the Shepherd bled,
  Are straying from the fold!

4 To comfort and to bless,
  To find a balm for woe,
  To tend the lone and fatherless
  Is angel's work below.

5 The captive to release,
  To God, the lost to bring,
  To teach the way of life and peace,
  It is a Christ-like thing.

SPECIAL OCCASIONS—NATIONAL FESTIVALS AND FASTS.

6 And we believe Thy word,
  Though dim our faith may be;
  Whate'er for Thine we do, O Lord,
  We do it unto Thee.

296   C.M.

1 O Fount of good, to own Thy love
  Our thankful hearts incline;
  What can we render, Lord, to Thee,
  When all the worlds are Thine?

2 But Thou hast needy brethren here,
  Partakers of Thy grace,
  Whose names Thou wilt Thyself confess
  Before the Father's face.

3 In each sad accent of distress
  Thy pleading voice is heard;
  In them Thou may'st be clothed and fed,
  And visited, and cheered.

4 Help us then, Lord, Thy yoke to wear,
  And joy to do Thy will;
  Each other's burdens gladly bear,
  And love's sweet law fulfil.

5 Thy face with reverence and with love
  We in Thy poor would see;
  And while we minister to them,
  Would do it as to Thee.

6 Do Thou, O Lord, our alms accept,
  And with Thy blessing speed;
  Bless us in giving; greatly bless
  Our gifts to them that need. Amen.

297   P.M.

1 Holy offerings, rich and rare,
  Offerings of praise and prayer,
  Purer life and purpose high,
  Claspèd hands, uplifted eye,
  Lowly acts of adoration
  To the God of our salvation:
  On His altar laid we leave them:
  Christ, present them! God, receive them!

2 Homage of each humble heart,
  Ere we from Thy house depart;
  Worship fervent, deep and high,
  Adoration, ecstasy;
  All that childlike love can render
  Of devotion true and tender;
  On Thine altar laid we leave them:
  Christ, present them! God, receive them!

3 To the Father, and the Son,
  And the Spirit, Three in One,
  Though our mortal weakness raise
  Offerings of imperfect praise,
  Yet with hearts bowed down most lowly,
  Crying, Holy! holy! holy!
  On Thine altar laid we leave them:
  Christ, present them! God, receive them!
                        Amen.

NATIONAL FESTIVALS AND FASTS.

298   C.M.

1 Lord, while for all mankind we pray,
  Of every clime and coast,
  Oh, hear us for our native land,
  The land we love the most!

2 Our fathers' sepulchres are here,
  And here our kindred dwell;
  Our children, too; how should we love
  Another's land so well?

3 Oh, guard our shores from every foe,
  With peace our borders bless;
  With prosperous times our cities crown,
  Our fields with plenteousness.

4 Unite us in the sacred love
  Of knowledge, truth, and Thee;
  And let our hills and valleys shout
  The songs of liberty.

5 Lord of the nations, thus to Thee
  Our country we commend;
  Be Thou our refuge and our trust,
  Our everlasting friend. Amen.

299   5,4.

1 God of our fathers,
  Bless this Thy land;
  Ocean to ocean
  Owneth Thy hand.
  Home of all nations
  From far and near,
  Give, to unite us,
  Thy faith and fear.
  God of our fathers
  Failing us never,
  God of our fathers,
  Be ours for ever.

SPECIAL OCCASIONS—NATIONAL FESTIVALS AND FASTS.

    2 Lord God of Sabaoth,
      Mighty in war,
      Boundless and numberless
      Thine armies are.
      Thy right hand conquereth
      All that oppose;
      Launch forth Thy thunderbolts,
      Smite down our foes;
      Lord God of Sabaoth,
      Failing us never,
      Lord God of Sabaoth,
      Fight for us ever.

    3 Lord God our Saviour,
      Thy love o'erflows.
      Making our wilderness
      Bloom as the rose.
      Thou with true liberty
      Makest us free,
      Knowing no master,
      No king, but Thee;
      Lord God our Saviour,
      Failing us never,
      Lord God our Saviour,
      Reign Thou for ever.

    4 Spirit of unity,
      Crown of all kings,
      Find us a resting place
      Under Thy wings:
      By Thine own presence
      Thy will be done,
      Millions of free men
      Banded as one.
      Lord God almighty,
      Failing us never,
      Thine be the glory,
      Now and for ever.   Amen.

300   6.6.4.6.6.6.4.

    1 God bless our native land!
      Firm may she ever stand,
      Through storm and night;
      When the wild tempests rave,
      Ruler of winds and wave,
      Do Thou our country save
      By Thy great might.

    2 For her our prayer shall rise
      To God, above the skies:
      On Him we wait;
      Thou Who art ever nigh,
      Guarding with watchful eye,
      To Thee aloud we cry,
      God save the state!   Amen.

---

301   L. M.

1 O Lord of Hosts! Almighty King!
  Behold the sacrifice we bring:
  To every arm Thy strength impart;
  Thy Spirit shed through every heart.

2 Wake in our breasts the living fires,
  The holy faith that warmed our sires;
  Thy hand hath made our nation free;
  To die for her is serving Thee.

3 Be Thou a pillared flame to show
  The midnight snare, the silent foe;
  And when the battle thunders loud,
  Still guide us in its moving cloud.

4 God of all nations! Sovereign Lord!
  In Thy dread Name we draw the sword,
  We lift the starry flag on high
  That fills with light our stormy sky.

5 From treason's rent, from murder's stain,
  Guard Thou its folds till peace shall reign,
  Till fort and field, till shore and sea,
  Join our loud anthem, praise to Thee!
                      Amen.

302   L. M.

1 O God of love, O King of peace,
  Make wars throughout the world to cease;
  The wrath of sinful man restrain,
  Give peace, O God, give peace again!

2 Remember, Lord, Thy works of old,
  The wonders that our fathers told:
  Remember not our sin's dark stain,
  Give peace, O God, give peace again!

3 Whom shall we trust but Thee, O Lord?
  Where rest but on Thy faithful word?
  None ever called on Thee in vain,
  Give peace, O God, give peace again!

4 Where saints and angels dwell above,
  All hearts are knit in holy love:
  Oh, bind us in that heavenly chain!
  Give peace, O God, give peace again!
                      Amen.

303   8.7.

1 Dread Jehovah, God of nations,
    From Thy temple in the skies,
  Hear Thy people's supplications,
    Now for their deliverance rise.

2 Lo, with deep contrition turning,
  Humbly at Thy feet we bend;
  Hear us, fasting, praying, mourning;
  Hear us, spare us, and defend.

3 Though our sins, our hearts confounding,
  Long and loud for vengeance call,
  Thou hast mercy more abounding,
  Jesus' blood can cleanse from all.

4 Let that love veil our transgression,
  Let that blood our guilt efface;
  Save Thy people from oppression,
  Save from spoil Thy holy place.   Amen.

THE OLD YEAR.

304   8.7.8.7.8.8.7.

1 Across the sky the shades of night
  This winter's eve are fleeting:
  We deck Thine altar, Lord, with light,
  In solemn worship meeting:
  And as the year's last hours go by
  We lift to Thee our earnest cry,
  Once more Thy love entreating.

2 Before the cross, subdued we bow,
  To Thee our prayers addressing;
  Recounting all Thy mercies now,
  And all our sins confessing;
  Beseeching Thee, this coming year,
  To hold us in Thy faith and fear,
  And crown us with Thy blessing.

3 And, while we kneel, we lift our eyes
  To dear ones gone before us;
  Safe housed with Thee in Paradise,
  Whose peace descendeth o'er us:
  And beg of Thee, when life is past,
  To re-unite us all, at last,
  And to our lost restore us.

4 We gather up, in this brief hour,
  The memory of Thy mercies;
  Thy wondrous goodness, love, and power,
  Our grateful song rehearses:
  For Thou hast been our strength and stay,
  In many a dark and dreary day
  Of sorrow and reverses.

5 In many an hour, when fear and dread,
  Like evil spells have bound us,
  And clouds were gathering overhead,
  Thy providence hath found us;
  In many a night when waves ran high,
  Thy gracious presence drawing nigh
  Hath made all calm around us.

6 Thou, O great God, in years to come,
  Whatever fate betide us,
  Right onward through our journey home
  Be Thou at hand to guide us:
  Nor leave us till, at close of life,
  Safe from all perils, toil, and strife,
  Heaven shall unfold and hide us.   Amen.

305   7.6.

1 O God, the Rock of ages,
  Who evermore hast been,—
  What time the tempest rages,—
  Our dwelling-place serene:
  Before Thy first creations,
  O Lord, the same as now,
  To endless generations
  The everlasting Thou!

2 Our years are like the shadows
  On sunny hills that lie,
  Or grasses in the meadows
  That blossom but to die:
  A sleep, a dream, a story
  By strangers quickly told,
  An unremaining glory
  Of things that soon are old.

3 O Thou, Who canst not slumber,
  Whose light grows never pale,
  Teach us aright to number
  Our years before they fail.
  On us Thy mercy lighten,
  On us Thy goodness rest,
  And let Thy Spirit brighten
  The hearts Thyself hast blest.

4 Lord, crown our faith's endeavor
  With beauty and with grace,
  Till, clothed in light for ever,
  We see Thee face to face:
  A joy no language measures;
  A fountain brimming o'er;
  An endless flow of pleasures;
  An ocean without shore.   Amen.

306   D.S.M.

1 A few more years shall roll,
   A few more seasons come,
  And we shall be with those that rest
   Asleep within the tomb;
  Then, O my Lord, prepare
   My soul for that great day;
  Oh, wash me in Thy precious blood,
   And take my sins away.

SPECIAL OCCASIONS—THE NEW YEAR.

2   A few more suns shall set
    O'er these dark hills of time,
    And we shall be where suns are not,
    A far serener clime:
    Then, O my Lord, prepare
    My soul for that blest day;
    Oh, wash me in Thy precious blood,
    And take my sins away.

3   A few more storms shall beat
    On this wild rocky shore,
    And we shall be where tempests cease,
    And surges swell no more :
    Then, O my Lord, prepare
    My soul for that calm day;
    Oh, wash me in Thy precious blood,
    And take my sins away.

4   A few more struggles here,
    A few more partings o'er,
    A few more toils, a few more tears,
    And we shall weep no more:
    Then, O my Lord, prepare
    My soul for that bright day;
    Oh, wash me in Thy precious blood,
    And take my sins away.

5   'Tis but a little while
    And He shall come again,
    Who died that we might live, Who lives
    That we with Him may reign:
    Then, O my Lord, prepare
    My soul for that glad day:
    Oh, wash me in Thy precious blood,
    And take my sins away.   Amen.

Also the following:

534 O God, our help in ages past.
642 Days and moments quickly flying.
645 I'm but a stranger here.

THE NEW YEAR.
307   7s.
1 For Thy mercy and Thy grace,
  Faithful through another year,
  Hear our song of thankfulness;
  Jesus, our Redeemer, hear.

2 In our weakness and distress,
  Rock of strength, be Thou our stay;
  In the pathless wilderness
  Be our true and living way.

3 Who of us death's awful road
  In the coming year shall tread,
  With Thy rod and staff, O God,
  Comfort Thou his dying bed.

4 Keep us faithful, keep us pure,
  Keep us evermore Thine own,
  Help, oh, help us to endure,
  Fit us for the promised crown!

5 So within Thy palace gate
  We shall praise, on golden strings,
  Thee the only Potentate,
  Lord of lords and King of kings.

308   7.6.
1 Another year is dawning,
  Dear Master, let it be
  In working and in waiting
  Another year with Thee.

2 Another year of leaning
  Upon Thy loving breast,
  Of ever deepening trustfulness,
  Of quiet, happy rest.

3 Another year of mercies,
  Of faithfulness and grace;
  Another year of gladness
  In the shining of Thy face.

4 Another year of progress,
  Another year of praise;
  Another year of proving
  Thy presence "all the days."

5 Another year of service,
  Of witness for Thy love :
  Another year of training
  For holier work above.

6 Another year is dawning,
  Dear Master, let it be,
  On earth, or else in heaven,
  Another year for Thee.   Amen.

Also the following :
572 Now a new year opens.

FOR THOSE AT SEA.
309   C.M.
1 O Lord, be with us when we sail
  Upon the lonely deep,
  Our guard when on the silent deck
  The nightly watch we keep.

95

SPECIAL OCCASIONS—FOR THOSE AT SEA.

2 We need not fear, though all around,
  'Mid rising winds, we hear
The multitude of waters surge;
  For Thou, O God, art near.

3 The calm, the breeze, the gale, the storm,
  The ocean and the land,
All, all are Thine, and held within
  The hollow of Thy hand.

4 As when on blue Gennesaret
  Rose high the angry wave,
And Thy disciples quailed in dread,
  One word of Thine could save;

5 So when the fiercer storms arise
  From man's unbridled will,
Be Thou, Lord, present in our hearts
  To whisper, "Peace, be still."

6 * If duty calls, from threatened strife
  To guard our native shore,
And shot and shell are answering
  The booming cannon's roar;

7 Be Thou the mainguard of our host
  Till war and dangers cease,
Defend the right, put up the sword,
  And through the world make peace.

8 Across this troubled tide of life
  Thyself our pilot be,
Until we reach that better land,
  The land that knows no sea. Amen.

* To be added in time of war.

310   8s.

1 Eternal Father! strong to save,
  Whose arm hath bound the restless wave,
  Who bid'st the mighty ocean deep
  Its own appointed limits keep;
    Oh, hear us when we cry to Thee
    For those who sail upon the sea!

2 O Christ! Whose voice the waters heard
  And hushed their raging at Thy word,
  Who walkedst on the foaming deep,
  And calm amidst its rage didst sleep;
    Oh, hear us when we cry to Thee
    For those who sail upon the sea!

3 Most Holy Spirit! Who didst brood
  Upon the chaos dark and rude,
  And bid its angry tumult cease,
  And give, for wild confusion, peace;
    Oh, hear us when we cry to Thee
    For those who sail upon the sea!

4 O Trinity of love and power!
  Our brethren shield in danger's hour;
  From rock and tempest, fire and foe,
  Protect them wheresoe'er they go;
    Thus evermore shall rise to Thee
    Glad hymns of praise from land and sea!
        Amen.

311   L.M.

1 Almighty Father, hear our cry,
  As o'er the trackless deep we roam;
  Be Thou our haven always nigh,
  On homeless waters, Thou our home.

2 O Jesus, Saviour, at Whose voice
  The tempest sank to perfect rest,
  Bid Thou the fearful heart rejoice,
  And cleanse and calm the troubled breast.

3 O Holy Ghost, beneath Whose power
  The ocean woke to life and light,
  Command Thy blessing in this hour,
  Thy fostering warmth, Thy quickening
      might.

4 Great God of our salvation, Thee
  We love, we worship, we adore;
  Our refuge on time's changeful sea,
  Our joy on heaven's eternal shore. Amen.

312   7s.

1 On the waters, dark and drear,
  Jesus, Saviour, Thou art near,
  With our ship where'er it roam,
  As with loving friends at home.

2 Thou hast walked the heaving wave;
  Thou art mighty still to save;
  With one gentle word of peace
  Thou canst bid the tempest cease.

SPECIAL OCCASIONS—FOR TRAVELLERS BY LAND OR SEA.

3 Safely from the boisterous main
Bring us back to port again:
In our haven we shall be,
Jesus, if we have but Thee.

4 Only by Thy power and love
Fit us for the port above:
Still the deadly storm within,
Gusts of passion, waves of sin:

5 So, when breaks the glorious dawn
Of the Resurrection morn,
When the night of toil is o'er,
We shall see Thee on the shore. Amen.

313   L.M.

1 While o'er the deep Thy servants sail,
Send Thou, O Lord, the prosperous gale;
And on their hearts, where'er they go,
Oh, let Thy heavenly breezes blow.

2 If on the morning's wings they fly,
They will not pass beyond Thine eye:
The wanderer's prayer Thou bend'st to hear,
And faith exults to know Thee near.

3 When tempests rock the groaning bark,
Oh, hide them safe in Jesus' ark!
When in the tempting port they ride,
Oh, keep them safe at Jesus' side!

4 If life's wide ocean smile or roar,
Still guide them to the heavenly shore;
And grant their dust in Christ may sleep,
Abroad, at home, or in the deep. Amen.

314   7s.

1 Safe upon the billowy deep,
Loving Lord, Thy servants keep;
Helpless, trusting pilgrims they,
Guard them on their watery way.

2 In the morning fill their sails,
Mid the dark send favoring gales;
If their sky be overcast,
Calm the waves, and still the blast.

3 Let Thy sunshine guide by day;
Send at eve the starry ray:
Through the watches of the night,
Be Thou, Lord, their shining light.

4 Thus as hour by hour rolls by
Watch with Thine unslumbering eye:
Guide with Thine almighty hand
Safe unto the haven-land.

5 And at last, life's voyage o'er,
Take us to the heavenly shore,
Safe in port, to dwell with Thee
Where there shall be "no more sea."
                          Amen.

FOR TRAVELLERS BY LAND OR SEA.

315   8.8.8.8.8.8.8.7.

1 O mighty God, Creator, King,
Who rulest over sea and land,
And dost the ocean deeps sustain
Within the hollow of Thine hand;
Oh, hear us as we cry to Thee
For those who traverse land or sea,
That they may now and ever be
Safe in Thy holy keeping.

2 And Thou Who can'st on earth to breathe
The breath of peace o'er heath and hill,
Didst walk upon the angry wave,
And bid the troubled sea "be still;"
Oh, hear us as we cry to Thee
For those who traverse land or sea,
That they may now and ever be
Safe in Thy holy keeping.

3 Wherever danger threatens, then,
O Holy Spirit, be Thou there,
And breathe into each trembling heart
The will and power of fervent prayer;
That we and all who cry to Thee,
With those who traverse land or sea,
Both now and evermore may be,
O ever Blessèd Trinity,
Safe in Thy holy keeping. Amen.

VI. The Christian Life.

316 L.M.

1 O Thou that hear'st when sinners cry,
  Though all my crimes before Thee lie,
  Behold them not with angry look,
  But blot their memory from Thy book.

2 Create my nature pure within,
  And form my soul averse to sin:
  Let Thy good Spirit ne'er depart,
  Nor hide Thy presence from my heart.

3 I cannot live without Thy light,
  Cast out and banished from Thy sight:
  Thy holy joys, my God, restore,
  And guard me that I fall no more.

4 A broken heart, my God, my King,
  Is all the sacrifice I bring;
  The God of grace will ne'er despise
  A broken heart for sacrifice.

5 Oh, may Thy love inspire my tongue!
  Salvation shall be all my song:
  And all my powers shall join to bless
  The Lord, my strength and righteousness.

317 C.M.

1 O Jesus, Saviour of the lost,
  My rock and hiding-place,
  By storms of sin and sorrow tossed,
  I seek Thy sheltering grace.

2 Guilty, forgive me, Lord, I cry;
  Pursued by foes, I come:
  A sinner, save me, or I die;
  An outcast, take me home.

3 Once safe in Thine almighty arms,
  Let storms come on amain;
  There danger never, never harms;
  There death itself is gain.

4 And when I stand before Thy throne,
  And all Thy glory see,
  Still be my righteousness alone
  To hide myself in Thee.

318 S.M.

1 Lord Jesus, think on me,
  And purge away my sin;
  From earthborn passions set me free,
  And make me pure within.

2 Lord Jesus, think on me,
  With many a care opprest,
  Let me Thy loving servant be,
  And taste Thy promised rest.

3 Lord Jesus, think on me,
  Nor let me go astray;
  Through darkness and perplexity
  Point Thou the heavenly way.

4 Lord Jesus, think on me,
  That, when the flood is past,
  I may the eternal brightness see,
  And share Thy joy at last. Amen.

319 10s.

1 Weary of earth, and laden with my sin,
  I look at heaven and long to enter in,
  But there no evil thing may find a home:
  And yet I hear a voice that bids me "Come."

2 It is the voice of Jesus that I hear,
  His are the hands stretched out to draw me near,
  And His the blood that can for all atone,
  And set me faultless there before the throne.

3 'Twas He Who found me on the deathly wild,
  And made me heir of heaven, the Father's child,
  And day by day, whereby my soul may live,
  Gives me His grace of pardon, and will give.

4 O great Absolver, grant my soul may wear
  The lowliest garb of penitence and prayer,
  That in the Father's courts my glorious dress
  May be the garment of Thy righteousness.

5 Yea, Thou wilt answer for me, righteous Lord;
  Thine all the merits, mine the great reward;
  Thine the sharp thorns, and mine the golden crown;
  Mine the life won, through Thine the life laid down.

320 7s.

1 Jesus, lover of my soul,
    Let me to Thy bosom fly,
  While the nearer waters roll,
    While the tempest still is high:
  Hide me, O my Saviour, hide,
    Till the storm of life be past;
  Safe into the haven guide,
    Oh, receive my soul at last!

THE CHRISTIAN LIFE.

2 Other refuge have I none,
  Hangs my helpless soul on Thee;
  Leave, ah! leave me not alone,
  Still support and comfort me:

All my trust on Thee is stayed;
  All my help from Thee I bring;
  Cover my defenceless head
  With the shadow of Thy wing.

3 Plenteous grace with Thee is found,
  Grace to cover all my sin;
  Let the healing streams abound,
  Make and keep me pure within:

Thou of life the fountain art,
  Freely let me take of Thee:
  Spring Thou up within my heart,
  Rise to all eternity. Amen.

321   7s.

1 Rock of ages, cleft for me,
  Let me hide myself in Thee;
  Let the water and the blood,
  From Thy side, a healing flood,
  Be of sin the double cure,
  Save from wrath, and make me pure.

2 Should my tears for ever flow,
  Should my zeal no languor know,
  All for sin could not atone,
  Thou must save, and Thou alone;
  In my hand no price I bring,
  Simply to Thy cross I cling.

3 While I draw this fleeting breath,
  When mine eyelids close in death,
  When I rise to worlds unknown,
  And behold Thee on Thy throne,
  Rock of ages, cleft for me,
  Let me hide myself in Thee. Amen.

322   8.8.8.6.

1 O Thou, the contrite sinners' friend,
  Who, loving, lov'st them to the end,
  On this alone my hopes depend,
  That Thou wilt plead for me.

2 When, weary in the Christian race,
  Far off appears my resting place,
  And, fainting, I mistrust Thy grace,
  Then, Saviour, plead for me.

3 When I have erred and gone astray
  Afar from Thine and wisdom's way,
  And see no glimmering, guiding ray,
  Still, Saviour, plead for me.

4 When Satan, by my sins made bold,
  Strives from Thy cross to loose my hold,
  Then with Thy pitying arms enfold,
  And plead, oh, plead for me!

5 And when my dying hour draws near,
  Darkened with sorrow, pain, and fear,
  Then to my fainting sight appear,
  Pleading in heaven for me.

6 When the full light of heavenly day
  Reveals my sins in dread array,
  Thou Who hast washed them all away;
  My Saviour, plead for me! Amen.

323   C.M.

1 Oh, help us, Lord; each hour of need
  Thy heavenly succor give;
  Help us in thought, and word, and deed,
  Each hour on earth we live!

2 Oh, help us when our spirits cry
  With contrite anguish sore;
  And when our hearts are cold and dry,
  Oh, help us, Lord, the more!

3 Oh, help us through the prayer of faith
  More firmly to believe!
  For still the more the servant hath,
  The more shall he receive.

4 Oh, help us, Saviour, from on high:
  Friend we have none but Thee!
  Oh, help us so to live and die
  As Thine in heaven to be! Amen.

324   L.M.

1 O Thou to Whose all-searching sight
  The darkness shineth as the light,
  Search, prove my heart: it pants for Thee;
  Oh, burst these bonds, and set it free!

2 Wash out its stains, refine its dross,
  Nail my affections to the cross;
  Hallow each thought; let all within
  Be clean, as Thou, my Lord, art clean.

3 If in this darksome wild I stray,
  Be Thou my light, be Thou my way;
  No foes, no violence I fear,
  No harm, while Thou, my God, art near.

4 When rising floods my soul o'erflow,
  When sinks my heart in waves of woe,
  Jesus, Thy timely aid impart,
  And raise my head, and cheer my heart.

THE CHRISTIAN LIFE.

5 Saviour, where'er Thy steps I see,
    Dauntless, untired, I follow Thee:
  Oh, let Thy hand support me still,
    And lead me to Thy holy hill! Amen.

325   6.5.

1 In the hour of trial,
    Jesus, plead for me;
  Lest by base denial
    I depart from Thee;
  When Thou see'st me waver,
    With a look recall,
  Nor for fear or favor
    Suffer me to fall.

2 With forbidden pleasures
    Would this vain world charm;
  Or its sordid treasures
    Spread to work me harm;
  Bring to my remembrance
    Sad Gethsemane,
  Or, in darker semblance,
    Cross-crowned Calvary.

3 Should Thy mercy send me
    Sorrow, toil, and woe;
  Or should pain attend me
    On my path below;
  Grant that I may never
    Fail Thy hand to see;
  Grant that I may ever
    Cast my care on Thee.

4 When my last hour cometh,
    Fraught with strife and pain,
  When my dust returneth
    To the dust again;
  On Thy truth relying,
    Through that mortal strife,
  Jesus, take me, dying,
    To eternal life. Amen.

326   L.M.

1 Ashamed of Thee! O dearest Lord,
  I marvel how such wrong can be:
  And yet how oft in deed and word
  Have I been found ashamed of Thee!

2 Ashamed of Thee! my King, my God,
    Who soughtest me with wondrous love
  Whose feet the way of sorrow trod
    To bring me to Thy home above:

3 Ashamed of Thee! of that blest Name
    Which speaks of mercy full and free!
  Nay, Lord, I would my only shame
    Might be to be ashamed of Thee.

4 Ashamed of Thee! Whose love divine
    Was not ashamed of our lost race,
  But even this cold heart of mine
    Dost make Thy home and dwelling-place:

5 Ashamed of Thee! O Lord, I pray
    This cruel wrong no more may be:
  And in Thy last great Advent-day
    Oh, be not Thou ashamed of me! Amen.

327   8.8.8.4.

1 Jesus, my Saviour! look on me,
    For I am weary and opprest;
  I come to cast myself on Thee:
    Thou art my Rest.

2 Look down on me, for I am weak;
    I feel the toilsome journey's length;
  Thine aid omnipotent I seek:
    Thou art my Strength.

3 I am bewildered on my way,
    Dark and tempestuous is the night;
  Oh, send Thou forth some cheering ray!
    Thou art my Light.

4 When Satan flings his fiery darts,
    I look to Thee: my terrors cease;
  Thy cross a hiding-place imparts:
    Thou art my Peace.

5 Standing alone on Jordan's brink,
    In that tremendous, latest strife,
  Thou wilt not suffer me to sink:
    Thou art my Life.

6 Thou wilt my every want supply,
    E'en to the end, whate'er befall;
  Through life, in death eternally,
    Thou art my All.

328   P.M.

1 Art thou weary, art thou languid,
    Art thou sore distrest?
  'Come to Me,' saith One, 'and coming,
    Be at rest.'

THE CHRISTIAN LIFE.

2 Hath He marks to lead me to Him,
   If He be my guide?
'In His feet and hands are wound-prints,
   And His side.'

3 Is there diadem, as monarch,
   That His brow adorns?
'Yea, a crown, in very surety,
   But of thorns.'

4 If I find Him, if I follow,
   What His guerdon here?
'Many a sorrow, many a labor,
   Many a tear.'

5 If I still hold closely to Him,
   What hath He at last?
'Sorrow vanquished, labor ended,
   Jordan passed.'

6 If I ask Him to receive me,
   Will He say me nay?
'Not till earth, and not till heaven
   Pass away.'

7 Finding, following, keeping, struggling,
   Is He sure to bless?
Saints, apostles, prophets, martyrs,
   Answer, 'Yes.'

329   8.8.8.6.

1 Just as I am, without one plea,
But that Thy blood was shed for me,
And that Thou bidd'st me come to Thee,
   O Lamb of God, I come.

2 Just as I am, and waiting not
To rid my soul of one dark blot,
To Thee, Whose blood can cleanse each spot,
   O Lamb of God, I come.

3 Just as I am, though tossed about
With many a conflict, many a doubt,
Fightings and fears within, without,
   O Lamb of God, I come.

4 Just as I am, poor, wretched, blind;
Sight, riches, healing of the mind,
Yea, all I need, in Thee to find,
   O Lamb of God, I come.

5 Just as I am: Thou wilt receive,
Wilt welcome, pardon, cleanse, relieve;
Because Thy promise I believe,
   O Lamb of God, I come.

6 Just as I am, Thy love unknown
Has broken every barrier down ;
Now to be Thine, yea, Thine alone,
   O Lamb of God, I come.

330   6s.

1 I hunger and I thirst ;
   Jesus, my Manna be:
Ye living waters, burst
   Out of the rock for me.

2 Thou bruised and broken Bread,
   My life-long wants supply;
As living souls are fed,
   Oh, feed me, or I die!

3 Thou true life-giving Vine,
   Let me Thy sweetness prove;
Renew my life with Thine,
   Refresh my soul with love.

4 Rough paths my feet have trod,
   Since first their course began ;
Feed me, Thou Bread of God ;
   Help me, Thou Son of Man.

5 For still the desert lies
   My thirsting soul before;
Oh, living waters, rise
   Within me evermore! Amen.

331   8.8.8.4.

1 My God, my Father, while I stray
Far from my home in life's rough way,
Oh, teach me from my heart to say,
   " Thy will be done ! "

2 Though dark my path, and sad my lot,
Let me be still and murmur not,
Or breathe the prayer divinely taught,
   " Thy will be done ! "

3 What though in lonely grief I sigh
For friends beloved, no longer nigh,
Submissive still would I reply,
   " Thy will be done ! "

4 If Thou should'st call me to resign
What most I prize, it ne'er was mine;
I only yield Thee what is Thine;
   " Thy will be done ! "

5 Let but my fainting heart be blest
   With Thy good Spirit for its guest,
   My God, to Thee I leave the rest;
   "Thy will be done!"

6 Renew my will from day to day,
   Blend it with Thine, and take away
   All that now makes it hard to say,
   "Thy will be done!"

7 Then, when on earth I breathe no more
   The prayer oft mixed with tears before,
   I'll sing upon a happier shore,
   "Thy will be done."

332   P.M.

1 Nearer, my God, to Thee,
   Nearer to Thee,
   E'en though it be a cross,
   That raiseth me;
   Still all my song shall be,
   Nearer, my God, to Thee,
   Nearer to Thee.

2 Oh, bring me near to God,
   Thou Christ, the Way!
   O Spirit, make my night
   Clear as the day!
   O Truth, O Light, bring me
   Nearer, my God, to Thee,
   Nearer to Thee.

3 Though like a wanderer,
   Weary and lone,
   Darkness comes over me,
   My rest a stone;
   Yet in my dreams I'd be
   Nearer, my God, to Thee,
   Nearer to Thee.

4 There let my way appear
   Steps unto heaven;
   All that Thou sendest me
   In mercy given;
   Angels to beckon me
   Nearer, my God, to Thee,
   Nearer to Thee.

5 Then with my waking thoughts
   Bright with Thy praise,
   Out of my stony griefs
   Altars I'll raise;
   So by my woes to be
   Nearer, my God, to Thee
   Nearer to Thee.

6 So will I ever sing,
   Jesus, my Lord:
   Closer to Thee still cling,
   Trusting Thy Word;
   Raised by Thy love to be
   Nearer, my God, to Thee,
   Nearer to Thee.

333   6.6.4.6.6.6.4.

1 My faith looks up to Thee,
   Thou Lamb of Calvary,
   Saviour divine!
   Now hear me while I pray;
   Take all my guilt away;
   Oh, let me from this day
   Be wholly Thine!

2 May Thy rich grace impart
   Strength to my fainting heart,
   My zeal inspire;
   As Thou hast died for me,
   Oh, may my love to Thee
   Pure, warm, and changeless be,
   A living fire!

3 While life's dark maze I tread,
   And griefs around me spread,
   Be Thou my guide;
   Bid darkness turn to day;
   Wipe sorrow's tears away;
   Nor let me ever stray
   From Thee aside!

4 When ends life's transient dream,
   When death's cold, sullen stream
   Shall o'er me roll;
   Blest Saviour, then in love,
   Fear and distrust remove;
   Oh, bear me safe above,
   A ransomed soul! Amen.

334   7s.

1 Lord, for ever at Thy side
   Let my place and portion be:
   Strip me of the robe of pride,
   Clothe me with humility.

2 Meekly may my soul receive,
   All Thy Spirit hath revealed;
   Thou hast spoken; I believe,
   Though the oracle be sealed.

3 Lowly as a little child,
   Weanèd from the mother's breast,
   By no subtleties beguiled,
   On Thy faithfulness I rest.

4 Saints, rejoicing evermore,
   In the Lord Jehovah trust;
   Him, in all His ways, adore,
   Wise, and wonderful, and just.

335   C.M.

1 Father of love, our guide and friend,
   Oh, lead us gently on,
   Until life's trial-time shall end,
   And heavenly peace be won!

2 We know not what the path may be
   As yet by us untrod;
   But we can trust our all to Thee,
   Our Father and our God.

3 If called, like Abraham's child, to climb
   The hill of sacrifice,
   Some angel may be there in time;
   Deliverance shall arise:

4 Or, if some darker lot be good,
   Oh, teach us to endure
   The sorrow, pain, or solitude,
   That make the spirit pure!

5 Christ by no flowery pathway came;
   And we, His followers here,
   Must do Thy will and praise Thy Name,
   In hope, and love, and fear.

6 And, till in heaven we sinless bow,
   And faultless anthems raise,
   O Father, Son, and Spirit, now
   Accept our feeble praise! Amen.

336   P.M.

1 The King of love my Shepherd is,
   Whose goodness faileth never;
   I nothing lack if I am His
   And He is mine for ever.

2 Where streams of living water flow
   My ransomed soul He leadeth,
   And, where the verdant pastures grow,
   With food celestial feedeth.

3 Perverse and foolish oft I strayed,
   But yet in love He sought me,
   And on His shoulder gently laid,
   And home, rejoicing, brought me.

4 In death's dark vale I fear no ill
   With Thee, dear Lord, beside me;
   Thy rod and staff my comfort still,
   Thy cross before to guide me.

5 Thou spread'st a table in my sight;
   Thy unction grace bestoweth;
   And oh, what transport of delight
   From Thy pure chalice floweth!

6 And so through all the length of days,
   Thy goodness faileth never;
   Good Shepherd, may I sing Thy praise
   Within Thy house for ever. Amen.

337   8.7.

1 Love divine, all love excelling,
   Joy of heaven, to earth come down!
   Fix in us Thy humble dwelling,
   All Thy faithful mercies crown.

2 Jesus, Thou art all compassion,
   Pure, unbounded love Thou art;
   Visit us with Thy salvation,
   Enter every longing heart.

3 Come, almighty to deliver,
   Let us all Thy life receive;
   Come to us, dear Lord, and never,
   Never more Thy temples leave.

4 Thee we would be alway blessing;
   Serve Thee as Thy hosts above;
   Pray, and praise Thee, without ceasing;
   Glory in Thy perfect love.

5 Finish then Thy new creation,
   Pure and spotless let us be;
   Let us see our whole salvation,
   Perfectly secured in Thee:

6 Changed from glory into glory,
   Till in heaven we take our place;
   Till we cast our crowns before Thee,
   Lost in wonder, love, and praise.

THE CHRISTIAN LIFE.

338 8.7.

1 Lord, with glowing heart I'd praise Thee
  For the bliss Thy love bestows,
For the pardoning grace that saves me,
  And the peace that from it flows:
Help, O God, my weak endeavor;
  This dull soul to rapture raise:
Thou must light the flame, or never
  Can my love be warmed to praise.

2 Praise, my soul, the God that sought thee,
  Wretched wanderer, far astray;
Found thee lost, and kindly brought thee
  From the paths of death away;
Praise, with love's devoutest feeling,
  Him Who saw thy guilt-born fear,
And, the light of hope revealing,
  Bade the blood-stained cross appear.

3 Lord, this bosom's ardent feeling
  Vainly would my lips express:
Low before Thy footstool kneeling,
  Deign Thy suppliant's prayer to bless:
Let Thy grace, my soul's chief treasure,
  Love's pure flame within me raise;
And, since words can never measure,
  Let my life show forth Thy praise.
  Amen.

339 6s.

1 When morning gilds the skies,
  My heart awaking cries,
  May Jesus Christ be praised:
  Alike at work and prayer
  To Jesus I repair;
  May Jesus Christ be praised!

2 Whene'er the sweet church bell
  Peals over hill and dell,
  May Jesus Christ be praised:
  Oh, hark to what it sings,
  As joyously it rings,
  May Jesus Christ be praised!

3 My tongue shall never tire
  Of chanting with the choir,
  May Jesus Christ be praised:
  This song of sacred joy,
  It never seems to cloy,
  May Jesus Christ be praised!

4 When sleep her balm denies,
  My silent spirit sighs,
  May Jesus Christ be praised:
  When evil thoughts molest,
  With this I shield my breast,
  May Jesus Christ be praised!

5 Does sadness fill my mind?
  A solace here I find,
  May Jesus Christ be praised:
  Or fades my earthly bliss?
  My comfort still is this,
  May Jesus Christ be praised!

6 The night becomes as day,
  When from the heart we say,
  May Jesus Christ be praised:
  The powers of darkness fear,
  When this sweet chant they hear,
  May Jesus Christ be praised!

7 In heaven's eternal bliss
  The loveliest strain is this,
  May Jesus Christ be praised:
  Let earth, and sea, and sky
  From depth to height reply,
  May Jesus Christ be praised!

8 Be this, while life is mine,
  My canticle divine,
  May Jesus Christ be praised:
  Be this the eternal song
  Through ages all along,
  May Jesus Christ be praised! Amen.

340 8.7.

1 Call Jehovah Thy salvation,
  Rest beneath th' Almighty's shade,
In His secret habitation
  Dwell, and never be dismayed.

2 There no tumult can alarm thee,
  Thou shalt dread no hidden snare;
Guile nor violence can harm thee,
  In eternal safeguard there.

3 God shall charge His angel legions
  Watch and ward o'er thee to keep:
Though thou walk through hostile regions,
  Though in desert wilds thou sleep.

4 Since, with pure and firm affection,
  Thou on God hast set thy love,
With the wings of His protection,
  He will shield thee from above.

THE CHRISTIAN LIFE.

5 Thou shalt call on Him in trouble,
   He will hearken, He will save;
   Here for grief reward thee double,
   Crown with life beyond the grave.

341   C. M.
1 O God of Bethel, by Whose hand
   Thy people still are fed ;
   Who through this weary pilgrimage
   Hast all our fathers led :

2 Our vows, our prayers, we now present
   Before Thy throne of grace:
   God of our fathers, be the God
   Of their succeeding race.

3 Through each perplexing path of life
   Our wandering footsteps guide;
   Give us each day our daily bread,
   And raiment fit provide.

4 Oh, spread Thy sheltering wings around,
   Till all our wanderings cease,
   And at our Father's loved abode
   Our souls arrive in peace!

5 Such blessings from Thy gracious hand
   Our humble prayers implore;
   And Thou shalt be our chosen God,
   And portion evermore.

342   S. M.
1 Heirs of unending life,
   While yet we sojourn here,
   Oh, let us our salvation work
   With trembling and with fear !

2 God will support our hearts
   With might before unknown :
   The work to be performed is ours,
   The strength is all His own.

3 'Tis He that works to will,
   'Tis He that works to do;
   His is the power by which we act,
   His be the glory too! Amen.

343   S. M.
1 My soul, be on thy guard!
   Ten thousand foes arise;
   The hosts of sin are pressing hard
   To draw thee from the skies.

2 Oh, watch, and fight, and pray!
   The battle ne'er give o'er ;
   Renew it boldly every day,
   And help divine implore.

3 Ne'er think the victory won,
   Nor lay thine armor down;
   Thy arduous work will not be done
   Till thou obtain thy crown.

4 Fight on, my soul, till death
   Shall bring thee to thy God!
   He'll take thee, at thy parting breath
   Up to His blest abode.

344   C. M.
1 Awake, my soul, stretch every nerve,
   And press with vigor on ;
   A heavenly race demands thy zeal,
   And an immortal crown.

2 A cloud of witnesses around
   Hold thee in full survey;
   Forget the steps already trod,
   And onward urge thy way.

3 'Tis God's all-animating voice
   That calls thee from on high,
   'Tis His own hand presents the prize
   To thine uplifted eye.

4 Then wake, my soul, stretch every nerve,
   And press with vigor on ;
   A heavenly race demands thy zeal,
   And an immortal crown.

345   7s.
1 Oft in danger, oft in woe,
   Onward, Christians, onward go:
   Fight the fight, maintain the strife,
   Strengthened with the bread of life.

2 Let your drooping hearts be glad ;
   March in heavenly armor clad :
   Fight, nor think the battle long.
   Victory soon shall tune your song.

3 Let not sorrow dim your eye,
   Soon shall every tear be dry;
   Let not fears your course impede,
   Great your strength, if great your need.

THE CHRISTIAN LIFE.

4 Onward then in battle move,
More than conquerors ye shall prove;
Though opposed by many a foe,
Christian soldiers, onward go.

346 S.M.

1 A charge to keep I have,
A God to glorify;
A never-dying soul to save,
And fit it for the sky.

2 From youth to hoary age,
My calling to fulfil:
Oh, may it all my powers engage
To do my Master's will!

3 Arm me with jealous care,
As in Thy sight to live,
And oh, Thy servant, Lord, prepare
A strict account to give!

4 Help me to watch and pray,
And on Thyself rely;
Sure, if my trust I keep alway,
To reign with Thee on high. Amen.

347 S.M.

1 Soldiers of Christ, arise,
And put your armor on;
Strong in the strength which God supplies,
Through His eternal Son.

2 Strong in the Lord of hosts,
And in His mighty power;
Who in the strength of Jesus trusts
Is more than conqueror.

3 Stand then in His great might,
With all His strength endued;
And take, to arm you for the fight,
The panoply of God.

4 From strength to strength go on,
Wrestle, and fight, and pray:
Tread all the powers of darkness down,
And win the well-fought day.

5 That having all things done,
And all your conflicts past,
Ye may o'ercome, through Christ alone,
And stand complete at last.

348 C.M.

1 The Son of God goes forth to war,
A kingly crown to gain:
His blood-red banner streams afar:
Who follows in His train?

2 Who best can drink his cup of woe,
Triumphant over pain;
Who patient bears his cross below,
He follows in His train.

3 The martyr first, whose eagle eye
Could pierce beyond the grave;
Who saw his Master in the sky,
And called on Him to save.

4 Like Him, with pardon on his tongue,
In midst of mortal pain,
He prayed for them that did the wrong:
Who follows in his train?

5 A glorious band, the chosen few,
On whom the spirit came:
Twelve valiant saints, their hope they knew,
And mocked the cross and flame.

6 They met the tyrant's brandished steel,
The lion's gory mane;
They bowed their necks the death to feel:
Who follows in their train?

7 A noble army: men and boys,
The matron and the maid;
Around the Saviour's throne rejoice,
In robes of light arrayed.

8 They climbed the steep ascent of heaven
Through peril, toil, and pain:
O God, to us may grace be given
To follow in their train. Amen.

349 7.6.

1 Go forward, Christian soldier,
Beneath His banner true!
The Lord Himself, thy Leader,
Shall all thy foes subdue.

His love foretells thy trials;
He knows thine hourly need;
He can with bread of heaven
Thy fainting spirit feed.

THE CHRISTIAN LIFE.

2 Go forward, Christian soldier!
Fear not the secret foe;
Far more o'er thee are watching
Than human eyes can know:
Trust only Christ, Thy Captain;
Cease not to watch and pray;
Heed not the treacherous voices
That lure thy soul astray.

3 Go forward, Christian soldier!
Nor dream of peaceful rest,
Till Satan's host is vanquished
And heaven is all possessed;
Till Christ Himself shall call thee
To lay thine armor by,
And wear in endless glory
The crown of victory.

4 Go forward, Christian soldier!
Fear not the gathering night:
The Lord has been thy shelter;
The Lord will be thy light.
When morn His face revealeth,
Thy dangers all are past;
Oh, pray that faith and virtue
May keep thee to the last!

350 7.6.

1 Looking upward every day,
Sunshine on our faces;
Pressing onward every day
Toward the heavenly places:

2 Growing every day in awe,
For Thy Name is holy;
Learning every day to love
With a love more lowly:

3 Walking every day more close
To our elder Brother;
Growing every day more true
Unto one another:

4 Leaving every day behind
Something which might hinder;
Running swifter every day,
Growing purer, kinder:

5 Lord, so pray we every day:
Hear us in Thy pity,
That at last we enter in
To the Holy City. Amen.

351 7.6.

1 O happy band of pilgrims,
If onward ye will tread
With Jesus as your Fellow
To Jesus as your Head!

2 Oh, happy if ye labor
As Jesus did for men!
Oh, happy it ye hunger
As Jesus hungered then!

3 The cross that Jesus carried,
He carried as your due:
The crown that Jesus weareth,
He weareth it for you.

4 The faith by which ye see Him,
The hope in which ye yearn,
The love that through all troubles
To Him alone will turn;

5 The trials that beset you,
The sorrows ye endure,
The manifold temptations
That death alone can cure;

6 What are they but His jewels,
Of right celestial worth?
What are they but the ladder
Set up to heaven on earth?

7 O happy band of pilgrims,
Look upward to the skies,
Where such a light affliction
Shall win so great a prize!

352 7s.

1 If thou wouldest life attain,
If with Christ thou wouldest reign,
Reaping wisdom from the past,
Know, that long as life may last,
Toil and conflict thee await
In thy present earthly state.

2 Labor, while it yet is day;
Labor, while you labor may;
Labor, for the night is long;
Labor, for the foe is strong;
Labor, for the prize is great;
Labor, for the hour is late.

THE CHRISTIAN LIFE.

3 Soon the struggle will be past ;
  Calm and peace will come at last ;
  Soon through death's transporting door,
  All thy pains and labors o'er,
  Thou shalt go to join the blest
  In the realms of endless rest ;

4 Rest, from toil and anxious care ;
  Rest, from earthly wear and tear ;
  Rest, from ever present sin ;
  Rest without, and rest within ;
  Rest, which no abatement knows ;
  Rest, and infinite repose.

5 Jesus, Who for me didst die
  On the cross of Calvary.
  Not in aught that is my own,
  But in Thy true blood alone,
  Do I put my trembling trust :
  Spare, oh, spare a child of dust ! Amen.

353   S. M.

1 Jesus, I live to Thee,
  The loveliest and best ;
  My life in Thee, Thy life in me,
  In Thy blest love I rest.

2 Jesus, I die to Thee,
  Whenever death shall come :
  To die in Thee is life to me,
  In my eternal home.

3 Whether to live or die,
  I know not which is best ;
  To live in Thee is bliss to me,
  To die is endless rest.

4 Living or dying, Lord,
  I ask but to be Thine ;
  My life in Thee, Thy life in me,
  Makes heaven for ever mine.

354   L. M.

1 Let me be with Thee where Thou art
  My Saviour, my eternal Rest :
  Then only will this longing heart
  Be fully and for ever blest.

2 Let me be with Thee where Thou art,
  Thine unveiled glory to behold ;
  Then only will this wandering heart
  Cease to be treacherous, faithless, cold.

3 Let me be with Thee where Thou art,
  Where spotless saints Thy Name adore;
  Then only will this evil heart
  Be sinful and defiled no more.

4 Let me be with Thee where Thou art,
  Where none can die, where none remove ;
  There neither life nor death can part
  Me from Thy presence and Thy love!
                                 Amen.

355   P. M.

1 One sweetly solemn thought
  Comes to me o'er and o'er ;
  I am nearer my home to-day
  Than I ever have been before.

2 Nearer the great white throne,
  Nearer the crystal sea,
  Nearer my Father's house,
  Where the "many mansions" be.

3 Nearer the bound of life,
  Where we lay our burdens down ;
  Nearer leaving the cross,
  Nearer gaining the crown.

4 But lying darkly between,
  Winding down through the night,
  Is the deep and unknown stream
  To be crossed ere we reach the light.

5 Jesus, perfect my trust.
  Strengthen the hand of my faith :
  Let me feel Thee near when I stand
  On the edge of the shore of death ;

6 Feel Thee near when my feet
  Are slipping over the brink ;
  For it may be I'm nearer home,
  Nearer now than I think.

356   S. M

1 For ever with the Lord !
  Amen ! so let it be!
  Life from the dead is in that word,
  And immortality!

2 Here in the body pent,
  Absent from Him I roam,
  Yet nightly pitch my moving tent
  A day's march nearer home.

GENERAL.

3 My Father's house on high,
  Home of my soul, how near,
At times, to faith's foreseeing eye,
  Thy golden gates appear !

4 Ah ! then my spirit faints
  To reach the land I love,
The bright inheritance of saints,
  Jerusalem above!

5 Then, then I feel, that He,
  Remembered or forgot,
The Lord, is never far from me,
  Though I perceive Him not.

6 So when my latest breath
  Shall rend the veil in twain,
By death I shall escape from death,
  And life eternal gain.

357 7.6.

1 Rise, my soul, and stretch thy wings.
  Thy better portion trace;
Rise from transitory things,
  Toward heaven, thy destined place;
Sun and moon and stars decay,
  Time shall soon this earth remove;
Rise, my soul, and haste away
  To seats prepared above.

2 Cease, my soul, oh, cease to mourn !
  Press onward to the prize;
Soon thy Saviour will return,
  To take thee to the skies :
There is everlasting peace,
  Rest, enduring rest, in heaven ;
There will sorrow ever cease,
  And crowns of joy be given.

Also the following:

40 Hark ! a thrilling voice is sounding.
77 In exile here we wander.
80 Blessed Saviour, Thou hast taught us.
87 With broken heart and contrite sigh.
94 Lord Jesus, when we stand afar.
138 Jesus calls us : o'er the tumult.
140 O Thou Who didst, with love untold.
143 O Son of Man, Thyself once crossed.
244 My God, accept my heart this day.
374 Lord, as to Thy dear cross we flee.
375 Sinful, sighing to be blest.
376 Out of the deep I call.
380 Heal me, O my Saviour heal.
440 Lead, kindly Light,

456 O Lamb of God, still keep me.
523 Not your own, but His ye are.
524 O Lord, our strength in weakness.
625 I lay my sins on Jesus.
629 O holy Saviour, friend unseen.
631 Prince of peace, control my will.
643 My hope is built on nothing less.
644 Onward Christian, through the region.
653 Oh, for a faith that will not shrink.
657 Though faint yet pursuing.
662 Lord Jesus by Thy Passion.
678 Thou hidden love of God, whose height.
680 O Thou from Whom all goodness flows.
686 I heard the voice of Jesus say.

VII. General.

358 11.10.

1 Ancient of days, Who sittest, throned in
    glory;
  To Thee all knees are bent, all voices pray;
Thy love has blessed the wide world's won-
    drous story,
  With light and life since Eden's dawning
    day.

2 O Holy Father, Who hast led Thy children
    In all the ages, with the Fire and Cloud,
  Through seas dry-shod ; through weary
    wastes bewildering ;
    To Thee, in reverent love, our hearts are
    bowed.

3 O Holy Jesus, Prince of peace and Saviour.
    To Thee we owe the peace that still pre-
    vails,
  Stilling the rude wills of men's wild behavior,
    And calming passion's fierce and stormy
    gales.

4 O Holy Ghost, the Lord and the Life-giver.
    Thine is the quickening power that gives
    increase.
  From Thee have flowed, as from a pleasant
    river,
    Our plenty, wealth, prosperity and peace.

5 O Triune God, with heart and voice adoring,
    Praise we the goodness that doth crown
    our days;
  Pray we, that Thou wilt hear us, still im-
    ploring
    Thy love and favor, kept to us always.
                                    Amen.

GENERAL.

359 S.M.
1 Creator of mankind!
Thy promised help we claim,
That so our life Thou may'st not find
Unworthy of Thy Name.

2 If Thou Thy grace deny,
In vain for Thee we strive;
In Thee alone to sin we die,
In Thee alone we live.

3 Our goings, Lord, uphold,
Till this dark vale be passed,
And in Thy love and fear made bold,
We reach our rest at last.

4 O happy, peaceful rest,
Prepared for saints above!
Where they, with endless quiet blest,
Drink of Thy streams of love.

5 O Trinity divine!
To Thee our hearts we raise!
May we Thy ransomed people join
And share their songs of praise.
Amen.

360 C.M.
1 Shine on our souls, eternal God,
With rays of beauty shine:
Oh, let Thy favor crown our days,
And all their round be Thine!

2 Did we not raise our hands to Thee,
Our hands might toil in vain;
Small joy success itself could give,
If Thou Thy love restrain.

3 With Thee let every week begin,
With Thee each day be spent,
For Thee each fleeting hour improved,
Since each by Thee is lent.

4 Thus cheer us through this desert road,
Till all our labors cease;
And heaven refresh our weary souls
With everlasting peace. Amen.

361 L.M.
1 Where'er have trod Thy sacred feet,
Teach us, O Lord, Thy steps to trace,
Where men in busy concourse meet,
Or in the lonely wilderness.

2 Bid us with Thee to watch and pray,
With Thee to die, with Thee to rise,
With Thee to bear our cross each day,
With Thee to soar beyond the skies.

3 Where'er Thou art may we remain;
Where'er Thou goest may we go:
With Thee, O Lord, no grief is pain;
Away from Thee, all joy is woe.

4 Oh, may we in each holy tide,
Each solemn season, dwell with Thee!
Content if only by Thy side
In life or death we still may be. Amen.

362 P.M.
1 Thou art coming, O my Saviour!
Thou art coming, O my King!
In Thy beauty all-resplendent,
In Thy glory all-transcendent;
Well may we rejoice and sing;
Coming: in the opening east
Herald brightness slowly swells;
Coming: O Thou glorious Priest!
Hear we not Thy golden bells?

2 Thou art coming, Thou art coming;
We shall meet Thee on Thy way;
We shall see Thee, we shall know Thee,
We shall bless Thee, we shall show Thee
All our hearts could never say;
What an anthem that will be,
Music rapturously sweet,
Pouring out our love to Thee
At Thine own all-glorious feet.

3 Thou art coming; at Thy table
We are witnesses for this;
While remembering hearts Thou meetest
In communion clearest, sweetest,
Earnest of our coming bliss;
Showing not Thy death alone,
And Thy love exceeding great,
But Thy coming, and Thy throne,
All for which we long and wait.

4 Thou art coming; we are waiting
With a hope that cannot fail;
Asking not the day or hour,
Resting on Thy word of power,
Anchored safe within the veil.
Time appointed may be long,
But the vision must be sure;
Certainty shall make us strong,
Joyful patience can endure.

5 Oh, the joy to see Thee reigning,
   Thee, our own belovèd Lord!
  Every tongue Thy Name confessing,
   Worship, honor, glory, blessing
  Brought to Thee with one accord;
  Thee, our Master, and our Friend,
   Vindicated and enthroned;
  Unto earth's remotest end
   Glorified, adored, and owned! Amen.

363   8.7.

1 Jesus came: the heavens adoring:
   Came with peace from realms on high;
  Jesus came for man's redemption,
   Lowly came on earth to die:
  Alleluia! Alleluia!
   Came in deep humility.

2 Jesus comes again in mercy,
   When our hearts are bowed with care:
  Jesus comes again in answer
   To an earnest, heart-felt prayer;
  Alleluia! Alleluia!
   Comes to save us from despair.

3 Jesus comes to hearts rejoicing,
   Bringing news of sins forgiven;
  Jesus comes in sounds of gladness,
   Leading souls redeemed to heaven;
  Alleluia! Alleluia!
   Now the gate of death is riven.

4 Jesus comes in joy and sorrow,
   Shares alike our hopes and fears;
  Jesus comes, whate'er befalls us,
   Glads our hearts, and dries our tears;
  Alleluia! Alleluia!
   Cheering e'en our failing years.

5 Jesus comes on clouds triumphant,
   When the heavens shall pass away;
  Jesus comes again in glory;
   Let us then our homage pay,
  Alleluia! ever singing,
   Till the dawn of endless day.   Amen.

364   P. M.

1 Thou didst leave Thy throne and Thy kingly
     crown
   When Thou camest to earth for me:
  But in Bethlehem's home was there found
     no room
   For Thy holy nativity.
     Oh, come to my heart, Lord Jesus!
     There is room in my heart for Thee.

2 Heaven's arches rang when the angels sang,
   Proclaiming Thy royal degree;
  But in lowly birth didst Thou come to earth,
   And in great humility.
     Oh, come to my heart, Lord Jesus!
     There is room in my heart for Thee.

3 The foxes found rest, and the birds had
     their nest
   In the shade of the forest tree;
  But Thy couch was the sod, O Thou Son of
     God,
   In the desert of Galilee.
     Oh, come to my heart, Lord Jesus!
     There is room in my heart for Thee.

4 Thou camest, O Lord, with the living word,
   That should set Thy people free;
  But with mocking scorn, and with crown of
     thorn,
   They bore Thee to Calvary.
     Oh, come to my heart, Lord Jesus!
     Thy cross is my only plea.

5 When the heavens shall ring, and the angels
     sing
   At Thy coming to victory,
  Let Thy voice call me home, saying, 'Yet
     there is room.
   There is room at My side for thee.'
     And my heart shall rejoice Lord Jesus,
     When Thou comest and callest for me.

365   8.7.

1 To the Name of our Salvation
   Laud and honor let us pay,
  Which for many a generation
   Hid in God's foreknowledge lay;
  But with holy exultation
   We may sing aloud to-day.

2 Jesus is the Name we treasure;
   Name beyond what words can tell;
  Name of gladness, Name of pleasure,
   Ear and heart delighting well;
  Name of sweetness, passing measure,
   Saving us from sin and hell.

3 'Tis the Name for adoration,
   Name for songs of victory,
  Name for holy meditation
   In this vale of misery,
  Name for joyful veneration
   By the citizens on high.

GENERAL.

4 'Tis the Name that whoso preacheth
Speaks like music to the ear ;
Who in prayer this Name beseecheth
Sweetest comfort findeth near ;
Who its perfect wisdom reacheth,
Heavenly joy possesseth here.

5 Therefore we in love adoring
This most blessèd Name revere;
Holy Jesus, Thee imploring
So to write it in us here,
That hereafter, heavenward soaring,
We may sing with angels there. Amen.

366   7s.

1 Conquering kings their titles take
From the foes they captive make:
Jesus, by a nobler deed,
From the thousands He hath freed.

2 Yes: none other Name is given
Unto mortals under heaven,
Which can make the dead arise,
And exalt them to the skies.

3 We would gladly for that Name
Bear the cross, endure the shame:
Joyfully for Him to die
Is not death but victory.

4 Jesus, Who dost condescend
To be called the sinner's Friend,
Hear us, as to Thee we pray,
Glorying in Thy Name to-day. Amen.

367   C. M.

1 There is a Name I love to hear;
I love to sing its worth ;
It sounds like music in mine ear,
The sweetest Name on earth.

2 It tells me of a Saviour's love
Who died to set me free;
It tells me of His precious blood,
The sinner's perfect plea.

3 It tells me of a Father's smile
Beaming upon His child ;
It cheers me through this little while,
Through desert, waste, and wild.

4 Jesus, the Name I love so well,
The Name I love to hear ;
No saint on earth its worth can tell,
No heart conceive how dear.

5 This Name shall shed its fragrance still
Along this thorny road,
Shall sweetly smooth the rugged hill,
That leads me up to God.

6 And there with all the blood-bought throng,
From sin and sorrow free,
I'll sing the new eternal song
Of Jesus' love to me.

368   L. M.

1 Jesus! the very thought is sweet ;
In that dear Name all heart-joys meet :
But oh, than honey sweeter far
The glimpses of His Presence are!

2 No word is sung more sweet than this,
No sound is heard more full of bliss,
No thought brings sweeter comfort nigh,
Than Jesus, Son of God most high.

3 Jesus, the hope of souls forlorn,
How good to them for sin that mourn !
To them that seek Thee, oh, how kind !
But what art Thou to them that find ?

4 No tongue of mortal can express,
No pen can write the blessedness,
He only who hath proved it knows
What bliss from love of Jesus flows.

5 O Jesus, King of wondrous might !
O Victor, glorious from the fight !
Sweetness that may not be expressed,
And altogether loveliest !

6 Abide with us, O Lord, to-day,
Fulfil us with Thy grace, we pray ;
And with Thine own true sweetness feed
Our souls from sin and darkness freed.
Amen.

369   7. 6.

1 O One with God the Father
In majesty and might,
The brightness of His glory,
Eternal Light of light ;
O'er this our home of darkness
Thy rays are streaming now;
The shadows flee before Thee,
The world's true light art Thou.

GENERAL.

2 Yet, Lord, we see but darkly:
  O heavenly Light, arise!
  Dispel these mists that shroud us,
  And hide Thee from our eyes!

We long to track the footprints
  That Thou Thyself hast trod:
We long to see the pathway
  That leads to Thee our God.

3 O Jesus, shine around us
  With radiance of Thy grace;
  O Jesus, turn upon us
  The brightness of Thy face.

We need no star to guide us,
  As on our way we press,
If Thou Thy light vouchsafest,
  O Sun of Righteousness.

370 C.M.

1 Joy to the world! the Lord is come:
  Let earth receive her King;
  Let every heart prepare Him room,
  And heaven and nature sing.

2 Joy to the world! the Saviour reigns:
  Let men their songs employ;
  While fields and floods, rocks, hills, and plains,
  Repeat the sounding joy.

3 No more let sins and sorrows grow,
  Nor thorns infest the ground;
  He comes to make His blessings flow
  Far as the curse is found.

4 He rules the world with truth and grace,
  And makes the nations prove
  The glories of His righteousness,
  And wonders of His love.

371 7.6.

1 Hail to the Lord's Anointed,
  Great David's greater Son!
  Hail, in the time appointed,
  His reign on earth begun!
  He comes to break oppression,
  To set the captive free;
  To take away transgression,
  And rule in equity.

2 He comes with succor speedy
  To those who suffer wrong,
  To help the poor and needy,
  And bid the weak be strong;
  To give them songs for sighing,
  Their darkness turn to light,
  Whose souls, condemned and dying,
  Were precious in His sight.

3 He shall come down like showers
  Upon the fruitful earth,
  And joy and hope, like flowers,
  Spring in His path to birth:
  Before Him on the mountains
  Shall peace, the herald, go;
  From hill to vale the fountains
  Of righteousness o'erflow.

4 Kings shall bow down before Him,
  And gold and incense bring;
  All nations shall adore Him.
  His praise all people sing;
  To Him shall prayer unceasing
  And daily vows ascend;
  His kingdom still increasing,
  A kingdom without end.

5 O'er every foe victorious,
  He on His throne shall rest;
  From age to age more glorious,
  All-blessing and all-blessed:
  The tide of time shall never
  His covenant remove;
  His Name shall stand for ever,
  His changeless Name of Love.

372 7s.

1 God of mercy, God of grace,
  Show the brightness of Thy face;
  Shine upon us, Saviour, shine,
  Fill Thy Church with light divine;
  And Thy saving health extend
  Unto earth's remotest end.

2 Let the people praise Thee, Lord;
  Be by all that live adored;
  Let the nations shout and sing
  Glory to their Saviour King;
  At Thy feet their tribute pay,
  And Thy holy will obey.

GENERAL.

3 Let the people praise Thee, Lord;
 Earth shall then her fruits afford;
 God to man His blessing give,
 Man to God devoted live;
 All below, and all above,
 One in joy, and light, and love.

373 S.M.

1 Far from my heavenly home,
 Far from my Father's breast,
 Fainting I cry, blest Spirit, come,
 And speed me to my rest.

2 My spirit homeward turns,
 And fain would thither flee;
 My heart, O Sion, droops and yearns,
 When I remember thee.

3 To thee, to thee I press,
 A dark and toilsome road;
 When shall I pass the wilderness,
 And reach the saints' abode?

4 God of my life, be near;
 On Thee my hopes I cast;
 Oh, guide me through the desert here,
 And bring me home at last! Amen.

374 C.M.

1 Lord, as to Thy dear cross we flee,
 And plead to be forgiven,
 So let Thy life our pattern be,
 And form our souls for heaven.

2 Help us, through good report and ill,
 Our daily cross to bear;
 Like Thee, to do our Father's will,
 Our brethren's grief to share.

3 Let grace our selfishness expel,
 Our earthliness refine;
 And kindness in our bosoms dwell,
 As free and true as Thine.

4 If joy shall at Thy bidding fly,
 And grief's dark day come on,
 We in our turn would meekly cry,
 "Father, Thy will be done."

5 Kept peaceful in the midst of strife,
 Forgiving and forgiven,
 Oh, may we lead the pilgrim's life,
 And follow Thee to heaven! Amen.

375 7s.

1 Sinful, sighing to be blest;
 Bound, and longing to be free;
 Weary, waiting for my rest;
 God be merciful to me.

2 Goodness I have none to plead,
 Sinfulness in all I see,
 I can only bring my need;
 God be merciful to me.

3 Broken heart and downcast eyes
 Dare not lift themselves to Thee;
 Yet Thou canst interpret sighs:
 God be merciful to me.

4 From this sinful heart of mine
 To Thy bosom I would flee:
 I am not my own but Thine:
 God be merciful to me.

5 There is One beside the throne,
 And my only hope and plea
 Are in Him, and Him alone;
 God be merciful to me.

6 He my cause will undertake,
 My Interpreter will be;
 He's my all; and for His sake
 God be merciful to me. Amen.

376 S.M.

1 Out of the deep I call
 To Thee, O Lord, to Thee;
 Before Thy Throne of grace I fall;
 Be merciful to me.

2 Out of the deep I cry,
 The woful deep of sin,
 Of evil done in days gone by,
 Of evil now within.

3 Out of the deep of fear,
 And dread of coming shame,
 From morning watch till night is near
 I plead the precious Name.

4 Lord, there is mercy now,
 As ever was, with Thee;
 Before Thy throne of grace I bow;
 Be merciful to me. Amen.

GENERAL.

377 S. 7. 8. 7. 4. 7.

1 Jesus, Lord of life and glory,
  Bend from heaven Thy gracious ear ;
While our waiting souls adore Thee,
  Friend of helpless sinners, hear :
    By Thy mercy,
  Oh, deliver us, good Lord.

2 From the depths of nature's blindness,
  From the hardening power of sin,
From all malice and unkindness,
  From the pride that lurks within,
    By Thy mercy,
  Oh, deliver us, good Lord.

3 When temptation sorely presses,
  In the day of Satan's power,
In our times of deep distresses,
  In each dark and trying hour,
    By Thy mercy,
  Oh, deliver us, good Lord.

4 When the world around is smiling,
  In the time of wealth and ease,
Earthly joys our hearts beguiling,
  In the day of health and peace,
    By Thy mercy,
  Oh, deliver us, good Lord.

5 In the weary hours of sickness,
  In the times of grief and pain,
When we feel our mortal weakness,
  When all human help is vain,
    By Thy mercy,
  Oh, deliver us, good Lord.

6 In the solemn hour of dying,
  In the awful judgment day,
May our souls, on Thee relying,
  Find Thee still our hope and stay;
    By Thy mercy,
  Oh, deliver us, good Lord. Amen.

378 S. M.

1 Have mercy, Lord, on me,
  As Thou wert ever kind ;
Let me, oppressed with loads of guilt,
  Thy wonted mercy find.

2 Wash off my foul offence,
  And cleanse me from my sin ;
For I confess my crime, and see
  How great my guilt has been.

3 Against Thee, Lord, alone,
  And only in Thy sight,
Have I transgressed; and, though condemn-
  Must own Thy judgment right.   [ed,

4 Blot out my crying sins,
  Nor me in anger view;
Create in me a heart that's clean,
  An upright mind renew.

5 Withdraw not Thou Thy help,
  Nor cast me from Thy sight ;
Nor let Thy Holy Spirit take
  His everlasting flight.

6 The joy Thy favor gives
  Let me, O Lord, regain ;
And Thy free Spirit's firm support
  My fainting soul sustain. Amen.

379 C. M.

1 Lord, when we bend before Thy throne,
  And our confessions pour,
Teach us to feel the sins we own,
  And hate what we deplore.

2 Our broken spirits, pitying, see ;
  True penitence impart ;
And let a kindling glance from Thee
  Beam hope upon the heart.

3 When we disclose our wants in prayer,
  May we our wills resign ;
And not a thought our bosom share
  Which is not wholly Thine.

4 Let faith each weak petition fill,
  And waft it to the skies,
And teach our hearts 'tis goodness still
  That grants it, or denies. Amen.

380 7s.

1 Heal me, O my Saviour, heal ;
  Heal me as I suppliant kneel ;
Heal me, and my pardon seal.

2 Fresh the wounds that sin hath made ;
  Hear the prayers I oft have prayed,
And in mercy send me aid.

3 Helpless, none can help me now ;
  Cheerless, none can cheer but Thou ;
Suppliant, Lord, to Thee I bow.

GENERAL.

4 Thou the true Physician art ;
  Thou, O Christ, canst health impart.
  Binding up the bleeding heart.

5 Other comforters are gone;
  Thou canst heal, and Thou alone,
  Thou for all my sin atone.

6 Heal me, then, my Saviour, heal ;
  Heal me, as I suppliant kneel ;
  To Thy mercy I appeal.

381 7s.

1 Son of Man, to Thee I cry;
  By the wondrous mystery
  Of Thy dwelling here on earth,
  By Thy pure and holy birth,
  Lord, Thy presence let me see ;
  Manifest Thyself to me.

2 Lamb of God, to Thee I cry;
  By Thy bitter agony,
  By Thy pangs, to us unknown,
  By Thy Spirit's parting groan,
  Lord, Thy presence let me see;
  Manifest Thyself to me.

3 Prince of Life, to Thee I cry;
  By Thy glorious majesty,
  By Thy triumph o'er the grave,
  Meek to suffer, strong to save,
  Lord, Thy presence let me see;
  Manifest Thyself to me.

4 Lord of glory, God most high,
  Man exalted to the sky,
  With Thy love my bosom fill ;
  Prompt me now to do Thy will ;
  Then Thy presence let me see;
  Manifest Thyself to me.   Amen.

382 7.6.

1 O Jesus, Thou art standing
    Outside the fast-closed door,
  In lowly patience waiting
    To pass the threshold o'er :
  Shame on us, Christian brothers,
    His Name and sign who bear :
  Oh, shame, thrice shame upon us,
    To keep Him standing there!

2 O Jesus, Thou art knocking :
    And lo! that hand is scarred,
  And thorns Thy brow encircle,
    And tears Thy face have marred :

O love that passeth knowledge,
  So patiently to wait !
O sin that hath no equal,
  So fast to bar the gate !

3 O Jesus, Thou art pleading
    In accents meek and low,
  'I died for you, My children,
    And will ye treat Me so?'
  O Lord, with shame and sorrow
    We open now the door ;
  Dear Saviour, enter, enter,
    And leave us nevermore. Amen.

383 C.M.

1 Lord! I beseech Thee on this day
    By Thine own life divine,
  To wash my many sins away
    In that dear blood of Thine:
  For I with tears in vain for them
    May struggle to atone;
  And nothing can their guilt redeem
    But that true blood alone.

2 Oh! in the years, if years there be,
    That yet to me remain,
  Before I cross the eternal sea,
    Not to return again ;
  Giver of all I to me, oh, give
    Thyself in all to see;
  And from henceforth by faith to live
    More worthily of Thee.

3 Thee suffering and Thee crucified,
    Thee dead and in the grave,
  Thee risen, ascended, glorified, ·
    Able all flesh to save;
  Thee I beseech, O Saviour God,
    To purge my soul within ;
  Nor let me faint beneath the load
    Of unforgiven sin! Amen.

384 C.5.

1 Glory be to Jesus,
    Who in bitter pains,
  Poured for me the lifeblood
    From His sacred veins!

  Grace and life eternal
    In that blood I find,
  Blest be His compassion
    Infinitely kind !

116

GENERAL.

2 Blest through endless ages
   Be the precious stream,
   Which from sin and sorrow
   Does the world redeem !
Abel's blood for vengeance
   Pleaded to the skies ;
But the blood of Jesus
   For our pardon cries.

3 Oft as earth exulting
   Wafts its praise on high,
   Angel hosts, rejoicing,
   Make their glad reply.
Lift ye then your voices;
   Swell the mighty flood ;
Louder still and louder,
   Praise the precious blood.

385 C. M.

1 There is a green hill far away,
   Without a city wall,
   Where the dear Lord was crucified
   Who died to save us all.

2 We may not know, we cannot tell,
   What pains He had to bear,
   But we believe it was for us
   He hung and suffered there.

3 He died that we might be forgiven.
   He died to make us good,
   That we might go at last to heaven,
   Saved by His precious blood.

4 There was no other good enough
   To pay the price of sin,
   He only could unlock the gate
   Of heaven, and let us in.

5 Oh, dearly, dearly has He loved,
   And we must love Him too,
   And trust in His redeeming blood,
   And try His works to do.

386 7. 6.

1 O Jesus, we adore Thee,
   Upon the cross, our King ;
   We bow our hearts before Thee;
   Thy gracious Name we sing :
That Name hath brought salvation,
   That Name, in life our stay;
Our peace, our consolation
   When life shall fade away.

2 Yet doth the world disdain Thee,
   Still pressing by Thy cross:
   Lord, may our hearts retain Thee,
   Counting all else but loss.
The grief Thy soul endurèd,
   Who can that grief declare?
Thy pains have thus assurèd
   That Thou Thy foes wilt spare.

3 Ah, Lord, our sins arraigned Thee,
   And nailed Thee to the tree:
   Our pride, O Lord, disdained Thee;
   Yet deign our hope to be.
O glorious King, we bless Thee,
   No longer pass Thee by;
O Jesus, we confess Thee
   Our Lord enthroned on high.

387 7. 6.

1 O Jesus! Lord most merciful,
   Low at Thy cross I lie;
   O sinner's friend, most pitiful,
   Hear my bewailing cry.
I come to Thee with mourning,
   I come to Thee in woe;
With contrite heart returning,
   And tears that overflow.

2 O gracious Intercessor !
   O Priest within the veil !
   Plead, for a lost transgressor,
   The blood that cannot fail.
I spread my sins before Thee,
   I tell them one by one;
Oh, for Thy Name's great glory,
   Forgive all I have done !

3 Oh, by Thy cross and passion,
   Thy tears and agony,
   And crown of cruel fashion,
   And death on Calvary;
By all that untold suffering
   Endured by Thee alone;
O Priest ! O spotless offering!
   Plead, for Thou didst atone!

4 And in this heart now broken
   Re-enter Thou and reign ;
   And say, by that dear token,
   I am absolved again ;
And build me up, and guide me,
   And guard me day by day;
And in Thy presence hide me,
   And keep my soul alway. Amen.

GENERAL.

388   8.7.8.7.7.7 7.7.

1 Christ, the Life of all the living,
    Christ, the Death of death our foe,
Who, Thyself for us once giving
    To the darkened depths of woe,
Patiently didst yield Thy breath,
Man to save from sin and death;
Thousand, thousand thanks shall be,
Blessèd Jesus, brought to Thee.

2 Thou, ah, Thou hast taken on Thee
    Bitter strokes, a cruel rod ;
Pain and scorn were heaped upon Thee,
    O Thou sinless Son of God ;
Only thus for us to win
Rescue from the bonds of sin ;
Thousand, thousand thanks shall be,
Blessèd Jesus, brought to Thee.

3 Thou didst bear the smiting, only
    That it might not fall on me;
Stoodest falsely charged and lonely,
    That I might be safe and free;
Comfortless, that I might know
Comfort from Thy boundless woe;
Thousand, thousand thanks shall be,
Blessèd Jesus, brought to Thee.

4 Then for all that wrought our pardon,
    For Thy sorrows deep and sore,
For Thine anguish in the garden,
    I will thank Thee evermore;
Thank Thee with the latest breath
For Thy sad and cruel death ;
For that last most bitter cry,
Praise Thee evermore on high.

389   8.8.6.

1 To Him Who for our sins was slain,
    To Him for all His dying pain.
        Sing we Alleluia!
To Him, the Lamb our sacrifice,
Who gave His blood our ransom-price,
        Sing we Alleluia!

2 To Him Who died that we might die
    To sin, and live with Him on high.
        Sing we Alleluia!
To Him Who rose that we might rise,
And reign with Him beyond the skies,
        Sing we Alleluia!

3 To Him Who now for us doth plead,
And helpeth us in all our need,
        Sing we Alleluia!
To Him Who doth prepare on high
Our home in immortality,
        Sing we Alleluia!

4 To Him be glory evermore:
Ye heavenly hosts, your Lord adore;
        Sing we Alleluia!
To Father, Son, and Holy Ghost,
Our God most great, our joy, our boast,
        Sing we Alleluia!
                Amen.

390   8.7.8.7.4.7.

1 Glory, glory everlasting
    Be to Him Who bore the cross,
Who redeemed our souls by tasting
    Death, the death deserved by us;
        Spread His glory,
Who redeemed His people thus!

2 Jesus' love is love unbounded,
    Without measure, without end;
Human thought is here confounded,
    'Tis too vast to comprehend ;
        Praise the Saviour ;
Magnify the sinner's friend !

3 While we hear the wondrous story
    Of the Saviour's cross and shame,
Sing we, 'everlasting glory
    Be to God and to the Lamb!'
        Saints and angels,
Give ye glory to His Name!

391   L. M.

1 Triumphant Lord, Thy work is done,
Thy toil is o'er, Thy victory won;
Oh, aid Thy servants in their strife;
Help us to win the crown of life!

2 Presenting Thine own sacrifice.
Our prayers like incense round Thee rise;
For 'Thou art Priest forever,' Thou
Art interceding for us now.

3 Oh, by Thy spotless, wondrous birth,
And by Thy bitter death on earth,
And by Thy rising from the grave,
Ascended Lord, Thy people save!

GENERAL.

4 "Thou art the King of Glory," Thine
All honor, praise, and power divine;
One with the Father now confessed,
And with the Spirit ever blest. Amen.

392 8.7.

1 Christ, above all glory seated!
King eternal, strong to save!
Dying, Thou hast death defeated,
Buried, Thou hast spoiled the grave.

2 Thou art gone, where now is given
What no mortal might could gain,
On the eternal throne of heaven
In Thy Father's power to reign.

3 There Thy kingdoms all adore Thee,
Heaven above and earth below;
While the depths of hell before Thee
Trembling and defeated bow.

4 We, O Lord, with hearts adoring,
Follow Thee above the sky;
Hear our prayers, Thy grace imploring,
Lift our souls to Thee on high;

5 So, when Thou again in glory
On the clouds of heaven shalt shine,
We Thy flock may stand before Thee,
Owned for evermore as Thine.

6 Hail! all hail! In Thee confiding,
Jesus, Thee shall all adore,
In Thy Father's might abiding
With one Spirit evermore!

393 C.M.

1 The Head, that once was crowned with thorns,
Is crowned with glory now;
A royal diadem adorns
The mighty Victor's brow.

2 The highest place that heaven affords
Is His, is His by right,
The King of kings and Lord of lords,
And heaven's eternal light.

3 The joy of all who dwell above;
The joy of all below,
To whom He manifests His love
And grants His Name to know.

4 To them the cross with all its shame,
With all its grace is given;
Their name, an everlasting name,
Their joy, the joy of heaven.

5 They suffer with their Lord below,
They reign with Him above,
Their profit and their joy to know
The mystery of His love.

6 The cross He bore is life and health,
Though shame and death to Him;
His people's hope, His people's wealth,
Their everlasting theme.

394 D.S.M.

1 Thou art gone up on high
To mansions in the skies;
And round Thy throne unceasingly
The songs of praise arise:
But we are lingering here,
With sin and care oppressed;
Lord, send Thy promised Comforter,
And lead us to Thy rest.

2 Thou art gone up on high;
But Thou didst first come down,
Through earth's most bitter misery,
To pass unto Thy crown;
And girt with griefs and fears
Our onward course must be;
But only let that path of tears
Lead us at last to Thee.

3 Thou art gone up on high;
But Thou shalt come again,
With all the bright ones of the sky
Attendant in Thy train.
Oh, by Thy saving power,
So make us live and die,
That we may stand, in that dread hour
At Thy right hand on high. Amen.

395 D.S.M.

1 Crown Him with many crowns,
The Lamb upon His throne:
Hark! how the heavenly anthem drowns
All music but its own:
Awake, my soul, and sing
Of Him Who died for Thee,
And hail Him as thy matchless King
Through all eternity.

119

GENERAL.

2 Crown Him the Son of God
   Before the worlds began,
  And ye, who tread where He hath trod,
   Crown Him the Son of Man,
  Who every grief hath known
   That wrings the human breast,
  And takes and bears them for His own,
   That all in Him may rest.

3 Crown Him the Lord of Life,
   Who triumphed o'er the grave,
  And rose victorious in the strife
   For those He came to save;
  His glories now we sing
   Who died, and rose on high,
  Who died, eternal life to bring,
   And lives, that death may die.

4 Crown Him of lords the Lord,
   Who over all doth reign,
  Who once on earth the incarnate Word
   For ransomed sinners slain,
  Now lives in realms of light,
   Where saints with angels sing
  Their songs before Him day and night,
   Their God, Redeemer, King.

5 Crown Him the Lord of heaven,
   Enthroned in worlds above;
  Crown Him the King to Whom is given
   The wondrous name of Love.
  Crown Him with many crowns
   As thrones before Him fall,
  Crown Him, ye kings, with many crowns,
   For He is King of all.

396   S.6.8.4.

1 Our blest Redeemer, ere He breathed
   His tender, last farewell,
  A Guide, a Comforter, bequeathed
   With us to dwell.

2 He came sweet influence to impart,
   A gracious, willing guest,
  While He can find one humble heart
   Wherein to rest.

3 And His that gentle voice we hear,
   Soft as the breath of even,
  That checks each thought, that calms each
   fear,
  And speaks of heaven.

4 And every virtue we possess,
   And every victory won,
  And every thought of holiness
   Are His alone.

5 Spirit of purity and grace,
   Our weakness, pitying, see:
  Oh, make our hearts Thy dwelling-place,
   And meet for Thee.   Amen.

397   S.M.

1 Come, Holy Spirit, come!
   Let Thy bright beams arise;
  Dispel the sorrow from our minds,
   The darkness from our eyes.

2 Revive our drooping faith,
   Our doubts and fears remove,
  And kindle in our breasts the flame
   Of never-dying love.

3 Convince us of our sin;
   Then lead to Jesus' blood,
  And to our wondering view reveal
   The secret love of God.

4 'Tis Thine to cleanse the heart,
   To sanctify the soul,
  To pour fresh life in every part,
   And new-create the whole.

5 Dwell therefore in our hearts,
   Our minds from bondage free;
  Then shall we know, and praise, and love
   The Father, Son, and Thee.   Amen.

398   7s.

1 Come, Thou Holy Spirit, come!
   And from Thy celestial home
   Shed a ray of light divine!
  Come, Thou Father of the poor!
  Come, Thou source of all our store!
   Come, within our bosoms shine!

2 Thou of comforters the best;
  Thou the soul's most welcome guest;
   Sweet refreshment here below;
  In our labor rest most sweet;
  Grateful coolness in the heat;
   Solace in the midst of woe.

GENERAL.

3 O most blessèd Light divine,
   Shine within these hearts of Thine,
   And our inmost being fill!
   Where Thou art not, man hath nought,
   Nothing good in deed or thought,
   Nothing free from taint of ill.

4 Heal our wounds; our strength renew;
   On our dryness pour Thy dew;
   Wash the stains of guilt away:
   Bend the stubborn heart and will;
   Melt the frozen, warm the chill;
   Guide the steps that go astray.

5 On the faithful, who adore
   And confess Thee, evermore
   In Thy sevenfold gifts descend;
   Give them virtue's sure reward;
   Give them Thy salvation, Lord;
   Give them joys that never end. Amen.

399   L.M.

1 Come, gracious Spirit, heavenly Dove,
   With light and comfort from above;
   Be Thou our guardian, Thou our guide,
   O'er every thought and step preside.

2 The light of truth to us display,
   And make us know and choose Thy way;
   Plant holy fear in every heart,
   That we from Thee may ne'er depart.

3 Lead us to Christ, the living Way,
   Nor let us from His precepts stray;
   Lead us to holiness, the road
   That we must take to dwell with God.

4 Lead us to heaven, that we may share
   Fulness of joy for ever there;
   Lead us to God, our final rest,
   To be with Him for ever blest. Amen.

400   L.M.

1 Come, Holy Ghost, Creator blest,
   Vouchsafe within our souls to rest,
   Come with Thy grace and heavenly aid,
   And fill the hearts which Thou hast made.

2 To Thee, the Comforter, we cry;
   To Thee, the gift of God most High;
   The fount of life, the fire of love,
   The soul's anointing from above.

3 O Finger of the Hand divine,
   The sevenfold gifts of grace are Thine;
   True promise of the Father Thou,
   Who dost the tongue with power endow.

4 Thy light to every sense impart,
   And shed Thy love in every heart;
   Thine own unfailing might supply
   To strengthen our infirmity.

5 Drive far away our ghostly foe,
   And Thine abiding peace bestow;
   If Thou be our preventing guide,
   No evil can our steps betide.

401   8s.

1 Creator Spirit, by Whose aid
   The world's foundations first were laid,
   Come, visit every humble mind;
   Come, pour Thy joys on human kind;
   From sin and sorrow set us free,
   And make Thy temples worthy Thee.

2 O source of uncreated light,
   The Father's promised Paraclete,
   Thrice holy fount, thrice holy fire,
   Our hearts with heavenly love inspire;
   Come, and Thy sacred unction bring
   To sanctify us while we sing.

3 Plenteous of grace, come from on high,
   Rich in Thy sevenfold energy;
   Make us eternal truth receive,
   And practise all that we believe;
   Give us Thyself, that we may see
   The Father and the Son by Thee. Amen.

402   C.M.

1 Spirit divine, attend our prayers,
   And make this house Thy home;
   Descend with all Thy gracious powers,
   Oh, come, great Spirit, come!

2 Come as the light: to us reveal
   Our emptiness and woe;
   And lead us in those paths of life,
   Whereon the righteous go.

3 Come as the fire, and purge our hearts
   Like sacrificial flame;
   Let our whole soul an offering be
   To our Redeemer's Name.

GENERAL.

4 Come as the dove, and spread Thy wings,
  The wings of peaceful love;
And let Thy Church on earth become
  Blest as the Church above.

5 Spirit divine, attend our prayers;
  Make a lost world Thy home;
Descend with all Thy gracious powers,
  Oh, come, great Spirit, come! Amen.

403 L.M.

1 Praises to Him, Whose love has given,
  In Christ, His Son, the life of heaven;
  Who for our darkness gives us light,
  And turns to day our deepest night.

2 Praises to Him, in grace Who came
  To bear our woe, and sin, and shame;
  Who lived to die, Who died to rise,
  The God-accepted sacrifice.

3 Praises to Him, Who sheds abroad
  Within our hearts the love of God;
  The Spirit of all truth and peace,
  Fountain of joy and holiness!

4 To Father, Son, and Spirit now
  Our hands we lift, our knees we bow;
  To Thee, Jehovah, thus we raise
  The sinner's endless song of praise.
            Amen.

404 P.M.

1 Holy, holy, holy! Lord God Almighty!
  Early in the morning our song shall rise
    to Thee:
  Holy, holy, holy! merciful and mighty!
  God in three Persons, blessèd Trinity!

2 Holy, holy, holy! All the saints adore Thee,
  Casting down their golden crowns around
    the glassy sea;
  Cherubim and seraphim falling down before
    Thee,
  Which wert, and art, and evermore shalt
    be.

3 Holy, holy, holy! though the darkness hide
    Thee,
  Though the eye of sinful man Thy glory
    may not see,
  Only Thou art holy; there is none beside
    Thee,
  Perfect in power, in love, and purity.

4 Holy, holy, holy! Lord God Almighty!
  All Thy works shall praise Thy Name, in
    earth, and sky, and sea;
  Holy, holy, holy! merciful and mighty!
  God in Three Persons, blessèd Trinity!

405 7s.

1 God, my Father, hear me pray,
  Wash my crimson guilt away;
  Wretched, helpless, lost, undone,
  Hear me for Thy blessèd Son;
  Lord, unnumbered sins are mine,
  But eternal love is Thine.

2 God, my Saviour, look on me;
  All my guilt I cast on Thee;
  Give my troubled spirit peace;
  Bid my fears and sorrows cease;
  Lord, unnumbered sins are mine,
  But eternal love is Thine.

3 God, my Comforter, my Light,
  Strengthen me with holy might,
  Make Thy dwelling in my heart:
  Faith, and joy, and hope impart.
  Lord, unnumbered sins are mine,
  But eternal love is Thine.

4 Blessèd, glorious Trinity!
  Holy, everlasting Three!
  Hear, oh, hear my earnest prayer,
  And my soul for heaven prepare!
  Lord, unnumbered sins are mine;
  But eternal love is Thine. Amen.

406 7s.

1 Holy, holy, holy, Lord,
  God of Hosts, eternal King,
  By the heavens and earth adored;
  Angels and archangels sing,
  Chanting everlastingly
  To the blessèd Trinity.

2 Since by Thee were all things made,
  And in Thee do all things live,
  Be to Thee all honor paid,
  Praise to Thee let all things give,
  Singing everlastingly
  To the blessèd Trinity.

GENERAL.

3 Thousands, tens of thousands stand,
   Spirits blest, before Thy throne,
Speeding thence at Thy command ;
   And when Thy command is done,
Singing everlastingly
To the blessèd Trinity.

4 Cherubim and seraphim
   Veil their faces with their wings;
Eyes of angels are too dim
   To behold the King of kings,
While they sing eternally
To the blessèd Trinity.

5 Thee, apostles, prophets, Thee,
   Thee, the noble martyr band,
Praise with solemn jubilee;
   Thee the Church in every land ;
Singing everlastingly
To the blessèd Trinity.

6 Alleluia! Lord, to Thee,
   Father, Son, and Holy Ghost,
Three in One, and One in Three,
   Join we with the heavenly host,
Singing everlastingly
To the blessèd Trinity. Amen.

407 8.7.

1 Round the Lord in glory seated
   Cherubim and seraphim
Filled His temple, and repeated
   Each to each the alternate hymn:
'Lord, Thy glory fills the heaven,
   Earth is with Thy fulness stored ;
Unto Thee be glory given,
   Holy, holy, holy Lord.'

2 Heaven is still with glory ringing,
   Earth takes up the angels' cry,
"Holy, holy, holy," singing,
   "Lord of Hosts, the Lord most High."
With His seraph train before Him,
   With His holy Church below,
Thus unite we to adore Him,
Bid we thus our anthem flow:

3 'Lord, Thy glory fills the heaven,
   Earth is with Thy fulness stored ;
Unto Thee be glory given,
   Holy, holy, holy Lord.'
Thus Thy glorious Name confessing,
   We adopt the angels' cry,
"Holy, holy, holy," blessing
   Thee, the Lord of Hosts most high.
                              Amen.

408 6.6.4.6.6.6.4.

1 Come, Thou almighty King,
   Help us Thy Name to sing,
   Help us to praise!
Father all glorious,
O'er all victorious,
Come and reign over us,
   Ancient of days!

2 Come, Thou incarnate Word,
   Gird on Thy mighty sword ;
   Our prayer attend!
Come, and Thy people bless;
Come, give Thy word success;
Spirit of holiness,
   On us descend !

3 Come, holy Comforter,
   Thy sacred witness bear,
   In this glad hour!
Thou, Who almighty art,
Now rule in every heart,
And ne'er from us depart,
   Spirit of power!

4 To Thee, great One in Three,
   The highest praises be,
   Hence evermore;
Thy sovereign majesty
May we in glory see,
And to eternity
   Love and adore. Amen.

409 7.7.7.5.

1 Three in One, and One in Three,
   Ruler of the earth and sea,
   Hear us, while we lift to Thee
   Holy chant and psalm.

2 Light of lights! with morning shine;
   Lift on us Thy light divine;
   And let charity benign
   Breathe on us her balm.

3 Light of lights! when falls the even,
   Let it close on sin forgiven ;
   Fold us in the peace of heaven ;
   Shed a holy calm.

4 Three in One and One in Three,
   Dimly here we worship Thee;
   With the saints hereafter we
   Hope to bear the palm. Amen.

GENERAL.

410   C.M.

1 Let saints on earth in concert sing
   With those whose work is done;
   For all the servants of our King
   In heaven and earth are one.

2 One family, we dwell in Him,
   One Church, above, beneath;
   Though now divided by the stream,
   The narrow stream of death.

3 One army of the living God,
   To His command we bow;
   Part of the host have crossed the flood,
   And part are crossing now.

4 E'en now to their eternal home
   There pass some spirits blest;
   While others to the margin come,
   Waiting their call to rest.

5 Jesus, be Thou our constant guide;
   Then, when the word is given,
   Bid Jordan's narrow stream divide,
   And bring us safe to heaven. Amen.

411   7s.

1 Soldiers, who are Christ's below,
   Strong in faith resist the foe:
   Boundless is the pledged reward
   Unto them who serve the Lord.

2 'Tis no palm of fading leaves
   That the conqueror's hand receives;
   Joys are his, serene and pure,
   Light that ever shall endure.

3 For the souls that overcome
   Waits the beauteous heavenly home,
   Where the blessèd evermore
   Tread, on high, the starry floor.

4 Passing soon and little worth
   Are the things that tempt on earth:
   Heavenward lift thy soul's regard;
   God Himself is thy reward.

5 Father, Who the crown dost give,
   Saviour, by Whose death we live,
   Spirit, Who our hearts dost raise,
   Three in One, Thy Name we praise.
                     Amen.

412   S.M.

1 Oh! what, if we are Christ's,
   Is earthly shame or loss?
   Bright shall the crown of glory be
   When we have borne the cross.

2 Keen was the trial once,
   Bitter the cup of woe,
   When martyred saints, baptized in blood,
   Christ's sufferings shared below.

3 Bright is their glory now,
   Boundless their joy above,
   Where, on the bosom of their God,
   They rest in perfect love.

4 Lord, may that grace be ours,
   Like them in faith to bear
   All that of sorrow, grief, or pain
   May be our portion here;

5 Enough if Thou at last
   The word of blessing give,
   And let us rest beneath Thy feet,
   Where saints and angels live.

413   C.M.

1 Not to the terrors of the Lord,
   The tempest, fire, and smoke;
   Not to the thunder of that word
   Which God on Sinai spoke:

2 But we are come to Sion's hill,
   The city of our God;
   Where milder words declare His will,
   And spread His love abroad.

3 Behold th' innumerable host
   Of angels clothed in light;
   Behold the spirits of the just,
   Whose faith is changed to sight.

4 Behold the blest assembly there
   Whose names are writ in heaven;
   Hear God, the Judge of all, declare
   Their sins, through Christ, forgiven.

5 Angels, and living saints and dead,
   But one communion make;
   All join in Christ, their living Head,
   And of His love partake.

GENERAL.

414 C.M.

1 Lo! what a cloud of witnesses
  Encompass us around!
  Men once like us with suffering tried,
  But now with glory crowned.

2 Let us, with zeal like theirs inspired,
  Strive in the Christian race;
  And, freed from every weight of sin,
  Their holy footsteps trace.

3 Behold a witness nobler still,
  Who trod affliction's path;
  Jesus, the author, finisher,
  Rewarder of our faith.

4 He, for the joy before Him set,
  And moved by pitying love,
  Endured the cross, despised the shame,
  And now He reigns above.

5 Thither, forgetting things behind,
  Press we to God's right hand;
  There, with the Saviour and His saints,
  Triumphantly to stand.

415 P.M.

1 Ten thousand times ten thousand
  In sparkling raiment bright,
  The armies of the ransomed saints
  Throng up the steeps of light:
  'Tis finished! all is finished,
  Their fight with death and sin.
  Fling open wide the golden gates,
  And let the victors in.

2 What rush of alleluias
  Fills all the earth and sky!
  What ringing of a thousand harps
  Bespeaks the triumph nigh!
  O day, for which creation
  And all its tribes were made!
  O joy, for all its former woes
  A thousand-fold repaid!

3 Oh, then what raptured greetings
  On Canaan's happy shore,
  What knitting severed friendships up,
  Where partings are no more!
  Then eyes with joy shall sparkle
  That brimmed with tears of late;
  Orphans no longer fatherless,
  Nor widows desolate.

4 Bring near Thy great salvation.
  Thou Lamb for sinners slain:
  Fill up the roll of Thine elect,
  Then take Thy power and reign!
  Appear, Desire of nations!
  Thine exiles long for home:
  Show in the heavens Thy promised sign!
  Thou Prince and Saviour, come! Amen.

416 7.6.

1 O heavenly Jerusalem,
  Of everlasting halls,
  Thrice blessèd are the people
  Thou storest in thy walls.

2 Thou art the golden mansion,
  Where saints for ever sing,
  The seat of God's own chosen,
  The palace of the king.

3 There God for ever sitteth,
  Himself of all the crown;
  The Lamb, the Light that shineth,
  And never goeth down.

4 Nought to this seat approacheth
  Their sweet peace to molest;
  They sing their God for ever,
  Nor day nor night they rest.

5 Sure hope doth thither lead us:
  Our longings thither tend;
  May short-lived toil ne'er daunt us
  For joys that cannot end.

6 To Christ, the Sun that lightens
  His Church above, below;
  To Father, and to Spirit
  All things created bow. Amen.

417 8.7.

1 Light's abode, celestial Salem,
  Vision whence true peace doth spring,
  Brighter than the heart can fancy,
  Mansion of the highest King;
  Oh, how glorious are the praises
  Which of thee the prophets sing!

2 There for ever and for ever
  Alleluia is out-poured;
  For unending, for unbroken
  Is the feast-day of the Lord;
  All is pure and all is holy
  That within thy walls is stored.

3 There no cloud nor passing vapor
    Dims the brightness of the air;
  Endless noon-day, glorious noon day,
    From the Sun of suns is there;
  There no night brings rest from labor,
    For unknown are toil and care.

4 Oh, how glorious and resplendent,
    Fragile body, shalt thou be,
  When endued with so much beauty,
    Full of health, and strong, and free,
  Full of vigor, full of pleasure
    That shall last eternally!

5 Now with gladness, now with courage,
    Bear the burden on thee laid,
  That hereafter these thy labors
    May with endless gifts be paid,
  And in everlasting glory
    Thou with brightness be arrayed.
      Amen.

418   C.M.

1 There is a land of pure delight,
    Where saints immortal reign ;
  Eternal day excludes the night,
    And pleasures banish pain.

2 There everlasting spring abides,
    And never-fading flowers;
  Death, like a narrow sea, divides
    This heavenly land from ours.

3 Bright fields beyond the swelling flood
    Stand dressed in living green ;
  So to the Jews fair Canaan stood,
    While Jordan rolled between.

4 But timorous mortals start and shrink
    To cross the narrow sea;
  And linger, trembling on the brink,
    And fear to launch away.

5 Oh, could we make our doubts remove,
    Those gloomy doubts that rise,
  And see the Canaan that we love,
    With faith's illumined eyes :

6 Could we but climb where Moses stood,
    And view the landscape o'er,
  Not Jordan's stream, nor death's cold flood,
    Should fright us from the shore.

419   10s.

1 Oh, what the joy and the glory must be,
  Those endless Sabbaths the blessèd ones see;
  Crown for the valiant, to weary ones rest ;
  God shall be all and in all ever blest.

2 What are the Monarch, His court, and His
    throne?
  What are the peace and the joy that they
    own?
  Oh, that the blest ones, who in it have share,
  All that they feel could as fully declare!

3 Truly Jerusalem name we that shore,
  Vision of peace, that brings joy evermore;
  Wish and fulfilment can severed be ne'er,
  Nor the thing prayed for come short of the
    prayer.

4 There, where no troubles distraction can
    bring,
  We the sweet anthems of Sion shall sing ;
  While for Thy grace, Lord, their voices of
    praise
  Thy blessèd people eternally raise.

5 There dawns no Sabbath, no Sabbath is o'er,
  Those Sabbath-keepers have one evermore;
  One and unending is that triumph-song
  Which to the angels and us shall belong.

6 Now, in the meanwhile, with hearts raised
    on high,
  We for that country must yearn and must
    sigh ;
  Seeking Jerusalem, dear native land,
  Through our long exile on Babylon's strand.

7 Low before Him with our praises we fall,
  Of Whom, and in Whom, and through
    Whom are all ;
  Of Whom, the Father ; and in Whom, the
    Son ;
  Through Whom, the Spirit, with Them ever
    One. Amen.

420   6.5.

1 Those eternal bowers
    Man hath never trod,
  Those unfading flowers
    Round the throne of God :
  Who may hope to gain them
    After weary fight ?
  Who at length attain them,
    Clad in robes of white?

GENERAL.

2 He who wakes from slumber
　At the Spirit's voice,
　Daring here to number
　Things unseen his choice:
　He who casts his burden
　Down at Jesus' cross ;
　Christ's reproach his guerdon,
　All beside but loss.

3 He who gladly barters
　All on earthly ground ;
　He who, like the martyrs,
　Says " I will be crowned ; "
　He whose one oblation
　Is a life of love,
　Knit in God's salvation
　To the blest above.

4 Shame upon you, legions
　Of the heavenly King,
　Citizens of regions
　Past imagining !
　What, with pipe and tabor
　Dream away the light!
　When He bids you labor,
　When He tells you, " Fight " ?

5 Jesus, Lord of glory,
　As we breast the tide,
　Whisper Thou the story
　Of the other side;
　Where the saints are casting
　Crowns before Thy feet,
　Safe for everlasting,
　In Thyself complete.
　　　　　Amen.

421　　　　　　　　　P.M.

1 O Paradise, O Paradise,
　Who doth not crave for rest ?
　Who would not seek the happy land,
　Where they that loved are blest ;
　Where loyal hearts, and true,
　Stand ever in the light,
　All rapture, through and through,
　In God's most holy sight ?

2 O Paradise, O Paradise,
　The world is growing old ;
　Who would not be at rest and free
　Where love is never cold ?
　Where loyal hearts, etc.

3 O Paradise, O Paradise,
　'Tis weary waiting here:
　We long to be where Jesus is,
　To feel, to see Him near ;
　Where loyal hearts, etc.

4 O Paradise, O Paradise,
　We shall not wait for long :
　E'en now the loving ear may catch
　Faint fragments of Thy song ;
　Where loyal hearts, etc.

5 Lord Jesus, King of Paradise,
　Oh, keep us in Thy love,
　And guide us to that happy land
　Of perfect rest above;
　Where loyal hearts, etc.　Amen.

422　　　　　　　　　7.6.

1 Awake, awake, O Sion.
　Put on thy strength divine.
　Thy garments bright in beauty ;
　The bridal dress, be thine:

　Jerusalem the holy,
　To purity restored ;
　Meek bride all fair and lowly,
　Go forth to meet thy Lord.

2 From henceforth pure and spotless,
　All glorious within,
　Prepared to meet the Bridegroom,
　And cleansed from every sin ;

　With love and wonder smitten,
　And bowed in guileless shame,
　Upon thy heart be written
　The new, mysterious Name.

3 Jerusalem the holy,
　In light and peace behold ;
　Her glowing altar flaming,
　Her candlesticks of gold ;

　The heavenly Bridegroom's dwelling,
　The place of David's throne ;
　Her solemn anthems swelling,
　Her pavement, precious stone.

4 The Lamb Who bore our sorrows
　Comes down to earth again ;
　No sufferer now, but victor,
　For evermore to reign ;

　To reign in every nation,
　To rule in every zone;
　O world-wide coronation,
　In every heart a throne!

5 Awake, awake, O Sion,
  Thy bridal day draws nigh,
The day of signs and wonders,
  And marvels from on high ;
Thy sun uprises slowly,
  But keep thou watch and ward,
Fair bride, all pure and lowly,
  Go forth to meet thy Lord.

423   7.6.
            Part I.

1 The world is very evil,
    The times are waxing late,
  Be sober and keep vigil,
    The Judge is at the gate:
  The Judge Who comes in mercy,
    The Judge Who comes with might,
  Who comes to end the evil,
    Who comes to crown the right.

2 Arise, arise, good Christian,
    Let right to wrong succeed ;
  Let penitential sorrow
    To heavenly gladness lead,
  To light that has no evening,
    That knows nor moon nor sun,
  The light so new and golden,
    The light that is but one:

3 The home of fadeless splendor,
    Of flowers that hide no thorn,
  Where they shall dwell as children
    Who here as exiles mourn ;
  'Midst power that knows no limit,
    Where wisdom has no bound,
  The beatific vision
    Shall glad the saints around.

4 O happy, holy portion,
    Refection for the blest,
  True vision of true beauty,
    True cure of the distrest ;
  Strive, man, to win that glory;
    Toil, man, to gain that light ;
  Send hope before to grasp it,
    Till hope be lost in sight.

424   7.6.
            Part II.

1 Brief life is here our portion,
    Brief sorrow, short-lived care;
  The life that knows no ending,
    The tearless life is there.

  O happy retribution !
    Short toil, eternal rest;
  For mortals and for sinners
    A mansion with the blest.

2 And now we fight the battle,
    But then shall wear the crown
  Of full and everlasting
    And passionless renown.

  But He Whom now we trust in
    Shall then be seen and known,
  And they that know and see Him
    Shall have Him for their own.

3 And there, when morn shall waken,
    And shadows shall decay,
  And each true-hearted servant
    Shall shine as doth the day.

  Then God, our King and Portion,
    In fulness of His grace,
  Shall we behold for ever,
    And worship face to face.

4 There grief is turned to pleasure;
    Such pleasure as below
  No human voice can utter,
    No human heart can know.

  And there is David's fountain,
    And life in fullest glow,
  And there the light is golden,
    And milk and honey flow.

5 Strive, man, to win that glory;
    Toil, man, to gain that light ;
  Send hope before to grasp it
    Till hope be lost in sight !

  Exult, O dust and ashes;
    The Lord shall be thy part,
  His only, His for ever,
    Thou shalt be, and thou art.

425   7.6.
            Part III.

1 For thee, O dear, dear country,
    Mine eyes their vigils keep ;
  For very love, beholding
    Thy happy name, they weep.

  The mention of thy glory
    Is unction to the breast,
  And medicine in sickness,
    And love, and life, and rest.

2 O one, O only mansion!
  O Paradise of joy!
 Where tears are ever banished,
  And smiles have no alloy:

 The Lamb is all thy splendor;
  The Crucified thy praise;
 His laud and benediction
  Thy ransomed people raise.

3 With jasper glow thy bulwarks,
  Thy streets with emeralds blaze;
 The sardius and the topaz
  Unite in thee their rays;

 Thine ageless walls are bonded
  With amethyst unpriced ;
 The saints build up its fabric,
  And the corner-stone is Christ.

4 Thou hast no shore, fair ocean!
  Thou hast no time, bright day!
 Dear fountain of refreshment
  To pilgrims far away!

 Upon the Rock of ages
  They raise Thy holy tower ;
 Thine is the victor's laurel,
  And thine the golden dower.

426   7.6.
Part IV.

1 Jerusalem, the golden !
  With milk and honey blest ;
 Beneath thy contemplation
  Sink heart and voice opprest.

 I know not, oh, I know not,
  What joys await us there!
 What radiancy of glory!
  What bliss beyond compare!

2 They stand, those halls of Sion,
  All jubilant with song,
 And bright with many an angel,
  And all the martyr throng.

 The Prince is ever in them,
  The daylight is serene;
 The pastures of the blessed
  Are decked in glorious sheen.

3 There is the throne of David ;
  And there, from care released,
 The shout of them that triumph,
  The song of them that feast.

9

And they, who with their Leader,
  Have conquered in the fight,
 For ever and for ever
  Are clad in robes of white.

The following may be sung here, and at the end of the other parts, preceding.

4 O sweet and blessed country,
  The home of God's elect !
 O sweet and blessed country,
  That eager hearts expect !

 Jesus, in mercy bring us
  To that dear land of rest !
 Who art, with God the Father,
  And Spirit, ever blest. Amen.

427   8.7.

1 Blessèd city, heavenly Salem,
  Vision dear of peace and love,
 Who of living stones art builded
  In the height of heaven above,
 And, with angel hosts encircled,
  As a bride dost earthward move;

2 From celestial realms descending,
  Bridal glory round thee shed,
 Meet for Him Whose love espoused thee,
  To thy Lord shalt thou be led ;
 All thy streets, and all thy bulwarks
  Of pure gold are fashionèd.

3 Bright thy gates of pearl are shining,
  They are open evermore ;
 And by virtue of His merits
  Thither faithful souls do soar,
 Who for Christ's dear Name, in this world
  Pain and tribulation bore.

4 Many a blow and biting sculpture
  Polished well those stones elect,
 In their places now compacted
  By the heavenly Architect,
 Who therewith hath willed for ever
  That His palace should be decked.

5 Laud and honor to the Father,
  Laud and honor to the Son,
 Laud and honor to the Spirit,
  Ever Three, and ever One,
 Consubstantial, Co-eternal,
  While unending ages run. Amen.

129

428   C.M.

1 Jerusalem, my happy home.
   Name ever dear to me,
  When shall my labors have an end
   In joy, and peace, and thee?

2 When shall these eyes thy heaven-built walls
   And gates of pearl behold?
  Thy bulwarks, with salvation strong,
   And streets of shining gold?

3 Apostles, martyrs, prophets, there
   Around my Saviour stand;
  And soon my friends in Christ below
   Will join the glorious band.

4 O Christ, do Thou my soul prepare
   For that bright home of love;
  That I may see Thee and adore,
   With all Thy saints above. Amen.

429   C.M.

1 O Mother dear, Jerusalem!
   When shall I come to thee?
  When shall my sorrows have an end?
   Thy joys when shall I see?

2 O happy harbor of God's saints!
   O sweet and pleasant soil!
  In thee no sorrow can be found,
   Nor grief, nor care, nor toil.

3 No murky cloud o'ershadows thee,
   Nor gloom, nor darksome night;
  But every soul shines as the sun;
   For God Himself gives light.

4 O my sweet home, Jerusalem!
   Thy joys when shall I see?
  The King that sitteth on thy throne
   In His felicity?

5 Thy gardens and thy goodly walks
   Continually are green,
  Where grow such sweet and pleasant flowers
   As nowhere else are seen.

6 Right through thy streets, with silver sound,
   The living waters flow,
  And on the banks, on either side,
   The trees of life do grow.

7 Those trees for evermore bear fruit,
   And evermore do spring;
  There evermore the angels are,
   And evermore do sing.

8 Jerusalem, my happy home,
   Would God I were in thee!
  Would God my woes were at an end,
   Thy joys that I might see! Amen.

430   6.6.6.6.4.4.4.4.

1 Jerusalem on high
   My song and city is,
  My home whene'er I die,
   The centre of my bliss:
    O happy place!
     When shall I be,
    My God, with Thee,
    To see Thy face?

2 There dwells my Lord, my King,
   Judged here unfit to live;
  There angels to Him sing,
   And lowly homage give:
    O happy place! etc.

3 The patriarchs of old
   There from their travels cease;
  The prophets there behold
   Their longed-for Prince of Peace:
    O happy place! etc.

4 The Lamb's apostles there
   I might with joy behold;
  The harpers I might hear
   Harping on harps of gold;
    O happy place! etc.

5 The bleeding martyrs, they
   Within those courts are found,
  Clothed in pure array,
   Their scars with glory crowned.
    O happy place! etc.

6 Ah me! ah me! that I
   In Kedar's tents here stay;
  No place like that on high;
   Lord, thither guide my way.
    O happy place!
     When shall I be,
    My God, with Thee,
    To see Thy face?

GENERAL.

431 C.M.

1 The roseate hues of early dawn,
The brightness of the day,
The crimson of the sunset sky,
How fast they fade away!

Oh, for the pearly gates of heaven!
Oh, for the golden floor!
Oh, for the Sun of righteousness
That setteth nevermore!

2 The highest hopes we cherish here,
How fast they tire and faint ;
How many a spot defiles the robe
That wraps an earthly saint !

Oh, for a heart that never sins!
Oh, for a soul washed white!
Oh, for a voice to praise our King,
Nor weary day nor night !

3 Here faith is ours, and heavenly hope,
And grace to lead us higher ;
But there are perfectness, and peace,
Beyond our best desire.

Oh, by Thy love and anguish, Lord,
And by Thy life laid down,
Grant that we fall not from Thy grace,
Nor cast away our crown! Amen.

432 C.M.

1 Lord, if on earth the thought of Thee
Be life, and strength, and peace,
How blessèd shall that vision be
Which never more can cease!

2 How blest when we Thy glory see
In light without a shade ;
The glory which surrounded Thee
Before the worlds were made!

3 Darkly to us, as through a glass,
Thy beauty now is shown ;
Then we shall see Thee face to face,
And know as we are known.

4 Then purge, O Lord, our hearts from sin,
Hallow Thine own abode,
That nought unclean be found within
The temple of our God. Amen.

433 S.M.

1 Blest are the pure in heart,
For they shall see our God ;
The secret of the Lord is theirs ;
Their soul is Christ's abode.

2 The Lord, Who left the heavens
Our life and peace to bring,
To dwell in lowliness with men
Their pattern and their King :

3 He to the lowly soul
Doth still Himself impart ;
And for His dwelling and His throne
Chooseth the pure in heart.

4 Lord, we Thy presence seek ;
May ours this blessing be;
Give us a pure and lowly heart,
A temple meet for Thee. Amen.

434 10s.

1 As pants the wearied hart for cooling springs,
That sinks exhausted in the summer's chase,
So pants my soul for Thee, great King of kings,
So thirsts to reach Thy sacred dwelling-place.

2 Lord, Thy sure mercies, ever in my sight,
My heart shall gladden through the tedious day;
And 'midst the dark and gloomy shades of night,
To Thee, my God, I'll tune the grateful lay.

3 Why faint, my soul ? why doubt Jehovah's aid ?
Thy God the God of mercy still shall prove;
Within His courts thy thanks shall yet be paid;
Unquestioned be His faithfulness and love.

435 7s.

1 Shepherd, with Thy tenderest love,
Guide me to Thy fold above;
Let me hear Thy gentle voice;
More and more in Thee rejoice;
From Thy fullness grace receive,
Ever in Thy Spirit live.

GENERAL.

2 Filled by Thee my cup o'erflows,
  For Thy love no limit knows;
  Guardian angels, ever nigh,
  Lead and draw my soul on high :
  Constant to my latest end,
  Thou my footsteps wilt attend.

3 Jesus, with Thy presence blest
  Death is life, and labor rest ;
  Guide me while I draw my breath;
  Guard me through the gate of death,
  And at last, oh, let me stand
  With the sheep at Thy right hand!
                Amen.

436   8.6.8.4.

1 The God of love my shepherd is,
  My gracious, constant guide;
  I shall not want, for I am His:
    In all supplied.

2 In His green pastures do I feed,
  And there lie down at will ;
  He leads me in my thirsty need
    By waters still.

3 His tenderness restores my soul,
  When sick and faint I roam ;
  Shows the right path and makes me whole,
    Bearing me home.

4 Yea! the dark valley when I tread
  No evil will I fear ;
  Thy rod and staff dispel my dread ;
    I feel Thee near.

5 Thou spread'st my table 'mid my foes ;
  The oil of grace is mine ;
  My cup with mercy overflows
    And love divine.

6 Goodness and mercy all my days
  My constant song shall be,
  Till heavenly anthems fill with praise
    Eternity.

437   8.7.

1 Guide me, O Thou great Jehovah,
  Pilgrim through this barren land,
  I am weak, but Thou art mighty;
  Hold me with Thy powerful hand.

2 Open now the crystal fountains
  Whence the living waters flow;
  Let the fiery, cloudy pillar
  Lead me all my journey through.

3 Feed me with the heavenly manna
  In this barren wilderness;
  Be my sword, and shield, and banner;
  Be the Lord my righteousness.

4 When I tread the verge of Jordan,
  Bid my anxious fears subside;
  Death of death, and hell's destruction,
  Land me safe on Canaan's side. Amen.

438   5.5.8.8.5.5.

1 Jesus, still lead on,
  Till our rest be won ;
  And, although the way be cheerless,
  We will follow calm and fearless;
    Guide us by Thy hand,
    To our Fatherland.

2 If the way be drear,
  If the foe be near,
  Let not faithless fears o'ertake us,
  Let not faith and hope forsake us;
    For through many a woe
    To our home we go.

3 When we seek relief
  From a long-felt grief :
  When temptations come alluring,
  Make us patient and enduring;
    Show us that bright shore
    Where we weep no more.

4 Jesus, still lead on,
  Till our rest be won ;
  Heavenly leader, still direct us,
  Still support, console, protect us,
    Till we safely stand
    In our Fatherland. Amen.

439   8.7.8.7.4.4.7.

1 Lead us, heavenly Father, lead us
  O'er the world's tempestuous sea;
  Guard us, guide us, keep us, feed us,
  For we have no help but Thee:
    Yet possessing
    Every blessing,
  If our God our Father be.

GENERAL.

2 Saviour, breathe forgiveness o'er us;
   All our weakness Thou dost know;
Thou didst tread this earth before us;
Thou didst feel its keenest woe;
   Lone and dreary,
   Faint and weary,
Through the desert Thou didst go.

3 Spirit of our God, descending,
   Fill our hearts with heavenly joy;
Love with every passion blending,
   Pleasure that can never cloy:
   Thus provided,
   Pardoned, guided,
Nothing can our peace destroy.

440   P.M.

1 Lead, kindly Light, amid the encircling gloom,
   Lead Thou me on !
The night is dark, and I am far from home,
   Lead Thou me on !
Keep Thou my feet ! I do not ask to see
The distant scene; one step enough for me.

2 I was not ever thus, nor prayed that Thou
   Shouldst lead me on ;
I loved to choose and see my path ; but now
   Lead Thou me on !
I loved the garish day; and, spite of fears,
Pride ruled my will : remember not past years.

3 So long Thy power has blest me, sure it still
   Will lead me on
O'er moor and fen, o'er crag and torrent, till
   The night is gone:
And with the morn those angel faces smile,
Which I have loved long since, and lost awhile.

441   C.M.

1 O very God of very God,
   And very Light of light,
Whose feet this earth's dark valley trod,
   That so it might be bright ;

2 Our hopes are weak, our fears are strong,
   Thick darkness blinds our eyes ;
Cold is the night ; Thy people long
   That Thou, their Sun, wouldst rise !

3 And even now, though dull and grey,
   The east is brightening fast,
And kindling to the perfect day,
   That never shall be past.

4 Oh, guide us till our path is done,
   And we have reached the shore
Where Thou, our everlasting Sun,
   Art shining evermore!

5 We wait in faith, and turn our face
   To where the daylight springs,
Till Thou shalt come our gloom to chase,
   With healing in Thy wings.

442   L.M.

1 O heavenly Word ! eternal Light !
   Begotten of the Father's might,
Who, in these latter days, art born
   For succor to a world forlorn ;

2 Our hearts enlighten from above,
   And kindle with Thine own true love;
That we, who hear Thy call to-day,
   May cast earth's vanities away.

3 And when as Judge Thou drawest nigh,
   The secrets of all hearts to try:
When sinners meet their awful doom,
   And saints attain their heavenly home;

4 Oh, let us not, for evil past,
   Be driven from Thy face at last ;
But with the blessèd evermore
   Behold Thee, love Thee, and adore.
                              Amen.

443   L.M.

1 All praise to Thee, eternal Lord,
   Who wore the garb of flesh and blood;
And chose a manger for Thy throne,
   While worlds on worlds were Thine alone.

2 Once did the skies before Thee bow;
   A virgin's arms contain Thee now;
While angels who in Thee rejoice
   Now listen for Thine infant voice.

3 A little child, Thou art our guest,
   That weary ones in Thee may rest:
Forlorn and lowly is Thy birth,
   That we may rise to heaven from earth.

GENERAL.

4 Thou comest in the darksome night
  To make us children of the light,
  To make us, in the realms divine,
  Like Thine own angels, round Thee shine.

5 All this for us Thy love hath done;
  By this to Thee our love is won;
  For this our joyful songs we raise,
  For this we sing Thee ceaseless praise.

444   7s.

1 Christ, Whose glory fills the skies,
  Christ, the true, the only light,
  Sun of Righteousness, arise!
  Triumph o'er the shades of night!
  Day-spring from on high, be near;
  Day-star, in our hearts appear.

2 Dark and cheerless is the morn
  Unillumined, Lord, by Thee;
  Joyless is the day's return,
  Till Thy mercy's beams we see;
  Till Thou inward light impart,
  Glad our eyes, and warm our heart.

3 Visit every soul of Thine!
  Pierce the gloom of sin and grief!
  Fill us, Radiancy divine!
  Scatter all our unbelief!
  More and more Thyself display,
  Shining to the perfect day! Amen.

445   L.M.

1 Lord of all being; throned afar,
  Thy glory flames from sun and star;
  Centre and soul of every sphere,
  Yet to each loving heart how near!

2 Sun of our life, Thy quickening ray
  Sheds on our path the glow of day;
  Star of our hope, Thy softened light
  Cheers the long watches of the night.

3 Our midnight is Thy smile withdrawn;
  Our noontide is Thy gracious dawn;
  Our rainbow arch, Thy mercy's sign;
  All, save the clouds of sin, are Thine!

4 Lord of all life, below, above,
  Whose light is truth, Whose warmth is love,
  Before Thy ever-blazing throne
  We ask no lustre of our own.

5 Grant us Thy truth to make us free,
  And kindling hearts that burn for Thee,
  Till all Thy living altars claim
  One holy light, one heavenly flame! Amen.

446   8.7.

1 God is love: His mercy brightens
  All the path in which we rove;
  Bliss He wakes and woe He lightens:
  God is wisdom, God is love.

2 Chance and change are busy ever;
  Man decays, and ages move;
  But His mercy waneth never;
  God is wisdom, God is love.

3 E'en the hour that darkest seemeth
  Will His changeless goodness prove;
  From the gloom His brightness streameth;
  God is wisdom, God is love.

4 He with earthly cares entwineth
  Hope and comfort from above;
  Everywhere His glory shineth;
  God is wisdom, God is love.

447   6s.

1 O love that casts out fear,
  O love that casts out sin,
  Tarry no more without,
  But come and dwell within!

2 True sunlight of the soul,
  Surround me as I go;
  So shall my way be safe,
  My feet no straying know.

3 Great love of God come in!
  Well-spring of heavenly peace;
  Thou Living Water, come!
  Spring up, and never cease.

4 Love of the living God,
  Of Father and of Son;
  Love of the Holy Ghost,
  Fill Thou each needy one. Amen.

448   L.M.

1 Jesus, Thou joy of loving hearts!
  Thou Fount of life! Thou Light of men!
  From the best bliss that earth imparts
  We turn unfilled to Thee again.

GENERAL.

2 Thy truth unchanged hath ever stood ;
  Thou savest those that on Thee call ;
  To them that seek Thee, Thou art good,
  To them that find Thee, all in all.

3 We taste Thee, O Thou living Bread!
  And long to feast upon Thee still ;
  We drink of Thee, the Fountain Head,
  And thirst from Thee our souls to fill.

4 Our restless spirits yearn for Thee,
  Where'er our changeful lot is cast ;
  Glad, when Thy gracious smile we see,
  Blest, when our faith can hold Thee fast.

5 O Jesus, ever with us stay!
  Make all our moments calm and bright!
  Chase the dark night of sin away!
  Shed o'er the world Thy holy light!
  Amen.

449 C.M.

1 How sweet the Name of Jesus sounds
  In a believer's ear!
  It soothes his sorrows, heals his wounds,
  And drives away his fear.

2 It makes the wounded spirit whole,
  And calms the troubled breast ;
  'Tis manna to the hungry soul,
  And to the weary rest.

3 Dear Name, the rock on which I build,
  My shield and hiding-place,
  My never-failing treasury, filled
  With boundless stores of grace.

4 Jesus! my Shepherd, Guardian, Friend,
  My Prophet, Priest, and King,
  My Lord, my Life, my Way, my End,
  Accept the praise I bring.

5 Weak is the effort of my heart,
  And cold my warmest thought :
  But when I see Thee as Thou art,
  I'll praise Thee as I ought.

6 Till then I would Thy love proclaim
  With every fleeting breath ;
  And may the music of Thy Name
  Refresh my soul in death. Amen.

450 C.M.

1 Jesus, the very thought of Thee
  With sweetness fills the breast ;
  But sweeter far Thy face to see,
  And in Thy presence rest.

2 No voice can sing, no heart can frame,
  Nor can the memory find,
  A sweeter sound than Jesus' Name,
  The Saviour of mankind.

3 O hope of every contrite heart,
  O joy of all the meek,
  To those who fall, how kind Thou art !
  How good to those who seek !

4 But what to those who find? Ah ! this
  Nor tongue nor pen can show ;
  The love of Jesus, what it is
  None but His loved ones know.

5 Jesus, our only joy be Thou,
  As Thou our prize wilt be ;
  In Thee be all our glory now,
  And through eternity. Amen.

451 C.M.

1 O Jesus, King most wonderful!
  Thou Conqueror renowned!
  O Christ, Thou true Anointed One,
  In Whom all joys are found !

2 When once Thou visitest the heart,
  Then truth begins to shine,
  Then earthly vanities depart,
  Then kindles love divine.

3 O Jesus, Light of all below!
  Thou Fount of living fire!
  Surpassing all the joys we know,
  And all we can desire ;

4 May every heart confess Thy Name,
  And ever Thee adore ;
  And, seeking Thee, itself inflame
  To seek Thee more and more.

5 Thee may our tongues for ever bless ;
  Thee may we love alone ;
  And ever in our lives express
  The image of Thine own.

GENERAL.

6 To Thee, our Light, our Life, our Lord,
All praise and glory be;
Thy Name for ever be adored,
Through all eternity. Amen.

452 C.M.

1 O Jesus, Thou the beauty art
Of angel-worlds above!
Thy Name is music to the heart,
Inflaming it with love.

2 Celestial sweetness unalloyed,
Who eat Thee hunger still ;
Who drink of Thee still feel a void,
Which only Thou canst fill.

3 O most sweet Jesus, hear the sighs
Which unto Thee we send!
To Thee our inmost spirit cries,
To Thee our prayers ascend.

4 Abide with us, and let Thy light
Shine, Lord, on every heart ;
Dispel the darkness of our night,
And joy to all impart.

5 Jesus, our Love and Joy, to Thee,
The Virgin's holy Son,
All might, and praise, and glory be,
While endless ages run. Amen.

453 C.M.

1 Eternal God ! we look to Thee,
To Thee for help we fly ;
Thine eye alone our wants can see,
Thy hand alone supply.

2 Lord ! let Thy fear within us dwell,
Thy love our footsteps guide:
That love will all vain love expel ;
That fear all fear beside.

3 Not what we wish, but what we want,
Oh, let Thy grace supply!
The good unasked in mercy grant ;
The ill, though asked, deny. Amen.

454 8.7.

1 Laboring and heavy laden,
Wanting help in time of need,
Fainting by the way from hunger,
"Bread of life!" on Thee we feed.

2 Thirsting for the springs of waters
That, by love's eternal law,
From the stricken Rock are flowing.
"Well of life!" from Thee we draw.

3 In the land of cloud and shadow,
Where no human eye can see,
Light to those who sit in darkness,
"Light of life!" we walk in Thee.

4 Thou the grace of life supplying,
Thou the crown of life wilt give;
Dead to sin, and daily dying,
"Life of life !" in Thee we live.

455 7.6.

1 'Come unto Me, ye weary,
And I will give you rest.'
Oh, blessèd voice of Jesus,
Which comes to hearts opprest!
It tells of benediction,
Of pardon, grace, and peace,
Of joy that hath no ending,
Of love which cannot cease.

2 'Come unto Me, ye wanderers,
And I will give you light.'
Oh, loving voice of Jesus,
Which comes to cheer the night !
Our hearts were filled with sadness,
And we had lost our way,
But morning brings us gladness,
And songs the break of day.

3 'Come unto Me, ye fainting,
And I will give you life.'
Oh, cheering voice of Jesus,
Which comes to aid our strife!
The foe is stern and eager,
The fight is fierce and long ;
But Thou hast made us mighty,
And stronger than the strong.

4 'And whosoever cometh,
I will not cast him out.'
Oh, welcome voice of Jesus,
Which drives away our doubt !
Which calls us, very sinners,
Unworthy though we be
Of love so free and boundless,
To come, O Lord, to Thee.

456 7.6.

1 O Lamb of God, still keep me
   Near to Thy wounded side!
   'Tis only there in safety
   And peace I can abide.
   What foes and snares surround me!
   What doubts and fears within!
   The grace that sought and found me,
   Alone can keep me clean.

2 'Tis only in Thee hiding,
   I feel my life secure;
   Only in Thee abiding,
   The conflict can endure:

   Thine arm the victory gaineth
   O'er every hateful foe;
   Thy love my heart sustaineth
   In all its care and woe.

3 Soon shall my eyes behold Thee,
   With rapture, face to face;
   One half hath not been told me
   Of all Thy power and grace:

   Thy beauty, Lord, and glory,
   The wonders of Thy love,
   Shall be the endless story
   Of all Thy saints above.

457 8.7.

1 Hail, Thou once-despised Jesus!
   Hail, Thou Galilean King!
   Thou didst suffer to release us:
   Thou didst free salvation bring.

   Hail, Thou agonizing Saviour,
   Bearer of our sin and shame!
   By Thy merit we find favor:
   Life is given through Thy Name.

2 Paschal Lamb, by God appointed,
   All our sins were on Thee laid:
   By almighty love anointed,
   Thou hast full atonement made.

   All Thy people are forgiven
   Through the virtue of Thy blood:
   Opened is the gate of heaven,
   Peace is made 'twixt man and God.

3 Jesus, hail! enthroned in glory,
   There for ever to abide,
   All the heavenly hosts adore Thee,
   Seated at Thy Father's side.

   There for sinners Thou art pleading:
   There Thou dost our place prepare:
   Ever for us interceding,
   Till in glory we appear.

4 Worship, honor, power, and blessing
   Thou art worthy to receive:
   Loudest praises, without ceasing,
   Meet it is for us to give.

   Help, ye bright angelic spirits!
   Bring your sweetest, noblest lays!
   Help to sing our Saviour's merits!
   Help to chant Emmanuel's praise!

458 8.7.

1 Alleluia! sing to Jesus!
   His the sceptre, His the throne;
   Alleluia! His the triumph,
   His the victory alone;
   Hark! the songs of peaceful Sion
   Thunder like a mighty flood;
   Jesus out of every nation
   Hath redeemed us by His blood.

2 Alleluia! not as orphans
   Are we left in sorrow now;
   Alleluia! He is near us,
   Faith believes, nor questions how:
   Though the cloud from sight received Him,
   When the forty days were o'er;
   Shall our hearts forget His promise,
   'I am with you evermore'?

3 Alleluia! Bread of angels,
   Thou on earth our Food, our Stay!
   Alleluia! here the sinful
   Flee to Thee from day to day;
   Intercessor, Friend of sinners,
   Earth's Redeemer, plead for me,
   Where the songs of all the sinless
   Sweep across the crystal sea.

4 Alleluia! King eternal,
   Thee the Lord of lords we own;
   Alleluia! born of Mary,
   Earth Thy footstool, heaven Thy throne:
   Thou within the veil hast entered,
   Robed in flesh, our great High Priest;
   Thou on earth both Priest and Victim
   In the Eucharistic feast.

GENERAL.

5 Alleluia! sing to Jesus!
  His the scepter, His the throne;
  Alleluia! His the triumph,
  His the victory alone;
Hark! the songs of peaceful Sion
  Thunder like a mighty flood;
  Jesus out of every nation
  Hath redeemed us by His blood.

459　　　　　　6.6.4.6.6.6.4.

1 Jesus, our risen King,
  Glory to Thee we sing,
    Praising Thy Name:
  Thy love and grace adore,
  Which all our sorrows bore;
    Singing for evermore,
    'Worthy the Lamb.'

2 O haste, ye ransomed race!
  For all His gifts of grace
    Praise ye His Name:
  He wondrous things hath done;
  Triumph o'er death hath won;
    Heaven's gate hath open thrown;
    'Worthy the Lamb.'

3 Come, all ye hosts above!
  Join in one song of love,
    Praising His Name:
  To Him ascribèd be
  Honor and majesty
    Through all eternity:
    'Worthy the Lamb.'

4 Blessèd and holy Three,
  Glorious Trinity,
    Praise to Thy Name:
  Father, Thy love we bless;
  Spirit of holiness,
    Thee we praise, and confess,
    'Worthy the Lamb.' Amen.

460　　　　　　S. M.

1 Awake, and sing the song
    Of glory to the Lamb!
  Wake every heart and every tongue
    To praise the Saviour's Name.

2 Sing of His dying love!
    Sing of His rising power!
  Sing how He intercedes above
    For those whose sins He bore!

138

3 Sing on your heavenly way!
    Ye ransomed sinners, sing!
  Sing on, rejoicing every day
    In Christ, the eternal King!

4 Soon shall ye hear Him say,
    "Ye blessèd children, come:'
  Soon will He call you hence away,
    And take His wanderers home.

5 There shall our raptured tongue
    His endless praise proclaim,
  And sweeter voices swell the song
    Of glory to the Lamb.

461　　　　　　7s.

1 Sing, my soul, His wondrous love,
  Who, from yon bright throne above,
  Ever watchful o'er our race,
  Still to man extends His grace.

2 Heaven and earth by Him were made;
  All is by His scepter swayed;
  What are we that He should show
  So much love to us below?

3 God, the merciful and good,
  Bought us with the Saviour's blood;
  And, to make our safety sure,
  Guides us by His Spirit pure.

4 Sing, my soul, adore His Name!
  Let His glory be thy theme:
  Praise Him till He calls thee home;
  Trust His love for all to come.

462　　　　　　L. M.

1 Come, magnify the Saviour's love!
  Come, praise our great Redeemer's Name!
  Who left the Father's throne above,
  And stooped for us to death and shame.

2 At God's right hand exalted now,
  With glory, majesty, and power,
  Let every knee before Him bow,
  And every tongue His Name adore.

3 Thy lowly spirit, Lord, impart,
  With holy fear our bosoms fill;
  Oh, give the meek, obedient heart,
  To suffer and to do Thy will!

GENERAL.

4 Thy cross, blest Saviour, may we bear;
  Mark the example Thou hast given;
  Follow in all Thy footsteps here;
  Rise to Thy glorious rest in heaven.
                  Amen.

463　　　　　　　　　　8.7.

1 Saviour, source of every blessing,
  Tune my heart to grateful lays:
  Streams of mercy, never ceasing,
  Call for ceaseless songs of praise.

2 Teach me some melodious measure,
  Sung by raptured saints above;
  Fill my soul with sacred pleasure,
  While I sing redeeming love.

3 Thou didst seek me when a stranger,
  Wandering from the fold of God;
  Thou to save my soul from danger,
  Didst redeem me with Thy blood.

4 By Thy hand restored, defended,
  Safe through life thus far I've come;
  Safe, O Lord, when life is ended.
  Bring me to my heavenly home. Amen.

464　　　　　　　　　　7.6.

1 O Saviour, precious Saviour,
  Whom yet unseen we love!
  O Name of might and favor,
  All other names above!
  We worship Thee, we bless Thee,
  To Thee alone we sing;
  We praise Thee, and confess Thee
  Our holy Lord and King.

2 O bringer of salvation,
  Who wondrously hast wrought,
  Thyself the revelation
  Of love beyond our thought;
  We worship Thee, we bless Thee,
  To Thee alone we sing;
  We praise Thee, and confess Thee
  Our gracious Lord and King.

3 In Thee all fulness dwelleth,
  All grace and power divine;
  The glory that excelleth,
  O Son of God, is Thine;
  We worship Thee, we bless Thee,
  To Thee alone we sing;
  We praise Thee, and confess Thee
  Our glorious Lord and King.

4 Oh, grant the consummation
  Of this our song above
  In endless adoration,
  And everlasting love!
  Then shall we praise and bless Thee
  Where perfect praises ring,
  And evermore confess Thee
  Our Saviour and our King.

465　　　　　　　　8.8.8.8.11.

1 Hosanna to the living Lord!
  Hosanna to the incarnate Word!
  To Christ, Creator, Saviour, King,
  Let earth, let heaven, Hosanna sing!
    Hosanna, Lord! Hosanna in the highest!

2 Hosanna, Lord! Thine angels cry;
  Hosanna, Lord! Thy saints reply;
  Above, beneath us, and around,
  The dead and living swell the sound;
    Hosanna, Lord! Hosanna in the highest!

3 O Saviour, with protecting care,
  Return to this Thy house of prayer;
  Assembled in Thy sacred Name,
  Where we Thy parting promise claim:
    Hosanna, Lord! Hosanna in the highest!

4 But, chiefest, in our cleansèd breast,
  Eternal! bid Thy Spirit rest;
  And make our secret soul to be
  A temple pure, and worthy Thee.
    Hosanna, Lord! Hosanna in the highest!

5 So in the last and dreadful day,
  When earth and heaven shall melt away,
  Thy flock, redeemed from sinful stain,
  Shall swell the sound of praise again.
    Hosanna, Lord! Hosanna in the highest!

466　　　　　　　　　　C.M.

1 Come, let us join our cheerful songs
  With angels round the throne!
  Ten thousand thousand are their tongues,
  But all their joys are one.

2 'Worthy the Lamb that died,' they cry,
  'To be exalted thus:'
  'Worthy the Lamb,' our lips reply,
  For He was slain for us.

GENERAL.

3 Jesus is worthy to receive
  Honor and power divine;
  And blessings more than we can give,
  Be, Lord, for ever Thine.

4 Let all that dwell above the sky,
  And air, and earth, and seas,
  Conspire to lift Thy glories high,
  And speak Thine endless praise!

5 The whole creation join in one
  To bless the sacred Name
  Of Him that sits upon the throne,
  And to adore the Lamb.

467 C.M.

1 Thou, God, all glory, honor, power,
  Art worthy to receive;
  Since all things by Thy power were made,
  And by Thy bounty live.

2 And worthy is the Lamb all power,
  Honor, and wealth to gain,
  Glory and strength; Who for our sins
  A sacrifice was slain.

3 All worthy Thou, Who hast redeemed
  And ransomed us to God,
  From every nation, every coast,
  By Thy most precious blood.

4 Blessing and honor, glory, power,
  By all in earth and heaven,
  To Him that sits upon the throne,
  And to the Lamb, be given. Amen.

468 L.M.

1 Come, let us sing the song of songs!
  The saints in heaven began the strain:
  The homage which to Christ belongs:
  " Worthy the Lamb, for He was slain!"

2 Slain to redeem us by His blood,
  To cleanse from every sinful stain,
  And make us kings and priests to God:
  " Worthy the Lamb, for He was slain!"

3 To Him Who suffered on the tree,
  Our souls, at His soul's price, to gain,
  Blessing, and praise, and glory be:
  " Worthy the Lamb, for He was slain!"

4 To Him, enthroned by filial right,
  All power in heaven and earth proclaim,
  Honor, and majesty, and might;
  " Worthy the Lamb, for He was slain!"

5 Long as we live, and when we die,
  And while in heaven with Him we reign;
  This song, our song of songs shall be:
  " Worthy the Lamb, for He was slain!"

469 C.M.

1 All hail the power of Jesus' Name!
  Let angels prostrate fall;
  Bring forth the royal diadem,
  And crown Him Lord of all!

2 Crown Him, ye martyrs of our God,
  Who from His altar call;
  Praise Him, Whose blood-stained path ye trod,
  And crown Him Lord of all!

3 Hail Him, the Heir of David's line,
  Whom David, Lord did call;
  The God incarnate! Man divine!
  And crown Him Lord of all!

4 Ye seed of Israel's chosen race,
  Ye ransomed of the fall,
  Hail Him Who saves you by His grace,
  And crown Him Lord of all!

5 Sinners, whose love can ne'er forget
  The wormwood and the gall,
  Go, spread your trophies at His feet,
  And crown Him Lord of all!

6 Let every kindred, every tribe,
  Before Him prostrate fall!
  To Him all majesty ascribe,
  And crown Him Lord of all! Amen.

470 L.M.

1 O Christ, our King, Creator, Lord,
  Saviour of all who trust Thy word,
  To them who seek Thee ever near,
  Now to our praises bend Thine ear.

2 In Thy dear cross a grace is found,
  It flows from every streaming wound,
  Whose power our inbred sin controls,
  Breaks the firm bond and frees our souls.

GENERAL.

3 Thou didst create the stars of night,
  Yet Thou hast veiled in flesh Thy light ;
  Hast deigned a mortal form to wear,
  A mortal's painful lot to bear.

4 When Thou didst hang upon the tree,
  The quaking earth acknowledged Thee;
  When Thou didst there yield up Thy breath,
  The world grew dark as shades of death.

5 Now in the Father's glory high,
  Great Conqueror, never more to die.
  Us by Thy mighty power defend,
  And reign through ages without end.
                              Amen.

471   7s.

1 Children of the heavenly King,
  As ye journey, sweetly sing!
  Sing your Saviour's worthy praise,
  Glorious in His works and ways!

2 We are traveling home to God,
  In the way the fathers trod :
  They are happy now, and we
  Soon their happiness shall see.

3 Lift your eyes, ye sons of light !
  Sion's city is in sight :
  There our endless home shall be,
  There our Lord we soon shall see.

4 Fear not, brethren ! Joyful stand
  On the borders of your land ;
  Jesus Christ, your Father's Son,
  Bids you undismayed go on.

5 Lord, obediently we go,
  Gladly leaving all below ;
  Only Thou our leader be,
  And we still will follow Thee.

472   8.7.8.7.8.7.

1 Praise, my soul, the King of heaven ;
  To His feet Thy tribute bring;
  Ransomed, healed, restored, forgiven,
  Evermore His praises sing:
    Alleluia! Alleluia!
  Praise the everlasting King.

2 Praise Him for His grace and favor
  To our fathers in distress;
  Praise Him still the same as ever,
  Slow to chide, and swift to bless:
    Alleluia! Alleluia!
  Glorious in His faithfulness.

3 Father-like He tends and spares us;
  Well our feeble frame He knows;
  In His hands He gently bears us,
  Rescues us from all our foes.
    Alleluia! Alleluia!
  Widely yet His mercy flows.

4 Angels in the height adore Him !
  Ye behold Him face to face;
  Saints triumphant bow before Him !
  Gathered in from every race.
    Alleluia! Alleluia!
  Praise with us the God of grace.

473   L. M.

1 Lift up your heads, ye mighty gates !
  Behold, the King of glory waits;
  The King of kings is drawing near;
  The Saviour of the world is here.

2 The Lord is just, a helper tried ;
  Mercy is ever at His side;
  His kingly crown is holiness;
  His scepter, pity in distress.

3 Oh, blest the land, the city blest,
  Where Christ the Ruler is confessed !
  Oh, happy hearts and happy homes
  To whom this King of triumph comes!

4 Fling wide the portals of your heart !
  Make it a temple, set apart
  From earthly use for heaven's employ,
  Adorned with prayer and love and joy.

5 Redeemer, come! I open wide
  My heart to Thee; here, Lord, abide!
  Let me Thy inner presence feel:
  Thy grace and love in me reveal.

6 So come, my Sovereign ! enter in!
  Let new and nobler life begin!
  Thy Holy Spirit guide us on,
  Until the glorious crown be won !
                              Amen.

474   C.C.6.6.8.8.

1   Rejoice, the Lord is King!
    Your Lord and King adore!
    Mortals, give thanks and sing,
    And triumph evermore;
  Lift up your heart ! lift up your voice!
  Rejoice ! again I say, rejoice!

2 Jesus the Saviour reigns,
　The God of truth and love;
　When He had purged our stains,
　He took His seat above.
Lift up your heart ! lift up your voice!
Rejoice ! again I say, rejoice!

3 He sits at God's right hand,
　Till all His foes submit,
　And bow to His command,
　And fall beneath His feet.
Lift up your heart ! lift up your voice!
Rejoice ! again I say, rejoice!

4 Rejoice in glorious hope!
　Jesus the Judge shall come,
　And take His servants up
　To their eternal home.
We soon shall hear the archangel's voice;
The trump of God shall sound: Rejoice!

475 L.M.

1 The Lord is King ! He wrought His will
　In heaven above, and earth below;
　His wonders the wide ocean fill,
　The caverned deeps His judgment show.

2 The Lord is King ! The word stands fast :
　Nature abides, for He is strong ;
　The perfect note He gave, shall last
　Till cadence of her even-song.

3 The Lord is King ! Ye worlds, rejoice!
　The waves of power, that from His shrine
　Thrill out in silence, have no choice:
　They harm not till He gives the sign.

4 The Lord is King ! Hush, wayward heart !
　Earth's wisdom fails, earth's daring faints.
　There seek Him whence He ne'er departs,
　And own Him greatest in His saints.

5 Thou, Lord, art King ! Crowned priests are we,
　To cast our crowns before the throne:
　By us the creature worships Thee,
　Yet we but bring Thee of Thine own.

6 To the great Maker, to the Son,
　Himself vouchsafing to be made,
　To the good Spirit, Three in One,
　All praise by all His works be paid.
　　　　　　　　　　　Amen.

142

476 L.M.

1 The Lord is King ! Lift up your voice,
　O earth, and all ye heavens, rejoice!
　From world to world the joy shall ring,
　The Lord omnipotent is King.

2 The Lord is King ! Who then shall dare
　Resist His will, distrust His care,
　Or murmur at His wise decrees,
　Or doubt His royal promises?

3 He reigns ! Ye saints, exalt your strains!
　Your God is King, your Father reigns ;
　And He is at the Father's side,
　The Man of love, the Crucified.

4 Come, make your wants, your burdens known!
　He will present them at the throne;
　And angel bands are waiting there
　His messages of love to bear.

5 Oh, when His wisdom can mistake,
　His might decay, His love forsake;
　Then may His children cease to sing,
　The Lord omnipotent is King !

477 8.7.8.7.8.8.7.

1 Sing praise to God Who reigns above,
　The God of all creation,
　The God of power, the God of love,
　The God of our salvation ;
　With healing balm my soul He fills,
　And every faithless murmur stills:
　　To God all praise and glory.

2 The angel host, O King of kings,
　Thy praise for ever telling,
　In earth and sky all living things
　Beneath Thy shadow dwelling,
　Adore the wisdom which could span,
　And power which formed creation's plan :
　　To God all praise and glory.

3 What God's almighty power hath made
　His gracious mercy keepeth ;
　By morning glow or evening shade
　His watchful eye ne'er sleepeth ;
　Within the kingdom of His might
　Lo! all is just and all is right :
　　To God all praise and glory.

GENERAL.

4 The Lord is never far away,
   But, through all grief distressing,
   An ever-present help and stay.
   Our peace and joy and blessing ;
   As with a mother's tender hand,
   He leads His own, His chosen band ;
   To God all praise and glory.

5 Thus all my toilsome way along
   I sing aloud Thy praises.
   That men may hear the grateful song
   My voice unwearied raises :
   Be joyful in the Lord, my heart ;
   Both soul and body bear your part ;
   To God all praise and glory. Amen.

478 P.M.

1 The God of Abraham praise,
   Who reigns enthroned above;
   Ancient of everlasting days,
   And God of love;
   Jehovah, great I AM,
   By earth and heaven confessed ;
   I bow and bless the sacred Name,
   For ever blest.

2 He by Himself hath sworn,
   I on His oath depend,
   I shall, on angel-wings upborne,
   To heaven ascend :
   I shall behold His face,
   I shall His power adore,
   And sing the wonders of His grace
   For evermore.

3 There dwells the Lord, our King,
   The Lord, our Righteousness,
   Triumphant o'er the world and sin,
   The Prince of Peace ;
   On Sion's sacred height
   His kingdom He maintains,
   And, glorious with His saints in light,
   For ever reigns.

4 The whole triumphant host
   Give thanks to God on high ;
   Hail, Father, Son, and Holy Ghost !
   They ever cry:
   Hail, Abraham's God and mine !
   I join the heavenly lays ;
   All might and majesty are Thine,
   And endless praise. Amen.

479 P.M.

1 God the all-terrible! King, Who ordainest
   Great winds Thy clarions, lightnings Thy
     sword ;
   Show forth Thy pity on high where Thou
     reignest :
   Grant to us peace, O most merciful Lord.

2 God the omnipotent ! mighty Avenger!
   Watching invisible, judging unheard ;
   Doom us not now in the hour of danger ;
   Grant to us peace, O most merciful Lord.

3 God the all-merciful ! earth hath forsaken
   Thy ways of blessedness, slighted Thy
     word ;
   Bid not Thy wrath in its terrors awaken :
   Grant to us peace, O most merciful Lord.

4 So shall Thy children, in thankful devotion,
   Praise Him Who saved them from peril
     and sword,
   Singing in chorus from ocean to ocean,
   Peace to the nations, and praise to the
     Lord.

480 10.10.11.11.

1 Oh, worship the King, all glorious above !
   Oh, gratefully sing His power and His
     love !
   Our shield and defender, the Ancient of
     days,
   Pavilioned in splendor, and girded with
     praise.

2 Oh, tell of His might! Oh, sing of His
     grace !
   Whose robe is the light ; whose canopy,
     space.
   His chariots of wrath the deep thunder-
     clouds form,
   And dark is His path on the wings of the
     storm.

3 Frail children of dust, and feeble as frail,
   In Thee do we trust, nor find Thee to fail ;
   Thy mercies, how tender ! how firm to the
     end !
   Our Maker, Defender, Redeemer, and
     Friend !

GENERAL.

4 O measureless might! ineffable love!
  While angels delight to hymn Thee above,
  The humbler creation, though feeble their lays,
  With true adoration shall lisp to Thy praise.

481   P. M.

1 The strain upraise of joy and praise,   Alleluia!
  To the glory of their King
  Shall the ransomed people sing,   Alleluia!
  And the choirs that dwell on high
  Shall re-echo through the sky   Alleluia!

2 They in the rest of Paradise who dwell,
  The blessèd ones with joy the chorus swell,   Alleluia!
  The planets beaming on their heavenly way,
  The shining constellations, join and say   Alleluia!

3   Ye clouds that onward sweep,
    Ye winds on pinions light,
    Ye thunders, echoing loud and deep,
    Ye lightnings, wildly bright,
  In sweet consent unite your   Alleluia!

4   Ye floods and ocean billows,
    Ye storms and winter snow,
    Ye days of cloudless beauty,
    Hoar frost and summer glow;
    Ye groves that wave in spring,
  And glorious forests, sing   Alleluia!

5 First let the birds, with painted plumage gay,
  Exalt their great Creator's praise, and say   Alleluia!
  Then let the beasts of earth, with varying strain,
  Join in creation's hymn, and cry again   Alleluia!

6 Here let the mountains thunder forth sonorous   Alleluia!
  There let the valleys sing in gentler chorus   Alleluia!
  Thou jubilant abyss of ocean cry   Alleluia!
  Ye tracts of earth and continents, reply   Alleluia!

7 To God, Who all creation made,
  The frequent hymn be duly paid: Alleluia!
  This is the strain, the eternal strain, the Lord almighty loves: Alleluia!

8 This is the song, the heavenly song, that Christ, the King, approves: Alleluia!
  Wherefore we sing, both heart and voice awaking.   Alleluia!
  And children's voices echo, answer making.   Alleluia!

9 Now from all men be outpoured
  Alleluia to the Lord;
  With Alleluia evermore
  The Son and Spirit we adore.
  Praise be done to the Three in One,
  Alleluia! Alleluia! Alleluia! Amen.

482   P. M.

1 Sing Alleluia forth in duteous praise,
  O citizens of heaven; and sweetly raise
      An endless Alleluia.

2 Ye Powers, who stand before the eternal Light,
  In hymning choirs re-echo to the height
      An endless Alleluia.

3 The holy city shall take up your strain,
  And with glad songs resounding wake again
      An endless Alleluia.

4 In blissful antiphons ye thus rejoice
  To render to the Lord with thankful voice
      An endless Alleluia.

5 Ye who have gained at length your palms in bliss,
  Victorious ones, your chant shall still be this,
      An endless Alleluia.

6 There, in one grand acclaim, for ever ring
  The strains which tell the honor of your King,
      An endless Alleluia.

7 This is the rest for weary ones brought back;
  This is the food and drink which none shall lack;
      An endless Alleluia.

8 While Thee, by Whom were all things made, we praise
  For ever, and tell out in sweetest lays
      An endless Alleluia.

9 Almighty Christ, to Thee our voices sing
  Glory for evermore; to Thee we bring
      An endless Alleluia.

GENERAL.

483 L. M.

1 All praise to Him Who built the hills;
 All praise to Him the streams Who fills;
 All praise to Him Who lights each star
 That sparkles in the blue afar.

2 All praise to Him Who makes the morn,
 And bids it glow with beams new-born;
 Who draws the shadows of the night,
 Like curtains, o'er our wearied sight.

3 All praise to Him Whose love hath given,
 In Christ His Son, the Life of heaven;
 Who gives us, for our darkness, light,
 And turns to day our deepest night.

4 All praise to Him in love Who came,
 To bear our woe, and sin, and shame;
 Who lived to die, Who died to rise,
 The all-prevailing sacrifice.

5 All praise to Him Who sheds abroad
 Within our hearts the love of God:
 The Spirit of all truth and peace,
 The fount of joy and holiness.

6 To Father, Son, and Spirit now
 Our hands we lift, our knees we bow;
 To Thee, blest Trinity, we raise,
 E'en here, in exile, songs of praise. Amen.

484 7s.

1 For the beauty of the earth,
 For the beauty of the skies,
 For the love which from our birth
 Over and around us lies;
 Christ, our God, to Thee we raise
 This our hymn of grateful praise.

2 For the beauty of each hour
 Of the day and of the night,
 Hill and vale, and tree and flower,
 Sun and moon and stars of light:
 Christ, our God, to Thee we raise
 This our hymn of grateful praise.

3 For the joy of ear and eye,
 For the heart and mind's delight,
 For the mystic harmony
 Linking sense to sound and sight:
 Christ, our God, to Thee we raise
 This our hymn of grateful praise.

4 For the joy of human love,
 Brother, sister, parent, child,
 Friends on earth, and friends above,
 For all gentle thoughts and mild:
 Christ, our God, to Thee we raise
 This our hymn of grateful praise.

5 For Thyself, best gift divine!
 To our race so freely given;
 For that great, great love of Thine,
 Peace on earth, and joy in heaven:
 Christ, our God, to Thee we raise
 This our hymn of grateful praise.

485 8.7.8.7.4.7.

1 God is love; that anthem olden
 Sing the glorious orbs of light,
 In their language glad and golden
 Telling to us, day and night,
 Their great story,
 God is love, and God is might.

2 And the teeming earth rejoices
 In that message from above,
 With ten thousand thousand voices
 Telling back, from hill and grove,
 Her glad story,
 God is might, and God is love.

3 Through these anthems of creation,
 Struggling up with gentle strife,
 Christian songs of Christ's salvation
 To the world, with blessings rife,
 Tell their story,
 God is love, and God is life.

4 Up to Him let each affection
 Daily rise, and round Him move;
 Our whole lives, one resurrection
 To the life of life above;
 Their glad story,
 God is life, and God is love.

486 8.7.

1 God, my King, Thy might confessing,
 Ever will I bless Thy Name;
 Day by day Thy throne addressing,
 Still will I Thy praise proclaim.

2 Honor great our God befitteth;
 Who His majesty can reach?
 Age to age His works transmitteth,
 Age to age His power shall teach.

GENERAL.

3 They shall talk of all Thy glory,
  On Thy might and greatness dwell,
  Speak of Thy dread acts the story,
  And Thy deeds of wonder tell.

4 Nor shall fail from memory's treasure,
  Works by love and mercy wrought,
  Works of love surpassing measure,
  Works of mercy passing thought.

5 Full of kindness and compassion,
  Slow to anger, vast in love,
  God is good to all creation;
  All His works His goodness prove.

6 All Thy works, O Lord, shall bless Thee,
  Thee shall all Thy saints adore;
  King supreme shall they confess Thee,
  And proclaim Thy sovereign power.

487   P.M.

1 Now thank we all our God,
  With heart and hands and voices!
  Who wondrous things hath done,
  In Whom His world rejoices;
  Who from our mother's arms
  Hath blessed us on our way
  With countless gifts of love;
  And still is ours to-day.

2 Oh, may this bounteous God
  Through all our life be near us!
  With ever joyful hearts
  And blessed peace to cheer us;
  And keep us in His grace,
  And guide us when perplexed,
  And free us from all ills
  In this world and the next. Amen.

488   8.7.

1 Praise the Lord! ye heavens, adore Him,
  Praise Him, angels, in the height;
  Sun and moon, rejoice before Him,
  Praise Him, all ye stars and light:

2 Praise the Lord! for He hath spoken;
  Worlds His mighty voice obeyed;
  Laws, which never shall be broken,
  For their guidance He hath made.

3 Praise the Lord! for He is glorious;
  Never shall His promise fail;
  God hath made His saints victorious,
  Sin and death shall not prevail.

4 Praise the God of our salvation;
  Hosts on high, His power proclaim!
  Heaven and earth, and all creation,
  Laud and magnify His Name! Amen.

489   L.M.

1 All people that on earth do dwell,
  Sing to the Lord with cheerful voice;
  Him serve with fear, His praise forth tell,
  Come ye before Him and rejoice.

2 Know that the Lord is God indeed;
  Without our aid He did us make;
  We are His flock, He doth us feed,
  And for His sheep He doth us take.

3 Oh, enter then His gates with praise,
  Approach with joy his courts unto;
  Praise, laud, and bless His Name always,
  For it is seemly so to do.

4 For why? the Lord our God is good,
  His mercy is for ever sure;
  His truth at all times firmly stood,
  And shall from age to age endure.

490   L.M.

1 Before Jehovah's awful throne,
  Ye nations, bow with sacred joy;
  Know that the Lord is God alone;
  He can create, and He destroy.

2 His sovereign power without our aid,
  Made us of clay, and formed us men;
  And when like wandering sheep we strayed,
  He brought us to His fold again.

3 We are His people, we His care,
  Our souls, and all our mortal frame:
  What lasting honors shall we rear,
  Almighty Maker, to Thy Name!

4 We'll crowd Thy gates with thankful songs,
  High as the heaven our voices raise:
  And earth, with her ten thousand tongues,
  Shall fill Thy courts with sounding praise.

5 Wide as the world is Thy command,
  Vast as eternity Thy love;
  Firm as a rock Thy truth must stand,
  When rolling years shall cease to move.

GENERAL.

491 L.M.

1 Oh, come, loud anthems let us sing!
Loud thanks to our almighty King;
And high our grateful voices raise,
As our salvation's Rock we praise.

2 Into His presence let us haste
To thank Him for His favors past;
To Him address, in joyful songs,
The praise that to His Name belongs.

3 For God the Lord, enthroned in state,
Is with unrivalled glory great;
The depths of earth are in His hand,
Her secret wealth at His command.

4 Oh, let us to His courts repair,
And bow with adoration there!
Down on our knees devoutly all
Before the Lord our Maker fall!

492 L.M.

1 Oh, render thanks to God above,
The fountain of eternal love;
Whose mercy firm through ages past
Has stood, and shall for ever last.

2 Who can His mighty deeds express,
Not only vast, but numberless?
What mortal eloquence can raise
His tribute of immortal praise?

3 Extend to me that favor, Lord,
Thou to Thy chosen dost afford;
When Thou return'st to set them free,
Let Thy salvation visit me.

4 Let Israel's God be ever blest!
His name eternally confessed!
Let all His saints, with full accord,
For ever sing Praise ye the Lord!

493 S.M.

1 Oh, bless the Lord, my soul!
His grace to thee proclaim!
And all that is within me join
To bless His holy Name!

2 Oh, bless the Lord, my soul!
His mercies bear in mind!
Forget not all His benefits!
The Lord to thee is kind.

3 He will not always chide;
He will with patience wait;
His wrath is ever slow to rise,
And ready to abate.

4 He pardons all Thy sins;
Prolongs Thy feeble breath;
He healeth thine infirmities,
And ransoms thee from death.

5 He clothes thee with His love;
Upholds thee with His truth;
And like the eagle He renews
The vigor of thy youth.

6 Then bless His holy Name,
Whose grace hath made thee whole;
Whose loving-kindness crowns thy days!
Oh, bless the Lord, my soul!

494 7s.

1 Songs of praise the angels sang;
Heaven with alleluias rang,
When Jehovah's work begun,
When He spake and it was done.

2 Songs of praise awoke the morn,
When the Prince of Peace was born;
Songs of praise arose, when He
Captive led captivity.

3 Heaven and earth must pass away;
Songs of praise shall crown that day;
God will make new heavens and earth;
Songs of praise shall hail their birth.

4 And shall man alone be dumb
Till that glorious kingdom come?
No; the Church delights to raise
Psalms, and hymns, and songs of praise.

5 Saints below, with heart and voice,
Still in songs of praise rejoice;
Learning here, by faith and love,
Songs of praise to sing above.

6 Borne upon their latest breath,
Songs of praise shall conquer death;
Then, amidst eternal joy,
Songs of praise their powers employ.

GENERAL.

495 L. M.

1 From all that dwell below the skies
   Let the Creator's praise arise!
   Let the Redeemer's Name be sung
   Through every land, by every tongue!

2 Eternal are Thy mercies, Lord,
   And truth eternal is Thy word :
   Thy praise shall sound from shore to shore,
   Till suns shall rise and set no more.

496 8.8.8.4.

1 O Lord of heaven, and earth, and sea,
   To Thee all praise and glory be ;
   How shall we show our love to Thee,
   Who givest all ?

2 The golden sunshine, vernal air,
   Sweet flowers and fruits Thy love declare,
   Where harvests ripen, Thou art there,
   Who givest all !

3 For peaceful homes, and healthful days,
   For all the blessings earth displays.
   We owe Thee thankfulness and praise,
   Who givest all !

4 Thou didst not spare Thine only Son,
   But gav'st Him for a world undone,
   And freely with that blessèd One
   Thou givest all.

5 Thou giv'st the Holy Spirit's dower,
   Spirit of life, and love, and power,
   And dost His seven-fold graces shower
   Upon us all.

6 For souls redeemed, for sins forgiven,
   For means of grace and hopes of heaven,
   Father, what can to Thee be given,
   Who givest all ?

7 We lose what on ourselves we spend;
   We have as treasure without end
   Whatever, Lord, to Thee we lend,
   Who givest all.

8 Whatever, Lord, we lend to Thee
   Repaid a thousandfold will be;
   Then gladly will we give to Thee,
   Who givest all ;

148

9 To Thee, from Whom we all derive
   Our life, our gifts, our power to give;
   Oh, may we ever with Thee live,
   Who givest all ! Amen.

497 6.6.6.6.4.4.4.4.

1 Lord of the worlds above,
   How pleasant and how fair,
   The dwellings of Thy love,
   Thy earthly temples are!
     To Thine abode
     My heart aspires
     With warm desires
     To see my God.

2 O happy souls, that pray
   Where God appoints to hear !
   O happy men, that pay
   Their constant service there!
     They praise Thee still :
     And happy they
     That love the way
     To Sion's hill.

3 They go from strength to strength
   Through this dark vale of tears,
   Till each arrives at length,
   Till each in heaven appears:
     O glorious seat!
     When God our King
     Shall thither bring
     Our willing feet.

4 God is our sun and shield,
   Our light and our defence;
   With gifts His hands are filled,
   We draw our blessings thence:
     Thrice happy he,
     O God of hosts,
     Whose spirit trusts,
     Alone in Thee.

498 6.6.4.6.6.6.4.

1 Shepherd of tender youth,
   Guiding in love and truth
     Through devious ways;
   Christ our triumphant King,
   We come Thy Name to sing ;
   Hither our children bring
     Tributes of praise.

GENERAL.

2 Thou art our holy Lord,
   The all-subduing Word,
     Healer of strife:
   Thou didst Thyself abase,
   That from sin's deep disgrace
   Thou mightest save our race,
     And give us life.

3 Thou art the great High Priest;
   Thou hast prepared the feast
     Of heavenly love;
   While in our mortal pain
   None calls on Thee in vain;
   Help Thou dost not disdain,
     Help from above.

4 Ever be Thou our guide,
   Our shepherd and our pride,
     Our staff and song:
   Jesus, Thou Christ of God,
   By Thy perennial word
   Lead us where Thou hast trod,
     Make our faith strong.

5 So now, and till we die,
   Sound we Thy praises high,
     And joyful sing.
   Let all the holy throng
   Who to Thy Church belong,
   Unite and swell the song
     To Christ our King! Amen.

499 7s.

1 Pleasant are Thy courts above
   In the land of light and love;
  Pleasant are Thy courts below
   In this land of sin and woe.

  Oh, my spirit longs and faints
   For the converse of Thy saints,
  For the brightness of Thy face,
   For Thy fulness, God of grace!

2 Happy birds that sing and fly
   Round Thy altars, O Most High!
  Happier souls that find a rest
   In a heavenly Father's breast!

  Like the wandering dove, that found
  No repose on earth around,
  They can to their ark repair
  And enjoy it ever there.

3 Happy souls! Their praises flow
   Ever in this vale of woe:
  Waters in the desert rise,
  Manna feeds them from the skies:

  On they go from strength to strength
  Till they reach Thy throne at length,
  At Thy feet adoring fall.
  Who hast led them safe through all.

4 Lord! be mine this prize to win;
  Guide me through a world of sin;
  Keep me by Thy saving grace;
  Give me at Thy side a place.

  Sun and shield alike Thou art;
  Guide and guard my erring heart,
  Grace and glory flow from Thee;
  Shower, oh, shower them, Lord, on me!
      Amen.

500 8s.

1 Lo! God is here! let us adore,
   And own how dreadful is this place!
  Let all within us feel His power,
   And silent bow before His face!
  Who know His power, His grace who prove,
  Serve Him with awe, with reverence, love.

2 Lo! God is here! Whom day and night
   United choirs of angels sing:
  To Him, enthroned above all height,
   Heaven's host their noblest praises bring:
  Disdain not, Lord, our meaner song,
  Who praise Thee with a stammering tongue.

3 Being of beings, may our praise
   Thy courts with grateful fragrance fill;
  Still may we stand before Thy face,
   Still hear and do Thy sovereign will;
  To Thee may all our thoughts arise,
  Ceaseless, accepted sacrifice! Amen.

501 8.7.

1 Christ is made the sure foundation,
   Christ the head and corner-stone,
  Chosen of the Lord, and precious,
   Binding all the Church in one;
  Holy Sion's help for ever,
   And her confidence alone.

149

GENERAL.

2 All that dedicated city,
Dearly loved of God on high,
In exultant jubilation
Pours perpetual melody;
God the One in Three adoring
In glad hymns eternally.

3 To this temple, where we call Thee,
Come, O Lord of hosts, to-day;
With Thy wonted loving-kindness,
Hear Thy servants as they pray;
And Thy fullest benediction
Shed within its walls alway.

4 Here vouchsafe to all Thy servants
What they ask of Thee to gain,
What they gain from Thee, for ever
With the blessèd to retain,
And hereafter in Thy glory
Evermore with Thee to reign. Amen.

502 6s.

1 We love the place, O God,
Wherein Thine honor dwells;
The joy of Thine abode
All other joy excels.

2 We love the house of prayer,
Wherein Thy servants meet;
For Thou, O Lord, art there
Thy chosen ones to greet.

3 We love the sacred font,
Wherein the holy Dove
Bestows, as He is wont,
His blessing from above.

4 We love Thine altar, Lord,
Its mysteries revere;
For there in faith adored,
We find Thy presence near.

5 We love Thy holy word,
The lamp Thou gav'st to guide
All wanderers home, O Lord,
Home to their Father's side.

6 Then let us sing the love
To us so freely given,
Until we sing above
The triumph-song of heaven! Amen.

503 S. M.

1 I love Thy kingdom, Lord,
The house of Thine abode.
The Church our blest Redeemer saved
With His own precious blood.

2 For her my tears shall fall;
For her my prayers ascend;
To her my cares and toils be given,
Till toils and cares shall end.

3 Beyond my highest joy
I prize her heavenly ways,
Her sweet communion, solemn vows,
Her hymns of love and praise.

4 Jesus, Thou friend divine,
Our Saviour and our King,
Thy hand from every snare and foe
Shall great deliverance bring.

5 Sure as Thy truth shall last,
To Sion shall be given
The brightest glories earth can yield,
And brighter bliss of heaven.

504 8.7.

1 Glorious things of thee are spoken,
Sion, city of our God;
He, Whose word cannot be broken.
Formed thee for His own abode:
On the Rock of ages founded,
What can shake thy sure repose?
With salvation's walls surrounded,
Thou may'st smile at all thy foes.

2 See, the streams of living waters
Springing from eternal love,
Well supply thy sons and daughters,
And all fear of want remove.
Who can faint, when such a river
Ever will their thirst assuage?
Grace which, like the Lord the giver,
Never fails from age to age!

3 On their way, around them hovering,
Pillared cloud and fire appear
For a glory and a covering,
Showing that the Lord is near.
Thus they march, the pillar leading,
Light by night, and shade by day,
Daily on the manna feeding,
Which He gives them when they pray.

GENERAL.

4 Blest inhabitants of Sion,
  Washed in the Redeemer's blood !
Jesus, Whom their souls rely on,
  Makes them kings and priests to God.

'Tis His love His people raises
  Over self to reign as kings:
And as priests His solemn praises
  Each for a thank-offering brings.

505 8.7.

1 Praise the Rock of our salvation,
    Laud His Name from zone to zone;
  On that Rock the Church is builded,
    Christ Himself the corner-stone:

  Vain against our rock-built Sion
    Winds and waters, fire and hail;
  Christ is in her midst; against her
    Sin and hell shall not prevail.

2 Framed of living stones, cemented
    By the Spirit's unity,
  Based on prophets and apostles,
    Firm in faith, and stayed on Thee,

  May Thy Church, O Lord incarnate,
    Grow in grace, in peace, in love :
  Emblem of the heavenly Sion,
    Our eternal home above.

3 Where Thou reignest, King of glory,
    Throned in everlasting light,
  Midst Thy saints, no more is needed
    Sun by day, nor moon by night :

  Soon may we those portals enter
    When this earthly strife is o'er:
  There to dwell with saints and angels
    In Thy presence evermore.

4 Join we now the voice of triumph
    To the throne of glory sent,
  Alleluia, Alleluia,
    To the Lord omnipotent.

  Praise to Thee, eternal Father,
    Praise to Thee, eternal Son,
  Praise to Thee, eternal Spirit,
    While unending ages run. Amen.

506 7.6.

1 The Church's one foundation
    Is Jesus Christ her Lord ;
  She is His new creation
    By water and the word :

  From heaven He came and sought her
    To be His holy bride:
  With His own blood He bought her,
    And for her life He died.

2 Elect from every nation,
    Yet one o'er all the earth,
  Her charter of salvation,
    One Lord, one faith, one birth;
  One holy Name she blesses,
    Partakes one holy food,
  And to one hope she presses,
    With every grace endued.

3 Though with a scornful wonder
    Men see her sore opprest,
  By schisms rent asunder,
    By heresies distrest ;
  Yet saints their watch are keeping,
    Their cry goes up " How long ?"
  And soon the night of weeping
    Shall be the morn of song.

4 'Mid toil and tribulation,
    And tumult of her war
  She waits the consummation
    Of peace for evermore:
  Till with the vision glorious
    Her longing eyes are blest,
  And the great Church victorious
    Shall be the Church at rest.

5 Yet she on earth hath union
    With God the Three in One,
  And mystic sweet communion
    With those whose rest is won:
  O happy ones and holy!
    Lord, give us grace that we
  Like them, the meek and lowly,
    On high may dwell with Thee.
                               Amen.

507 L.M

1 O Holy Ghost, Thou God of peace,
    Pity Thy Church, now rent in twain;
  Bid wrath, and strife, and variance cease,
    And let us all be one again;

2 One with our brethren here in love,
    And one with saints that are at rest,
  And one with angel hosts above,
    And one with God for ever blest.

GENERAL.

3 Oh, make on earth all churches one,
　One with the blessèd gone before.
　All knit in sweet communion,
　To love Thee, worship, and adore.

4 For one the Lord on Whom we call,
　The Spirit one which He hath given,
　One God and Father of us all,
　One faith on earth, one hope of heaven.

508　　　　　　　　　　　　8.8.8.4.

1 Father of all, from land and sea
　The nations sing, 'Thine, Lord, are we,
　Countless in number, but in Thee
　　May we be one.'

2 O Son of God, Whose love so free
　For men did make Thee Man to be,
　United to our God in Thee
　　May we be one.

3 Thou, Lord, didst once for all atone:
　Thee may both Jew and Gentile own
　Of their two walls the Corner Stone,
　　Making them one.

4 Thou art the fountain of all good,
　Cleansing with Thy most precious blood,
　And feeding us with angels' food,
　　Making us one.

5 Join high and low, join young and old,
　In love that never waxes cold ;
　Under one Shepherd, in one fold,
　　Make us all one.

6 O Spirit blest, Who from above
　Cam'st gently gliding like a dove,
　Calm all our strife, give faith and love ;
　　Oh make us one!

7 O Trinity in Unity,
　One only God, in Persons Three,
　Dwell ever in our hearts ; like Thee
　　May we be one.

8 So, when the world shall pass away,
　May we awake with joy and say,
　'Now in the bliss of endless day
　　We all are one. Amen.

509　　　　　　　　　　　　C.M.

1 What time the evening shadows fall
　　Around the Church on earth,
　When darker forms of doubt appal,
　　And new false lights have birth ;
　Then closer should her faithful band
　　For truth together hold,
　Hell's last devices to withstand,
　　And safely guard her fold.

2 O Father, in that hour of fear
　　Fail not Thy Church to keep,
　Thy altar to the last to rear,
　　And feed Thy fainting sheep :
　May she the holy truths attest,
　　Apostles taught of yore,
　Nor quit the faith by saints confest,
　　But love it more and more.

3 O Christ, Who for Thy flock didst pray,
　　That all might be as one,
　Unite us all ere fades the day,
　　Thou sole-begotten Son :
　The East, the West, together bind
　　In love's unbroken chain ;
　Give each one hope, one heart, one mind,
　　One glory, and one gain.

4 O Spirit, Lord of light and life,
　　The Church with strength renew,
　Compose the angry voice of strife,
　　All jealousies subdue:
　Do Thou in ever-quickening streams
　　Upon Thy saints descend,
　And warm them with reviving beams,
　　And guide them to the end.

5 Great Three in One, great One in Three,
　　Our hymns of prayer receive,
　And teach us all from sin to flee,
　　And live as we believe:
　So, pure in faith, our thoughts and speech
　　And acts that faith shall own ;
　So shall we to Thy presence reach,
　　And know as we are known. Amen.

510　　　　　　　　　　　　11.11.11.5.

1 Lord of our life, and God of our salvation,
　Star of our night, and hope of every nation,
　Hear and receive Thy Church's supplication,
　　Lord God almighty.

2 See round Thine Ark the hungry billows
curling!
See how Thy foes their banners are unfurling!
Lord, while their darts envenomed they are
hurling,
   Thou canst preserve us.

3 Lord, Thou canst help when earthly armor
faileth;
Lord, Thou canst save when deadly sin as-
saileth;
Lord, o'er Thy Rock nor death nor hell pre-
vaileth;
   Grant us Thy peace, Lord!

4 Peace in our hearts, our evil thoughts as-
suaging,
Peace in Thy Church, where brothers are
engaging,
Peace, when the world its busy war is wag-
ing;
   Calm Thy foes raging!

5 Grant us Thy help till backward they are
driven;
Grant them Thy truth, that they may be
forgiven;
Grant peace on earth, and after we have
striven,
   Peace in Thy heaven. Amen.

511　　　　　　　　　　　　　L. M.

1 Almighty God, Whose only Son
O'er sin and death the triumph won,
And ever lives to intercede
For souls who Thy sweet mercy need;

2 In His dear Name to Thee we pray
For all who err and go astray,
For sinners, wheresoe'er they be,
Who do not serve and honor Thee.

3 And some within Thy sacred fold,
To holy things are dead and cold,
And waste the precious hours of life
In selfish ease, or toil, or strife;

4 And many a quickened soul within
There lurks the secret love of sin,
A wayward will, or anxious fears,
Or lingering taint of bygone years:

5 Oh, give repentance true and deep
To all Thy lost and wandering sheep!
And kindle in their hearts the fire
Of holy love and pure desire:

6 That so from angel hosts above
May rise a sweeter song of love,
And we, with all the blest, adore
Thy Name, O God, for evermore. Amen.

512　　　　　　　　　　　　　6s.

1 Thy kingdom come, O God!
Thy reign, O Christ, begin!
Break with Thine iron rod
The tyrannies of sin!

2 Where is Thy rule of peace,
And purity, and love?
When shall all hatred cease,
As in the realms above?

3 When comes the promised time
That war shall be no more,
Oppression, lust, and crime
Shall flee Thy face before?

4 We pray Thee, Lord, arise,
And come in Thy great might;
Revive our longing eyes,
Which languish for Thy sight.

5 O'er heathen lands afar
Thick darkness broodeth yet;
Arise, O morning Star,
Arise, and never set. Amen.

513　　　　　　　　　6.6.4.6.6.6.4.

1 Thou, Whose almighty word
Chaos and darkness heard,
   And took their flight;
Hear us, we humbly pray,
And, where the Gospel day
Sheds not its glorious ray,
   Let there be light!

2 Thou Who didst come to bring
On Thy redeeming wing
   Healing and sight,
Health to the sick in mind,
Sight to the inly-blind,
Oh, now, to all mankind,
   Let there be light!

3 Spirit of truth and love,
Life-giving, holy Dove,
Speed forth Thy flight!
Move on the waters' face,
Bearing the lamp of grace,
And, in earth's darkest place
Let there be light!

4 Holy and blessèd Three,
Glorious Trinity,
Wisdom, Love, Might;
Boundless as ocean's tide,
Rolling in fullest pride,
Through the world, far and wide,
Let there be light! Amen.

514 7s.

1 Hark! the song of Jubilee,
Loud as mighty thunders roar:
Or the fulness of the sea,
When it breaks upon the shore.

Alleluia! for the Lord
God omnipotent shall reign;
Alleluia! let the word
Echo round the earth and main.

2 Alleluia! Hark! the sound,
From the depths unto the skies,
Wakes above, beneath, around,
All creation's harmonies:

See Jehovah's banners furled;
Sheathed His sword; He speaks; 'tis done.
And the kingdoms of this world
Are the kingdoms of His Son.

3 He shall reign from pole to pole
With illimitable sway;
He shall reign, when, like a scroll,
Yonder heavens have passed away:

Then the end; beneath His rod
Man's last enemy shall fall;
Alleluia! Christ in God,
God in Christ is all in all. Amen.

515 6.6.6.6.8.8.

1 Blow ye the trumpet, blow!
The gladly solemn sound;
Let all the nations know,
To earth's remotest bound,
The year of Jubilee is come:
Return, ye ransomed sinners, home!

2 Jesus, our great High-Priest,
Hath full atonement made;
Ye weary spirits, rest!
Ye mournful souls, be glad!
The year of Jubilee is come;
Return, ye ransomed sinners, home!

3 Extol the Lamb of God!
The all-atoning Lamb;
Redemption in His blood
Throughout the world proclaim!
The year of Jubilee is come;
Return, ye ransomed sinners, home!

516 6.6.4 6.6.6.4.

1 Lord of all power and might,
Father of love and light,
Speed on Thy word!
Oh, let the Gospel sound
All the wide world around,
Wherever man is found!
God speed His word!

2 Hail, blessèd Jubilee!
Thine, Lord, the glory be;
Alleluia!
Thine was the mighty plan:
From Thee the work began;
Away with praise of man!
Glory to God!

3 Lo, what embattled foes,
Stern in their hate, oppose
God's holy word!
One for His truth we stand,
Strong in His own right hand,
Firm as a martyr-band:
God shield His word!

4 Onward shall be our course,
Despite of fraud or force;
God is before.
His words ere long shall run
Free as the noon-day sun;
His purpose must be done:
God bless His word! Amen.

517 7.6.

1 O brothers, lift your voices,
Triumphant songs to raise;
Till heaven on high rejoices,
And earth is filled with praise.

Ten thousand hearts are bounding
With holy hopes and free;
The Gospel trump is sounding,
The trump of Jubilee.

2 O Christian brothers, glorious
   Shall be the conflict's close:
   The cross hath been victorious,
   And shall be o'er its foes.
  Faith is our battle-token:
   Our Leader all controls;
   Our trophies, fetters broken;
   Our captives, ransomed souls.

3 Not unto us: Lord Jesus,
   To Thee all praise be due!
   Whose blood-bought mercy frees us,
   Has freed our brethren too.
  Not unto us: in glory
   The angels catch the strain,
   And cast their crowns before Thee
   Exultingly again.

4 Captain of our salvation,
   Thy presence we adore:
   Praise, glory, adoration
   Be Thine for evermore!
  Still on in conflict pressing
   On Thee Thy people call,
   Thee, King of kings confessing,
   Thee, crowning Lord of all. Amen.

518 S.M.

1 To bless Thy chosen race,
   In mercy, Lord, incline;
   And cause the brightness of Thy face
   On all Thy saints to shine;

2 That so Thy wondrous way
   May through the world be known;
   While distant lands their tribute pay,
   And Thy salvation own.

3 Oh, let them shout and sing,
   With joy and pious mirth!
   For Thou, the righteous Judge and King,
   Shalt govern all the earth.

4 Let differing nations join
   To celebrate Thy fame!
   Let all the world, O Lord, combine
   To praise Thy glorious Name!

5 Then God upon our land
   Shall constant blessings shower:
   And all the world in awe shall stand
   Of His resistless power.

519 S.M.

1 How beauteous are their feet,
   Who stand on Sion's hill;
   Who bring salvation on their tongues,
   And words of peace reveal!

2 How charming is their voice!
   How sweet their tidings are!
   'Sion, behold thy Saviour-King!
   He reigns and triumphs here.'

3 How happy are our ears
   That hear this joyful sound,
   Which kings and prophets waited for,
   And sought, but never found!

4 How blessèd are our eyes
   That see this heavenly light!
   Prophets and kings desired it long,
   But died without the sight.

5 The watchmen join their voice,
   And tuneful notes employ;
   Jerusalem breaks forth in songs,
   And deserts learn the joy.

6 The Lord makes bare His arm
   Through all the earth abroad;
   Let every nation now behold
   Their Saviour and their God.

520 8.8.7.8.8.7

1 Come, pure hearts, in sweetest measures
   Sing of those who spread the treasures
   In the holy gospels shrined!
   Blessèd tidings of salvation,
   Peace on earth their proclamation,
   Love from God to lost mankind.

2 See the rivers four that gladden
   With their streams the better Eden
   Planted by our Lord most dear;
   Christ the fountain, these the waters;
   Drink, O Sion's sons and daughters,
   Drink and find salvation here.

3 Oh, that we, Thy truth confessing,
   And Thy holy word possessing,
   Jesus, may Thy voice adore!
   Unto Thee our voices raising,
   Thee with all Thy ransomed praising,
   Ever and for evermore. Amen.

GENERAL.

521 C.M.

1 Upon the holy mount they stood
That wondrous, awful night;
They saw, and knew that it was good
To see that vision bright.

2 No man of sorrows stands there now;
But, keen as lightning-flame,
The streams of heavenly radiance flow
From that transfigured frame.

3 Beneath that mount another scene
They saw, when morning smiled:
A father, torn with anguish keen,
Sought mercy for his child.

4 No more the blaze of glistering light
Enwraps the form divine,
But tender love and healing might
Around Him softly shine.

5 He came from hours of rapture high
To care for human woe:
So angels from God's presence fly
To succor men below.

6 O Jesus, be our life like Thine;
Blest labor, doubly blest
By communings with things divine
Upon the mountain's crest.

7 Lord, we would pass from hours of prayer,
That lift our souls above,
To go where want and sorrow are
With lowly deeds of love.

8 Let no self-will within us lurk,
Nor faithless sloth be there;
But prayer give life to all our work,
And work crown all our prayer.
Amen.

522 8.7.

1 All unseen the Master walketh
By the toiling servant's side;
Comfortable words He speaketh,
While His hands uphold and guide.

2 Grief nor pain nor any sorrow
Rends thy heart, to Him unknown;
He to-day, and He to-morrow,
Grace sufficient gives His own.

3 Holy strivings nerve and strengthen;
Long endurance wins the crown;
When the evening shadows lengthen,
Thou shalt lay thy burden down.

523 7s.

1 Not your own, but His ye are,
Who has paid a price untold
For your life, exceeding far
All earth's store of gems and gold;

With the precious blood of Christ,
Ransom treasure all unpriced,
Full redemption is procured,
Full salvation is assured.

2 Not your own; to Him ye owe
All your life and all your love;
Live, that ye His praise may show
Who is yet all praise above.

Every day and every hour,
Every gift and every power,
Consecrate to Him alone
Who hath claimed you for His own.

3 Teach us, Master, how to give
All we have and are to Thee;
Grant us, Saviour, while we live
Wholly, only, Thine to be.

Henceforth be our calling high,
Thee to serve and glorify;
Thine for ever, not our own;
Thine for ever, Thine alone. Amen.

[TEMPERANCE.]

524 7.6.

1 O Lord, our strength in weakness,
We pray to Thee for grace;
For power to fight the battle,
For speed to run the race:

When Thy baptismal waters
Were poured upon our brow,
We then were made Thy children,
And pledged our earliest vow;

2 We then were sealed and hallowed
By Thy life-giving word;
Were made the Spirit's temples,
And members of the Lord;

With His own blood He bought us,
And made the purchase sure;
His are we; may He keep us
Sober, and chaste, and pure.

GENERAL.

3 Conformed to His own likeness
    May we so live and die,
  That in the grave our bodies
    In holy peace may lie;
  And at the resurrection
    Forth from those graves may spring,
  Like to the glorious body
    Of Christ, our Lord and King.

4 The pure in heart are blessèd,
    For they shall see the Lord
  For ever and for ever
    By seraphim adored;
  And they shall drink the pleasures,
    Such as no tongue can tell,
  From the clear crystal river,
    And life's eternal well.

[TEMPERANCE.]
525   L. M.

1 When, doomed to death, the apostle lay
    At night in Herod's dungeon cell,
  A light shone round him like the day,
    And from his limbs the fetters fell.

2 A messenger from God was there,
    To break his chain and bid him rise;
  And lo! the saint, as free as air,
    Walked forth beneath the open skies.

3 Chains yet more strong and cruel bind
    The victims of that deadly thirst
  Which drowns the soul, and from the mind
    Blots the bright image stamped at first.

4 O God of love and mercy, deign
    To look on those with pitying eye
  Who struggle with that fatal chain,
    And send them succor from on high!

5 Send down, in its resistless might,
    Thy gracious Spirit, we implore,
  And lead the captive forth to light,
    A rescued soul, a slave no more!   Amen.

[ORPHANS.]
526   8s.

1 O Thou, who madest land and sea,
    And guidest all, in all their ways,
  Who hearest those who bring to Thee
    Their sacrifice of prayer and praise;
  Oh, hear Thy children as they bring
    Themselves a lowly offering!

2 Great God, Who with a Father's love
    Dost watch o'er all created things,
  And gatherest all, below, above,
    Beneath the shadow of Thy wings;
  Protect, we pray Thee, now and bless
    Thy children who are fatherless.

3 Thou hearest still the eagles' cry,
    And notest e'en a sparrow's fall.
  Thy listening ear doth heed on high,
    And hearken to the raven's call;
  Then, heavenly Father, hear and bless
    Thy children who are fatherless.

4 Come, heavenly Father, come to-day,
    For we Thy children come to Thee,
  And Thou wilt never say us, nay!
    If come we in humility;
  New-born in Thee, O Father, bless
    Thy children who are fatherless.

5 Cast forth upon the barren strand
    Of this lone world, to Thee we fly;
  In faith and hope, we fain would stand
    Beneath Thy sheltering arm for aye;
  Stretch forth Thy hand, and pitying bless
    Thy children who are fatherless.

6 And may we all with joyful mind
    Our hearts as living offerings bring,
  The first-fruits of our life, to find
    A Father in our heavenly King;
  And learn in life and death to bless
    Thee, "Father of the fatherless."
                                        Amen.

[ORPHANS.]
527   6s.

1 Thou Who with dying lips
    Thy mother didst commend
  Unto the tender care
    Of Thy beloved friend;
  Thou Who by Lazarus' grave
    In human grief didst groan,
  Turn, Lord, Thine eyes on those
    Left in the world alone.

2 Thou Who didst call Thy Twelve
    Their home and friends to leave,
  And in Thy kingdom all,
    Yea, more than all, receive,
  To those bereft of all,
    Thy pitying love extend,
  And let them find in Thee
    Father, and home, and friend.

3 Thou Who didst say of old,
  'Thine orphans lend to Me;
  Unto the fatherless
  I will a Father be,'
  Thy promises are sure ;
  Help us to trust Thee still ;
  To those who need Thee sore,
  That faithful word fulfil.

4 Thou Who in Thy still rest
  Our dear ones safe dost keep ;
  Thou Who shalt bring them back
  One day from their long sleep,
  Oh, keep us by Thy grace,
  That we at last may be,
  When that bright morning dawns,
  At home with them and Thee.
              Amen.

528   C.M.

1 We walk by faith, and not by sight ;
  No gracious words we hear
  From Him Who spake as man ne'er spake,
  But we believe Him near.

2 We may not touch His hands and side,
  Nor follow where He trod ;
  But in His promise we rejoice,
  And cry, "My Lord and God!"

3 Help then, O Lord, our unbelief ;
  And may our faith abound,
  To call on Thee when Thou art near,
  And seek where Thou art found:

4 That, when our life of faith is done,
  In realms of clearer light
  We may behold Thee as Thou art,
  With full and endless sight. Amen.

529   8s.

1 O Light, Whose beams illumine all
  From twilight dawn to perfect day,
  Shine Thou before the shadows fall,
  That lead our wandering feet astray:
  At morn and eve Thy radiance pour,
  That youth may love, and age adore.

2 O Way, through Whom our souls draw near
  To yon eternal home of peace,
  Where perfect love shall cast out fear,
  And earth's vain toil and wandering cease;
  In strength or weakness may we see
  Our heavenward path, O Lord, through Thee.

3 O Truth, before Whose shrine we bow,
  Thou priceless pearl for all who seek,
  To Thee our earliest strength we vow,
  Thy love will bless the pure and meek ;
  When dreams or mists beguile our sight,
  Turn Thou our darkness into light.

4 O Life, the well that ever flows
  To slake the thirst of those that faint,
  Thy power to bless, what seraph knows?
  Thy joy supreme, what words can paint?
  In earth's last hour of fleeting breath
  Be Thou our conqueror over death.

5 O Light, O Way, O Truth, O Life,
  O Jesus, born mankind to save,
  Give Thou Thy peace in deadliest strife;
  Shed Thou Thy calm on stormiest wave;
  Be Thou our hope, our joy, our dread,
  Lord of the living and the dead. Amen.

530   C.M.

1 Thou art the Way, to Thee alone
  From sin and death we flee;
  And he who would the Father seek,
  Must seek Him, Lord, by Thee.

2 Thou art the Truth, Thy word alone
  True wisdom can impart ;
  Thou only canst inform the mind
  And purify the heart.

3 Thou art the Life, the rending tomb
  Proclaims Thy conquering arm ;
  And those who put their trust in Thee
  Nor death nor hell shall harm.

4 Thou art the Way, the Truth, the Life;
  Grant us that way to know,
  That truth to keep, that life to win,
  Whose joys eternal flow. Amen.

[SPRING.]
531   P.M.

1 For all Thy love and goodness, so bountiful
    and free,
  Thy Name, Lord, be adored!
  On the wings of joyous praise our hearts
    soar up to Thee;
  Glory to the Lord!

GENERAL.

2 The spring-time breaks all round about, waking from winter's night:
Thy Name, Lord, be adored!
The sunshine, like God's love, pours down in floods of golden light;
Glory to the Lord!

3 A voice of joy is in all the earth, a voice is in all the air;
Thy Name, Lord, be adored!
All nature singeth aloud to God; there is gladness everywhere;
Glory to the Lord!

4 The flowers are strewn in field and copse, on the hill and on the plain;
Thy Name, Lord, be adored!
The soft air stirs in the tender leaves that clothe the trees again;
Glory to the Lord!

5 The works of Thy hands are very fair; and for all Thy bounteous love,
Thy Name, Lord, be adored!
But what, if this world is so fair, is the better land above?
Glory to the Lord!

6 Oh, to awake from death's short sleep, like the flowers from their wintry grave!
Thy Name, Lord, be adored!
And to rise all glorious in the day when Christ shall come to save!
Glory to the Lord!

7 Oh, to dwell in that happy land, where the heart cannot choose but sing!
Thy Name, Lord, be adored!
And where the life of the blessèd ones is a beautiful endless Spring!
Glory to the Lord! Amen.

532 [SUMMER.] 6.5.

1 Summer suns are glowing
Over land and sea,
Happy light is flowing
Bountiful and free.

Everything rejoices
In the mellow rays,
All earth's thousand voices
Swell the psalm of praise.

2 God's free mercy streameth
Over all the world,
And His banner gleameth
Everywhere unfurled.

Broad and deep and glorious
As the heaven above,
Shines in might victorious
His eternal love.

3 Lord, upon our blindness
Thy pure radiance pour;
For Thy loving-kindness
Make us love Thee more.

And when clouds are drifting
Dark across our sky,
Then, the veil uplifting,
Father, be Thou nigh.

4 We will never doubt Thee,
Though Thou veil Thy light;
Life is dark without Thee;
Death with Thee is bright.

Light of light! shine o'er us
On our pilgrim way;
Go Thou still before us
To the endless day. Amen.

533 [AUTUMN.] 7.6.

1 The year is swiftly waning;
The summer days are past;
And life, brief life, is speeding;
The end is nearing fast.

2 The ever-changing seasons
In silence come and go;
But Thou, eternal Father,
No time or change canst know.

3 Oh, pour Thy grace upon us,
That we may worthier be,
Each year that passes o'er us,
To dwell in heaven with Thee!

4 Behold the bending orchards
With bounteous fruit are crowned;
Lord, in our hearts more richly
Let heavenly fruits abound.

5 Oh, by each mercy sent us,
And by each grief and pain,
By blessings like the sunshine,
And sorrows like the rain,

6 Our barren hearts make fruitful
   With every goodly grace,
   That we Thy Name may hallow,
   And see at last Thy face. Amen.

534 C.M.

1 O God, our help in ages past,
   Our hope for years to come,
   Our shelter from the stormy blast
   And our eternal home:

2 Under the shadow of Thy throne
   Thy saints have dwelt secure;
   Sufficient is Thine arm alone,
   And our defence is sure.

3 Before the hills in order stood,
   Or earth received her frame,
   From everlasting Thou art God,
   To endless years the same.

4 A thousand ages in Thy sight
   Are like an evening gone;
   Short as the watch that ends the night
   Before the rising sun.

5 Time, like an ever-rolling stream,
   Bears all its sons away;
   They fly forgotten, as a dream
   Dies at the opening day.

6 O God, our help in ages past,
   Our hope for years to come,
   Be Thou our guard while life shall last,
   And our eternal home. Amen.

535 P.M.

1 'Soon and for ever:'
   Such promise our trust,
   Though ashes to ashes,
   And dust unto dust ;
   'Soon and for ever'
   Our union shall be
   Made perfect, our glorious
   Redeemer, in Thee:
   When the sins and the sorrows
   Of time shall be o'er,
   Its pangs, and its partings
   Remembered no more.
   Where life cannot fail, and where
   Death cannot sever,
   Christians with Christ shall be
   'Soon and for ever.'

2 'Soon and for ever'
   The breaking of day
   Shall drive all the night-clouds
   Of sorrow away;
   'Soon and for ever'
   We'll see as we're seen,
   And learn the deep meaning
   Of things that have been:
   When fightings without us,
   And fears from within,
   Shall weary no more in
   The warfare of sin ;
   Where fears, and where tears, and where
   Death shall be never,
   Christians with Christ shall be
   'Soon and for ever.'

3 'Soon and for ever'
   The work shall be done ;
   The warfare accomplished,
   The victory won:
   'Soon and for ever'
   The soldier lays down
   His sword for a harp, and
   His cross for a crown:
   Then droop not in sorrow,
   Despond not in fear;
   A glorious to-morrow
   Is brightening and near;
   When (blessèd reward of each
   Faithful endeavor)
   Christians with Christ shall be
   'Soon and for ever.' Amen.

536 7s.

1 When our heads are bowed with woe,
   When our bitter tears o'erflow,
   When we mourn the lost, the dear,
   Jesus, Son of Mary, hear !

2 Thou our throbbing flesh hast worn,
   Thou our mortal griefs hast borne,
   Thou hast shed the human tear ;
   Jesus, Son of Mary, hear !

3 When the solemn death-bell tolls
   For our own departing souls,
   When our final doom is near,
   Jesus, Son of Mary, hear !

4 Thou hast bowed the dying head,
   Thou the blood of life hast shed,
   Thou hast filled a mortal bier ;
   Jesus, Son of Mary, hear !

5 When the heart is sad within
    With the thought of all its sin,
    When the spirit shrinks with fear,
    Jesus, Son of Mary, hear!

6 Thou the shame, the grief, hast known,
    Though the sins were not Thine own;
    Thou hast deigned their load to bear;
    Jesus, Son of Mary, hear! Amen.

537 S. M.
1 Oh, where shall rest be found,
    Rest for the weary soul?
    'Twere vain the ocean-depths to sound,
    Or pierce to either pole.

2 The world can never give
    The bliss for which we sigh;
    'Tis not the whole of life to live,
    Nor all of death to die.

3 Beyond this vale of tears
    There is a life above,
    Unmeasured by the flight of years,
    And all that life is love.

4 There is a death, whose pang
    Outlasts the fleeting breath;
    Oh, what eternal horrors hang
    Around the second death!

5 Lord God of truth and grace,
    Teach us that death to shun,
    Lest we be banished from Thy face,
    For evermore undone.

6 Here would we end our quest:
    Alone are found in Thee
    The life of perfect love, the rest
    Of immortality.

538 L. M.
1 For Thee, O God, our constant praise
    In Sion waits, Thy chosen seat:
    Our promised altars there we'll raise,
    And all our zealous vows complete.

2 Thou, Who to every humble prayer
    Dost always bend Thy listening ear,
    To Thee shall all mankind repair,
    And at Thy gracious throne appear.

3 Our sins, though numberless, in vain
    To stop Thy flowing mercy try;
    Whilst Thou o'erlook'st the guilty stain,
    And washest out the crimson dye.

4 Blest is the man who, near Thee placed,
    Within Thy sacred dwelling lives!
    'Tis there abundantly we taste
    The vast delights Thy temple gives.

VIII. Processionals.

539 P. M.
We march, we march to victory!
    With the cross of the Lord before us,
    With His loving eye looking down from the sky,
    And His holy arm spread o'er us.

1 We come in the might of the Lord of light,
    In reverent train to meet Him;
    And we put to flight the armies of night,
    That the sons of the day may greet Him.
    We march, we march, etc.

2 Our sword is the Spirit of God on high,
    Our helmet is His salvation,
    Our banner the Cross of Calvary,
    Our watchword, the Incarnation.
    We march, we march, etc.

3 And the choir of angels with song awaits
    Our march to the golden Sion;
    For our Captain has broken the brazen gates,
    And burst the bars of iron.
    We march, we march, etc.

4 Then onward we march, our arms to prove,
    With the banner of Christ before us,
    With His eye of love looking down from above,
    And His holy arm spread o'er us.

We march, we march to victory!
    With the cross of the Lord before us,
    With His loving eye looking down from the sky,
    And His holy arm spread o'er us.

540   6.5.

1 Brightly gleams our banner
  Pointing to the sky,
  Waving wanderers onward
    To their home on high.
  Journeying o'er the desert,
    Gladly thus we pray,
  And with hearts united
    Take our heavenward way.
      Brightly gleams our banner
      Pointing to the sky,
      Waving wanderers onward
        To their home on high.

2 Jesus, Lord and Master,
    At Thy sacred feet,
  Here with hearts rejoicing
    See Thy children meet:
  Often have we left Thee,
    Often gone astray;
  Keep us, mighty Saviour,
    In the narrow way.
      Brightly gleams, etc.

3 All our days direct us
    In the way we go,
  Lead us on victorious
    Over every foe:
  Bid Thine angels shield us
    When the storm-clouds lower,
  Pardon, Lord, and save us
    In the last dread hour.
      Brightly gleams, etc.

4 Then with saints and angels
    May we join above,
  Offering prayers and praises
    At Thy throne of love;
  When the toil is over,
    Then come rest and peace,
  Jesus in His beauty,
    Songs that never cease.
      Brightly gleams, etc.

541   8.7.

1 Come, ye faithful, raise the anthem:
  Cleave the skies with shouts of praise;
Sing to Him Who brought salvation,
  Wondrous in His works and ways:
God eternal, Word incarnate,
  Whom the heaven of heavens obeys.

2 Ere He raised the lofty mountains,
  Formed the sea, or spread the sky,
Love eternal, free and boundless,
  Moved the Lord of life to die;
Foreordained the Prince of princes
  For the throne of Calvary.

3 Now above the sapphire pavement,
  High in unapproached light,
Lo! He lives and reigns for ever,
  Victor after hard-won fight,
Where the song of the redeemed
  Rings unceasing day and night.

4 Yet this earth He still remembers,
  Still by Him the flock are fed:
Yea, He gives them food immortal,
  Gives Himself, the living Bread:
Leads them where the precious fountain
  From the smitten Rock is shed.

5 Trust Him then, ye fainting pilgrims!
  Who shall pluck you from His hand?
Pledged He stands for your salvation,
  Pledged to give the promised land,
Where among the ransomed nations
  Ye too round His throne shall stand.

542   6.5.

1 On our way rejoicing,
  As we homeward move,
  Hearken to our praises,
    O Thou God of love!
  Is there grief or sadness?
    Thine it cannot be!
  Is our sky beclouded?
    Clouds are not from Thee!
      On our way rejoicing,
        As we homeward move,
      Hearken to our praises,
        O Thou God of love!

2 If with honest-hearted
    Love for God and man,
  Day by day Thou find us
    Doing what we can,
  Thou Who giv'st the seed-time
    Wilt give large increase,
  Crown the head with blessings,
    Fill the heart with peace.
      On our way rejoicing, etc.

3 On our way rejoicing
  Gladly let us go,
  Conquered hath our Leader,
  Vanquished is our foe!
  Christ without, our safety,
  Christ within, our joy:
  Who, if we be faithful.
  Can our hope destroy?
    On our way rejoicing, etc.

4 Unto God the Father
  Joyful songs we sing;
  Unto God the Saviour
  Thankful hearts we bring:
  Unto God the Spirit
  Bow we and adore,
  On our way rejoicing
  Now and evermore!
    On our way rejoicing, etc.

543   6,5.
            Part I.

1 Forward! be our watchword,
  Steps and voices joined;
  Seek the things before us,
  Not a look behind;
  Burns the fiery pillar
  At our army's head;
  Who shall dream of shrinking,
  By our Captain led?
    Forward through the desert!
    Through the toil and fight;
    Jordan flows before us;
    Sion beams with light.

2 Glories upon glories
  Hath our God prepared,
  By the souls that love Him
  One day to be shared;
  Eye hath not beheld them,
  Ear hath never heard;
  Nor of these hath uttered
  Thought or speech a word;
    Forward! marching eastward
    Where the heaven is bright,
    Till the veil be lifted,
    Till our faith be sight.

3 Far o'er yon horizon
  Rise the city towers,
  Where our God abideth;
  That fair home is ours;

Flash the streets with jasper.
  Shine the gates with gold;
  Flows the gladdening river
  Shedding joys untold.
    Thither, onward thither,
    In the Spirit's might!
    Pilgrims to your country,
    Forward into light!

            Part II.

4 Into God's high temple
  Onward as we press,
  Beauty spreads around us.
  Born of holiness;
  Arch, and vault, and carving,
  Lights of varied tone;
  Softened words and holy,
  Prayer and praise alone;
    Every thought upraising
    To our city bright,
    Where the tribes assemble
    Round the throne of light.

5 Nought that city needeth
  Of these aisles of stone;
  Where the Godhead dwelleth,
  Temple there is none;
  All the saints, that ever
  In these courts have stood,
  Are but babes, and feeding
  On the children's food.
    On through sign and token!
    Stars amidst the night;
    Forward through the darkness!
    Forward into light!

6 To the eternal Father
  Loudest anthems raise;
  To the Son and Spirit
  Echo songs of praise:
  To the Lord of glory.
  Blessèd Three in One,
  Be by men and angels
  Endless honor done.
    Weak are earthly praises.
    Dull the songs of night;
    Forward into triumph!
    Forward into light!

544   8,7.

1 Through the night of doubt and sorrow
  Onward goes the pilgrim band,
  Singing songs of expectation.
  Marching to the promised land.

Clear before us through the darkness
  Gleams and burns the guiding light;
Brother clasps the hand of brother,
  Stepping fearless through the night.

2 One, the light of God's own presence,
  O'er His ransomed people shed,
Chasing far the gloom and terror,
  Brightening all the path we tread:
One, the object of our journey,
  One, the faith which never tires,
One, the earnest looking forward,
  One, the hope our God inspires.

3 One, the strain the lips of thousands
  Lift us from the heart of one;
One the conflict, one the peril,
  One, the march in God begun:
One, the gladness of rejoicing
  On the far eternal shore,
Where the one almighty Father
  Reigns in love for evermore.

4 Onward therefore, pilgrim brothers!
  Onward, with the Cross our aid!
Bear its shame, and fight its battle,
  Till we rest beneath its shade!
Soon shall come the great awaking;
  Soon the rending of the tomb:
Then, the scattering of all shadows,
  And the end of toil and gloom!

545 8.7.

1 In the Name of God the Father,
  In the Name of God the Son,
In the Name of God the Spirit,
  One in Three, and Three in One;
In the Name which highest angels
  Speak not ere they veil their face,
Crying, "Holy, holy, holy."
  Come we to this sacred place.

2 Lo, in wondrous condescension,
  Jesus seeks His altar-throne;
Though in lowly symbols hidden,
  Faith and love His presence own.

164

When the Lord His temple visits,
  Let the listening earth be still;
May the Spirit's sweet indwelling
  Each believing heart fulfil.

3 Here, in figure represented,
  See the Passion once again;
Here behold the Lamb most holy,
  As for our redemption slain;
Here the Saviour's body broken,
  Here the blood which Jesus shed,
Mystic food of life eternal,
  See for our refreshment spread.

4 Here shall highest praise be offered,
  Here shall meekest prayer be poured,
Here, with body, soul, and spirit,
  God incarnate be adored.
Holy Jesus, for Thy coming
  May Thy love our hearts prepare;
Thine we fain would have them wholly;
  Enter, Lord, and tarry there. Amen.

546 8.7.

1 Sing, ye faithful! sing with gladness!
  Wake your noblest, sweetest strain!
With the praises of your Saviour
  Let His house resound again!
Him let all your music honor,
  And your songs exalt His reign!

2 Sing how He came forth from heaven,
  Bowed Himself to Bethlehem's cave,
Stooped to wear the servant's vesture,
  Bore the pain, the cross, the grave,
Passed within the gates of darkness,
  Thence His banished ones to save!

3 So He tasted death for all men,
  He of all mankind the Head,
Sinless one among the sinful,
  Prince of life among the dead;
So He wrought the full redemption,
  And the captor captive led.

4 Now on high, yet ever with us,
  From His Father's throne, the Son
Rules and guides the world He ransomed,
  Till the appointed work be done,
Till He see, renewed and perfect,
  All things gathered into one.

5 Day of promised restitution !
　Fruit of all His sorrows past!
　When the crown of His dominions
　He before the throne shall cast,
　And throughout the wide creation
　God be "all in all" at last.

647　　　　　　　　　　7s.

1 Forward go in glad accord,
　Ye who know your risen Lord!
　Let the strain of fervent love
　Lift each drooping heart above!
　Dark and troublous though the day,
　Cast unworthy care away!
　Trust in Him Whose mighty hand
　Guards the Church and rules the land!

2 Forward still! and let the strain
　Tell of triumph yet again!
　For the Lord, Who reigns on high,
　Leads His own to victory:
　Through the world's opposing might,
　Through the gathering gloom of night,
　Strong in faith, let holy song
　Cheer us as we march along.

3 Forward go! despond no more!
　Jesus calls, and goes before.
　He will guard His chosen Bride,
　He will never leave her side:
　Kingdoms flourish and decay,
　Heaven and earth will pass away;
　Evermore the Church shall raise
　Songs of triumph, joy, and praise.

4 Forward go! the saints above
　Still prolong the strain of love;
　Soon may we, within the gate,
　See with them our King in state:
　There will He His choir unite,
　All arrayed in robes of white;
　There will songs of purest joy
　All their blissful life employ.

648　　　　　　　　　　6.5.

1 Saviour, blessèd Saviour,
　　Listen while we sing ;
　Hearts and voices raising
　　Praises to our King.
　All we have we offer,
　　All we hope to be,
　Body, soul, and spirit,
　　All we yield to Thee.

2 Nearer, ever nearer,
　　Christ, we draw to Thee,
　Deep in adoration
　　Bending low the knee :
　Thou for our redemption
　　Cam'st on earth to die :
　Thou, that we might follow,
　　Hast gone up on high.

3 Great and ever greater
　　Are Thy mercies here,
　True and everlasting
　　Are the glories there:
　Where no pain, or sorrow,
　　Toil, or care, is known,
　Where the angel legions
　　Circle round Thy throne.

4 Clearer still, and clearer,
　　Dawns the light from heaven,
　In our sadness bringing
　　News of sins forgiven;
　Life has lost its shadows,
　　Pure the light within;
　Thou hast shed Thy radiance
　　On a world of sin.

5 Brighter still, and brighter,
　　Glows the western sun,
　Shedding all its gladness
　　O'er our work that's done ;
　Time will soon be over,
　　Toil and sorrow past,
　May we, blessèd Saviour,
　　Find a rest at last !

6 Onward, ever onward,
　　Journeying o'er the road
　Worn by saints before us,
　　Journeying on to God!
　Leaving all behind us,
　　May we hasten on,
　Backward never looking
　　Till the prize is won.

7 Bliss, all bliss excelling,
　　When the ransomed soul,
　Earthly toils forgetting,
　　Finds its promised goal ;
　Where in joys unheard of
　　Saints with angels sing,
　Never weary raising
　　Praises to their King.

PROCESSIONALS.

549   S.M.

1 Rejoice, ye pure in heart!
   Rejoice, give thanks, and sing!
   Your glorious banner wave on high,
   The cross of Christ your King!

2 Bright youth, and snow-crowned age,
   Strong men and maidens meek:
   Raise high your free, exulting song!
   God's wondrous praises speak!

3 With all the angel choirs,
   With all the saints of earth,
   Pour out the strains of joy and bliss,
   True rapture, noblest mirth!

4 Your clear hosannas raise,
   And alleluias loud!
   Whilst answering echoes upward float,
   Like wreaths of incense cloud.

5 Yes, on through life's long path!
   Still chanting as ye go;
   From youth to age, by night and day,
   In gladness and in woe.

6 Still lift your standard high!
   Still march in firm array!
   As warriors through the darkness toil
   Till dawns the golden day!

7 At last the march shall end;
   The wearied ones shall rest;
   The pilgrims find their Father's house.
   Jerusalem the blest.

8 Then on, ye pure in heart!
   Rejoice, give thanks, and sing!
   Your glorious banner wave on high,
   The cross of Christ your King!

550   6.5.

1 Onward, Christian soldiers,
   Marching as to war,
   With the cross of Jesus
   Going on before!
   Christ the royal Master
   Leads against the foe;
   Forward into battle,
   See, His banners go.
     Onward, Christian soldiers,
     Marching as to war,
     With the cross of Jesus
     Going on before!

2 At the sign of triumph
   Satan's host doth flee;
   On, then, Christian soldiers,
   On to victory!
   Hell's foundations quiver
   At the shout of praise;
   Brothers, lift your voices,
   Loud your anthems raise!
     Onward, etc.

3 Like a mighty army
   Moves the Church of God;
   Brothers, we are treading
   Where the saints have trod;
   We are not divided,
   All one body we,
   One in hope and doctrine,
   One in charity.
     Onward, etc.

4 Crowns and thrones may perish,
   Kingdoms rise and wane,
   But the Church of Jesus
   Constant will remain;
   Gates of hell can never
   'Gainst that Church prevail;
   We have Christ's own promise,
   And that cannot fail.
     Onward, etc.

5 Onward, then, ye people!
   Join our happy throng!
   Blend with ours your voices
   In the triumph song!
   Glory, laud, and honor,
   Unto Christ the King;
   This through countless ages
   Men and angels sing.
     Onward, Christian soldiers,
     Marching as to war,
     With the cross of Jesus
     Going on before!

551   6.5.

1 At the Name of Jesus
   Every knee shall bow,
   Every tongue confess Him
   King of glory now:
   'Tis the Father's pleasure
   We should call Him Lord,
   Who from the beginning
   Was the mighty Word.

2 At His voice creation
   Sprang at once to sight,
   All the angel faces,
   All the hosts of light,
   Thrones and dominations,
   Stars upon their way,
   All the heavenly orders,
   In their great array.

3 Humbled for a season,
   To receive a Name
   From the lips of sinners
   Unto whom He came,
   Faithfully He bore it
   Spotless to the last,
   Brought it back victorious,
   When from death He passed;

4 Bore it up triumphant,
   With its human light,
   Through all ranks of creatures,
   To the central height;
   To the throne of Godhead,
   To the Father's breast,
   Filled it with the glory
   Of that perfect rest.

5 In your hearts enthrone Him;
   There let Him subdue
   All that is not holy,
   All that is not true :
   Crown Him as your Captain
   In temptation's hour;
   Let His will enfold you
   In its light and power.

6 Brothers, this Lord Jesus
   Shall return again,
   With His Father's glory,
   With His angel train;
   For all wreaths of empire
   Meet upon His brow,
   And our hearts confess Him
   King of glory now.

Also the following:

345 Oft in danger, oft in woe.
348 The Son of God goes forth to war.
349 Go forward, Christian soldier.
351 O happy band of pilgrims.
358 Ancient of days.
362 Thou art coming, O my Saviour.
371 Hail to the Lord's anointed.
395 Crown Him with many crowns.
398 Come Thou Holy Spirit, come.

402 Spirit divine, attend our prayers.
403 Praises to Him Whose love has given.
406 Holy, holy, holy Lord.
415 Ten thousand times ten thousand.
419 Oh, what the joy and the glory must be.
420 Those eternal bowers.
422 Awake, awake, O Sion.
425 For thee, O dear, dear country.
426 Jerusalem the golden.
427 Blessèd city, heavenly Salem.
429 O mother dear, Jerusalem.
438 Jesus, still lead on.
445 Lord of all being throned afar.
451 O Jesus, King most wonderful.
457 Hail, Thou once despisèd Jesus.
458 Alleluia! sing to Jesus.
459 Jesus, our risen King.
464 O Saviour, precious Saviour.
472 Praise my soul the King of heaven.
473 Lift up your heads, ye mighty gates.
477 Sing praise to God Who reigns above.
499 Pleasant are Thy courts above.
504 Glorious things of Thee are spoken.
505 Praise the Rock of our salvation.
506 The Church's one foundation.
517 O brothers, lift your voices.

IX. Litanies.

LITANY OF THE HOLY GHOST.

552 7.7.7.6.

1 Holy Spirit, heavenly Dove,
   Dew descending from above,
   Breath of life, and fire of love ;
      Hear us, Holy Spirit.

2 Source of strength, of knowledge clear,
   Wisdom, godliness sincere,
   Understanding, counsel, fear ;
      Hear us, Holy Spirit.

3 Source of meekness, love, and peace,
   Patience, pureness, faith's increase,
   Hope and joy that cannot cease ;
      Hear us, Holy Spirit.

4 Spirit guiding us aright,
   Spirit making darkness light,
   Spirit of resistless might ;
      Hear us, Holy Spirit.

LITANIES.

5 Thou by Whom the Virgin bore
  Him Whom heaven and earth adore,
  Sent our nature to restore;
      Hear us, Holy Spirit.

6 Thou Whom Jesus from His throne
  Gave to cheer and help His own,
  That they might not be alone;
      Hear us, Holy Spirit.

7 Thou Whose grace the Church doth fill,
  Showing her God's perfect will,
  Making Jesus present still;
      Hear us, Holy Spirit.

8 Coming with Thy power to save,
  Moving on baptismal wave,
  Raising us from sin's dark grave;
      Hear us, Holy Spirit.

9 Thou by Whom our souls are fed
  With the true and living Bread,
  Even Him Who for us bled;
      Hear us, Holy Spirit.

10 All Thy sevenfold gifts bestow,
   Gifts of wisdom God to know,
   Gifts of strength to meet the foe;
       Hear us, Holy Spirit.

11 All our evil passions kill,
   Bend aright our stubborn will,
   Though we grieve Thee, patient still;
       Hear us, Holy Spirit.

12 Come to raise us when we fall,
   And, when snares our souls enthrall,
   Lead us back with gentle call;
       Hear us, Holy Spirit.

13 Come to strengthen all the weak,
   Give Thy courage to the meek,
   Teach our faltering tongues to speak;
       Hear us, Holy Spirit.

14 Come to aid the souls who yearn
   More of truth divine to learn,
   And with deeper love to burn;
       Hear us, Holy Spirit.

15 Keep us in the narrow way,
   Warn us when we go astray,
   Plead within us when we pray;
       Hear us, Holy Spirit.

16 Holy, loving, as Thou art,
   Come, and live within our heart;
   Never more from us depart;
       Hear us, Holy Spirit. Amen.

LITANY OF THE CHURCH.
553   7.7.7.6.

1 Jesus, with Thy Church abide,
  Be her Saviour, Lord, and Guide,
  While on earth her faith is tried:
      We beseech Thee, hear us.

2 Keep her life and doctrine pure,
  Help her, patient to endure,
  Trusting in Thy promise sure:
      We beseech Thee, hear us.

3 Be Thou with her all the days,
  May she, safe from error's ways,
  Toil for Thine eternal praise:
      We beseech Thee, hear us.

4 May her voice be ever clear,
  Warning of a judgment near,
  Telling of a Saviour dear:
      We beseech Thee, hear us.

5 All her fettered powers release,
  Bid our strife and envy cease,
  Grant the heavenly gift of peace:
      We beseech Thee, hear us.

6 May she one in doctrine be,
  One in truth and charity,
  Winning all to faith in Thee:
      We beseech Thee, hear us.

7 May she guide the poor and blind,
  Seek the lost until she find,
  And the broken-hearted bind:
      We beseech Thee, hear us.

8 Save her love from growing cold,
  Make her watchmen strong and bold,
  Fence her round, Thy peaceful fold:
      We beseech Thee, hear us.

9 May her priests Thy people feed,
  Shepherds of the flock indeed,
  Ready, where Thou call'st, to lead:
      We beseech Thee, hear us.

10 Judge her not for work undone,
Judge her not for fields unwon.
Bless her works in Thee begun :
    We beseech Thee, hear us.

11 For the past give deeper shame,
Make her jealous for Thy Name,
Kindle zeal's most holy flame:
    We beseech Thee, hear us.

12 Raise her to her calling high,
Let the nations far and nigh
Hear Thy heralds' warning cry:
    We beseech Thee, hear us.

13 May her lamp of truth be bright,
Bid her bear aloft its light
Through the realms of heathen night :
    We beseech Thee, hear us.

14 May her scattered children be
From reproach of evil free,
Blameless witnesses for Thee:
    We beseech Thee, hear us.

15 Arm her soldiers with the cross,
Brave to suffer toil or loss,
Counting earthly gain but dross :
    We beseech Thee, hear us.

16 May she holy triumphs win,
Overthrow the hosts of sin,
Gather all the nations in :
    We beseech Thee, hear us.

17 May she soon all glorious be,
Spotless and from wrinkle free,
Pure, and bright, and worthy Thee:
    We beseech Thee, hear us.

18 Fit her all Thy joy to share
In the home Thou dost prepare,
And be ever blessèd there:
    We beseech Thee, hear us.
                Amen.

LITANY FOR CHILDREN.
554   7.7.7.6.

1 Jesus, Saviour ever mild,
Born for us a little child
Of the Virgin undefiled;
    Hear us, holy Jesus.

2 Jesus, by the Mother-Maid
In Thy swaddling-clothes arrayed,
And within a manger laid;
    Hear us, holy Jesus.

3 Jesus, at Whose infant feet
Shepherds, coming Thee to greet,
Knelt to pay their worship meet;
    Hear us, holy Jesus.

4 Jesus, unto Whom of yore
Wise men, hastening to adore,
Gold and myrrh and incense bore;
    Hear us, holy Jesus.

5 Jesus, to Thy temple brought,
Whom, by Thy good Spirit taught,
Simeon and Anna sought;
    Hear us, holy Jesus.

6 Jesus, Who didst deign to flee
From King Herod's cruelty
In Thy earliest infancy;
    Hear us, holy Jesus.

7 Jesus, Whom Thy mother found
'Midst the doctors sitting round,
Marvelling at Thy words profound;
    Hear us, holy Jesus.

PART II.

8 From all pride and vain conceit,
From all spite and angry heat,
From all lying and deceit;
    Save us, holy Jesus.

9 From all sloth and idleness,
From not caring for distress,
From all lust and greediness;
    Save us, holy Jesus.

10 From refusing to obey,
From the love of our own way,
From forgetfulness to pray;
    Save us, holy Jesus.

PART III.

11 By Thy birth and early years,
By Thine infant wants and fears,
By Thy sorrows and Thy tears;
    Save us, holy Jesus.

LITANIES.

12 By Thy pattern bright and pure,
   By the pains Thou didst endure
   Our salvation to procure;
     Save us, holy Jesus.

13 By Thy wounds and thorn-crowned head,
   By Thy blood for sinners shed,
   By Thy rising from the dead;
     Save us, holy Jesus.

14 By the Name we bow before,
   Human Name, which evermore
   All the hosts of heaven adore;
     Save us, holy Jesus.

15 By Thine own unconquered might,
   By Thy glory in the height,
   By Thy mercies infinite;
     Save us, holy Jesus.   Amen.

LITANY FOR CHILDREN.

555   7.7.7.6.

1 Jesus, from Thy throne on high,
  Far above the bright blue sky,
  Look on us with loving eye;
    Hear us, holy Jesus.

2 Little children need not fear,
  When they know that Thou art near:
  Thou dost love us, Saviour dear;
    Hear us, holy Jesus.

3 Little hearts may love Thee well,
  Little lips Thy love may tell,
  Little hymns Thy praises swell:
    Hear us, holy Jesus.

4 Little lives may be divine,
  Little deeds of love may shine,
  Little ones be wholly Thine:
    Hear us, holy Jesus.

5 Jesus, once an infant small,
  Cradled in the oxen's stall,
  Though the God and Lord of all:
    Hear us, holy Jesus.

6 Once a child so good and fair,
  Feeling want, and toil, and care,
  All that we may have to bear:
    Hear us, holy Jesus.

7 Jesus, Thou dost love us still,
  And it is Thy holy will
  That we should be safe from ill:
    Hear us, holy Jesus.

8 Be Thou with us every day,
  In our work and in our play,
  When we learn and when we pray:
    Hear us, holy Jesus.

9 When we lie asleep at night,
  Ever may Thy angels bright
  Keep us safe till morning's light:
    Hear us, holy Jesus.

10 Make us brave without a fear,
   Make us happy, full of cheer,
   Sure that Thou art always near:
     Hear us, holy Jesus.

11 May we prize our Christian name,
   May we guard it free from blame,
   Fearing all that causes shame:
     Hear us, holy Jesus.

12 May we grow from day to day,
   Glad to learn each holy way,
   Ever ready to obey:
     Hear us, holy Jesus.

13 May we ever try to be
   From our sinful tempers free,
   Pure and gentle, Lord, like Thee:
     Hear us, holy Jesus.

14 May our thoughts be undefiled,
   May our words be true and mild,
   Make us each a holy child:
     Hear us, holy Jesus.

15 Jesus, Son of God most high,
   Who didst in a manger lie,
   Who upon the cross didst die:
     Hear us, holy Jesus.

16 Jesus, from Thy heavenly throne,
   Watching o'er each little one,
   Till our life on earth is done:
     Hear us, holy Jesus.

17 Jesus, Whom we hope to see
   Calling us in heaven to be
   Happy evermore with Thee:
     Hear us, holy Jesus.   Amen.

LITANIES.

LITANY OF THE INCARNATE LIFE.
556 7.7.7.5.

1 Lord of mercy and of might,
Of mankind the life and light,
Maker, Teacher infinite,
  Jesus, hear and save.

2 Strong Creator, Saviour mild,
Humbled to a mortal child,
Captive, beaten, bound, reviled,
  Jesus, hear and save.

3 Throned above celestial things,
Borne aloft on angels' wings,
Lord of lords, and King of kings,
  Jesus, hear and save.

4 Soon to come to earth again,
Judge of angels and of men,
Hear us now, and hear us then,
  Jesus, hear and save. Amen.

LITANY OF THE INCARNATE LIFE.
557 8.7.
Part I.

1 Pity on us, heavenly Father,
  For the love of Jesus take,
And with Thine own Holy Spirit,
  Save us for Thy mercies' sake.

2 By the lowly cradle manger
  Over which the angels spake
Songs of peace, and words of wonder;
  Save us for Thy mercies' sake.

3 By the tender human nature
  He for us did stoop and take,
All His travail, thirst and hunger;
  Save us for Thy mercies' sake.

4 By the tears, whose loving kindness
  From His human eyes did brake
When He stood by human sorrow;
  Save us for Thy mercies' sake.

5 By the words, whose free forgiveness
  In the dying thief did wake
Hope of Paradise and pardon;
  Save us for Thy mercies' sake.

6 By the thorns, that mocking crowned Him,
  By the bloody sweat that brake
From His brow, in bitter anguish;
  Save us for Thy mercies' sake.

7 By His limbs outstretched and wounded,
  By the cleft the spear did make,
By the blood and by the water;
  Save us for Thy mercies' sake.

Part II.

8 From a heart by sin deceived,
  Bent, with froward will, to take
Its own downward course of madness;
  Save us for Thy mercies' sake.

9 From a soul whose death-like slumber
  Will not at Thy call awake,
But sleep on, nor heed its danger;
  Save us for Thy mercies' sake.

10 From foul hands, and thoughts uncleanly
  That their resting place would make
In the souls redeemed by Jesus;
  Save us for Thy mercies' sake.

11 In the time of tears, and laughter,
  When we sleep, and when we wake,
Rising, resting, coming, going,
  Save us for Thy mercies' sake.

12 In the hour of our departure,
  When life's lingering sands do shake,
In the grave, and Rest remaining,
  Save us for Thy mercies' sake.

13 In the glorious Resurrection,
  When the dead in Christ awake
At the voice of the archangel,
  Save us for Thy mercies' sake.

14 In the dreadful day of Judgment,
  When the worlds before Thee quake,
Plead our cause, O God our Saviour;
  Save us for Thy mercies' sake. Amen.

LITANY OF THE INCARNATE LIFE.
558 7.7.7.6.

1 Son of God, for man decreed
To be born the woman's Seed,
Very God, and Man indeed;
  Hear us, holy Jesus.

2 Thou Whose wisdom all things planned,
Held by Whose almighty hand
All things in their order stand;
  Hear us, holy Jesus.

3 God with us, Emmanuel,
 Coming here as man to dwell,
 Saving us when Adam fell;
  Hear us, holy Jesus.

4 Saviour, full of truth and grace,
 Leaving Thine eternal place
 To restore our fallen race;
  Hear us, holy Jesus.

5 Image of the God unseen,
 Still what Thou hadst ever been
 Though in form of infant mean;
  Hear us, holy Jesus.

6 Word, by Whom the worlds were made,
 In a lowly manger laid,
 Taught on earth a humble trade;
  Hear us, holy Jesus.

7 Jesus, led by love to share
 All the forms of grief and care,
 That we sinful mortals bear;
  Hear us, holy Jesus.

8 Good Physician, come to cure
 All the ills that men endure,
 And to make our nature pure;
  Hear us, holy Jesus.

9 Man of sorrows, weak and worn
 With Thy woes for sinners borne,
 Lest we should for ever mourn;
  Hear us, holy Jesus.

10 Shepherd, Who Thy watch dost keep,
 Guarding still Thy chosen sheep
 From the spoiler's malice deep;
  Hear us, holy Jesus.

11 Lamb, from earth's foundation slain,
 By Whose bitter stripes of pain
 We are freed from guilty stain;
  Hear us, holy Jesus.

12 Only victim we can plead,
 Our High-Priest to intercede,
 Advocate in all our need;
  Hear us, holy Jesus.

13 Standing now before the throne,
 Pleading that which can alone
 For the sin of man atone;
  Hear us, holy Jesus.

14 Only hope of those who pray,
 Only help while here we stay,
 Life of those who pass away;
  Hear us, holy Jesus. Amen.

LITANY OF THE INCARNATE LIFE.

559   7.7.7.6.

1 God the Father, God the Son,
 God the Spirit, Three in One,
 Hear us from Thy heavenly throne,
  Spare us, holy Trinity.

2 Thou Who leaving crown and throne
 Camest here, an outcast lone,
 That Thou mightest save Thine own,
  Hear us, holy Jesus.

3 Thou with sinners wont to eat,
 Who with loving words didst greet
 Mary weeping at Thy feet,
  Hear us, holy Jesus.

4 Thou Whose saddened look did chide
 Peter when he thrice denied,
 Till with bitter tears he cried,
  Hear us, holy Jesus.

5 Thou Who hanging on the tree
 To the thief saidst, "Thou shalt be
 To-day in Paradise with Me,"
  Hear us, holy Jesus.

6 Thou, despised, denied, refused,
 And for man's transgressions bruised,
 Sinless, yet of sin accused,
  Hear us, holy Jesus.

7 Thou Who on the cross didst reign,
 Dying there in bitter pain,
 Cleansing with Thy blood our stain,
  Hear us, holy Jesus.

8 Shepherd of the straying sheep,
 Comforter of them that weep,
 Hear us crying from the deep,
  Hear us, holy Jesus.

9 That in Thy pure innocence
 We may wash our souls' offence,
 And find truest penitence,
  We beseech Thee, Jesus.

10 That we give to sin no place,
 That we never quench Thy grace,
 That we ever seek Thy face,
  We beseech Thee, Jesus.

11 That denying evil lust,
 Living godly, meek, and just,
 In Thee only we may trust,
   We beseech Thee, Jesus.

12 That to sin for ever dead
 We may live to Thee instead,
 And the narrow pathway tread,
   We beseech Thee, Jesus.

13 When shall end the battle sore,
 When our pilgrimage is o'er,
 Grant Thy peace for evermore,
   We beseech Thee, Jesus. Amen.

LITANY OF PENITENCE.

560   7.7.7.6.
     Part I.

1 Father, hear Thy children's call:
 Humbly at Thy feet we fall,
 Prodigals, confessing all :
   We beseech Thee, hear us.

2 Christ, beneath Thy Cross we blame
 All our life of sin and shame:
 Penitent we breathe Thy Name:
   We beseech Thee, hear us.

3 Holy Spirit, grieved and tried,
 Oft forgotten and defied,
 Now we mourn our stubborn pride:
   We beseech Thee, hear us.

4 Love, that caused us first to be,
 Love, that bled upon the tree,
 Love, that draws us lovingly: ·
   We beseech Thee, hear us.

5 We Thy call have disobeyed,
 Into paths of sin have strayed,
 And repentance have delayed :
   We beseech Thee, hear us.

6 Sick, we come to Thee for cure,
 Guilty, seek Thy mercy sure,
 Evil, long to be made pure:
   We beseech Thee, hear us.

7 Blind, we pray that we may see,
 Bound, we pray to be made free,
 Stained, we pray for sanctity:
   We beseech Thee, hear us.

8 Thou Who hear'st each contrite sigh,
 Bidding sinful souls draw nigh,
 Willing not that one should die,
   We beseech Thee, hear us.

     Part II.

9 By the gracious saving call
 Spoken tenderly to all
 Who have shared in Adam's fall,
   We beseech Thee, hear us.

10 By the nature Jesus wore,
 By the stripes and death He bore,
 By His life for evermore,
   We beseech Thee, hear us.

11 By the love that longs to bless,
 Pitying our sore distress,
 Leading us to holiness,
   We beseech Thee, hear us.

12 By the love so calm and strong,
 Patient still to suffer wrong
 And our day of grace prolong,
   We beseech Thee, hear us.

13 By the love that speaks within,
 Calling us to flee from sin,
 And the joy of goodness win,
   We beseech Thee, hear us.

14 By the love that bids Thee spare,
 By the heaven Thou dost prepare,
 By Thy promises to prayer,
   We beseech Thee, hear us.

     Part III.

15 Teach us what Thy love has borne,
 That with loving sorrow torn
 Truly contrite we may mourn :
   We beseech Thee, hear us.

16 Gifts of light and grace bestow,
 Help us to resist the foe,
 Fearing what alone is woe :
   We beseech Thee, hear us.

17 Let not sin within us reign,
 May we gladly suffer pain,
 If it purge away our stain :
   We beseech Thee, hear us.

18 May we to all evil die,
 Fleshly longings crucify,
 Fix our hearts and thoughts on high :
   We beseech Thee, hear us.

LITANIES.

19 Grant us faith to know Thee near,
    Hail Thy grace, Thy judgment fear,
    And through trial persevere:
    We beseech Thee, hear us.

20 Grant us hope from earth to rise,
    And to strain with eager eyes
    Towards the promised heavenly prize:
    We beseech Thee, hear us.

21 Grant us love Thy love to own,
    Love to live for Thee alone,
    And the power of grace make known:
    We beseech Thee, hear us.

22 All our weak endeavors bless,
    As we ever onward press,
    Till we perfect holiness:
    We beseech Thee, hear us.

23 Lead us daily nearer Thee,
    Till at last Thy face we see,
    Crowned with Thine own purity:
    We beseech Thee, hear us. Amen.

LITANY OF THE PASSION.
561   7.7.7.6.

1 Jesus, Who for us didst bear
   Scorn and sorrow, toil and care,
   Hearken to our lowly prayer;
   Hear us, holy Jesus.

2 By that hour of agony,
   Spent while Thine apostles three
   Slumbered in Gethsemane,
   Hear us, holy Jesus.

3 By the prayer Thou thrice didst pray
   That the cup might pass away,
   So Thou mightest still obey,
   Hear us, holy Jesus.

4 By the kiss of treachery,
   To Thy foes betraying Thee,
   By Thy harsh captivity,
   Hear us, holy Jesus.

5 By the scourging Thou hast borne,
   By the purple robe of scorn,
   By the reed and crown of thorn,
   Hear us, holy Jesus.

6 By the insult of the Jews,
   When Barabbas they would choose,
   And did Thee their King refuse,
   Hear us, holy Jesus.

7 By Thy going forth to die,
   When they raised the wicked cry,
   "Crucify Him, crucify!"
   Hear us, holy Jesus.

8 By the cross which Thou didst bear,
   By the cup they bade Thee share,
   Mingled gall and vinegar,
   Hear us, holy Jesus.

9 By Thy nailing to the tree,
   By the title over Thee,
   By the gloom of Calvary,
   Hear us, holy Jesus.

10 By the parting of Thy clothes,
   By the mocking of Thy foes,
   As they watched Thy dying woes,
   Hear us, holy Jesus.

11 By Thy seven words then said,
   By the bowing of Thy head,
   By Thy numbering with the dead,
   Hear us, holy Jesus.

12 By the piercing of Thy side,
   By the stream of double tide,
   Blood and water, thence supplied,
   Hear us, holy Jesus.

13 Cleansing us from outward sin,
   And from evil thoughts within,
   That we may true pureness win,
   Save us, holy Jesus.

14 When temptation sore is rife,
   When we faint amidst the strife,
   Thou, Whose death hath been our life,
   Save us, holy Jesus.

15 While on stormy seas we toss,
   Let us count all things as loss,
   But Thee only on Thy cross;
   Save us, holy Jesus.

16 So, with hope in Thee made fast,
   When death's bitterness is past,
   We may see Thy face at last;
   Save us, holy Jesus.

562   7.7.7.6.
(THE WORDS ON THE CROSS.)
Part I.

"Father forgive them, for they know not what they do."—St. Luke, xxiii. 34.

1 Jesus, in Thy dying woes,
Even while Thy life-blood flows,
Craving pardon for Thy foes :
  Hear us, holy Jesus.

2 Saviour, for our pardon sue,
When our sins Thy pangs renew,
For we know not what we do :
  Hear us, holy Jesus.

3 Oh, may we, who mercy need,
Be like Thee in heart and deed,
When with wrong our spirits bleed :
  Hear us, holy Jesus.

Part II.

"To-day shalt thou be with Me in Paradise."
St. Luke, xxiii. 43.

1 Jesus, pitying the sighs
Of the thief, who near Thee dies,
Promising him Paradise :
  Hear us, holy Jesus.

2 May we, in our guilt and shame,
Still Thy love and mercy claim,
Calling humbly on Thy Name :
  Hear us, holy Jesus.

3 Oh, remember us who pine,
Looking from our cross to Thine;
Cheer our souls with hope divine :
  Hear us, holy Jesus.

Part III.

"Woman behold thy Son." "Behold thy mother."
St. John, xix. 26, 27.

1 Jesus, loving to the end
Her whose heart Thy sorrows rend,
And Thy dearest human friend :
  Hear us, holy Jesus.

2 May we in Thy sorrows share,
And for Thee all peril dare,
And enjoy Thy tender care :
  Hear us, holy Jesus.

3 May we all Thy loved ones be,
All one holy family,
Loving for the love of Thee :
  Hear us, holy Jesus.

Part IV.

"My God, My God, why hast Thou forsaken Me."
St. Matt. xxvii. 46.

1 Jesus, whelmed in fears unknown,
With our evil left alone,
While no light from heaven is shown :
  Hear us, holy Jesus.

2 When we vainly seem to pray,
And our hope seems far away,
In the darkness be our stay :
  Hear us, holy Jesus.

3 Though no Father seem to hear,
Though no light our spirits cheer,
Tell our faith that God is near :
  Hear us, holy Jesus.

Part V.

"I thirst." - St. John. xix. 28.

1 Jesus, in Thy thirst and pain,
While Thy wounds Thy life-blood drain,
Thirsting more our love to gain :
  Hear us, holy Jesus.

2 Thirst for us in mercy still;
All Thy holy work fulfil :
Satisfy Thy loving will :
  Hear us, holy Jesus.

3 May we thirst Thy love to know;
Lead us in our sin and woe
Where the healing waters flow :
  Hear us, holy Jesus.

Part VI.

"It is finished."—St. John, xix. 30.

1 Jesus, all our ransom paid,
All Thy Father's will obeyed,
By Thy sufferings perfect made :
  Hear us, holy Jesus.

2 Save us in our soul's distress,
Be our help to cheer and bless,
While we grow in holiness :
  Hear us, holy Jesus.

3 Brighten all our heavenward way,
With an ever holier ray,
Till we pass to perfect day :
  Hear us, holy Jesus.

PART VII.
"Father into Thy hands I commend My Spirit."
ST. LUKE, xxiii. 46.

1 Jesus, all Thy labor vast,
All Thy woe and conflict past,
Yielding up Thy soul at last :
  Hear us, holy Jesus.

2 When the death shades round us lower,
Guard us from the tempter's power,
Keep us in that trial hour :
  Hear us, holy Jesus.

3 May Thy life and death supply
Grace to live and grace to die,
Grace to reach the home on high.
  Hear us, holy Jesus.
                            Amen.

LITANY OF THE FOUR LAST THINGS.

563

1 Jesus, life of those who die,
Advocate with God on high,
Hope of immortality:
  Hear us, holy Jesus.

2 Thou Whose death to mortals gave
Power to triumph o'er the grave,
Living now, from death to save:
  Hear us, holy Jesus.

3 Thou before Whose great white throne
All our doings must be shown,
Pleading now for us Thine own:
  Hear us, holy Jesus.

4 Thou Whose death was borne that we,
From the power of Satan free,
Might not die eternally;
  Hear us, holy Jesus.

5 Thou Who dost a place prepare,
That in heavenly mansions fair
Sinners may Thy glory share:
  Hear us, holy Jesus.

DEATH.

6 We are dying day by day ;
Soon from earth we pass away ;
Lord of life, to Thee we pray :
  Hear us, holy Jesus.

7 Ere we hear the angel's call,
And the shadows round us fall,
Be our Saviour, be our all :
  Hear us, holy Jesus.

8 Wean our hearts from things below;
Make us all Thy love to know;
Guard us from our ghostly foe :
  Hear us, holy Jesus.

9 Shelter us with angel's wing ;
To our souls Thy pardon bring ;
So shall death have lost its sting :
  Hear us, holy Jesus.

10 In the gloom Thy light provide ;
Safely through the valley guide;
Thee we trust, for Thou hast died:
  Hear us, holy Jesus.

JUDGMENT.

11 When Thy summons we obey
On the dreadful Judgment day,
Let not fear our soul dismay:
  Hear us, holy Jesus.

12 While the lost in terror fly,
May we see with joyful eye
Our redemption drawing nigh:
  Hear us, holy Jesus.

13 May we see Thee on Thy throne
As the Saviour we have known,
And have followed as our own:
  Hear us, holy Jesus.

14 May we then, among the blest
Who Thy Name on earth confessed,
Hear Thee calling us to rest :
  Hear us, holy Jesus.

HELL.

15 From the awful place of doom,
Where in rayless outer gloom
Dead souls lie as in a tomb,
Save us, holy Jesus.

16 From the black, the dull despair
Ruined men and angels share,
From the dread companions there,
Save us, holy Jesus.

17 From the unknown agonies
Of the soul that helpless lies;
From the worm that never dies,
Save us, holy Jesus.

18 From the lusts that none can tame.
From the fierce mysterious flame,
From the everlasting shame,
Save us, holy Jesus.

HEAVEN.

19 Where Thy saints in glory reign,
Free from sorrow, free from pain,
Pure from every guilty stain,
Bring us, holy Jesus.

20 Where the captives find release,
Where all foes from troubling cease,
Where the weary rest in peace,
Bring us, holy Jesus.

21 Where the pleasures never cloy,
Where in angels' holy joy
Thy redeemed their powers employ,
Bring us, holy Jesus.

22 Where in wondrous light are shown
All Thy dealings with Thine own,
Who shall know as they are known,
Bring us, holy Jesus.

23 Where, with loved ones gone before,
We may love Thee and adore
In Thy presence evermore,
Bring us, holy Jesus. Amen.

X. Appendix.

CHILDREN'S SERVICES AND
SUNDAY SCHOOLS.

564   6.5.

1 Jesus, King of glory
  Throned above the sky,
Jesus, tender Saviour,
  Hear Thy children cry.
Pardon our transgressions,
  Cleanse us from our sin ;
By Thy Spirit help us
  Heavenly life to win.
Jesus, King of glory
  Throned above the sky,
Jesus, tender Saviour,
  Hear Thy children cry.

2 On this day of gladness,
  Bending low the knee
In Thine earthly temple,
  Lord, we worship Thee ;
Celebrate Thy goodness,
  Mercy, grace, and truth,
All Thy loving guidance
  Of our heedless youth;
Jesus, King of glory
  Throned above the sky,
Jesus, tender Saviour,
  Hear our grateful cry.

3 For the little children,
  Who have come to Thee;
For the glad, bright spirits
  Who Thy glory see;
For the loved ones resting
  In Thy dear embrace ;
For the pure and holy
  Who behold Thy face,
Jesus, King of glory
  Throned above the sky,
Jesus, tender Saviour,
  Hear our grateful cry.

4 For Thy faithful servants
  Who have entered in;
For Thy fearless soldiers
  Who have conquered sin ;
For the countless legions
  Who have followed Thee,
Heedless of the danger,
  On to victory;
Jesus, King of glory
  Throned above the sky,
Jesus, tender Saviour,
  Hear our grateful cry.

CHILDREN'S SERVICES AND SUNDAY SCHOOLS.

5 When the shadows lengthen,
   Show us, Lord. Thy way;
Through the darkness lead us
   To the heavenly day.
When our course is finished,
   Ended all the strife,
Grant us with the faithful
   Palms and crowns of life.
Jesus, King of glory
   Throned above the sky,
Jesus, tender Saviour,
   Hear Thy children cry. Amen.

565　　　　　　　　　　　7.6.

1 Come, praise your Lord and Saviour
   In strains of holy mirth;
Give thanks to Him, O children,
   Who lived a child on earth.

He loved the little children,
   And called them to His side,
His loving arms embraced them,
   And for their sake He died.

2 O Jesus, we would praise Thee
   With songs of holy joy;
For Thou on earth didst sojourn
   A pure and spotless boy.

Make us like Thee, obedient,
   Like Thee from sin-stains free,
Like Thee in God's own temple,
   In lowly home like Thee.

3 O Jesus, we would praise Thee,
   The lowly maiden's son;
In Thee all gentlest graces
   Are gathered into one.

Oh, give that best adornment
   That Christian child can wear,
The meek and quiet spirit
   Which shone in Thee so fair!

4 O Lord, with voices lifted
   We sing our songs of praise;
Be Thou the light and pattern
   Of all our childhood's days;

And lead us ever onward,
   That, while we stay below,
We may, like Thee, O Jesus,
   In grace and wisdom grow. Amen.

566　　　　　　　　　　　7s.

1 Now the dreary night is done,
Comes again the glorious sun;
Crimson clouds and silver white
Wait upon his breaking light.

2 Child of Mary, Thou dost know
What of danger, joy, or woe
Shall to-day my portion be;
Let me meet it all in Thee.

3 Thou wast meek and undefiled;
Make me holy too, and mild:
Thou didst foil the tempter's power;
Help me in temptation's hour.

4 Thou didst love Thy mother here:
Make me gentle, kind and dear:
Thou wast subject to her word;
Teach me to obey. O Lord.

5 Fretful feelings, passion, pride,
Never did with Thee abide;
Make me watch myself to-day,
That they lead me not astray. Amen.

567　　　　　　　　　　　8.7.

1 Jesus, tender Shepherd, hear me;
   Bless Thy little lamb to-night;
Through the darkness be Thou near me;
   Keep me safe till morning light.

2 All this day Thy hand has led me,
   And I thank Thee for Thy care;
Thou hast warmed me, clothed and fed me;
   Listen to my evening prayer!

3 Let my sins be all forgiven;
   Bless the friends I love so well:
Take us all at last to heaven,
   Happy there with Thee to dwell. Amen.

568　　　　　　　　　　　S.M.

1 We come, Lord, to Thy feet
   On this Thy holy day;
Oh, come to us, while here we meet
   To learn, and praise, and pray!

2 Our many sins forgive;
   The Holy Spirit send;
And teach us to begin to live
   The life that knows no end.

3 Lord fill our hearts with love;
   Our teachers' labors own;
That we and they may meet above,
   To sing before Thy throne. Amen.

569   7s.

1 Suppliant, lo! Thy children bend,
   Father, for Thy blessing now;
   Thou canst teach us, guide, defend;
   We are weak, almighty Thou.

2 With the peace Thy word imparts
   Be the taught and teacher blest:
   In their lives and in their hearts,
   Father, be Thy laws impressed.

3 Pour into each longing mind
   Light and knowledge from above;
   Charity for all mankind,
   Trusting faith, enduring love. Amen.

570   8.5.7.5.

1 Glory to the blessèd Jesus!
   Who for us was born,
   In the stable, cold and poor,
   On glad Christmas morn.

2 Glory to the blessèd Jesus!
   Who was crucified
   On Good Friday for our sins:
   Loving us He died.

3 Glory to the blessèd Jesus!
   Who for sinners lay
   In the tomb, and rose upon
   Happy Easter day.

4 Glory to the blessèd Jesus!
   He Who is our Way
   Went up in a cloud to heaven
   On Ascension day.

5 Glory to the blessèd Jesus!
   Who at Whitsuntide
   Sent His Holy Spirit down
   With us to abide.

6 Glory to the blessèd Jesus!
   We will praise His love,
   All our days on earth below,
   And for aye above. Amen.

571   8.7.8.7.7.7.

1 Once in royal David's city
   Stood a lowly cattle shed,
   Where a mother laid her baby,
   In a manger for His bed;
   Mary was that mother mild,
   Jesus Christ her little child.

2 He came down to earth from heaven
   Who is God and Lord of all,
   And His shelter was a stable,
   And His cradle was a stall;
   With the poor, and mean, and lowly,
   Lived on earth our Saviour holy.

3 And, through all His wondrous childhood,
   He would honor and obey,
   Love, and watch the lowly maiden
   In whose gentle arms He lay;
   Christian children all must be
   Mild, obedient, good as He.

4 For He is our childhood's pattern;
   Day by day like us He grew;
   He was little, weak and helpless,
   Tears and smiles like us He knew;
   And He feeleth for our sadness,
   And He shareth in our gladness.

5 And our eyes at last shall see Him,
   Through His own redeeming love;
   For that child so dear and gentle
   Is our Lord in heaven above;
   And He leads his children on
   To the place where He is gone.

6 Not in that poor lowly stable,
   With the oxen standing by,
   We shall see Him; but in heaven,
   Set at God's right hand on high;
   When like stars His children crowned,
   All in white shall wait around.

572   6.5.

1 Now a new year opens,
   Now we newly turn
   To the holy Saviour,
   Lessons fresh to learn.

2 This the holy lesson
   On the year's first day;
   Jesus by obedience
   Teaches to obey.

3 Of Thy cross thus early
   Tokens Thou dost give;
   By Thy wounds Thou healest;
   By Thy death we live.

4 Not to suffer only,
   Jesus, didst Thou come,
   But to leave us way-marks
   Pointing to our home.

CHILDREN'S SERVICES AND SUNDAY SCHOOLS.

5 In Thy blessèd footsteps
  Ever may we tread ;
Safe wher' keeping near Thee,
  By Thy Spirit led. Amen.

573   8.7.

1 Saw you never, in the twilight,
  When the sun had left the skies,
Up in heaven the clear stars shining
  Through the gloom, like silver eyes?
So of old the wise men, watching,
  Saw a little stranger star,
And they knew the King was given,
  And they followed it from far.

2 Heard you never of the story
  How they crossed the desert wild,
Journeyed on by plain and mountain,
  Till they found the holy Child?
How they opened all their treasure,
  Kneeling to that infant King ;
Gave the gold and fragrant incense,
  Gave the myrrh in offering.

3 Know ye not that lowly baby
  Was the bright and morning Star?
He Who came to light the Gentiles,
  And the darkened isles afar?
And, we too, may seek His cradle ;
  There our hearts' best treasures bring ;
Love, and faith, and true devotion,
  For our Saviour, God, and King.

574   7s.

1 Lamb of God, for sinners slain ;
  By Thy mercy born again,
For Thy guidance still we pray,
  Lest from grace we fall away.

2 By the mystic, cleansing flood,
  By the Water and the Blood,
Washed and sanctified to Thee,
  Holy may we ever be.

3 Aid us with Thy daily grace
  Steadfastly to run our race ;
Grant us victory in the strife,
  And the prize of endless life.

4 Praise to Thee, from all on earth,
  God, Who gavest us new birth ;
Praise from all the heavenly host;
  Father, Son, and Holy Ghost. Amen.

575   6.5.

1 Golden harps are sounding,
  Angel voices sing,
Pearly gates are opened,
  Opened for the King;
Jesus, King of glory,
  Jesus, King of love,
Is gone up in triumph
  To His throne above.
All His work is ended,
  Joyfully we sing ;
Jesus hath ascended!
  Glory to our King!

2 He Who came to save us,
  He Who bled and died,
Now is crowned with glory,
  At His Father's side.
Never more to suffer,
  Never more to die ;
Jesus, King of glory,
  Is gone up on high!
All His work, etc.

3 Praying for His children
  In that blessèd place,
Calling them to glory,
  Sending them His grace;
His bright home preparing,
  Faithful ones, for you ;
Jesus ever liveth,
  Ever loveth too.
All His work, etc. Amen.

576   7.7.5.7.7.7.5.

1 Great Creator, Lord of all,
Father, Friend, on Thee we call;
  Hear Thy children's prayer.
Guide us, rule us, as is best,
With Thy loving favor blest,
  Till we reach Thy home of rest,
  And are with Thee there.

2 Jesus, Who for man didst die,
Who dost plead Thy death on high,
  And our place prepare:
From sin's bondage set us free,
Lead us onward after Thee,
  Till with joy Thy face we see,
  And Thy likeness wear.

CHILDREN'S SERVICES AND SUNDAY SCHOOLS.

3 Holy Spirit, Life, and Light,
  Wisdom, Pureness, Love, and Might,
    Fallen souls restore ;
  Guide our spirits when we pray,
  Cheer us, help us on our way,
  Make us holier day by day,
    Till we sin no more.

4 Ever blessèd Three in One,
  May Thy will in us be done,
    Show in us Thy love ;
  Keep us Thine while here below,
  Make us in Thy grace to grow,
  And at last Thy glory know
    In the world above. Amen.

577   7s.

1 Glory to the Father give,
  God in Whom we move and live;
  Children's prayers He deigns to hear,
  Children's songs delight His ear.

2 Glory to the Son we bring,
  Christ our Prophet, Priest, and King:
  Children raise your sweetest strain
  To the Lamb, for He was slain.

3 Glory to the Holy Ghost !
  He reclaims the sinner lost;
  Children's minds may He inspire,
  Touch their tongues with holy fire.

4 Glory in the highest be
  To the blessèd Trinity,
  For the Gospel from above,
  For the word that "God is love." Amen.

578   8.7.8.7.4.7.

1 God almighty, in Thy temple
  Low before Thy throne we bow;
  From Thy dwelling-place in glory
  Hear our supplications now,
    While we offer
  Earnest prayer and solemn vow.

2 Christ our Saviour, Thou Who carest
  For the youngest of Thy fold,
  Give us now Thy heavenly blessing,
  As Thou didst in days of old ;
    Priceless treasure,
  Richer far than gems or gold.

3 God the Holy Ghost, be near us:
  Ever dwell our hearts within ;
  Keep them pure, and brave, and earnest,
  Give us grace to conquer sin,
    And, through Jesus,
  Heaven's eternal crown to win.

4 Holy Trinity, defend us
  In a world with evil rife ;
  Let Thine angel-guards surround us,
  In each sore and bitter strife :
    Oh, preserve us
  Unto everlasting life!

579   L.M.

1 God hath two families of love;
  One is on earth and one above:
  One is in battle sharp and sore;
  And one at rest for evermore.

2 The Church on earth maintains the fight
  Against the devil and his might;
  The Church at rest with war hath done;
  And yet the two are only one.

3 For they who loved their Saviour here,
  And died in God's true faith and fear,
  Are waiting now in Paradise
  To join the Church beyond the skies.

4 We thank Thee, Saviour, for the grace
  By which they reached that blessèd place;
  Oh, teach us so to live, that we
  May follow them, as they did Thee!

5 Teach us to live in faith and love,
  Until Thou callest us above,
  To see Thee as Thou art, and stand
  Before Thee in the far-off land. Amen.

580   7s.

1 King of glory! Saviour dear !
  Grant us grace to persevere ;
  Leader of the hosts of God,
  May we tread where Thou hast trod !

2 Once for Thee, the Crucified,
  Many a faithful martyr died :
  How can we, Thy children, show
  All our love for all Thy woe?

3 They for Thee faced axe and wheel,
  Fire. and beasts, and piercing steel;
  Like them, may we suffer shame,
  Pain or loss for Thy dear Name.

4 Bearing calmly for our Lord
  Thoughtless jest or bitter word ;
  Curbing angry speech and tear,
  Strong in Thee to persevere.

5 Persevere, Thy yoke is light!
  Persevere, Thy crown is bright!
  Persevere, and we shall sing
  In the palace of our King!

581 6,5.

1 Jesus, high in glory,
    Lend a listening ear ;
  When we bow before Thee,
    Children's praises hear.

2 Though Thou art so holy,
    Heaven's almighty King,
  Thou wilt stoop to listen,
    When Thy praise we sing.

3 We are little children,
    Weak and apt to stray;
  Saviour, guide and keep us
    In the heavenly way.

4 Save us, Lord, from sinning ;
    Watch us day by day;
  Help us now to love Thee;
    Take our sins away.

5 Then, when Thou dost call us
    To our heavenly home,
  We shall gladly answer,
    Saviour, Lord, we come.

582 7,5.

1 Hear Thy children's hymn of praise,
    Lord of earth and sea,
  Which our joyful voices raise,
    Father, unto Thee.

2 Gentle Jesus, Thou didst love
    Little children here:
  Bid Thine angels guard us well
    From all harm and fear.

3 Blessèd Spirit, be Thou near
    When temptations rise ;
  Keep Thy little ones from sin,
    Fix their wandering eyes.

4 Thy dear cross, salvation's sign,
    On our brow we bear ;
  Christ's own infant soldier-band
    Christ's own cross should share.

5 When the battle's fought and won,
    Weary warfare o'er,
  Angels bright will bear us home
    Safe to heaven's shore.

6 Alleluia! let us sing
    To the Father, Son,
  With the Holy Spirit blest,
    Ever Three in One. Amen.

583 7s.

1 God of mercy, throned on high,
  Listen from Thy lofty seat ;
  Hear, oh, hear our lowly cry!
  Guide, oh, guide our wandering feet!

2 Young and erring travelers, we
  All our dangers do not know;
  Scarcely fear the stormy sea,
  Hardly feel the tempest blow.

3 Jesus, lover of the young,
  Cleanse us with Thy blood divine;
  Ere the tide of sin grow strong,
  Take us, keep us, make us Thine.

4 When perplexed in danger's snare,
  Thou alone our guide canst be:
  When oppressed with deepest care,
  Whom have we to trust but Thee?

5 Let us ever hear Thy voice,
  Ask Thy counsel every day;
  Saints and angels will rejoice,
  If we walk in wisdom's way.

6 Saviour, give us faith, and pour
  Hope and love on every soul ;
  Hope, till time shall be no more ;
  Love, while endless ages roll. Amen.

584   7s.

1 Loving Shepherd of Thy sheep,
Keep Thy lambs, in safety keep;
Nothing can Thy power withstand;
None can pluck us from Thy Hand.

2 Loving Saviour, Thou didst give
Thine own life that we might live;
And the hands outstretched to bless
Bear the cruel nails' impress.

3 We would praise Thee every day,
Gladly all Thy will obey,
Like Thy blessèd ones above
Happy in Thy precious love.

4 Loving Shepherd, ever near,
Teach Thy lambs Thy voice to hear;
Suffer not our steps to stray
From the strait and narrow way.

5 Where Thou leadest we would go,
Walking in Thy steps below,
Till before our Father's throne
We shall know as we are known.

585   8.7.

1 Day by day we magnify Thee,
When to Thee our hymns we raise;
Daily work begun and ended
With the daily voice of praise.

2 Day by day we magnify Thee,
Not in words of praise alone;
Truthful lips and meek obedience
Show Thy glory in Thine own.

3 Day by day we magnify Thee,
When for Jesus' sake, we try
Every wrong to bear with patience,
Every sin to mortify.

4 Day by day we magnify Thee,
Till our days on earth shall cease,
Till we rest from these our labors,
Waiting for Thy Day in peace.

5 Then, on that eternal morning,
With Thy great redeemèd host,
May we fully magnify Thee,
Father, Son, and Holy Ghost! Amen.

586   7.6.

1 There's a friend for little children
Above the bright blue sky,
A friend Who never changes,
Whose love will never die;
Our earthly friends may fail us,
And change with changing years,
This friend is always worthy
Of that dear Name He bears.

2 There's a rest for little children,
Above the bright blue sky,
Who love the blessèd Saviour,
And to the Father cry:
A rest from every turmoil,
From sin and sorrow free,
Where every little pilgrim
Shall rest eternally.

3 There's a home for little children
Above the bright blue sky,
Where Jesus reigns in glory,
A home of peace and joy;
No home on earth is like it,
Nor can with it compare;
For every one is happy,
Nor could be happier there.

4 There's a song for little children
Above the bright blue sky,
A song that will not weary,
Though sung continually;
A song which even angels
Can never, never sing;
They know not Christ as Saviour,
But worship Him as King.

5 There's a crown for little children
Above the bright blue sky,
And all who look for Jesus
Shall wear it by and by;
All, all above is treasured,
And found in Christ alone;
Lord, grant Thy little children
To know Thee as their own. Amen.

587   C.M.

1 Come, Christian children, come and raise
Your voice with one accord;
Come, sing in joyful songs of praise
The glories of your Lord.

2 Sing of the wonders of His love,
    And loudest praises give
  To Him Who left His throne above,
    And died that you might live.

3 Sing of the wonders of His truth,
    And read in every page
  The promise made to earliest youth,
    Fulfilled to latest age.

4 Sing of the wonders of His power,
    Who with His own right arm
  Upholds and keeps you hour by hour,
    And shields from every harm.

5 Sing of the wonders of His grace,
    Who made and keeps you His,
  And guides you to the appointed place
    At His right hand in bliss.

588   8.7.
1 Gracious Saviour, gentle Shepherd,
    Little ones are dear to Thee;
  Gathered with Thine arms and carried
    In Thy bosom may we be;
  Sweetly, fondly, safely tended,
    From all want and danger free.

2 Tender Shepherd, never leave us
    From Thy fold to go astray;
  By Thy look of love directed
    May we walk the narrow way;
  Thus direct us, and protect us,
    Lest we fall an easy prey.

3 Cleanse our hearts from sinful folly
    In the stream Thy love supplied,
  Mingled stream of blood and water,
    Flowing from Thy wounded side;
  And to heavenly pastures lead us,
    Where Thy own still waters glide.

4 Let Thy holy word instruct us;
    Guide us daily by its light ;
  Let Thy love and grace constrain us
    To approve whate'er is right:
  Take Thine easy yoke, and wear it,
    Strengthened with Thy heavenly might.

5 Taught to lisp the holy praises
    Which on earth Thy children sing,
  Both with lips and hearts unfeigned,
    May we our thank-offerings bring;
  Then with all the saints in glory
    Join to praise our Lord and King. Amen.

589   7s.
1 God eternal, mighty King,
  Unto Thee our praise we bring ;
  All the earth doth worship Thee ;
  We amid the throng would be.

2 Holy, holy, holy! cry
  Angels round Thy throne on high :
  Lord of all the heavenly powers,
  Be the same loud anthem ours.

3 Glorified apostles raise
  Night and day continual praise :
  Hast Thou not a mission too
  For Thy children here to do ?

4 With the prophets' goodly line
  We in mystic bond combine ;
  For Thou hast to babes revealed
  Things that to the wise were sealed.

5 Martyrs, in a noble host,
  Of the cross are heard to boast :
  Oh, that we our cross may bear,
  And a crown of glory wear! Amen.

590   8.7.
1 Heavenly Father, send Thy blessing
    On Thy children gathered here,
  May they all, Thy Name confessing,
    Be to Thee for ever dear ;
  May they be like Joseph, loving,
    Dutiful, and chaste, and pure ;
  And their faith, like David, proving,
    Steadfast unto death endure.

2 Holy Saviour, Who in meekness
    Didst vouchsafe a child to be,
  Guide their steps and help their weakness,
    Bless and make them like to Thee ;
  Bear Thy lambs when they are weary
    In Thine arms and at Thy breast;
  Through life's desert dry and dreary,
    Bring them to Thy heavenly rest.

3 Spread Thy golden pinions o'er them,
    Holy Spirit from above ;
  Guide them, lead them, go before them,
    Give them peace, and joy, and love:
  Temples of Thy glorious Godhead,
    May they with Thy presence shine,
  And immortal bliss inherit,
    And for evermore be Thine. Amen.

591 C.M.

1 Hosanna! raise the pealing hymn
　To David's Son and Lord:
　With cherubim and seraphim,
　Exalt the incarnate Word.

2 Hosanna! Lord, our feeble tongue
　No lofty strains can raise;
　But Thou wilt not despise the young,
　Who meekly chant Thy praise.

3 Hosanna! Sovereign, Prophet, Priest,
　How vast Thy gifts, how free!
　Thy blood, our life; Thy Word, our feast;
　Thy Name, our only plea.

4 Hosanna! once Thy gracious ear
　Approved a lisping throng;
　Be gracious still, and deign to hear
　Our ever grateful song. Amen.

592 P.M.

1 Hosanna we sing, like the children dear,
　In the olden days when the Lord lived here;
　He blessed little children, and smiled on them,
　While they chanted His praise in Jerusalem.

2 Alleluia we sing, like the children bright,
　With their harps of gold and their raiment white,
　As they followed their Shepherd, with loving eyes,
　Through the beautiful valleys of Paradise.

3 Hosanna we sing, for He bends His ear,
　And rejoices the hymns of His own to hear;
　We know that His heart will never wax cold
　To the lambs that He feeds in His earthly fold.

4 Alleluia we sing in the Church we love,
　Alleluia resounds in the Church above;
　To Thy little ones, Lord, may such grace be given,
　That we lose not our part in the song of heaven.
　　　　Amen.

593 7s.

1 Father, lead us, day by day,
　Ever in Thine own sweet way;
　Teach us to be pure and true,
　Show us what we ought to do.

2 When in danger make us brave;
　Make us know that Thou canst save;
　Keep us safe by Thy dear side;
　Let us in Thy love abide.

3 When we're tempted to do wrong,
　Make us steadfast, wise, and strong;
　And, when all alone we stand,
　Shield us with Thy mighty hand.

4 When our hearts are full of glee,
　Help us to remember Thee;
　Happy most of all to know
　That our Father loves us so.

5 When our work seems hard and dry,
　May we press on cheerily;
　Help us patiently to bear
　Pain and hardship, toil and care.

6 May we do the good we know,
　Be Thy children true below,
　Then at last go home to be
　Children still, dear Lord, to Thee.
　　　　Amen.

594 7s.

1 Saviour! teach me, day by day,
　Love's sweet lesson to obey;
　Sweeter lessons cannot be,
　Loving Him Who first loved me.

2 With a childlike heart of love,
　At Thy bidding may I move;
　Prompt to serve and follow Thee,
　Loving Him Who first loved me.

3 Teach me all Thy steps to trace,
　Strong to follow in Thy grace;
　Learning how to love from Thee;
　Loving Him Who first loved me.

4 Love in loving finds employ,
　In obedience all her joy;
　Ever new that joy will be,
　Loving Him Who first loved me.

5 Thus may I rejoice to show
  That I feel the love I owe ;
  Singing, till Thy face I see,
  Of His love Who first loved me. Amen.

595   7s.

1 Lamb of God, I look to Thee :
  Thou shalt my example be ;
  Thou art gentle, meek, and mild,
  Thou wast once a little child.

2 Fain I would be as Thou art ;
  Give me Thy obedient heart ;
  Thou art pitiful and kind,
  Let me have Thy loving mind.

3 Let me, above all, fulfill
  God my heavenly Father's will,
  Never His good Spirit grieve,
  Only to His glory live.

4 Loving Jesus, gentle Lamb,
  In Thy gracious hands I am ;
  Make me, Saviour, what Thou art,
  Live Thyself within my heart.

5 I shall then show forth Thy praise,
  Serve Thee all my happy days ;
  Then the world shall always see
  Christ the holy Child in me.

596   6.5.

1 Jesus, meek and gentle,
  Son of God most high,
  Pitying, loving Saviour,
  Hear Thy children's cry.

2 Pardon our offenses,
  Loose our captive chains,
  Break down every idol
  Which our soul detains.

3 Give us holy freedom,
  Fill our hearts with love;
  Draw us, holy Jesus,
  To the realms above.

4 Lead us on our journey,
  Be Thyself the way
  Through terrestrial darkness
  To celestial day.

5 Jesus, meek and gentle,
  Son of God most high,
  Pitying, loving Saviour,
  Hear Thy children's cry. Amen.

597   6.6.6.6.8.8.

1 Hushed was the evening hymn,
  The temple courts were dark,
  The lamp was burning dim,
  Before the sacred ark :
  When suddenly a voice divine
  Rang through the silence of the shrine.

2 The old man, meek and mild,
  The priest of Israel, slept ;
  His watch the temple-child,
  The little Levite, kept :
  And what from Eli's sense was sealed,
  The Lord to Hannah's son revealed.

3 Oh, give me Samuel's ear,
  The open ear. O Lord,
  Alive and quick to hear
  Each whisper of Thy word!
  Like him to answer at Thy call,
  And to obey Thee first of all.

4 Oh, give me Samuel's heart,
  A lowly heart, that waits
  Where in Thy house Thou art,
  Or watches at Thy gates!
  By day and night, a heart that still
  Moves at the breathing of Thy will.

5 Oh, give me Samuel's mind,
  A sweet, unmurmuring faith,
  Obedient and resigned
  To Thee in life and death!
  That I may read with childlike eyes
  Truths that are hidden from the wise.
                                        Amen.

598   S. M.

1 Fair waved the golden corn
  In Canaan's pleasant land,
  When, full of joy, some shining morn,
  Went forth the reaper-band.

2 To God so good and great
  Their cheerful thanks they pour ;
  Then carry to His temple-gate
  The choicest of their store.

186

CHILDREN'S SERVICES AND SUNDAY SCHOOLS.

3 Like Israel, Lord, we give
  Our earliest fruits to Thee,
And pray that, long as we shall live,
  We may Thy children be.

4 Thine is our youthful prime,
  And life and all its powers;
Be with us in our morning time,
  And bless our evening hours.

5 In wisdom let us grow,
  As years and strength are given,
That we may serve Thy Church below,
  And join Thy saints in heaven. Amen.

599   6.6.6.6.4.4.4.4.

1 Above the clear blue sky,
    In heaven's bright abode,
  The angel host on high
    Sing praises to their God:
      Alleluia!
    They love to sing
    To God their King
      Alleluia!

2 But God from children's tongues
    On earth receiveth praise;
  We then our cheerful songs
    In sweet accord will raise:
      Alleluia!
    We too will sing
    To God our King
      Alleluia!

3 O blessed Lord, Thy truth
    To all Thy flock impart,
  And teach us in our youth
    To know Thee as Thou art.
      Alleluia!
    Then shall we sing
    To God our King
      Alleluia!

4 Oh, may Thy holy word
    Spread all the world around!
  And all with one accord
    Uplift the joyful sound:
      Alleluia!
    All then shall sing
    To God their King
      Alleluia!

600   6.8.

1 O Jesus, God and Man,
    For love of children once a child!
  O Jesus, God and Man,
    We hail Thee, Saviour, sweet and mild!

2 O Jesus, God and Man!
    We children all are dear to Thee:
  Oh, lead us to Thyself,
    To love Thee for eternity!

3 O Jesus, Lord and God!
    The friend of children ever sure;
  Thy blood has washed us clean
    From guilt; oh, keep us always pure!

4 O Jesus, Saviour dear!
    We thank Thee ever for Thy love.
  And pray that to the Faith
    We may all true and faithful prove.

5 O Jesus, Mary's Son!
    On Thee for grace we children call,
  That we each other love,
    But Thee above, and chief of all.

6 O Jesus, bless our work;
    Our sorrows soothe, our sins forgive!
  Oh, happy, happy they
    Who in the love of Jesus live!

7 O God most great and good,
    At work, at play, by night, by day,
  Make us remember Thee,
    Who so rememberest us alway. Amen.

601   6s.

1 Great Shepherd of the sheep,
    Who all Thy flock doth keep,
      Leading by waters calm;
    Do Thou my footsteps guide,
    To follow by Thy side;
      Make me Thy little lamb.

2 I fear I may be torn
    By many a sharp-set thorn,
      As far from Thee I stray;
    My weary feet may bleed,
    For rough are paths which lead
      Out of Thy pleasant way.

3 But when the road is long,
   Thy tender arm, and strong,
   The weary one will bear;
   And Thou wilt wash me clean,
   And lead to pastures green.
   Where all the flowers are fair.

4 Till, from the soil of sin
   Cleansed and made pure within,
   Dear Saviour, Who hast died,
   Thou bringest me in love,
   Safe to Thy fold above,
   For ever to abide. Amen.

2 Thou hast promised to receive us,
   Poor and sinful though we be;
   Thou hast mercy to relieve us,
   Grace to cleanse, and power to free:
   Blessèd Jesus!
   Let us early turn to Thee.

3 Early let us seek Thy favor,
   Early let us learn Thy will;
   Do Thou, Lord, our only Saviour,
   With Thy love our bosoms fill:
   Blessèd Jesus!
   Thou hast loved us; love us still. Amen.

602   7s.

1 Lord, Thy children guide and keep,
   As with feeble steps they press
   On the pathway rough and steep
   Through the weary wilderness.
   Holy Jesus, day by day,
   Lead us in the narrow way.

2 There are stony ways to tread;
   Give the strength we sorely lack.
   There are tangled paths to tread;
   Light us, lest we miss the track.
   Holy Jesus, etc.

3 There are sandy wastes that lie
   Cold and sunless, vast and drear.
   Where the feeble faint and die;
   Grant us grace to persevere.
   Holy Jesus, etc.

4 There are soft and flowery glades
   Decked with golden-fruited trees,
   Sunny slopes and scented shades;
   Keep us, Lord, from slothful ease.
   Holy Jesus, etc.

5 Upward still to purer heights!
   Onward yet to scenes more blest,
   Calmer regions, clearer lights,
   Till we reach the promised rest!
   Holy Jesus, etc. Amen.

603   8.7.8.7.4.7.

1 Saviour, like a shepherd lead us,
   Much we need Thy tender care;
   In Thy pleasant pastures feed us;
   For our use Thy folds prepare:
   Blessèd Jesus!
   Thou hast bought us, Thine we are.

604   8.7.

1 Grant us, O our heavenly Father,
   Now in these our early days,
   Thee in all things to remember,
   Thee to serve, and Thee to praise.

2 With the cross of Christ, our Saviour,
   Stamped upon our infant brows,
   May we in the battle's dawning
   Heed His word, and keep our vows.

3 Then in holy Confirmation,
   By the laying on of hands,
   Strength may we receive, and blessing,
   To obey our Lord's commands.

4 Drawing nearer still and nearer,
   May we close and closer cling
   To our Lord, and to His altar
   There ourselves an offering bring.

5 Step by step in life advancing,
   Onward, upward, as we move
   Through the world unharmed, rejoicing
   In His all-redeeming love:

6 Blest in joy, upheld in sorrow,
   At our work as in His sight,
   May His presence still be with us,
   As we do it with our might.

7 Serving Thee, our heavenly Father,
   From the dawn to set of sun,
   Serving Thee in life's young morning,
   Till our work on earth is done:

8 Till the shadows of the evening
   Shall for ever pass away,
   And the Resurrection-morning
   Kindle into perfect day. Amen.

CHILDREN'S SERVICES AND SUNDAY SCHOOLS.

605 6.5.

1 Jesus, gentlest Saviour,
God of might and power,
Thou Thyself art dwelling
With us at this hour.

2 Nature cannot hold Thee,
Heaven is all too strait
For Thine endless glory,
And Thy royal state.

3 Out beyond the shining
Of the farthest star,
Thou art ever stretching
Infinitely far.

4 Yet the hearts of children
Hold what worlds cannot,
And the God of wonders
Loves the lowly spot.

5 Jesus, gentlest Saviour,
Thou art with us now;
Fill us with Thy goodness
Till our hearts o'erflow.

6 Multiply our graces :
Give us love and fear,
And, dear Lord, the chiefest,
Grace to persevere !

7 Oh, how can we thank Thee
For a gift like this,
Gift that truly maketh
Heaven's eternal bliss?

606 7s.

1 Son of God, eternal Word,
Glorious Day-spring, Christ the Lord :
Shine upon us with Thy rays,
While we celebrate Thy praise.

2 When Thou didst arise from death,
We were quickened by Thy breath ;
We arose with Thee, our Head,
First-begotten from the dead.

3 Send to us the Holy Ghost ;
Give the light of Pentecost ;
That we may for ever bless
Thee, the Sun of Righteousness.

4 Keep us safe from harm and sin,
Foes around us and within ;
May we know Thee ever nigh,
Ever walk as in Thine eye.

5 Lead us onward, Lord, we pray,
To the pure and perfect day,
Where we may the glory see
Of the blessèd Trinity. Amen.

607 L.M.

1 How beauteous were the marks divine,
That in Thy meekness used to shine,
That lit Thy lowly pathway, trod
In wondrous love, O Son of God !

2 Oh, who like Thee, so calm, so bright,
So pure, so made to live in light?
Oh, who like Thee did ever go
So patient through a world of woe?

3 Oh, who like Thee so humbly bore
The scorn, the scoffs of men before ?
So meek, forgiving, godlike, high,
So glorious in humility ?

4 Oh, in Thy light be mine to go,
Illuming all my way of woe!
And give me ever on the road
To trace Thy footsteps, Son of God !
Amen.

608 L.M.

1 Saviour, Who didst from heaven come down,
A little child awhile to be:
Whose precious blood and thorny crown,
From death and sin have ransomed me:

2 Teach me, dear Saviour, some return
Of lowly service for Thy love,
Such as a thankful child may learn,
Such as Thy Spirit shall approve.

3 The hearts of little ones are claimed
For Thine own altar by Thy word ;
May I lay there my own unblamed,
And wilt Thou lift it heavenward, Lord ?
Amen.

609 8.7.8.7.4.7.

'1 In the vineyard of our Father
  Daily work we find to do:
Scattered gleanings we may gather.
  Though we are but young and few:
    Little clusters
  Help to fill the garners too.

2 Toiling early in the morning,
  Catching moments through the day.
Nothing small or lowly scorning
  While we work, and watch, and pray;
    Gathering gladly
  Free-will offerings by the way.

3 Not for selfish praise or glory,
  Not for objects nothing worth,
But to send the blessed story
  Of the Gospel o'er the earth.
    Telling mortals
  Of our Lord and Saviour's birth.

4 Up and ever at our calling,
  Till in death our lips are dumb,
Or till, sin's dominion falling,
  Christ shall in His kingdom come,
    And His children
  Reach their everlasting home.

5 Steadfast, then, in our endeavor,
  Heavenly Father, may we be;
And for ever, and for ever,
  We will give the praise to Thee;
    Alleluia!
  Singing, all eternity. Amen.

610 8.7.

1 God in heaven, hear our singing!
  Only little ones are we:
Yet a great petition bringing.
  Father, now we come to Thee.

2 Let Thy kingdom come, we pray Thee;
  Let the world in Thee find rest!
Let all know Thee and obey Thee,
  Loving, praising, blessing, blest!

3 Let the sweet and joyful story
  Of the Saviour's wondrous love,
Wake on earth a song of glory,
  Like the angels' song above!

4 Father, send the glorious hour!
  Every heart be Thine alone!
For the kingdom, and the power,
  And the glory are Thine own. Amen.

19)

611 7s.

1 Jesus loves me; this I know.
  For the Bible tells me so:
  Little ones to Him belong:
  They are weak, but He is strong.

2 Jesus loves me, He Who died
  Heaven's gate to open wide;
  He will wash away my sin,
  Let His little child come in.

3 Jesus loves me; He will stay
  Close beside me all the way:
  If I love Him, when I die
  He will take me home on high.
                        Amen.

  Also the following:

554 Jesus, Saviour ever mild.
555 Jesus, from Thy throne on high.
556 Lord of mercy and of might.

Parochial Missions.

612 8.7.8.7.3.

1 Lord. I hear of showers of blessing.
  Thou art scattering full and free!
  Showers the thirsty land refreshing;
  Let some portion fall on me,
                        Even me!

2 Pass me not, O gracious Father!
  Sinful though my heart may be;
  Thou might'st punish, but the rather
  Let Thy mercy light on me,
                        Even me!

3 Pass me not, O tender Saviour!
  Let me love and cling to Thee;
  I am longing for Thy favor;
  Whilst Thou'rt calling, oh, call me,
                        Even me!

4 Pass me not, O mighty Spirit!
  Thou canst make the blind to see;
  Witnesser of Jesus' merit,
  Speak the word of power to me,
                        Even me!

5 Have I long in sin been sleeping?
  Long been slighting, grieving Thee?
  Has the world my heart been keeping?
  Oh, forgive and rescue me,
                        Even me!

6 Love of God, so pure and changeless:
  Blood of God, so rich and free ;
  Grace of God, so strong and boundless,
  Magnify it all in me,
                    Even me!

7 Pass me not ! this lost one bringing.
  'Tis but one more. Lord, for Thee !
  All my heart to Thee is springing;
  Blessing others, oh, bless me,
                    Even me!
                    Amen.

613   7.6.

1 To-day Thy mercy calls us
  To wash away our sin.
  However great our trespass,
  Whatever we have been ;

  However long from mercy
  Our hearts have turned away,
  Thy precious blood can cleanse us.
  And make us white to-day.

2 To-day Thy gate is open,
  And all who enter in
  Shall find a Father's welcome,
  And pardon for their sin.

  The past shall be forgotten.
  A present joy be given.
  A future grace be promised.
  A glorious crown in heaven.

3 To-day our Father calls us.
  His Holy Spirit waits;
  His blessed angels gather
  Around the heavenly gates:

  No question will be asked us
  How often we have come ;
  Although we oft have wandered.
  It is our Father's home.

4 Oh, all-embracing mercy !
  Oh, ever-open door !
  What should we do without Thee
  When heart and eyes run o'er?

  When all things seem against us.
  To drive us to despair.
  We know one gate is open.
  One ear will hear our prayer.

614   L.M.

1 When at Thy footstool, Lord, I bend.
  And plead with Thee for mercy there,
  Think of the sinner's dying friend,
  And for His sake receive my prayer.

2 Oh, think not of my shame and guilt.
  My thousand stains of deepest dye!
  Think of the blood which Jesus spilt,
  And let that blood my pardon buy.

3 Think, Lord, how I am still Thine own.
  The trembling creature of Thy hand ;
  Think how my heart to sin is prone,
  And what temptations round me stand.

4 Oh, think upon Thy holy Word,
  And every plighted promise there!
  How prayer should evermore be heard.
  And how Thy glory is to spare.

5 Oh, think not of my doubts and fears.
  My strivings with Thy grace divine ;
  Think upon Jesus' woes and tears.
  And let His merits stand for mine.

6 Thine eye, Thine ear, they are not dull ;
  Thine arm can never shortened be ;
  Behold me here ; my heart is full ;
  Behold, and spare, and succor me.
                    Amen.

615   7s.

1 Jesus Christ is passing by ;
  Sinner, lift to Him thine eye:
  As the precious moments flee.
  Cry, " Be merciful to me."

2 Jesus Christ is passing by :
  Will He always be so nigh?
  Now is the accepted day ;
  Seek for healing while you may.

3 Fearest thou He will not hear?
  Art thou bidden to forbear?
  Let no obstacle defeat ;
  Yet more earnestly entreat.

4 Lo ! He stands and calls to thee.
  " What wilt thou then have of Me ? "
  Rise and tell Him all thy need ;
  Rise, He calleth thee indeed.

5 "Lord, I would Thy mercy see;
   Lord, reveal Thy love to me:
   Let it penetrate my soul;
   All my heart and life control."

6 Oh, how sweet! the touch of power
   Comes; it is salvation's hour:
   Jesus gives from guilt release;
   Faith hath saved thee, go in peace.

7 Glory to the Saviour's Name!
   He is ever still the same;
   To His matchless honor raise
   Never-ending songs of praise.

616 S.M.

1 Only one prayer to-day.
   One earnest, tearful plea;
   A litany from out the heart.
   Have mercy, Lord, on me.

2 Although my sin is great,
   Still to my God I flee;
   Yes, I can dare look up, and say,
   "Have mercy, Lord, on me."

3 Because of Jesus' cross,
   And that unfathomed sea,
   The crimson tide which laves the world,
   Have mercy, Lord, on me.

4 No other Name than His,
   My hope, my help may be;
   Oh, by that one all-saving Name,
   Have mercy, Lord, on me!

5 In garb of sorrow clad
   I crave Thy pardon free;
   In life to die, in death to live;
   Have mercy, Lord, on me. Amen.

617 S.M.

1 The Spirit, in our hearts,
   Is whispering, Sinner, come:
   The Bride, the Church of Christ, proclaims
   To all His children, Come.

2 Let him that heareth say
   To all about him, Come;
   Let him that thirsts for righteousness,
   To Christ, the fountain, come.

3 Yes, whosoever will,
   Oh, let him freely come,
   And freely drink the stream of life!
   'Tis Jesus bids him come.

4 Lo, Jesus, Who invites,
   Declares, I quickly come,
   Lord! even so; I wait Thy hour!
   Jesus, my Saviour, come. Amen.

618 7s.

1 Hark, my soul! it is the Lord;
   'Tis thy Saviour, hear His word;
   Jesus speaks, and speaks to thee,
   Speaks to each one, "Lov'st thou Me?"

2 He delivered thee when bound,
   And when wounded, healed thy wound;
   Sought thee wandering, set thee right,
   Turned thy darkness into light.

3 Can a woman's tender care
   Cease towards the child she bare?
   Yes, she may forgetful be;
   Yet will He remember thee.

4 His is an unchanging love,
   Higher than the heights above,
   Deeper than the depths beneath,
   Free and faithful, strong as death.

5 We shall see His glory soon,
   When the work of grace is done;
   Partners of His throne shall be;
   Hear Him asking, "Lov'st thou Me?"

6 Lord, it is my chief complaint
   That my love is weak and faint;
   Yet I love Thee and adore;
   Oh, for grace to love Thee more!

619 8s.

1 Jesus, my Lord, my God, my all,
   Hear me, blest Saviour, when I call;
   Hear me, and from Thy dwelling-place
   Pour down the riches of Thy grace.
   Jesus, my Lord, I Thee adore;
   Oh, make me love Thee more and more!

2 Jesus, too late I Thee have sought,
   How can I love Thee as I ought?
   And how extol Thy matchless fame,
   The glorious beauty of Thy Name?
   Jesus, my Lord, I Thee adore;
   Oh, make me love Thee more and more!

3 Jesus, what didst Thou find in me
   That Thou hast dealt so lovingly?
   How great the joy that Thou hast brought!
   Oh, far exceeding hope or thought!
       Jesus, my Lord, I Thee adore;
       Oh, make me love Thee more and more!

4 Jesus, of Thee shall be my song,
   To Thee my heart and soul belong:
   All that I am or have is Thine;
   And Thou, my Saviour, Thou art mine.
       Jesus, my Lord, I Thee adore;
       Oh, make me love Thee more and more!
                                         Amen.

620   6.6.6.6.4.4.4.4.

1 My song is love unknown;
   My Saviour's love to me;
   Love to the loveless shown,
   That they might lovely be.
       Oh, who am I,
       That for my sake,
       My Lord should take
       Frail flesh, and die?

2 He came from His blest throne,
   Salvation to bestow;
   But men made strange, and none
   The longed-for Christ would know.
       But oh, my friend!
       My friend indeed,
       Who at my need
       His life did spend.

3 Sometimes they strew His way,
   And His sweet praises sing;
   Resounding all the day,
   Hosannas to their King.
       Then "Crucify!"
       Is all their breath,
       And for His death
       They thirst and cry.

4 Why, what hath my Lord done?
   What makes this rage and spite?
   He made the lame to run,
   He gave the blind their sight.
       Sweet injuries!
       Yet they at these
       Themselves displease,
       And 'gainst Him rise.

5 They rise, and needs will have
   My dear Lord made away:
   A murderer they save;
   The Prince of Life they slay.
       Yet cheerful He
       To suffering goes,
       That He His foes
       From thence might free.

6 In life no house, no home
   My Lord on earth might have;
   In death no friendly tomb,
   But what a stranger gave.
       What may I say?
       Heaven was His home;
       But mine the tomb
       Wherein He lay.

7 Here might I stay and sing:
   No story so divine.
   Never was love, dear King,
   Never was grief like Thine!
       This is my friend,
       In Whose sweet praise
       I all my days
       Could gladly spend.

621   7.7.8.5.

1 Light that from that dark abyss
   Madest all things, none amiss,
   To share Thy beauty, share Thy bliss,
       Come to us: oh, come!

2 Light that dost o'er all things reign,
   Life that dost all life maintain;
   Oh, Life that doth create again,
       Come to us: oh, come!

3 Light of men, that left the skies,
   Light that looked through human eyes,
   And died in darkness as man dies,
       Come to us: oh, come!

4 Light that stooped to rise and raise,
   Soared to God above our gaze,
   And still art near us, all the days,
       Come to us: oh, come!

5 Light that makest manifest,
   Beautifiest, hallowest,
   Light in Thy joyous strength at rest,
       Come to us: oh, come!

6 Leave us not to say we see,
While we shut our eyes to Thee.
Who knockest very patiently;
Enter, Lord, and come!

7 All our good is Thine alone;
All our evil is our own;
Oh, drive it from before Thy throne!
Come to us: oh, come!

8 Works of darkness put away;
With Thy harness us array
To walk in light and wait for day,
And for Thee to come!

9 We have done great wrong to Thee,
Yet we do belong to Thee;
Oh, make our life one song to Thee!
Come to us: oh, come!

10 Come in all the majesty
Of Thy great humility!
Come! the whole earth cries out to Thee.
Come to us: oh, come! Amen.

622 7.6.

1 I need Thee, precious Jesus,
For I am full of sin;
My soul is dark and guilty,
My heart is dead within.

I need the cleansing fountain
Where I can always flee,
The blood of Christ most precious,
The sinner's perfect plea.

2 I need Thee, precious Jesus,
For I am very poor;
A stranger and a pilgrim,
I have no earthly store.

I need the love of Jesus
To cheer me on my way,
To guide my doubting footsteps,
To be my strength and stay.

3 I need Thee, precious Jesus,
I need a friend like Thee,
A friend to soothe and pity,
A friend to care for me.

I need the heart of Jesus
To feel each anxious care,
To tell my every trouble,
And all my sorrow share.

4 I need Thee, precious Jesus,
Thou joy of all Thine own;
Who through such toil and sorrow
Hast mounted to Thy throne:

There, with Thy blood-bought children,
My joy shall ever be,
To sing Thy praises, Jesus,
To gaze, my Lord, on Thee.

623 7.6.

1 I could not do without Thee,
O Saviour of the lost,
Whose precious blood redeemed me
At such tremendous cost;

Thy righteousness, Thy pardon,
Thy precious blood, must be
My only hope and comfort,
My glory and my plea.

2 I could not do without Thee,
I cannot stand alone,
I have no strength or goodness,
No wisdom of my own;

But Thou, beloved Saviour,
Art all in all to me,
And weakness will be power
If leaning hard on Thee.

3 I could not do without Thee,
For, oh, the way is long,
And I am often weary,
And sigh replaces song;

How could I do without Thee?
I do not know the way;
Thou knowest, and Thou leadest,
And wilt not let me stray.

4 I could not do without Thee,
O Jesus, Saviour dear;
E'en when my eyes are holden,
I know that Thou art near.

How dreary and how lonely
This changeful life would be
Without the sweet communion,
The secret rest with Thee!

5 I could not do without Thee:
  No other friend can read
The spirit's strange deep longings,
  Interpreting its need ;
No human heart could enter
  Each dim recess of mine,
And soothe, and hush, and calm it,
  O blessèd Lord, but Thine.

6 I could not do without Thee,
  For years are fleeting fast,
And soon in solemn loneliness
  The river must be passed ;
But Thou wilt never leave me,
  And though the waves roll high,
I know Thou wilt be near me,
  And whisper, "It is I."

624   6s.

1 Thy life was given for me!
    Thy blood, O Lord, was shed
  That I might ransomed be,
    And quickened from the dead.
  Thy life was given for me:
    What have I given for Thee?

2 Long years were spent for me
    In weariness and woe,
  That through eternity
    Thy glory I might know.
  Long years were spent for me:
    Have I spent one for Thee?

3 Thy Father's home of light,
    Thy rainbow-circled throne,
  Were left for earthly night,
    For wanderings sad and lone.
  Yea, all was left for me:
    Have I left aught for Thee?

4 And Thou hast brought to me
    Down from Thy home above
  Salvation full and free,
    Thy pardon and Thy love.
  Great gifts Thou broughtest me:
    What have I brought to Thee?

5 Oh, let my life be given,
    My years for Thee be spent!
  World-fetters all be riven,
    And joy with suffering blent.
  Thou gavest Thyself for me :
    I give myself to Thee.

625   7.6.

1 I lay my sins on Jesus,
    The spotless Lamb of God;
  He bears them all, and frees us
    From the accursed load.
  I bring my guilt to Jesus,
    To wash my crimson stains
  White in His blood most precious,
    Till not a spot remains.

2 I lay my wants on Jesus;
    All fullness dwells in Him ;
  He heals all my diseases,
    He doth my soul redeem.
  I lay my griefs on Jesus,
    My burdens and my cares;
  He from them all releases:
    He all my sorrows shares.

3 I rest my soul on Jesus,
    This weary soul of mine:
  His right hand me embraces,
    I on His breast recline.
  I love the Name of Jesus,
    Emmanuel, Christ, the Lord;
  Like fragrance on the breezes.
    His Name abroad is poured.

4 I long to be like Jesus,
    Meek, loving, lowly, mild ;
  I long to be like Jesus,
    The Father's holy Child ;
  I long to be with Jesus,
    Amid the heavenly throng ;
  To sing with saints His praises,
    To learn the angels' song.

626   7s.

1 Love of Jesus, all divine,
  Fill this longing heart of mine:
  Ceaseless struggling after life,
  Weary with the endless strife.

  Saviour, Jesus, lend Thine aid;
  Lift Thou up my fainting head;
  Lead me to my long-sought rest,
  Pillowed on Thy loving breast.

2 Thou alone my trust shall be,
Thou alone canst comfort me;
Only, Jesus, let Thy grace
Be my shield and hiding-place;
Let me know Thy saving power
In temptation's fiercest hour:
Then, my Saviour, at Thy side
Let me evermore abide.

3 Thou hast wrought this fond desire,
Kindled here this sacred fire,
Weaned my heart from all below,
Thee, and Thee alone to know.
Thou, Who hast inspired the cry,
Thou alone canst satisfy:
Love of Jesus, all divine,
Fill this longing heart of mine. Amen.

627 6.5.

1 Lo! the voice of Jesus
 Fondly speaks to all:
He it is Who frees us
 From sin's bitter thrall;
He it is Whose nature,
 Human as our own,
Pleads for every creature
 By the Father's throne.

2 Lo! the voice of Jesus,
 Heard within the breast,
Tells us He will ease us,
 Howsoe'er distrest:
Tells us that our sorrow
 For the night may last,
But a glad to-morrow
 Breaks upon us fast.

3 Lo! the voice of Jesus
 Bids us still endure:
Seek not what will please us,
 But things just and pure;
Strive through self-denial
 Upwards to the light,
Where faith's years of trial
 Shall be lost in sight. Amen.

628 7.5.7.5.7.5.7.5.8.8.

1 When the weary, seeking rest,
 To Thy goodness flee;
When the heavy-laden cast
 All their load on Thee;
When the troubled, seeking peace,
 On Thy Name shall call;
When the sinner, seeking life,
 At Thy feet shall fall:
Hear then in love, O Lord, the cry,
In heaven, Thy dwelling-place on high.

2 When the worldling, sick at heart,
 Lifts his soul above;
When the prodigal looks back
 To his father's love;
When the proud man from his pride
 Stoops to seek Thy face;
When the burdened brings his guilt
 To Thy throne of grace:
Hear then in love, O Lord, the cry,
In heaven, Thy dwelling-place on high.

3 When the stranger asks a home,
 All his toils to end;
When the hungry craveth food,
 And the poor a friend;
When the sailor on the wave
 Bows the fervent knee;
When the soldier on the field
 Lifts his heart to Thee:
Hear then in love, O Lord, the cry,
In heaven, Thy dwelling-place on high.

4 When the child, with loving heart,
 Youth, or maiden fair;
When the aged, trusting still,
 Seek Thy face in prayer;
When the widow weeps to Thee,
 Sad and lone and low;
When the orphan brings to Thee
 All his orphan woe:
Hear then in love, O Lord, the cry,
In heaven, Thy dwelling-place on high.
 Amen.

629 8.8.8.6.

1 O holy Saviour, friend unseen,
The faint, the weak, on Thee may lean;
Help me, throughout life's varying scene,
 By faith to cling to Thee.

2 Blest with communion so divine,
Take what Thou wilt, shall I repine,
When, as the branches to the vine,
 My soul may cling to Thee?

3 What though the world deceitful prove,
 And earthly friends and joys remove,
 With patient, uncomplaining love,
  Still would I cling to Thee.

4 Oft when I seem to tread alone
 Some barren waste with thorns o'ergrown,
 A voice of love in gentle tone
  Whispers, "Still cling to Me."

5 Though faith and hope awhile be tried.
 We ask not, need not aught beside.
 So safe, so calm, so satisfied,
  The souls that cling to Thee.

6 They fear not life's rough storms to brave,
 Since Thou art near and strong to save,
 Nor shudder e'en at death's dark wave,
  Because they cling to Thee.

630   7s.

1 Jesus, merciful and mild,
 Lead me as a helpless child :
 On no other arm but Thine
 Would my weary soul recline.

 Thou art ready to forgive,
 Thou canst bid the sinner live;
 Guide the wanderer, day by day,
 In the strait and narrow way.

2 Thou canst fit me by Thy grace
 For the heavenly dwelling place ;
 All Thy promises are sure,
 Ever shall Thy love endure :

 Then what more could I desire,
 How to greater bliss aspire?
 All I need, in Thee I see;
 Thou art all in all to me.

3 Jesus, Saviour, all divine,
 Hast Thou made me truly Thine?
 Hast Thou bought me by Thy blood?
 Reconciled my heart to God?

 Hearken to my humble prayer,
 Let me Thine own image bear,
 Let me love Thee more and more,
 Till I reach heaven's blissful shore.
                     Amen.

631   7s.

1 Prince of Peace, control my will ;
 Bid this struggling heart be still ;
 Bid my fears and doubtings cease ;
 Hush my spirit into peace.

2 Thou hast bought me with Thy blood,
 Opened wide the gate to God ;
 Peace I ask ; but peace must be,
 Lord, in being one with Thee.

3 May Thy will, not mine, be done ;
 May Thy will and mine be one ;
 Chase these doubtings from my heart;
 Now Thy perfect peace impart.

4 Saviour, at Thy feet I fall ;
 Thou my life, my God, my all!
 Let Thy happy servant be
 One for evermore with Thee!
                     Amen

632   7.6.

1 O Jesus, I have promised
  To serve Thee to the end ;
 Be Thou for ever near me,
  My Master and my Friend !
 I shall not fear the battle
  If Thou art by my side,
 Nor wander from the pathway
  If Thou wilt be my guide.

2 Oh, let me feel Thee near me!
  The world is ever near ;
 I see the sights that dazzle,
  The tempting sounds I hear ;
 My foes are ever near me,
  Around me and within ;
 But, Jesus, draw Thou nearer,
  And shield my soul from sin.

3 Oh, let me hear Thee speaking
  In accents clear and still,
 Above the storms of passion.
  The murmurs of self-will !
 Oh, speak to re-assure me,
  To hasten or control !
 Oh, speak, and make me listen,
  Thou guardian of my soul!

4 O Jesus, Thou hast promised
  To all who follow Thee,
That where Thou art in glory
  There shall Thy servant be;
And, Jesus, I have promised
  To serve Thee to the end;
Oh, give me grace to follow,
  My Master and my Friend!

5 Oh, let me see Thy foot-marks,
  And in them plant mine own!
My hope to follow duly
  Is in Thy strength alone.
Oh, guide me, call me, draw me,
  Uphold me to the end!
At last in heaven receive me,
  My Saviour and my Friend!
    Amen.

633.   L.M.

1 He leadeth me! O blessed thought!
O words with heavenly comfort fraught!
Whate'er I do, where'er I be,
Still 'tis God's hand that leadeth me.

Refrain:
  He leadeth me! He leadeth me!
  By His own hand He leadeth me;
  His faithful follower I would be,
  For by His hand He leadeth me.

2 Sometimes 'mid scenes of deepest gloom,
Sometimes where Eden's bowers bloom,
By waters calm, o'er troubled sea,
Still 'tis His hand that leadeth me.

3 Lord, I would clasp Thy hand in mine,
Nor ever murmur nor repine:
Content, whatever lot I see,
Since 'tis my God that leadeth me.

4 And when my task on earth is done,
When, by Thy grace, the victory's won,
E'en death's cold wave I will not flee,
Since God through Jordan leadeth me.

634.   8.7.8.7.4.7.

1 Glory be to God the Father!
  Glory be to God the Son!
Glory be to God the Spirit!
  Great Jehovah, Three in One!
    Glory, glory,
  While eternal ages run!

2 Glory be to Him Who loved us,
  Washed us from each spot and stain!
Glory be to Him Who bought us,
  Made us kings with Him to reign!
    Glory, glory,
  To the Lamb that once was slain!

3 Glory to the King of angels!
  Glory to the Church's King!
Glory to the King of nations!
  Heaven and earth your praises bring:
    Glory, glory,
  To the King of glory bring!

4 Glory, blessing, praise eternal!
  Thus the choir of angels sings;
Honor, riches, power, dominion!
  Thus its praise creation brings;
    Glory, glory,
  Glory to the King of kings!   Amen.

635   P.M.

1 Praise, praise ye the Name of Jehovah our God!
Declare, oh, declare ye His glories abroad!
Proclaim ye His mercy from nation to nation,
Till the uttermost islands have heard His salvation!
  For His love floweth on free and full as a river,
  And His mercy endureth for ever and ever.

2 Praise, praise ye the Lamb, Who for sinners was slain!
Who went down to the grave, and ascended again;
And Who soon shall return when these dark days are o'er,
To set up His kingdom in glory and power;
  For His love floweth on free and full as a river,
  And His mercy endureth for ever and ever.

3 Then the heaven and the earth and the sea shall rejoice,
The field and the forest shall lift the glad voice,
The sands of the desert shall bloom and be green,
And Lebanon's glory be shed o'er the scene:
  For His love floweth on free and full as a river,
  And His mercy endureth for ever and ever.

4 Her bridal attire and her festal array,
　All nature shall wear on that glorious day,
　For her King cometh down with His people
　　to reign,
　And His presence shall bless her with Eden
　　again;
　For His love floweth on free and full as a
　　river.
　And His mercy endureth for ever and ever.
　　　　　　　　　　　　　　　　Amen.

636　　　　　　　　　　　　　　C.M.

1 Praise to the Holiest in the height,
　And in the depth be praise :
　In all His words most wonderful,
　Most sure in all His ways.

2 O loving wisdom of our God!
　When all was sin and shame,
　A second Adam to the fight
　And to the rescue came.

3 O wisest love! that flesh and blood,
　Which did in Adam fail,
　Should strive afresh against their foe,
　Should strive and should prevail:

4 And that a higher gift than grace
　Should flesh and blood refine;
　God's presence and His very self,
　And essence all-divine.

5 O generous love! that He, Who smote
　In man for man the foe:
　The double agony in man
　　For man should undergo;

6 And in the garden secretly,
　And on the cross on high,
　Should teach His brethren, and inspire
　To suffer and to die.

7 Praise to the Holiest in the height,
　And in the depth be praise;
　In all His words most wonderful,
　Most sure in all His ways.　Amen.

637　　　　　　　　　　　　　　S.M.

1 Revive Thy work, O Lord,
　Thy mighty arm make bare ;
　Speak with the voice that wakes the dead,
　And make Thy people hear.

2 Revive Thy work, O Lord.
　Disturb this sleep of death;
　Quicken the smouldering embers now
　By Thine almighty breath.

3 Revive Thy work, O Lord,
　Create soul-thirst for Thee;
　And hungering for the bread of life,
　Oh, may our spirits be!

4 Revive Thy work, O Lord,
　Exalt Thy precious Name;
　And, by the Holy Ghost, our love
　For Thee and Thine inflame.

5 Revive Thy work, O Lord,
　And give refreshing showers;
　The glory shall be all Thine own.
　The blessing, Lord, be ours.　Amen.

638　　　　　　　　　　　　7.6.7.5.

1 Work, for the night is coming,
　Work through the morning hours:
　Work while the dew is sparkling,
　Work 'mid springing flowers;

　Work when the day grows brighter,
　Work in the glowing sun ;
　Work, for the night is coming,
　When man's work is done.

2 Work, for the night is coming,
　Work through the sunny noon ;
　Fill brightest hours with labor,
　Rest comes sure and soon :

　Give every flying minute
　Something to keep in store:
　Work, for the night is coming,
　When man works no more.

3 Work, for the night is coming,
　Under the sunset skies;
　While their bright tints are glowing,
　Work, for daylight flies:

　Work till the last beam fadeth,
　Fadeth to shine no more;
　Work while the night is darkening,
　When man's work is o'er.

639 8.7.

1 Call them in! the poor, the wretched.
  Sin-stained wanderers from the fold;
  Peace and pardon freely offer!
  Can you weigh their worth with gold?

  Call them in! the weak, the weary,
  Laden with the doom of sin;
  Bid them come and rest in Jesus!
  He is waiting: call them in!

2 Call them in! the Jew, the Gentile;
  Bid the stranger to the feast!
  Call them in! the rich, the noble,
  From the highest to the least.

  Forth the Father runs to meet them,
  He hath all their sorrows seen;
  Robe, and ring, and kiss of pardon,
  Wait the lost ones: call them in!

3 Call them in! the broken-hearted,
  Cowering 'neath the brand of shame;
  Speak love's message low and tender!
  'Twas for sinners Jesus came.

  See the shadows lengthen round us,
  Soon the day-dawn will begin;
  Call them in! the lost and lonely:
  Christ is coming: call them in!

640 7.6.

1 Stand up, stand up, for Jesus.
  Ye soldiers of the cross!
  Lift high His royal banner!
  It must not suffer loss:

  From victory unto victory
  His army shall He lead;
  Till every foe is vanquished,
  And Christ is Lord indeed.

2 Stand up, stand up, for Jesus!
  The trumpet call obey!
  Forth to the mighty conflict
  In this His glorious day!

  Ye that are men now serve Him
  Against unnumbered foes!
  Your courage rise with danger,
  And strength to strength oppose.

3 Stand up, stand up, for Jesus!
  Stand in His strength alone!
  The arm of flesh will fail you,
  Ye dare not trust your own:

  Put on the gospel armor,
  And watching unto prayer,
  When duty calls, or danger,
  Be never wanting there!

4 Stand up, stand up, for Jesus!
  The strife will not be long:
  This day, the noise of battle;
  The next, the victor's song.

  To him that overcometh
  A crown of life shall be;
  He with the King of glory
  Shall reign eternally.

641 7.6.8.6.8.6.8.6.

1 Beneath the cross of Jesus
  I fain would take my stand,
  The shadow of a mighty Rock
  Within a weary land;
  A home within the wilderness,
  A rest upon the way,
  From the burning of the noon-tide heat,
  And the burden of the day.

2 Upon the cross of Jesus,
  Mine eye at times can see
  The very dying form of One
  Who suffered there for me.
  And from my smitten heart with tears,
  These wonders I confess,
  The wonder of His glorious love,
  And my own worthlessness.

3 I take, O cross, thy shadow
  For my abiding-place;
  I ask no other sunshine than
  The sunshine of His face:
  Content to let the world go by,
  To know no gain nor loss,
  My sinful self my only shame,
  My glory all the cross.

642 P.M.

1 Days and moments quickly flying
  Speed us onward to the dead;
  Oh, how soon shall we be lying
  Each within his narrow bed!

2 Jesus, merciful Redeemer,
  Rouse dead souls to hear Thy voice;
  Wake, oh, wake each idle dreamer
  Now to make th' eternal choice!

3 Mark we whither we are wending;
　Ponder how we soon must go
　To inherit bliss unending,
　Or eternity of woe.

4 As a shadow life is fleeting;
　As a vapor so it flies:
　For the bygone years retreating
　Pardon grant, and make us wise;

5 Wise that we our days may number,
　Strive and wrestle with our sin;
　Stay not in our work nor slumber
　Till Thy holy rest we win.

6 Soon before the Judge all glorious
　We with all the dead shall stand;
　Saviour, over death victorious,
　Place us then on Thy right hand.

(After fourth and sixth verses.)

　Life passeth soon;
　　Death draweth near;
　Keep us, good Lord,
　　Till Thou appear;
　With Thee to live,
　　With Thee to die,
　With Thee to reign
　　Through eternity!　Amen.

643　8s.

1 My hope is built on nothing less
　Than Jesus' blood and righteousness;
　I dare not trust the sweetest frame,
　But wholly lean on Jesus' Name.
　On Christ, the solid rock, I stand;
　All other ground is shifting sand.

2 When clouds and darkness veil His face,
　I rest on His unchanging grace;
　In every high and stormy gale
　My anchor holds within the veil.
　On Christ, the solid rock, I stand;
　All other ground is shifting sand.

3 His word, His covenant, His blood,
　Support me in the 'whelming flood;
　When all around my soul gives way,
　He then is all my hope and stay.
　On Christ, the solid rock, I stand;
　All other ground is shifting sand.

4 When He shall come, with trumpet sound,
　Oh, may I then in Him be found!
　Clothed in His righteousness alone,
　Faultless to stand before the throne.
　On Christ, the solid rock, I stand;
　All other ground is shifting sand.

644　8.7.

1 Onward, Christian! though the region
　Where thou art be drear and lone;
　God has set a guardian legion
　Very near thee; press thou on!

2 Listen, Christian! their hosanna
　Rolleth o'er thee: "God is love;"
　Write upon thy red-cross banner,
　"Upward ever; heaven's above."

3 By the thorn-road, and none other,
　Is the mount of vision won;
　Tread it without shrinking, brother!
　Jesus trod it; press thou on!

4 Be this world the wiser, stronger,
　For thy life of pain and peace,
　While it needs thee; oh, no longer
　Pray thou for thy quick release!

5 Pray thou, Christian, daily rather,
　That thou be a faithful son;
　By the prayer of Jesus, "Father,
　Not my will, but Thine, be done." Amen

645　6.4.6.4.6.6.6.4.

1 I'm but a stranger here,
　　Heaven is my home;
　Earth is a desert drear,
　　Heaven is my home.
　Danger and sorrow stand
　Round me on every hand.
　Heaven is my fatherland,
　　Heaven is my home.

2 What though the tempest rage,
　　Heaven is my home:
　Short is my pilgrimage,
　　Heaven is my home.
　And time's wild wintry blast
　Soon will be over-past;
　I shall reach home at last,
　　Heaven is my home.

3 Therefore I murmur not,
   Heaven is my home;
   Whate'er my earthly lot,
   Heaven is my home.
   And I shall surely stand
   There at my Lord's right hand ;
   Heaven is my fatherland,
   Heaven is my home.

       Also the following:

16 At even when the sun did set.
88 Lord, in this Thy mercy's day.
97 When I survey the wondrous cross,
244 My God, accept my heart this day.
273 Look from Thy sphere of endless day.
306 A few more years shall roll.
320 Jesus lover of my soul.
321 Rock of ages.
328 Art thou weary.
382 O Jesus Thou art standing.
384 Glory be to Jesus.
387 O Jesus, Lord most merciful.
447 O love that casts out fear.
451 O Jesus, King most wonderful.
455 Come unto Me, ye weary.
456 O Lamb of God, still keep me.
457 Hail! Thou once despised Jesus.
468 Come, let us sing the song of songs.
473 Lift up your heads, ye mighty gates.
485 God is love : that anthem olden.
493 Oh, bless the Lord, my soul.
517 O brothers, lift your voices.
523 Not your own, but His ye are.
535 Soon and for ever.
537 Oh, where shall rest be found.
544 Through the night of doubt and sorrow.
686 I heard the voice of Jesus say.

      Lay Helpers.
646   7s.

1 Soldiers of the cross, arise!
   Gird you with your armor bright!
   Mighty are your enemies,
   Hard the battle ye must fight.

2 O'er a faithless fallen world
   Raise your banner in the sky!
   Let it float there wide unfurled!
   Bear it onward! lift it high!

3 'Mid the homes of want and woe,
   Strangers to the living word,
   Let the Saviour's herald go!
   Let the voice of hope be heard!

4 Where the shadows deepest lie,
   Carry truth's unsullied ray!
   Where are crimes of blackest dye,
   There the saving sign display!

5 To the weary and the worn
   Tell of realms where sorrows cease!
   To the outcast and forlorn
   Speak of mercy and of peace!

6 Guard the helpless! seek the strayed!
   Comfort troubles! banish grief!
   In the might of God arrayed,
   Scatter sin and unbelief!

7 Be the banner still unfurled,
   Still unsheathed the Spirit's sword,
   Till the kingdoms of the world
   Are the kingdom of the Lord! Amen.

647   L.M.

1 Go, labor on! spend and be spent!
   Thy joy to do the Father's will ;
   It is the way the Master went ;
   Should not the servant tread it still?

2 Go, labor on! 'tis not for naught ;
   Thine earthly loss is heavenly gain;
   Men heed thee, love thee, praise thee not:
   The Master praises: what are men?

3 Go, labor on! enough, while here,
   If He shall praise thee, if He deign
   The willing heart to mark and cheer :
   No toil for Him shall be in vain.

4 Go, labor on, while it is day!
   The world's dark night is hastening on :
   Speed, speed thy work! cast sloth away!
   It is not thus that souls are won.

5 Toil on! faint not! keep watch, and pray!
   Be wise the erring soul to win!
   Go forth into the world's highway!
   Compel the wanderer to come in!

6 Toil on, and in thy toil rejoice!
   For toil comes rest, for exile home;
   Soon shalt thou hear the Bridegroom's voice,
   The midnight peal, " Behold, I come!"

DEDICATION OF PLACES AND THINGS.

648   6.6.4.6.6.4.

1 Christ for the world we sing;
The world to Christ we bring,
With loving zeal;
The poor, and them that mourn,
The faint and overborne,
Sin-sick and sorrow-worn,
Whom Christ doth heal.

2 Christ for the world we sing;
The world to Christ we bring,
With fervent prayer;
The wayward and the lost,
By restless passions tost,
Redeemed at countless cost,
From dark despair.

3 Christ for the world we sing;
The world to Christ we bring,
With one accord;
With us the work to share,
With us reproach to dare,
With us the cross to bear,
For Christ our Lord.

4 Christ for the world we sing;
The world to Christ we bring,
With joyful song;
The new-born souls, whose days,
Reclaimed from error's ways,
Inspired with hope and praise,
To Christ belong.

649   C.M.

1 How blessèd from the bonds of sin
And earthly fetters free,
In singleness of heart and aim,
Thy servants, Lord, to be!

The hardest toil to undertake
With joy at Thy command,
The meanest office to receive
With meekness at Thy hand:

2 With willing heart and longing eyes
To watch before Thy gate,
Ready to run the weary race,
To bear the heavy weight:

No voice of thunder to expect,
But follow, calm and still;
For love can easily divine
The one beloved's will.

3 Thus may we serve Thee, gracious Lord!
Thus ever Thine alone,
Our souls and bodies given to Thee,
The purchase Thou hast won.

Through evil or through good report
Still keeping by Thy side,
By life or death, in this poor flesh
Let Christ be magnified!

4 How happily the working days
In this dear service fly!
How rapidly the closing hour,
The time of rest, draws nigh:

When all the faithful gather home,
A joyful company!
And ever where the Master is
Shall His blest servants be! Amen.

Also the following:

163 O Son of God, our Captain of salvation.
164 The son of consolation.
517 O brothers, lift your voices.
521 Upon the holy mount they stood.
522 All unseen the Master walketh.
523 Not your own, but His ye are.

Dedication of Places and Things.

[BURIAL GROUND.]

650   8s.

1 O Thou, in Whom Thy saints repose,
When life's brief conflict finds its close:
Behold us met before Thy face
To hallow this their resting-place:
Safe are the souls whom Thou dost keep;
And safely here their dust shall sleep.

2 Thou knowest, Lord,—for Thou hast wept
Beside the tomb where Lazarus slept,—
What tears must flow, what hearts must bleed,
When here we sow the precious seed:
Thou still rememberest, on Thy throne,
Thy garden grave and sealèd stone.

3 Bid then Thy hosts encamp around
This chosen spot of holy ground :
Here let calm hope with memory dwell,
And faith, of heavenly comfort tell :
No thought of ill, no footstep rude
Profane the sacred solitude.

FOR THE SICK AND AFFLICTED.

4 Here when Thy mourners shall repair
  In lonely grief and trembling prayer,
  Lift Thou sad hearts and streaming eyes
  To those fair glades of Paradise,
  Where safe within the guarded gate
  Thy ransomed souls in patience wait.

5 And when the valley, thick with corn,
  Shall joy to see Thy harvest-morn,
  Here may the angel-reapers find
  Full many a sheaf for Thee to bind,
  And in Thy golden garner store,
  Gathered and safe for evermore. Amen.

[CHURCH BELLS.]
651   8.7.

1 Raised between the earth and heaven,
  Now our bells are set on high ;
  In the Name of Him Who giveth
  Skill, and strength, and industry.

2 For His praise we meekly lay them
  As a gift beneath His throne;
  All their sweet and noblest music
  Shall resound for Him alone.

3 Faithful men afar shall listen,
  'Mid their daily toil or rest,
  While the melody shall bid them
  Love the Church where all are blest.

4 Earth's rejoicings, bright and holy,
  Shall be signed with joyful peal;
  And the music from the steeple
  Shall our faith and love reveal.

5 They who languish, sick and lonely,
  Shall be minded, as they sigh,
  Of the Church's one communion,
  God's true home and family.

6 When the spirits of the faithful
  Pass away to light and peace;
  Solemn tones shall then forewarn us,
  Soon our life and work must cease.

7 May these loud and well-tuned voices,
  Pealing forth in grand accord,
  Lift our hearts through joy and sorrow
  To Thy throne, most gracious Lord.
                              Amen.

[AN ORGAN.]
652   P.M.

1 Angel-voices, ever singing
  Round Thy throne of light:
  Angel-harps, for ever ringing,
  Rest not day nor night ;
  Thousands only live to bless Thee,
  And confess Thee
  Lord of might !

2 Lord, we know Thy love rejoices
  O'er each work of Thine;
  Thou didst ears, and hands, and voices
  For Thy praise combine;
  Craftsman's art and music's measure
  For Thy pleasure
  Didst design.

3 Here, great God, to-day we offer
  Of Thine own to Thee;
  And for Thine acceptance proffer,
  All unworthily,
  Hearts and minds, and hands and voices,
  In our choicest
  Melody.

4 Honor, glory, might, and merit,
  Thine shall ever be!
  Father, Son, and Holy Spirit,
  Blessèd Trinity!
  Of the best that Thou hast given,
  Earth and heaven
  Render Thee! Amen.

For the Sick and Afflicted.

653   C.M.

1 Oh, for a faith that will not shrink
  Though pressed by every foe,
  That will not tremble on the brink
  Of any earthly woe!

2 That will not murmur nor complain
  Beneath the chastening rod,
  But, in the hour of grief or pain,
  Will lean upon its God ;

3 A faith that shines more bright and clear
  When tempests rage without ;
  That, when in danger, knows no fear,
  In darkness, feels no doubt.

FOR THE SICK AND AFFLICTED.

4 Lord, give us such a faith as this ;
  And then, whate'er may come,
We'll taste, ev'n here, the hallowed bliss
  Of an eternal home. Amen.

654 8.4.

1 My God, I thank Thee, Who hast made
    The earth so bright ;
  So full of splendor and of joy,
    Beauty and light ;
  So many glorious things are here,
    Noble and right.

2 I thank Thee too that Thou hast made
    Joy to abound ;
  So many gentle thoughts and deeds
    Circling us round,
  That in the darkest spot of earth
    Some love is found.

3 I thank Thee more that all our joy
    Is touched with pain ;
  That shadows fall on brightest hours ;
    That thorns remain ;
  So that earth's bliss may be our guide,
    And not our chain.

4 For Thou Who knowest, Lord, how soon
    Our weak heart clings,
  Hast given us joys, tender and true,
    Yet all with wings ;
  So that we see, gleaming on high,
    Diviner things.

5 I thank Thee, Lord, that Thou hast kept
    The best in store;
  We have enough, yet not too much
    To long for more;
  A yearning for a deeper peace,
    Not known before.

6 I thank Thee, Lord, that here our souls,
    Though amply blest,
  Can never find, although they seek,
    A perfect rest ;
  Nor ever shall, until they lean
    On Jesus' breast.

655 S. M.

1 "My times are in Thy hand : "
    My God, I wish them there;
  My life, my friends, my soul, I leave
    Entirely to Thy care.

2 "My times are in Thy hand,"
    Whatever they may be;
  Pleasing or painful, dark or bright,
    As best may seem to Thee.

3 "My times are in Thy hand : "
    Why should I doubt or fear?
  My Father's hand will never cause
    His child a needless tear.

4 "My times are in Thy hand,"
    Jesus, the crucified !
  The hand my cruel sins had pierced
    Is now my guard and guide.

656 L. M.

1 O Love divine, that stooped to share
    Our sharpest pang, our bitterest tear!
  On Thee we cast each earth-born care;
    We smile at pain while Thou art near.

2 Though long the weary way we tread,
    And sorrow crown each lingering year,
  No path we shun, no darkness dread,
    Our hearts still whispering, Thou art near.

3 When drooping pleasure turns to grief,
    And trembling faith is changed to fear,
  The murmuring wind, the quivering leaf,
    Shall softly tell us, Thou art near.

4 On Thee we rest our burdening woe,
    O Love divine, for ever dear !
  Content to suffer, while we know,
    Living and dying, Thou art near.

657 11s.

1 Tho' faint, yet pursuing, we go on our way;
  The Lord is our leader, His word is our stay;
  Though suffering, and sorrow, and trial be
    near,
  The Lord is our refuge, and whom can we
    fear?

2 He raiseth the fallen, he cheereth the faint ;
  The weak, and oppressed, He will bear
    their complaint;
  The way may be weary, and thorny the
    road,
  But how can we falter? our help is in God !

FOR THE SICK AND AFFLICTED.

3 And to His green pastures our footsteps He
leads;
His flock in the desert how kindly He feeds!
The lambs in His bosom He tenderly bears,
And brings back the wanderers safe from
the snares.

4 Though clouds may surround us, our God is
our light;
Though storms rage around us, our God is
our might;
So faint, yet pursuing, still onward we
come;
The Lord is our leader, and heaven is our
home!

658 11.10.

1 We would see Jesus: for the shadows
lengthen
Across this little landscape of our life;
We would see Jesus, our weak faith to
strengthen
For the last weariness, the final strife.

2 We would see Jesus, the great rock founda-
tion
Whereon our feet were set by sovereign
grace;
Nor life nor death, with all their agitation,
Can thence remove us, if we see His face.

3 We would see Jesus: other lights are paling,
Which for long years we have rejoiced to
see;
The blessings of our pilgrimage are failing;
We would not mourn them, for we go to
Thee.

4 We would see Jesus; yet the spirit lingers
Round the dear objects it has loved so
long,
And earth from earth can scarce unclasp its
fingers;
Our love to Thee makes not this love less
strong.

5 We would see Jesus: sense is all too binding,
And heaven appears too dim, too far
away;
We would see Thee, Thyself our hearts
reminding
What Thou hast suffered, our great debt
to pay.

206

6 We would see Jesus: this is all we're needing;
Strength, joy, and willingness come with
the sight;
We would see Jesus, dying, risen, pleading;
Then welcome day, and farewell mortal
night.

659 11.10.

1 Thou knowest, Lord, the weariness and sor-
row
Of the sad heart that comes to Thee for
rest;
Cares of to-day, and burdens of to-morrow,
Blessings implored, and sins to be con-
fest;
We come before Thee at Thy gracious word,
And lay them at Thy feet: Thou knowest,
Lord.

2 Thou knowest all the past; how long and
blindly
On the dark mountains the lost wanderer
strayed;
How the Good Shepherd followed, and how
kindly
He bore it home, upon His shoulders laid;
And healed the bleeding wounds, and sooth-
ed the pain,
And brought back life, and hope, and
strength again.

3 Thou knowest all the present; each tempta-
tion,
Each toilsome duty, each foreboding fear;
All to each one assigned, of tribulation,
Or to belovèd ones, than self more dear;
All pensive memories, as we journey on,
Longings for vanished smiles and voices
gone.

4 Thou knowest all the future; gleams of
gladness
By stormy clouds too quickly overcast;
Hours of sweet fellowship and parting sad-
ness,
And the dark river to be crossed at last.
Oh, what could hope and confidence afford
To tread that path! but this, Thou knowest,
Lord.

5 Thou knowest, not alone as God, all-knowing;
   As Man, our mortal weakness Thou hast proved ;
On earth, with purest sympathies o'erflowing.
   O Saviour, Thou hast wept, and Thou hast loved ;
And love and sorrow still to Thee may come,
   And find a hiding-place, a rest, a home.

6 Therefore we come, Thy gentle call obeying,
   And lay our sins and sorrows at Thy feet;
On everlasting strength our weakness staying,
   Clothed in Thy robe of righteousness complete:
Then rising and refreshed we leave Thy throne,
   And follow on to know as we are known.

660   L.M.

1 With tearful eyes I look around ;
   Life seems a dark and stormy sea;
Yet, 'mid the gloom, I hear a sound,
   A heavenly whisper, "Come to Me."

2 It tells me of a place of rest ;
   It tells me where my soul may flee :
Oh, to the weary, faint, oppressed,
   How sweet the bidding, "Come to Me !"

3 "Come, for all else must fail and die!
   Earth is no resting-place for thee;
To heaven direct thy weeping eye,
   I am thy portion ; Come to Me."

4 O voice of mercy! voice of love!
   In conflict, grief, and agony,
Support me, cheer me from above;
   And gently whisper, "Come to Me!"
                       Amen.

661   6s.

1 Thy way, not mine, O Lord,
   However dark it be:
Lead me by Thine own hand,
   Choose out the path for me.

Smooth let it be or rough,
   It will be still the best ;
Winding or straight, it leads
   Right onward to Thy rest.

2 I dare not choose my lot :
   I would not, if I might ;
Choose Thou for me, my God :
   So shall I walk aright.

Take Thou my cup, and it
   With joy or sorrow fill,
As best to Thee may seem ;
   Choose Thou my good and ill.

3 Choose Thou for me my friends,
   My sickness or my health ;
Choose Thou my cares for me,
   My poverty or wealth.

Not mine, not mine the choice,
   In things or great or small ;
Be Thou my guide, my strength,
   My wisdom, and my all. Amen.

662   7.6

1 Lord Jesus by Thy Passion,
   To Thee I make my prayer;
Thou Who in mercy smitest,
   Have mercy, Lord, and spare.

2 Oh, wash me in the fountain,
   That floweth from Thy side!
Oh, clothe me in the raiment
   Thy blood hath purified!

3 Oh, hold Thou up my goings,
   And lead from strength to strength,
That unto Thee in Sion
   I may appear at length!

4 Oh, hearken to my knocking,
   And open wide the door,
That I may enter freely
   And never leave Thee more!

5 Oh, bring me, loving Jesus,
   To that most blessèd place,
Where angels and archangels
   Look ever on Thy face;

6 Where gladsome alleluias
   Unceasingly resound;
Where martyrs, now triumphant,
   Walk robed in white and crowned!

7 Oh, make my spirit worthy,
   To join that ransomed throng!
Oh, teach my lips to utter
   That everlasting song!

HOME AND PERSONAL USE.

8 Oh, give that last, best blessing,
 That even saints can know,
To follow in Thy footsteps
 Wherever Thou dost go!

9 Not wisdom, might, or glory,
 I ask to win above;
I ask for Thee, Thee only,
 O Thou eternal love!

Home and Personal Use.

663 8s.

1 As every day, Thy mercy spares,
 Will bring its trials and its cares,
 O Saviour, till my life shall end,
 Be Thou my counselor and friend!
 Teach me Thy precepts all divine,
 And be Thy great example mine.

2 When each day's scenes and labors close,
 And wearied nature seeks repose,
 With pardoning mercy richly blest,
 Guard me, my Saviour, while I rest;
 And as each morning sun shall rise,
 Oh, lead me onward to the skies!

3 And at my life's last setting sun,
 My conflicts o'er, my labors done,
 Jesus, Thy heavenly radiance shed,
 To cheer and bless my dying bed;
 Then from death's gloom my spirit raise,
 To see Thy face and sing Thy praise. Amen.

664 C.M.

1 My Father, for another night
 Of quiet sleep and rest,
For all the joy of morning light,
 Thy holy Name be blest.

2 Now with the new-born day I give
 Myself anew to Thee,
That as Thou willest I may live,
 And what Thou willest be.

3 Whate'er I do, things great or small,
 Whate'er I speak or frame,
Thy glory may I seek in all,
 Do all in Jesus' Name.

4 My Father, for His sake, I pray,
 Thy child accept and bless;
And lead me by Thy grace to-day
 In paths of righteousness. Amen.

665 C.M.

1 The morning bright with rosy light
 Has waked me from my sleep;
Father, I own Thy love alone
 Thy little one doth keep.

2 All through the day, I humbly pray,
 Be Thou my guard and guide;
My sins forgive, and let me live,
 Lord Jesus, near Thy side.

3 Oh, make Thy rest within my breast,
 Great Spirit of all grace!
Make me like Thee; then shall I be
 Prepared to see Thy face. Amen.

666 L.M.

1 Saviour, when night involves the skies,
 My soul, adoring, turns to Thee;
Thee, self-abased in mortal guise,
 And wrapt in shades of death for me.

2 On Thee my waking raptures dwell,
 When crimson gleams the east adorn,
Thee, victor of the grave and hell,
 Thee, source of life's eternal morn.

3 When noon her throne in light arrays,
 To Thee my soul triumphant springs;
Thee, throned in glory's endless blaze,
 Thee, Lord of lords and King of kings.

4 O'er earth, when shades of evening steal,
 To death and Thee my thoughts I give;
To death, whose power I soon must feel,
 To Thee, with Whom I trust to live.

667 8.7.

1 Tarry with me, O my Saviour!
 For the day is passing by;
See! the shades of evening gather,
 And the night is drawing nigh.

2 Deeper, deeper grow the shadows,
 Paler now the glowing west,
Swift the night of death advances;
 Shall it be the night of rest?

3 Lonely seems the vale of shadow;
 Sinks my heart with troubled fear;
 Give me faith for clearer vision.
 Speak Thou, Lord, in words of cheer.

4 Let me hear Thy voice behind me,
 Calming all these wild alarms;
 Let me, underneath my weakness,
 Feel the everlasting arms.

5 Feeble, trembling, fainting, dying,
 Lord, I cast myself on Thee;
 Tarry with me through the darkness;
 While I sleep, still watch by me.

6 Tarry with me, O my Saviour!
 Lay my head upon Thy breast
 Till the morning; then awake me!
 Morning of eternal rest. Amen.

668 8s.

1 Inspirer and hearer of prayer,
  Thou shepherd and guardian of Thine,
  My all to Thy covenant care,
  I, sleeping or waking, resign.

2 If Thou art my shield and my sun,
  The night is no darkness to me;
  And, fast as my minutes roll on,
  They bring me but nearer to Thee.

3 A sovereign protector I have,
  Unseen, yet for ever at hand;
  Unchangeably faithful to save,
  Almighty to rule and command.

4 His smiles and His comforts abound,
  His grace, as the dew, shall descend;
  And walls of salvation surround
  The soul He delights to defend.

669 L.M.

1 Great God, to Thee my evening song
  With humble gratitude I raise:
  Oh, let Thy mercy tune my tongue,
  And fill my heart with lively praise.

2 My days unclouded as they pass,
  And every onward rolling hour,
  Are monuments of wondrous grace,
  And witness to Thy love and power.

3 And yet this thoughtless, wretched heart,
 Too oft regardless of Thy love,
 Ungrateful, can from Thee depart,
 And from the path of duty rove.

4 Seal my forgiveness in the blood
 Of Christ my Lord; His Name alone
 I plead for pardon, gracious God,
 And kind acceptance at Thy throne.

5 With hope in Him mine eyelids close;
 With sleep refresh my feeble frame;
 Safe in Thy care may I repose,
 And wake with praises to Thy Name.
                            Amen.

670 8.7.8.7.7.7.

1 Through the day Thy love has spared us;
  Now we lay us down to rest;
  Through the silent watches guard us,
  Let no foe our peace molest;
  Jesus, Thou our guardian be;
  Sweet it is to trust in Thee.

2 Pilgrims here on earth, and strangers,
  Dwelling in the midst of foes;
  Us and ours preserve from dangers;
  In Thine arms may we repose;
  And, when life's short day is past,
  Rest with Thee in heaven at last.
                            Amen.

671 C.M.

1 To Sion's hill I lift my eyes,
  From thence expecting aid;
  From Sion's hill, and Sion's God,
  Who heaven and earth has made.

2 He will not let Thy foot be moved,
  Thy guardian will not sleep;
  Behold, the God who slumbers not
  Will favored Israel keep.

3 Sheltered beneath th' Almighty's wings,
  Thou shalt securely rest,
  Where neither sun nor moon shall Thee
  By day or night molest.

4 At home, abroad, in peace, in war,
  Thy God shall thee defend;
  Conduct thee through life's pilgrimage,
  Safe to thy journey's end.

672   S.M.

1 Jesus, my strength, my hope,
  On Thee I cast my care:
With humble confidence look up,
  And know Thou hear'st my prayer.

Give me on Thee to wait,
  Till I can all things do;
On Thee, almighty to create,
  Almighty to renew.

2 Give me a true regard,
  A single, steady aim,
Unmoved by threatening or reward,
  To Thee and Thy great Name;

A jealous, just concern
  For Thine immortal praise;
A pure desire that all may learn
  And glorify Thy grace.

3 I rest upon Thy word;
  The promise is for me;
My succor and salvation, Lord,
  Shall surely come from Thee:

But let me still abide,
  Nor from my hope remove,
Till Thou my patient spirit guide
  Into Thy perfect love. Amen.

673   C.M.

1 Approach, my soul, the mercy-seat,
  Where Jesus answers prayer;
There humbly fall before His feet,
  For none can perish there.

2 Thy promise is my only plea,
  With this I venture nigh;
Thou callest burdened souls to Thee,
  And such, O Lord, am I.

3 Bowed down beneath a load of sin,
  By Satan sorely pressed,
By war without, and fears within,
  I come to Thee for rest.

4 Be Thou my shield and hiding-place;
  That, sheltered near Thy side,
I may my fierce accuser face,
  And tell him, Thou hast died!

5 O wondrous love! to bleed and die,
  To bear the cross and shame,
That guilty sinners, such as I,
  Might plead Thy gracious Name.

674   8s.

1 Jesus, Thy boundless love to me
  No thought can reach, no tongue declare;
Oh, knit my thankful heart to Thee,
  And reign without a rival there!
Thine wholly, Thine alone, I am;
  Be Thou alone my constant flame.

2 Oh, grant that nothing in my soul
  May dwell, but Thy pure love alone!
Oh, may Thy love possess me whole,
  My joy, my treasure, and my crown:
Strange flames far from my heart remove;
  May every act, word, thought, be love!

3 O love, how cheering is Thy ray!
  All pain before Thy presence flies:
Care, anguish, sorrow, melt away,
  Where'er Thy healing beams arise.
O Jesus, nothing may I see,
  Nothing desire or seek, but Thee!

4 Still let Thy love point out my way!
  What wondrous things Thy love hath wrought!
Still lead me, lest I go astray;
  Direct my word, inspire my thought;
And if I fall, soon may I hear
  Thy voice, and know that love is near.

5 In suffering, be Thy love my peace;
  In weakness, be Thy love my power;
And when the storms of life shall cease,
  Jesus, in that dark, final hour
Of death, be Thou my guide and friend,
  That I may love Thee without end.
                Amen.

675   C.M.

1 My God, I love Thee: not because
  I hope for heaven thereby;
Nor yet because if I love not
  I must for ever die.

2 But, O my Jesus, Thou didst me
  Upon the cross embrace;
For me didst bear the nails and spear,
  And manifold disgrace.

3 And griefs and torments numberless,
  And sweat of agony,
E'en death itself; and all for me
  Who was Thine enemy.

4 Then why, O blessèd Jesus Christ,
  Should I not love Thee well?
Not for the hope of winning heaven,
  Nor of escaping hell ;

5 Not with the hope of gaining aught ;
  Not seeking a reward :
But as Thyself hast lovèd me,
  O ever-loving Lord!

6 E'en so I love Thee, and will love,
  And in Thy praise will sing ;
Solely because Thou art my God,
  And my eternal King.

676   L. M.

1 No change of time shall ever shock
  My firm affection, Lord, to Thee ;
For Thou hast always been my rock,
  A fortress and defence to me.

2 Thou my deliverer art, my God ;
  My trust is in Thy mighty power :
Thou art my shield from foes abroad,
  At home my safeguard and my tower.

3 To Thee I will address my prayer,
  To Whom all praise we justly owe ;
So shall I, by Thy watchful care,
  Be guarded safe from every foe.

677   C. M.

1 When all Thy mercies, O my God,
  My rising soul surveys,
Transported with the view, I'm lost
  In wonder, love, and praise.

2 Oh, how shall words with equal warmth
  The gratitude declare
That glows within my ravished heart?
  But Thou canst read it there.

3 Ten thousand thousand precious gifts
  My daily thanks employ ;
Nor is the least a cheerful heart,
  That tastes those gifts with joy.

4 Through every period of my life
  Thy goodness I'll pursue ;
And after death, in distant worlds,
  The glorious theme renew.

5 When nature fails, and day and night
  Divide Thy works no more,
My ever grateful heart, O Lord,
  Thy mercy shall adore.

6 Through all eternity, to Thee
  A joyful song I'll raise ;
But oh, eternity's too short
  To utter all Thy praise!

678   8s.

1 Thou hidden love of God, whose height,
  Whose depth unfathomed no man knows :
I see from far Thy beauteous light,
  Inly I sigh for Thy repose :
My heart is pained, nor can it be
At rest till it find rest in Thee.

2 Is there a thing beneath the sun
  That strives with Thee my heart to share?
Ah! tear it thence, and reign alone,
  The Lord of every motion there.
Then shall my heart from earth be free,
When it hath found repose in Thee.

3 Oh, hide this self from me, that I
  No more, but Christ in me, may live!
My base affections crucify,
  Nor let one favorite sin survive ;
In all things nothing may I see,
Nothing desire, or seek, but Thee.

4 Each moment draw from earth away
  My heart, that lowly waits Thy call!
Speak to my inmost soul, and say
  I am thy love, thy God, thy all !
To feel Thy power, to hear Thy voice,
To taste Thy love, be all my choice! Amen.

679   L. M.

1 Let me with light and truth be blest ;
  Be these my guides to lead the way,
Till on Thy holy hill I rest,
  And in Thy sacred temple pray.

2 Then will I there fresh altars raise
  To God, Who is my only joy ;
And well-tuned harps, with songs of praise,
  Shall all my grateful hours employ.

HOME AND PERSONAL USE.

3 Why then cast down, my soul? and why
  So much oppressed with anxious care?
On God, thy God, for aid rely,
  Who will thy ruined state repair.

680 C.M.

1 O Thou, from Whom all goodness flows,
    I lift my heart to Thee;
  In all my sorrows, conflicts, woes,
    Dear Lord, remember me.

2 When on my aching, burdened heart
    My sins lie heavily,
  Thy pardon grant, Thy peace impart :
    In love, remember me.

3 When trials sore obstruct my way,
    And ills I cannot flee,
  Oh, let my strength be as my day!
    For good, remember me.

4 If worn with pain, disease, and grief,
    This feeble frame should be,
  Grant patience, rest, and kind relief :
    Hear and remember me.

5 And oh, when in the hour of death
    I own Thy just decree,
  Be this the prayer of my last breath,
    Dear Lord, remember me. Amen.

681 S.M.

1 My spirit, on Thy care,
    Blest Saviour, I recline;
  Thou wilt not leave me to despair,
    For Thou art love divine.

2 In Thee I place my trust,
    On Thee I calmly rest ;
  I know Thee good, I know Thee just,
    And count Thy choice the best.

3 Whate'er events betide,
    Thy will they all perform :
  Safe in Thy breast my head I hide,
    Nor fear the coming storm.

4 Let good or ill befall,
    It must be good for me;
  Secure of having Thee in all,
    Of having all in Thee.

682 7s.

1 Sovereign ruler of the skies,
  Ever gracious, ever wise;
  All our times are in Thy hand,
  All events at Thy command.

2 He that formed us in the womb,
  He shall guide us to the tomb;
  All our ways shall ever be
  Ordered by His wise decree.

3 Times of sickness, times of health,
  Blighting want and cheerful wealth,
  All our pleasures, all our pains,
  Come, and end, as God ordains.

4 May we always own Thy hand,
  Still to Thee surrendered stand,
  Know that Thou art God alone,
  We and ours are all Thy own ! Amen.

683 C.M.

1 Father, whate'er of earthly bliss
    Thy sovereign will denies,
  Accepted at Thy throne of grace
    Let this petition rise.

2 Give me a calm and thankful heart,
    From every murmur free;
  The blessings of Thy grace impart,
    And make me live to Thee.

3 Let the sweet hope that Thou art mine
    My path of life attend :
  Thy presence through my journey shine,
    And crown my journey's end. Amen.

684 C.M.

1 While Thee I seek, protecting power,
    Be my vain wishes stilled ;
  And may this consecrated hour
    With better hopes be filled.

2 Thy love the power of thought bestowed,
    To Thee my thoughts would soar :
  Thy mercy o'er my life has flowed,
    That mercy I adore.

3 In each event of life, how clear
    Thy ruling hand I see;
  Each blessing to my soul more dear,
    Because conferred by Thee.

4 In every joy that crowns my days,
   In every pain I bear,
 My heart shall find delight in praise,
   Or seek relief in prayer.

5 When gladness wings my favored hour,
   Thy love my thoughts shall fill;
 Resigned when storms of sorrow lower,
   My soul shall meet Thy will.

6 My lifted eye, without a tear,
   The gathering storms shall see;
 My steadfast heart shall know no fear,
   That heart will rest on Thee.

685 S.M.

1 Blest be the tie that binds
   Our hearts in Jesus' love:
 The fellowship of Christian minds
   Is like to that above.

2 Before our Father's throne
   We pour united prayers;
 Our fears, our hopes, our aims are one;
   Our comforts and our cares.

3 We share our mutual woes,
   Our mutual burdens bear;
 And often for each other flows
   The sympathizing tear.

4 When we at death must part,
   Not like the world's, our pain;
 But one in Christ, and one in heart,
   We part to meet again.

5 From sorrow, toil, and pain,
   And sin, we shall be free;
 And perfect love and friendship reign
   Throughout eternity.

686 C.M.

1 I heard the voice of Jesus say,
   Come unto Me and rest;
 Lay down, thou weary one, lay down
   Thy head upon My breast.

 I came to Jesus as I was,
   Weary and worn and sad,
 I found in Him a resting-place,
   And He has made me glad.

2 I heard the voice of Jesus say,
   Behold I freely give
 The living water; thirsty one,
   Stoop down and drink, and live.

 I came to Jesus, and I drank
   Of that life-giving stream;
 My thirst was quenched, my soul revived,
   And now I live in Him.

3 I heard the voice of Jesus say,
   I am this dark world's light;
 Look unto Me, thy morn shall rise,
   And all thy day be bright.

 I looked to Jesus, and I found
   In Him my Star, my Sun;
 And in that light of life I'll walk,
   Till traveling days are done.

687 L.M.

1 As, when the weary traveller gains
   The height of some commanding hill,
 His heart revives, if o'er the plains
   He sees his home, though distant still;

2 Thus, when the Christian pilgrim views
   By faith his mansion in the skies,
 The sight his fainting strength renews,
   And wings his speed to reach the prize.

3 The thought of heaven his spirit cheers;
   No more he grieves for troubles past;
 Nor any future trial fears,
   So he may safe arrive at last.

4 Jesus, on Thee our hopes we stay,
   To lead us on to Thine abode;
 Assured Thy love will far o'erpay
   The hardest labors of the road.

688 6s.

1 There is a blessèd home
   Beyond this land of woe,
 Where trials never come,
   Nor tears of sorrow flow;
 Where faith is lost in sight,
   And patient hope is crowned,
 And everlasting light
   Its glory throws around.

2 There is a land of peace:
　　Good angels know it well;
　Glad songs that never cease
　　Within its portals swell;
　Around its glorious throne
　　Ten thousand saints adore
　Christ, with the Father One,
　　And Spirit, evermore.

3 O joy all joys beyond,
　　To see the Lamb Who died,
　And count each sacred wound
　　In hands, and feet, and side!

　To give to Him the praise
　　Of every triumph won,
　And sing through endless days
　　The great things He hath done!

4 Look up, ye saints of God!
　　Nor fear to tread below
　The path your Saviour trod
　　Of daily toil and woe!
　Wait but a little while
　　In uncomplaining love!
　His own most gracious smile
　　Shall welcome you above.

DOXOLOGIES.

Note.—After the Long, Common, and Short Metres, the Doxologies follow in numerical order; first the simple numbers, then the double, and then the mixed. And the sequence is always from the higher to the lower, as 10s, 8s, 7s; 8.7, 7.6, 6.5, etc.

L.M.

Praise God, from Whom all blessings flow !
Praise Him, all creatures here below !
Praise Him above, ye heavenly host !
Praise Father, Son, and Holy Ghost ! Amen.

L.M.

To Father, Son, and Holy Ghost,
The God Whom earth and heaven adore.
Be glory, as it was of old,
Is now, and shall be evermore. Amen.

C.M.

To Father, Son, and Holy Ghost,
The God Whom we adore,
Be glory, as it was, is now,
And shall be evermore. Amen.

D.C.M.

To praise the Father, and the Son,
And Spirit all-divine,
The One in Three, and Three in One
Let saints and angels join :
Glory to Thee, blest Three in One,
The God Whom we adore,
As was, and is, and shall be done,
When time shall be no more. Amen. 8s.

S.M.

To God, the Father, Son,
And Spirit, ever blest,
The One in Three, the Three in One,
Be endless praise addressed. Amen.

D.S.M.

Praise, as in ages past,
Praise, as in glory now,
Praise, while eternity shall last,
To Thee, O God, we vow ;
Whom all the heavenly host
And saints on earth adore ;
To Father, Son, and Holy Ghost,
Be glory evermore. Amen.

1   10s.

To God the Father, and to God the Son,
To God the Holy Spirit, Three in One,
Be praise from all on earth and all in heaven,
As was, and is, and ever shall be given.
Amen.

2   8s.

All praise to the Father, the Son,
And Spirit, thrice holy and blest,
Th' eternal, supreme Three in One,
Was, is, and shall still be addressed.
Amen.

3   8.8.8.8.8.8.

To God the Father, God the Son,
And God the Spirit, Three in One,
Be glory in the highest given,
By all in earth, and all in heaven,
As was through ages heretofore,
Is now, and shall be evermore. Amen.

4   8.8.8.8.8.8.

To Father, Son, and Holy Ghost,
The God Whom heaven's triumphant host
And suffering saints on earth adore,
Be glory as in ages past,
As now it is, and so shall last
When time itself shall be no more.
Amen.

5   D.8s.

Eternal Father ! throned above,
Thou fountain of redeeming love !
Eternal Word ! Who left Thy throne
For man's rebellion to atone ;
Eternal Spirit, Who dost give
That grace whereby our spirits live ;
Thou God of our salvation, be
Eternal praises paid to Thee. Amen.

DOXOLOGIES.

6   7s.
Holy Father, Holy Son,
Holy Spirit, Three in One !
Glory, as of old, to Thee,
Now, and evermore shall be. Amen.

11   8.7.
Praise the Father, earth and heaven,
Praise the Son, the Spirit praise,
As it was, and is, be given
Glory through eternal days. Amen.

7s.   **7**   7.7.7.7.7.7.
Praise the Name of God most high,
Praise Him, all below the sky,
Praise Him, all ye heavenly host,
Father, Son, and Holy Ghost :
As through countless ages past,
Evermore His praise shall last. Amen.

8.7.   **12**   8.7.8.7.8.7.
Praise and honor to the Father,
Praise and honor to the Son,
Praise and honor to the Spirit,
Ever Three and ever One;
One in might and one in glory
While eternal ages run. Amen.

8   D.7s.
Holy Father, fount of light,
God of wisdom, goodness, might ;
Holy Son, Who cam'st to dwell,
God with us, Emmanuel :
Holy Spirit, heavenly Dove,
God of comfort, peace, and love;
Evermore be Thou adored,
Holy, holy, holy Lord. Amen.

13   D.8.7.
Let the voice of all creation,
Earth and heaven's triumphant host,
Praise the God of our salvation,
Father, Son, and Holy Ghost.
See the heavenly elders casting
Golden crowns before His throne :
Alleluias everlasting
Be to Him, and Him alone. Amen.

9   6s.
To Father, and to Son,
And, Holy Ghost, to Thee,
Eternal Three in One,
Eternal glory be. Amen.

14   7.6.
To Father, Son, and Spirit,
The God Whom we adore,
Be loftiest praises given,
Now and for evermore. Amen.

6s.   **10**   D.6s.   7.6.
To Father and to Son,
And, Holy Ghost, to Thee,
Eternal Three in One,
Eternal glory be:
As hath been, and is now,
And shall be evermore :
Before Thy throne we bow,
And Thee our God adore. Amen.

15   D 7.6.
O Father ever glorious.
O everlasting Son,
O Spirit all victorious,
Thrice holy Three in One,
Great God of our salvation,
Whom earth and heaven adore,
Praise, glory, adoration,
Be Thine for evermore. Amen.

DOXOLOGIES.

16   6.5.

Glory to the Father,
Glory to the Son,
And to Thee, blest Spirit,
Whilst all ages run. Amen.

17   D.6.5. or 11s.

O Father almighty, to Thee be addressed,
With Christ and the Spirit, one God ever
  blest,
All glory and worship, from earth and
  from heaven,
As was, and is now, and shall ever be
  given. Amen.

18   8.7.8.7.4.7.

Great Jehovah! we adore Thee,
  God the Father, God the Son,
God the Spirit, joined in glory
  On the same eternal throne:
    Endless praises
  To Jehovah, Three in One. Amen.

19   8.7.8.7.7.7.

Praise the Father throned in heaven;
  Praise the everlasting Son;
Praise the Spirit freely given;
  Praise the blessed Three in One.
As of old, the Trinity
  Still is worshipped, still shall be. Amen.

20   8.7.8.7.8.8.7.

To Father, Son, and Spirit blest,
  Supreme o'er earth and heaven,
Eternal Three in One confest,
  Be highest glory given,
As hath been from the ages past,
As shall be while the ages last,
  By all in earth and heaven. Amen.

21   8.8.8.6.

O Holy Father, Holy Son,
And Holy Spirit, Three in One,
As was, and is, and shall be done,
Glory to Thee, O Lord. Amen.

22   7.7.7.5.

Holy Father, Holy Son,
Holy Spirit, Three in One,
Alleluias round Thy throne
  Rise eternally. Amen.

23   6.6.6.6.8.8.

To God the Father's throne
  Your highest honors raise;
Glory to God the Son;
  To God, the Spirit, praise:
With all our powers, eternal King,
Thy Name we sing, while faith adores.
                Amen.

24   6.6.4.6.6.6.4.

To Father and to Son
And Spirit, Three in One,
  All praise be given,
As hath been heretofore
And shall be evermore:
Let all His Name adore
  In earth and heaven. Amen.

25

Come, let us adore Him; come, bow at His
  feet!
Oh, give Him the glory, the praise that is meet!
Let joyful hosannas unceasing arise,
And join the full chorus that gladdens the
  skies! Amen.

INDEX OF FIRST LINES.

	HYMN
A charge to keep I have	346
A few more years shall roll	306
A voice is heard on earth of kinsfolk weeping	253
Abide with me! fast falls the eventide	15
Above the clear blue sky	599
According to Thy gracious word	226
Across the sky the shades of night	304
All glory, laud and honor	89
All glory to the Father be	132
All hail the power of Jesus' Name	469
All people that on earth do dwell	489
All praise to Him Who built the hills	488
All praise to Thee, eternal Lord	443
All praise to Thee, my God, this night	11
All praise to Thee, O Lord	73
All unseen the Master walketh	522
Alleluia! Alleluia! hearts to heaven and voices raise	110
Alleluia! sing to Jesus!	458
Alleluia! song of sweetness	76
Almighty Father, bless the word	37
Almighty Father, hear our cry	311
Almighty God Whose only Son	511
An exile for the faith	145
Ancient of days, Who sittest throned in glory	358
Angels from the realms of glory	60
Angel voices ever singing	652
And now, O Father, mindful of the love	218
And now the wants are told, that brought	35
And will the great eternal God	268
Another year is dawning	308
Approach, my soul, the mercy seat	673
Arise, O Lord, and shine	270
Arm of the Lord, awake, awake	284
Art thou weary, art thou languid	328
As every day Thy mercy spares	663
As the sun doth daily rise	8
As Thou didst rest, O Father	29
As pants the wearied hart for cooling springs	484
As when the weary traveler gains	687
As with gladness men of old	70
Ashamed of Thee, O dearest Lord!	326
Asleep in Jesus! blessed sleep!	252
At even, when the sun did set	16
At the cross her station keeping	100
At the Lamb's high feast we sing	115
At the Name of Jesus	551

	HYMN
Awake, and sing the song	460
Awake! Awake! O Sion	422
Awake, my soul, stretch every nerve	344
Awake, my soul, and with the sun	2
Awhile in spirit, Lord to Thee	84
Before Jehovah's awful throne	490
Behold a humble train	155
Behold, the Master passeth by	175
Behold us, Lord, before Thee met	237
Beneath the cross of Jesus	641
Bishop of the souls of men	157
Blessed art Thou who passed before	255
Blessed city, heavenly Salem	427
Blessed Saviour, Thou hast taught us	80
Blessing, honor, thanks and praise	248
Blest are the pure in heart	493
Blest be, O Lord, the grace of love	162
Blest be the tie that binds	685
Blow ye the trumpet, blow	315
Bow down Thine ear, almighty Lord	257
Bowed down with sorrow, sin and shame	83
Bread of heaven on Thee we feed	223
Bread of the world in mercy broken	222
Brief life is here our portion	424
Brightest and best of the sons of the morning	68
Brightly gleams our banner	540
Call Jehovah thy salvation	346
Call them in, the poor, the wretched	639
Children of the heavenly King	471
Christ above all glory seated	392
Christ by heavenly hosts adored	203
Christ for the world, we sing	648
Christ is coming! let creation	47
Christ is made the sure foundation	501
Christ is risen! Christ is risen!	111
Christ our King to heaven ascendeth	125
Christ, the life of all the living	388
Christ the Lord is risen again	112
Christ the Lord is risen to-day	109
Christ, Whose glory fills the skies	444
Come, Christian children, come and raise	587
Come, gracious Spirit, heavenly Dove	390
Come, Holy Ghost, Creator blest	400
Come, Holy Ghost, our souls inspire	250
Come, Holy Spirit, come	397
Come, let us join our cheerful songs	466
Come, let us sing the song of songs	468

219

INDEX OF FIRST LINES.

First Line	HYMN
Come, Lord, and tarry not	49
Come, magnify the Saviour's love	462
Come, my soul, thou must be waking	5
Come, O Saviour, to Thy table	219
Come, praise your Lord and Saviour	565
Come, pure hearts, in sweetest measures	520
Come, quickly come, dread Judge of all	42
Come, Thou almighty King	408
Come, Thou Holy Spirit, come	398
Come to our poor nature's night	130
Come unto Me, ye weary	455
Come, ye faithful, raise the anthem	541
Come, ye faithful, raise the strain	108
Come, ye thankful people, come	210
Conquering kings their titles take	366
Creator of mankind	359
Creator Spirit, by Whose aid	401
Crown Him with many crowns	395
Day by day we magnify Thee	585
Day of wrath! oh, day of mourning!	44
Days and moments quickly flying	642
Draw, Holy Ghost, Thy sevenfold veil	239
Draw nigh, and take the body of the Lord	212
Dread Jehovah, God of nations	303
Earth has many a noble city	65
Eternal Father! strong to save	310
Eternal God! we look to Thee	453
Every morning mercies new	7
Fair waved the golden corn	598
Far from my heavenly home	373
Father, before Thy throne of light	178
Father, hear Thy children's call	560
Father, lead us day by day	593
Father of all, from land and sea	508
Father of heaven, Whose love profound	135
Father of heaven, Who hast created all	229
Father of love, our guide and friend	335
Father of mercies, God of love	207
Father of mercies in Thy Word	263
Father, whate'er of earthly bliss	683
Father, Who mak'st Thy suffering sons	292
Fierce raged the storm of wind	74
Fling out the banner, let it float	274
For all the saints, who from their labors rest	185
For all Thy love and goodness, so bountiful and free	531
For all Thy saints, a noble throng	170
For ever with the Lord	356
For the beauty of the earth	484
For Thee, O dear, dear country	425
For Thee, O God, our constant praise	538
For Thy dear saint, O Lord	191
For Thy mercy and Thy grace	307
Forward! be our watchword	548
Forward go in glad accord	547
Framer of the light	4
From all that dwell below the skies	493
From all Thy saints in warfare	183
From Greenland's icy mountains	275
From the eastern mountains	64
Glorious things of thee are spoken	504
Glory be to God the Father	634
Glory be to Jesus	384
Glory, glory everlasting	390
Glory to the blessed Jesus	570
Glory to the Father give	577
Glory to Thee, O Lord	148
Go forward, Christian soldier	349
Go, labor on, spend and be spent	647
God almighty, in Thy temple	578
God bless our native land	300
God eternal, mighty King	589
God hath two families of love	579
God in heaven hear our singing	610
God is love; His mercy brightens	446
God is love; that anthem olden	485
God, my Father, hear me pray	405
God, my King, Thy might confessing	486
God of mercy, God of grace	372
God of mercy, throned on high	583
God of our fathers, bless this land	299
God of that glorious gift of grace	231
God of the living, in Whose eyes	249
God, that madest earth and heaven	23
God the all-terrible! King, Who ordainest	479
God the Father, God the Son	559
Golden harps are sounding	575
Gracious Saviour, gentle Shepherd	588
Gracious Spirit, Holy Ghost	79
Grant us, O our heavenly Father	604
Great Creator, Lord of all	576
Great God of our salvation	270
Great God, to Thee my evening song	669
Great God, what do I see and hear	43
Great King of nations, hear our prayer	199
Great Shepherd of the sheep	601
Guide me, O Thou great Jehovah	437
Guide Thou, O God, the guardian hands	193
Hail the day that sees Him rise	123
Hail ! Thou long expected Jesus	62
Hail! Thou once despised Jesus	457
Hail, Thou source of every blessing	69
Hail to the Lord's Anointed	371
Hail to the Lord Who comes	156
Hark! a thrilling voice is sounding	40
Hark, my soul! it is the Lord	618
Hark! ten thousand voices sounding	121

INDEX OF FIRST LINES.

First Line	HYMN
Hark! the glad sound! the Saviour comes	51
Hark! the herald angels sing	54
Hark! the loud celestial hymn	136
Hark! the song of Jubilee	514
Hark! the sound of holy voices	189
Hark! the swelling breezes	283
Hark! the voice eternal	39
Hark! what mean those holy voices	61
Have mercy, Lord, on me	378
He is risen, He is risen	114
He leadeth me, O blessed thought	633
Heal me, O my Saviour, heal	380
Hear Thy children's hymn of praise	582
Hear us, Thou that broodest	128
Heavenly Father, send Thy blessing	500
Heavenly Shepherd, Thee we pray	260
Heirs of unending life	342
Here, O my Lord, I see Thee face to face	211
Holy Father, cheer our way	12
Holy, holy, holy Lord	406
Holy, holy, holy, Lord God almighty	404
Holy offerings rich and rare	297
Holy Spirit, heavenly Dove	552
Holy Spirit, Lord of glory	240
Holy Spirit, Lord of love	238
Hosanna! raise the pealing hymn	591
Hosanna to the living Lord	465
Hosanna we sing, like the children dear	592
How beauteous are their feet	519
How beauteous were the marks divine	607
How blessed from the bonds of sin	649
How oft, O Lord, Thy face hath shone	141
How sweet the Name of Jesus sounds	449
Hushed was the evening hymn	597
I am not worthy, holy Lord	220
I could not do without Thee	623
I heard the voice of Jesus say	686
I hunger and I thirst	330
I lay my sins on Jesus	625
I love Thy kingdom, Lord	503
I need Thee, precious Jesus	622
If thou wouldest life attain	352
I'm but a stranger here	645
In exile here we wander	77
In grief and fear to Thee, O Lord	200
In His temple now behold Him!	153
In the hour of trial	325
In the Name of God the Father	545
In the Name which earth and heaven	266
In the vineyard of our Father	609
In token that thou shalt not fear	233
Inspirer and hearer of prayer	668
It is finished! blessed Jesus	104
Jerusalem, my happy home	428

First Line	HYMN
Jerusalem on high	430
Jerusalem the golden	426
Jesus calls us: o'er the tumult	138
Jesus came; the heavens adoring	363
Jesus Christ is passing by	615
Jesus Christ is risen to-day	110
Jesus, from Thy throne on high	555
Jesus, gentlest Saviour	605
Jesus, high in glory	581
Jesus, I have promised	632
Jesus, I live to Thee	353
Jesus, in Thy dying woes	562
Jesus, King of glory	564
Jesus, life of those who die	563
Jesus lives! Thy threatening woe	118
Jesus, Lord of life and glory	377
Jesus, Lord, Thy praise we sing	142
Jesus, lover of my soul	320
Jesus loves me: this I know	611
Jesus, meek and gentle	596
Jesus, merciful and mild	630
Jesus, my Lord, my God, my all	619
Jesus, my Saviour, look on me	327
Jesus, my strength, my hope	672
Jesus, Name of wondrous love	150
Jesus, our risen King	459
Jesus, Saviour, ever mild	554
Jesus shall reign where'er the sun	281
Jesus, still lead on	438
Jesus, tender Shepherd, hear me	567
Jesus, the very thought is sweet	368
Jesus, the very thought of Thee	450
Jesus, Thou joy of loving hearts	448
Jesus, Thy boundless love to me	674
Jesus to Thy table led	216
Jesus, where'er Thy people meet	271
Jesus, Who for us didst bear	561
Jesus, with Thy Church abide	553
Joy to the world! the Lord is come	370
Just as I am, without one plea	329
King of glory. Saviour dear	580
King of saints. O Lord incarnate	139
King of saints, to Whom the number	174
Laboring and heavy laden	454
Lamb of God, for sinners slain	574
Lamb of God, I look to Thee	595
Lamp of our feet, whereby we trace	261
Lead, kindly Light, amid the encircling gloom	440
Lead us, heavenly Father, lead us	439
Let me be with Thee where Thou art	354
Let me with light and truth be blessed	679
Let no hopeless tears be shed	254
Let saints on earth in concert sing	410

INDEX OF FIRST LINES.

First Line	HYMN
Lift the strain of high thanksgiving	272
Lift up your heads, ye mighty gates	473
Light's abode, celestial Salem	417
Light that from that dark abyss	621
Lo! God is here! let us adore	500
Lo! He comes with clouds descending	41
Lo! round the throne a glorious band	187
Lo! the voice of Jesus	627
Lo! what a cloud of witnesses	414
Look from Thy sphere of endless day	273
Looking upward every day	350
Lord, a Saviour's love displaying	279
Lord, as to Thy dear cross we flee	374
Lord, dismiss us with Thy blessing	38
Lord, for ever at Thy side	334
Lord, her watch Thy Church is keeping	277
Lord! I beseech Thee on this day	383
Lord, I hear of showers of blessing	612
Lord, if on earth the thought of Thee	482
Lord, in this Thy mercy's day	88
Lord, in Thy Name Thy servants plead	202
Lord, it is good for us to be	171
Lord Jesus, by Thy Passion	602
Lord Jesus, think on me	318
Lord Jesus, when we stand afar	94
Lord, lead the way the Saviour went	293
Lord of all being; throned afar	445
Lord of all power and might	516
Lord of glory, Who hast bought us	294
Lord of mercy and of might	356
Lord of our life, and God of our salvation	510
Lord of the Church, we humbly pray	192
Lord of the harvest, hear	197
Lord of the harvest, once again	208
Lord of the harvest, Thee we hail	204
Lord of the hearts of men	78
Lord of the living harvest	256
Lord of the worlds above	497
Lord, pour Thy Spirit from on high	195
Lord, Thy children guide and keep	602
Lord, Thy word abideth	262
Lord, to Thee glad songs of praise	147
Lord, when we bend before Thy throne	370
Lord, while for all mankind we pray	298
Lord, Who at Cana's wedding feast	245
Lord! Who throughout these forty days	83
Lord, with glowing heart I'd praise Thee	338
Love divine, all love excelling	337
Love of Jesus, all divine	626
Loving Shepherd of Thy sheep	584
My faith looks up to Thee	383
My Father, for another night	604
My God, accept my heart this day	244
My God, and is Thy table spread	221
My God, I love Thee : not because	675

First Line	HYMN
My God, I thank Thee, Who hast made	654
My God, my Father, while I stray	331
My hope is built on nothing less	643
My song is love unknown	620
My soul, be on thy guard	343
My spirit on Thy care	681
My times are in Thy hand	655
Nearer, my God, to Thee	332
New every morning is the love	1
No change of time shall ever shock	676
Not by Thy mighty hand	75
Not to the terrors of the Lord	413
Not your own, but His ye are	523
Now a new year opens	372
Now thank we all our God	487
Now that the daylight fills the sky	6
Now the day is over	26
Now the dreary night is done	566
Now the laborer's task is o'er	250
O blessèd day, when first was poured	149
O Bread of life, from heaven	217
O Brightness of the immortal Father's face	10
O brothers, lift your voices	517
O Christ, our King, Creator, Lord	470
O come, all ye faithful	53
O come and mourn with me awhile	102
O come, O come, Emmanuel	48
O day of rest and gladness	31
O Father, all-creating	246
O Fount of good, to own Thy love	296
O God, in Whose all-searching eye	285
O God of Bethel, by Whose hand	341
O God of life, Whose power benign	134
O God of love, O King of Peace	302
O God of mercy, God of might	288
O God, our help in ages past	534
O God, our strength, our hope, our rock	232
O God, the Rock of ages	305
O God, unseen yet ever near	214
O gracious Master, bless us	241
O happy day that stays my choice	243
O heavenly Father, mindful of the love	218
O heavenly Jerusalem	416
O heavenly Word, eternal Light	442
O holy, holy, holy Lord	183
O holy Jesus, Prince of peace	225
O Holy Ghost, Thou God of peace	507
O holy Saviour, friend unseen	629
O Jesus, crucified for man	9
O Jesus, God and Man	600
O Jesus, I have promised	632
O Jesus, King most wonderful	451
O Jesus, Lord most merciful	387
O Jesus, Lord of heavenly grace	3

INDEX OF FIRST LINES.

First line	HYMN
O Jesus, Saviour of the lost	317
O Jesus, Thou art standing	382
O Jesus, Thou the beauty art	452
O Jesus, we adore Thee	886
O King eternal, King most high	124
O Lamb of God! still keep me	436
O Light, whose beams illumine all	529
O little town of Bethlehem	59
O Lord, be with us when we sail	309
O Lord of heaven, and earth, and sea	496
O Lord of Hosts! almighty King	301
O Lord of Hosts, Whose glory fills	265
O Lord our strength in weakness	524
O Love divine, that stooped to share	656
O Love that casts out fear	447
O mighty God, Creator, King	315
O mother dear, Jerusalem	429
O One with God the Father	369
O Paradise, O Paradise	421
O Rock of ages, one Foundation	168
O sacred head surrounded	99
O Saviour, bless us ere we go	18
O Saviour! precious Saviour	464
O Saviour, Who for man hast trod	126
O sinner, lift the eye of faith	93
O Son of God, our captain of salvation	163
O Son of Man, Thyself once crossed	143
O Spirit of the living God	258
O Thou, from Whom all goodness flows	680
O Thou, in Whom alone is found	267
O Thou, in Whom Thy saints repose	650
O Thou, that hear'st when sinners cry	316
O Thou, the contrite sinners' friend	322
O Thou, through suffering perfect made	289
O Thou, to Whose all-searching sight	324
O Thou, Who by a star didst guide	66
O Thou, Who didst with love untold	140
O Thou, Who dost to man accord	85
O Thou, Who gav'st Thy servant grace	144
O Thou, Who madest land and sea	526
O Thou, Who through this holy week	92
O Thou, Whose own vast temple stands	269
O Very God of Very God	441
O wondrous type! O vision fair	173
O Word of God incarnate	264
O'er the distant mountains breaking	52
Of the Father sole-begotten	56
Oft in danger, oft in woe	345
Oh, bless the Lord, my soul	493
Oh, blest was He, whose earlier skill	179
Oh, come loud anthems let us sing	491
Oh, for a faith that will not shrink	658
Oh, happy band of pilgrims	351
Oh, help us Lord; each hour of need	323
Oh, render thanks to God above	492
Oh, that the Lord's salvation	285
Oh, what if we are Christ's	412
Oh, what the joy and the glory must be	419
Oh, where shall rest be found	537
Oh, who are they, so pure and bright	146
Oh, why should Israel's sons once blessed	287
Oh, worship the King	480
On Jordan's bank the Baptist's cry	45
On our way rejoicing as we homeward move	542
On the resurrection morning	251
On the waters dark and drear	312
On this day, the first of days	27
Once in royal David's city	571
Once, only once, and once for all	213
One sweetly solemn thought	355
Only one prayer to-day	616
Onward, Christian soldiers	550
Onward, Christian, though the region	644
Our blest Redeemer, ere He breathed	396
Our day of praise is done	24
Our Lord is risen from the dead	127
Out of the deep I call	376
Pity on us, heavenly Father	557
Pleasant are Thy courts above	499
Praise my soul, the King of heaven	472
Praise, praise ye the Name of Jehovah our God	635
Praise the Lord! ye heavens adore Him	488
Praise the Rock of our salvation	505
Praise to God, immortal praise	209
Praise to the Holiest in the height	636
Praise we the Lord this day	159
Praises to Him Whose love has given	403
Prince of peace, control my will	631
Raised between the earth and heaven	651
Rejoice, rejoice, believers	46
Rejoice, the Lord is King	474
Rejoice, ye pure in heart	549
Rejoice, ye sons of men	154
Resting from His work to-day	103
Revive Thy work, O Lord	637
Ride on! ride on in majesty!	90
Rise, my soul, and stretch thy wings	357
Rock of ages, cleft for me	321
Round the Lord in glory seated	407
Safe upon the billowy deep	314
Saviour, again to Thy dear Name we raise	36
Saviour, blessed Saviour	548
Saviour, breathe an evening blessing	20
Saviour, like a shepherd lead us	603
Saviour, source of every blessing	463
Saviour, sprinkle many nations	278
Saviour, teach me day by day	594
Saviour, when in dust to Thee	86

223

INDEX OF FIRST LINES.

	HYMN		HYMN
Saviour, when night involves the skies	666	The God of Abraham, praise	478
Saviour, Who didst from heaven come down	608	The God of love my Shepherd is	436
		The grave itself a garden is	106
Saviour, Who Thy flock art feeding	230	The head that once was crowned with thorns	393
Saw you never in the twilight	573		
See the Conqueror mounts in triumph	122	The heavenly King must come	166
See the destined day arise	95	The King of love my Shepherd is	336
Shepherd of souls, refresh and bless	227	The Lord is King; He wrought His will	475
Shepherd of tender youth	498	The Lord is King; lift up your voice	476
Shepherd, with Thy tenderest love	435	The morning bright with rosy light	665
Shine on our souls, eternal God	360	The radiant morn hath passed away	13
Shout the glad tidings, exultingly sing	58	The roseate hues of early dawn	431
Sinful, sighing to be blest	375	The royal banners forward go	91
Sing Alleluia forth in duteous praise	482	The saints of God, their conflict past	184
Sing, my soul, His wondrous love	461	The shadows of the evening hours	17
Sing, oh sing, this blessed morn	55	The son of consolation	104
Sing praise to God Who reigns above	477	The Son of God goes forth to war	348
Sing with all the sons of glory	120	The Spirit in our hearts	617
Sing, ye faithful, sing with gladness	546	The strain upraise of joy and praise	481
So rest, our rest	105	The strife is o'er, the battle done	117
Softly now the light of day	19	The sun is sinking fast	21
Soldiers of Christ, arise	347	The world is very evil	423
Soldiers of the cross, arise!	646	The year is swiftly waning	533
Soldiers, who are Christ's below	411	Thee we adore, O hidden Saviour, Thee	215
Son of God, for man decreed	558	Their names are names of kings	186
Son of God, eternal Word	606	There is a blessed home	688
Son of Man, to Thee I cry	381	There is a green hill far away	385
Songs of praise the angels sang	494	There is a land of pure delight	418
Songs of thankfulness and praise	71	There is a Name I love to hear	367
Soon and for ever	585	There is one way, and only one	161
Souls in heathen darkness lying	280	There's a friend for little children	586
Sound aloud Jehovah's praises	137	Thine arm, O Lord, in days of old	290
Sovereign ruler of the skies	682	Thine for ever: God of love	242
Speed Thy servants, Saviour, speed them	282	This day, by Thy creative word	28
Spirit divine, attend our prayers	402	This day the wondrous mystery	98
Spirit of mercy, truth, and love	131	This is the day of light	34
Stand, soldier of the cross	234	Those eternal bowers man hath never trod	420
Stand up, stand up for Jesus	640		
Stars of the morning, so gloriously bright	176	Thou art coming, O my Saviour	362
Summer suns are glowing	532	Thou art gone up on high	394
Sun of my soul, Thou Saviour dear	14	Thou art the Christ, O Lord	167
Suppliant lo! Thy children bend	569	Thou art the Way, to Thee alone	530
Sweet the moments rich in blessing	101	Thou didst leave Thy throne and Thy kingly crown	364
Sweet Saviour, bless us, ere we go	18		
		Thou glorious Sun of Righteousness	30
Tarry with me, O my Saviour	667	Thou, God, all glory, honor, power	467
Ten thousand times ten thousand	415	Thou hidden love of God, whose height	678
The angel sped on wings of light	158	Thou knowest Lord, the weariness and sorrow	659
The Church has waited long	50		
The Church's one foundation	506	Thou standest at the altar	224
The cross is on our brow	236	Thou to Whom the sick and dying	291
The day is gently sinking to a close	25	Thou, Who on that wondrous journey	81
The day is past and over	22	Thou Who sentest Thine apostles	181
The day of resurrection!	113	Thou Who the night in prayer didst spend	196
The earth, O Lord, is one wide field	194	Thou Who with dying lips	527
The foe behind, the deep before	116	Thou Whose almighty word	513

INDEX OF FIRST LINES.

	HYMN		HYMN
Though faint, yet, pursuing, we go on our way	657	We would see Jesus; for the shadows lengthen	658
Three in One, and One in Three	409	Weary of earth and laden with my sin	819
Through the day Thy love has spared us	670	Welcome, happy morning, age to age shall say	107
Through the night of doubt and sorrow	544		
Thy kingdom come, O God	512	Welcome, sweet day of rest	33
Thy life was given for me	624	What thanks and praise to Thee we owe	180
Thy way, not mine, O Lord	661	What time the evening shadows fall	509
Till He come : oh, let the words	228	When all Thy mercies, O my God	677
To bless Thy chosen race	518	When at Thy footstool, Lord, I bend	614
To-day Thy mercy calls us	613	When Christ the Lord would come on earth	165
To hail Thy rising Sun of life	63		
To Him Who for our sins was slain	389	When, doomed to death the apostle lay	525
To Sion's hill I lift my eyes	671	When from the East the wise men came	67
To the Name of our salvation	365	When I survey the wondrous cross	97
To Thee, O Comforter divine	129	When morning gilds the skies	339
To Thee, O Father, throned on high	247	When our heads are bowed with woe	536
To Thee, O God, we Gentiles pay	151	When the weary, seeking rest	628
To Thee, O Lord, our hearts we raise	206	When Thou, O Lord, didst send the twelve	182
To Thee our God we fly	201	Where'er have trod Thy sacred feet	361
Triumphant Lord, Thy work is done	391	Where the angel hosts adore Thee	177
		While o'er the deep Thy servants sail	818
Upon the holy mount they stood	521	While shepherds watched their flocks by night	57
Wake, harp of Sion, wake again	286	While Thee I seek, protecting power	684
We come, Lord, to Thy feet	568	Who are these in bright array	190
We give thee but Thine own	295	Who are these like stars appearing	188
We love the place, O God	502	With broken heart and contrite sigh	87
We march, we march to victory	539	With joy we hail the sacred day	32
We plough the fields and scatter	205	With tearful eyes I look around	660
We praise Thy grace, O Saviour	160	With trembling awe the chosen three	172
We praise Thy Name, O Lord most high	169	Within the Father's house	73
We sing the glorious conquest	152	Work, for the night is coming	638
We sing the praise of Him Who died	96		
We walk by faith and not by sight	528	Ye servants of the Lord	198

225

INDEX OF SUBJECTS.

Adoration, 35, 384, 391. 392, 393. 395. 406, 407, 457, 458, 459, 464, 466, 467, 468, 469, 546.
Aspiration, 27, 70, 130. 305, 318. 324, 330, 332, 356, 381, 431, 432. 448, 621, 626.
Associations or Guilds, 162, 163, 164, 166, 168, 174, 182, 295 at vs. 3, 351, 352, 521, 522, 523, 646, 647, 649.
Autumn, 533.

Christ's Call, 138, 175, 455, 613. 617, 660, 686.
Church, Intercession for the, 181, 276, 277, 509, 510, 511, 512, 516, 553.
Church Militant, 186, 197, 348, 503, 5 4, 505, 506, 544, 550, 648.
Church at rest, 13, 184, 187, 189. 190, 249, 306, 410, 413, 415, 421. 424, 579, 688.
Church Triumphant. 77, 120, 416, 417, 425, 426, 427, 429, 430.
Clergy, The, 165, 168, 192, 193, 194, 195, 196, 257, 258.
Confession of Christ, 166, 168 at vs. 2, 169, 328, 386, 640.
Consecration, 21, 97, 246, 332, 333, 348. 349, 350, 353, 420, 473, 497, 523, 631.
Country, Our, 199, 201, 203, 298, 299, 300, 301, 479.

Doubt, 140, 141, 444, 508.

Faith, 13 at vs. 2, 25, 49, 50, 94, 333. 355, 356, 418, 453, 645, 653.
Fellowship with God, 15. 360, 361, 369, 374, 381, 432, 433. 445, 448, 454.
Following Christ, 348, 349, 351, 369, 471, 547, 632.

Guidance, 318, 323. 327, 328, 330, 335, 341, 359, 373, 397, 399, 400, 435, 437, 438, 439, 440. 441.

Hope, 46, 47, 355, 356, 357, 363, 411, 418, 419, 585.
Hospitals, 16, 179, 289, 290, 291. 292.
House of God, 499, 500, 501, 502, 546.
Humility, 334, 433, 623.

Joy, 46, 47, 51, 474.
Judgment, Day of, 43, 44.

Love of God, 96, 337, 368, 446, 447, 450, 485, 620, 674.
Love to God, 78, 79. 80, 81, 101, 338, 354, 362, 451, 594, 619. 674, 675.
Love to Man, 80, 294. 296.

Name of Jesus, 150, 365, 366, 367, 449, 551.

Orphans, 526, 527.

Peace, 17, 36, 360, 510. 631.
Penitence, 87, 316. 317. 319. 375, 376, 377. 378, 379. 380, 387, 405, 559.
Perseverance, 347, 359, 580.
Praise. 24, 338. 339, 384. 389. 390, 403, 460. 461, 462, 463, 471, 472, 478, 481, 482, 483, 484, 486, 488, 493, 635, 636.
Preparation for Christ, 40, 45, 46, 52, 423, 465.
Progress, 345, 347, 349, 350, 414, 543, 644.
Protection, 8. 20, 23, 340. 341. 453, 479, 480, 534. 608.
Providence, 202, 205, 207, 475, 477, 488, 496.

Spring. 531.
Summer, 532.
Submission, 331, 374. 629, 655, 661.
Sympathy, 162, 163, 164, 288, 291, 292, 296, 659.

Temperance, 524, 525.
Thanksgiving, 388, 654.
Triumph of Christ, 41, 125, 392, 474.
Trust, 143, 305, 320. 321, 322, 324, 325, 327, 329, 335, 336. 436, 456, 476, 613, 643, 655, 657. 667, 681.

Unity, 507, 508, 509.

Watchfulness, 198, 343, 346, 347, 423.
Work, 351, 352, 521, 522, 523, 638, 639, 640, 646, 647, 648, 649.

Zeal, 182, 344, 414.

227

APPENDIX.

PREFACE.

The Hymnal revised is herewith offered to the General Convention by the Committee appointed for this work.

The leading principles which have guided the Committee in the compilation of the Book are these:

1. To conform the contents and the arrangement of the Hymnal to the Book of Common Prayer.

2. To provide for the present needs and demands of the Church in her public worship and her increased activities, as the conditions have changed within the last twenty years.

3. To provide so fully for hymns in the various departments of Church life and work as to make unnecessary the purchase of additional books for special occasions.

4. To meet the necessities not merely of the larger City Parishes, but to include hymns which would satisfy the wants of smaller and remote missions and the needs of individual souls for the deepening, cultivation and expression of their personal devotion.

5. To include, as far as possible, the expression of the varying schools of theological thought and phases of religious feeling in the Church.

6. To place as many as possible of the hymns for the various seasons under the heading of "General," where they can readily be found by means of the first-line references, and where yet they will naturally come into use throughout the year.

The Committee has had constantly in mind three canons by which to test the value of a hymn:

(a) That while undoubtedly one object of a hymn is to rouse devotional feeling, as indicated by the Apostolic injunction, "Speaking to one another in Psalms and spiritual songs," and as abundantly illustrated by the texture of the Psalter; yet *expression* rather than *impression* should be the chief characteristic of a good hymn as a direct utterance of prayer or praise to God.

(b) That it was the duty of a Committee to criticize every hymn, and to present only such as come up to the recognized standards of the best authorities in hymnology, without *too* much regard to the prejudices or the associations of the past, or to the passing popularity of the present, based, both of them, upon the insecure and insufficient ground of sentiment; and also to dissever the actual merits of each hymn from the accident of an attractive tune, which often sings into favor words quite unmeaning and unworthy of use.

(c) That while other things being equal, a return to the original form of a hymn is desirable, it is perfectly legitimate, when the authors are not named in connection with the hymns, to change the language of a hymn, which the Church chooses to adopt as part of its public worship.

PREFACE.

Dr. Martineau, in the preface to his "Hymns of Praise and Prayer," argues for this liberty in the following language, on which the Committee is content to rest this claim : "In common with earlier Christians who turned the Psalter to their use, Watts altered David, and Wesley altered Watts ; Jeremy Taylor, as well as Tate and Brady, was corrected by Bishop Heber ; George Herbert by Bishop Horne ; and the Moravian Hymns appear in their successive editions with various transformations. In the absence of this liberty there could be no literature of devotion common to Christendom. The whole hope of any gathering together of Christians in a comprehensive 'City of God' depends on a gradual falling away of transitory from permanent elements in the *sacra* transmitted from the past ; and they can never be sifted out and lay bare the imperishable residuum, unless each Communion is free to take what it can from the life of the rest, and so test the real range of possible sympathy."

The increased number of hymns is due to the actual need of meeting the exigencies, emergencies and diversities already alluded to, and is justified by the size of those Hymnals which have secured the largest use.

The writing of this Preface brings to an end the work of the Committee, whose only further duty is to present the Report to the body which appointed it. And it brings to an end an association of much labor, of mutual counsel and concession, of earnest interest and high aims, clouded by only two events : the removal from very valuable service to our American Church of the Bishop of Nova Scotia, who brought most cultivated taste and thought to our labors ; and, to us, the far sadder removal, to the rest of Paradise, of our beloved brother, Albert Zabriskie Gray, in whom a character of most intense devoutness lent consecration to his ripe scholarship, his rich poetic feeling, and his rare and exquisite taste.

W. C. DOANE, D.D., Bp. of Albany, *Chairman.*
B. H. PADDOCK, D.D., Bp. of Massachusetts.
S. BENEDICT, D.D.
H. W. NELSON, JR., *Secretary.*
HENRY COPPÉE, LL.D.
JAMES S BIDDLE.
W. K. ACKERMAN.

NOTE.

At a meeting of the Committee on the Revision of the Hymnal, held in New York on the 13th and 14th of June, 1889, this preliminary Report was amended as follows:

(a) By striking out Hymns Nos. 4, 8, 29, 30, 49, 82, 84, 85, 93, 124, 132, 146, 149, 162, 165, 169, 172, 186, 213, 231, 237, 246, 383, 403, 411, 419, 430, 432, 452, 475, 479, 480, 505, 521, 523, 545, 556, 558, 561, 579, 585, 589, 608, 611, 620, 621, 636, 641.

(b) By restoring from the present Hymnal the following:

D.C.M.

1 Once more, O Lord, Thy sign shall be
  Upon the heavens displayed,
  And earth and its inhabitants
  Be terribly afraid;
  For, not in weakness clad, Thou com'st,
  Our woes, our sins to bear,
  But girt with all Thy Father's might,
  His judgment to declare.

2 The terrors of that awful day,
  Oh, who can understand?
  Or who abide, when Thou in wrath
  Shalt lift Thy holy hand?
  The earth shall quake, the sea shall roar,
  The sun in heaven grow pale;
  But Thou hast sworn, and wilt not change,
  Thy faithful shall not fail.

3 Then grant us, Saviour, so to pass
  Our time in trembling here,
  That when upon the clouds of heaven
  Thy glory shall appear,
  Uplifting high our joyful heads,
  In triumph we may rise,
  And enter, with Thine angel train,
  Thy palace in the skies.

2 Still through the cloven skies they come,
  With peaceful wings unfurled;
  And still their heavenly music floats
  O'er all the weary world;
  Above its sad and lowly plains
  They bend on hovering wing,
  And ever o'er its Babel sounds
  The blessed angels sing.

3 O ye, beneath life's crushing load,
  Whose forms are bending low,
  Who toil along the climbing way
  With painful steps and slow!
  Look now, for glad and golden hours
  Come swiftly on the wing;
  Oh, rest beside the weary road,
  And hear the angels sing.

4 For lo, the days are hastening on,
  By prophets seen of old,
  When with the ever-circling years,
  Shall come the time foretold,
  When the new heaven and earth shall own
  The Prince of Peace their King,
  And the whole world send back the song
  Which now the angels sing.

C.M.

D.C.M.

1 It came upon the midnight clear,
  That glorious song of old,
  From angels bending near the earth
  To touch their harps of gold;
  Peace on the earth, good-will to men,
  From heaven's all-gracious King;
  The world in solemn stillness lay
  To hear the angels sing.

1 Calm on the listening ear of night
  Come heaven's melodious strains,
  Where wild Judea stretches far
  Her silver-mantled plains.

2 Celestial choirs from courts above
  Shed sacred glories there;
  And angels, with their sparkling lyres,
  Make music on the air.

APPENDIX.

3 The answering hills of Palestine
　Send back the glad reply;
　And greet, from all their holy heights,
　The Day-spring from on high.

4 O'er the blue depths of Galilee
　There comes a holier calm,
　And Sharon waves in solemn praise,
　Her silent groves of palm.

5 "Glory to God!" the sounding skies
　Loud with their anthems ring,
　"Peace to the earth, good-will to men,
　From heaven's eternal King!"

6 Light on thy hills, Jerusalem!
　The Saviour now is born!
　And bright on Bethlehem's joyous plains
　Breaks the first Christmas morn.

S. M.

1 The ancient law departs
　And all its terrors cease;
　For Jesus makes with faithful hearts
　A covenant of peace.

2 The Light of Light divine,
　True Brightness undefiled,
　He bears for us the shame of sin,
　A holy, spotless Child.

3 To-day the Name is Thine,
　At which we bend the knee;
　They call Thee Jesus, Child divine!
　Our Jesus deign to be.

10s.

1 Rise, crowned with light, imperial Salem, rise;
　Exalt thy towering head and lift thine eyes;
　See heaven its sparkling portals wide display,
　And break upon thee in a flood of day.

2 See a long race thy spacious courts adorn,
　See future sons, and daughters yet unborn,
　In crowding ranks on every side arise,
　Demanding life, impatient for the skies.

3 See barbarous nations at thy gates attend,
　Walk in thy light, and in thy temple bend;
　See thy bright altars thronged with prostrate kings,
　While every land its joyous tribute brings.

6

4 The seas shall waste, the skies to smoke decay,
　Rocks fall to dust, and mountains melt away;
　But fixed His word, His saving power remains;
　Thy realm shall last, thy own Messiah reigns.

7s.

1 Forty days and forty nights
　Thou wast fasting in the wild;
　Forty days and forty nights
　Tempted and yet undefiled.

2 Shall not we Thy sorrow share,
　And from earthly joys abstain,
　Fasting with unceasing prayer,
　Glad with Thee to suffer pain?

3 And if Satan, vexing sore,
　Flesh or spirit should assail,
　Thou, his Vanquisher before,
　Grant we may not faint or fail.

4 So shall we have peace divine;
　Holier gladness ours shall be;
　Round us, too, shall angels shine,
　Such as ministered to Thee.

5 Keep, oh, keep us, Saviour dear,
　Ever constant by Thy side;
　That with Thee we may appear
　At th' eternal Eastertide.

L. M.

1 My God, permit me not to be
　A stranger to myself and Thee:
　Amidst a thousand thoughts I rove,
　Forgetful of my highest love.

2 Why should my passions mix with earth,
　And thus debase my heavenly birth?
　Why should I cleave to things below,
　And all my purest joys forego?

3 Call me away from flesh and sense;
　Thy grace, O Lord, can draw me thence;
　I would obey the voice divine,
　And all inferior joys resign.

8s.

1 Weary of wandering from my God,
　And now made willing to return,
　I hear and bow me to the rod;
　For Thee, not without hope, I mourn;
　I have an Advocate above,
　A friend before the throne of love.

APPENDIX.

2 O Jesus, full of pardoning grace,
   More full of grace than I of sin;
   Yet once again I seek Thy face:
   Open Thine arms and take me in;
   And freely my backslidings heal,
   And love the faithless sinner still.

3 Thou know'st the way to bring me back,
   My fallen spirit to restore:
   Oh, for Thy truth and mercy's sake,
   Forgive, and bid me sin no more:
   The ruins of my soul repair,
   And make my heart a house of prayer.

C. M.

1 Come, Holy Spirit, heavenly Dove,
   With all Thy quickening powers;
   Kindle a flame of sacred love
   In these cold hearts of ours.

2 See how we grovel here below,
   Fond of these earthly toys:
   Our souls, how heavily they go,
   To reach eternal joys.

3 In vain we tune our lifeless songs,
   In vain we strive to rise:
   Hosannas languish on our tongues,
   And our devotion dies.

4 Come, Holy Spirit, heavenly Dove,
   With all Thy quickening powers;
   Come, shed abroad a Saviour's love,
   And that shall kindle ours.

C. M.

1 Blest day of God! most calm, most bright,
   The first, the best of days:
   The laborer's rest, the saint's delight,
   The day of prayer and praise.

2 My Saviour's face made thee to shine;
   His rising thee did raise,
   And made thee heavenly and divine
   Beyond all other days.

3 The first-fruits oft a blessing prove
   To all the sheaves behind;
   And they the day of Christ who love,
   A happy week shall find.

4 This day I must with God appear;
   For, Lord, the day is Thine;
   Help me to spend it in Thy fear,
   And thus to make it mine.

L. M.

1 Another six days' work is done,
   Another Lord's day has begun;
   Return, my soul, enjoy thy rest,
   Improve the hours thy God hath blest.

2 This day may our devotion rise,
   As grateful incense to the skies;
   And heaven that sweet repose bestow,
   Which none but they who feel it know.

3 This peaceful calm within the breast
   Is the sure pledge of heavenly rest,
   Which for the Church of God remains,
   The end of cares, the end of pains.

4 In holy duties, let the day,
   In holy pleasures pass away;
   How sweet a Sabbath thus to spend,
   In hope of one that ne'er shall end!

L. M.

1 Jesus, and shall it ever be,
   A mortal man ashamed of Thee?
   Ashamed of Thee, Whom angels praise,
   Whose glories shine through endless days?

2 Ashamed of Jesus! sooner far
   Let night disown each radiant star;
   'Tis midnight with my soul, till He,
   Bright Morning Star, bid darkness flee.

3 Ashamed of Jesus! oh, as soon
   Let morning blush to own the sun;
   He sheds the beams of light divine
   O'er this benighted soul of mine.

4 Ashamed of Jesus! that dear friend
   On Whom my hopes of heaven depend!
   No; when I blush, be this my shame,
   That I no more revere His Name.

5 Ashamed of Jesus! empty pride!
   I'll boast a Saviour crucified;
   And oh, may this my portion be,
   My Saviour not ashamed of me.

P. M.

1 I think when I read that sweet story of old,
   When Jesus was here among men,
   How He called little children as lambs to His fold,
   I should like to have been with them then.

APPENDIX.

2 I wish that His hands had been placed on my head,
That His arm had been thrown around me,
And that I might have seen His kind look when He said,
" Let the little ones come unto Me."

3 Yet still to His footstool in prayer I may go,
And ask for a share in His love;
And if I thus earnestly seek Him below,
I shall see Him and hear Him above.

4 In that beautiful place He has gone to prepare
For all who are washed and forgiven;
And many dear children shall be with Him there,
For "of such is the kingdom of heaven."

5 But thousands and thousands who wander and fall,
Never heard of that heavenly home;
I wish they could know there is room for them all,
And that Jesus has bid them to come.

L. M.

1 Father of mercies, how Thine ear,
Attentive to our earnest prayer:
We plead for those who plead for Thee;
Successful pleaders may they be!

2 How great their work, how vast their charge!
Do Thou their anxious souls enlarge;
Their best acquirements are our gain;
We share the blessings they obtain.

3 Clothe, then, with energy divine
Their words, and let those words be Thine;
To them Thy sacred truth reveal,
Suppress their fear, inflame their zeal.

4 Teach them to sow the precious seed;
Teach them Thy chosen flock to feed;
Teach them immortal souls to gain,
Souls that will well reward their pain.

5 Let thronging multitudes around
Hear from their lips the joyful sound;
In humble strains Thy grace implore,
And feel Thy now-creating power.

6 Let sinners break their massy chains,
Distressèd souls forget their pains;
Let light through distant realms be spread,
And Sion rear her drooping head.

8

L. M.

1 With one consent let all the earth
To God their cheerful voices raise;
Glad homage pay with awful mirth,
And sing before Him songs of praise.

2 Convinced that He is God alone,
From Whom both we and all proceed;
We, whom He chooses for His own,
The flock that He vouchsafes to feed.

3 Oh, enter then His temple gate,
Thence to His courts devoutly press:
And still your grateful hymns repeat,
And still His Name with praises bless.

4 For He's the Lord, supremely good,
His mercy is for ever sure;
His truth, which always firmly stood,
To endless ages shall endure.

C. M.

1 Now from the altar of our hearts
Let flames of love arise;
Assist us, Lord, to offer up
Our evening sacrifice.

2 Minutes and mercies multiplied
Have made up all this day;
Minutes came quick, but mercies were
More swift, more free than they.

3 New time, new favors, and new joys
Do a new song require;
Till we shall praise Thee as we would,
Accept our hearts' desire.

C. M.

1 There is a fountain filled with blood
Drawn from Emmanuel's veins;
And sinners plunged beneath that flood
Lose all their guilty stains.

2 The dying thief rejoiced to see
That fountain in his day;
And there may I, as vile as he,
Wash all my sins away.

3 Dear, dying Lamb, Thy precious blood
Shall never lose its power,
Till all the ransomed Church of God
Be saved to sin no more.

APPENDIX.

4 E'er since, by faith, I saw the stream
   Thy flowing wounds supply,
   Redeeming love has been my theme,
   And shall be till I die.

5 Then in a nobler, sweeter song,
   I'll sing Thy power to save.
   When this poor, lisping, stammering tongue
   Lies silent in the grave.

7s.

1 Come, my soul, thy suit prepare;
   Jesus loves to answer prayer;
   He Himself has bid thee pray,
   Therefore will not say thee, Nay.

2 Thou art coming to a King:
   Large petitions with thee bring;
   For His grace and power are such,
   None can ever ask too much.

3 With my burden I begin:
   Lord, remove this load of sin;
   Let Thy blood, for sinners spilt,
   Set my conscience free from guilt.

4 Lord, I come to Thee for rest;
   Take possession of my breast;
   There Thy blood-bought right maintain,
   And without a rival reign.

5 While I am a pilgrim here,
   Let Thy love my spirit cheer;
   As my guide, my guard, my friend,
   Lead me to my journey's end.

6 Show me what I have to do;
   Every hour my strength renew;
   Let me live a life of faith,
   Let me die Thy people's death.

C. M.

1 Oh, for a closer walk with God,
   A calm and heavenly frame:
   A light to shine upon the road
   That leads me to the Lamb.

2 Return, O holy Dove, return,
   Sweet messenger of rest;
   I hate the sins that made Thee mourn,
   And drove Thee from my breast.

3 The dearest idol I have known,
   Whate'er that idol be,
   Help me to tear it from Thy throne,
   And worship only Thee.

4 So shall my walk be close with God,
   Calm and serene my frame;
   So purer light shall mark the road
   That leads me to the Lamb.

S. M.

1 Come, ye that love the Lord,
   And let your joys be known;
   Join in a song with sweet accord,
   And thus surround the throne.

2 Let those refuse to sing
   That never knew our God,
   But children of the heavenly King
   May speak their joys abroad.

3 The God of heaven is ours,
   Our Father and our love;
   His care shall guard life's fleeting hours,
   Then waft our souls above.

4 There shall we see His face,
   And never, never sin;
   There, from the rivers of His grace,
   Drink endless pleasures in.

5 Yes, and before we rise
   To that immortal state,
   The thought of such amazing bliss
   Shall constant joys create.

6 Children of grace have found
   Glory begun below;
   Celestial fruits on earthly ground
   From faith and hope may grow.

7 The hill of Sion yields
   A thousand sacred sweets,
   Before we reach the heavenly fields,
   Or walk the golden streets.

8 Then let our songs abound,
   And every tear be dry;
   We're travelling through Emmanuel's ground,
   To fairer worlds on high.

C. M.

1 God moves in a mysterious way
   His wonders to perform:
   He plants His footsteps in the sea,
   And rides upon the storm.

APPENDIX.

2 Deep in unfathomable mines,
   With never-failing skill,
   He treasures up His bright designs,
   And works His sovereign will.

3 Ye fearful saints, fresh courage take;
   The clouds ye so much dread
   Are big with mercy, and shall break
   In blessings on your head.

4 Judge not the Lord by feeble sense,
   But trust Him for His grace;

   Behind a frowning providence
   He hides a smiling face.

5 His purposes will ripen fast,
   Unfolding every hour:
   The bud may have a bitter taste,
   But sweet will be the flower.

6 Blind unbelief is sure to err,
   And scan His work in vain;
   God is His own interpreter,
   And He will make it plain.

By adding from other sources the following, viz.:

L.M.

1 Lord, speak to me, that I may speak
   In living echoes of Thy tone;
   As Thou hast sought, so let me seek,
   Thy erring children lost and lone.

2 Oh, lead me, Lord, that I may lead
   The wandering and the wavering feet;
   Oh, feed me, Lord, that I may feed
   Thy hungering ones with manna sweet.

3 Oh, strengthen me, that while I stand
   Firm on the Rock, and strong in Thee,
   I may stretch out a loving hand
   To wrestlers with the troubled sea.

4 Oh, teach me, Lord, that I may teach
   The precious things Thou dost impart;
   And wing my words, that they may reach
   The hidden depths of many a heart.

5 Oh, give Thine own sweet rest to me,
   That I may speak with soothing power
   A word in season, as from Thee,
   To weary ones in needful hour.

6 Oh, fill me with Thy fullness, Lord,
   Until my very heart o'erflow
   In kindling thought and glowing word,
   Thy love to tell, Thy praise to show.

7 Oh, use me, Lord, use even me,
   Just as Thou wilt, and when, and where;
   Until Thy blessèd face I see,
   Thy rest, Thy joy, Thy glory share.

7.6.

1 From glory unto glory! Be this our joyous
   song;
   As on the King's own highway, we bravely
   march along.
   From glory unto glory! O word of stirring
   cheer,
   As dawns the solemn brightness of another
   glad New Year.

2 From glory unto glory! What great things
   He hath done,
   What wonders He hath shown us, what triumphs He hath won!
   From glory unto glory! What mighty
   blessings crown
   The lives for which our Lord hath laid His
   own so freely down!

3 The fullness of His blessing encompasseth
   our way;
   The fullness of His promises crowns every
   bright'ning day;
   The fullness of His glory is beaming from
   above,
   While more and more we learn to know the
   fullness of His love.

4 And closer yet and closer the golden bonds
   shall be,
   Uniting all who love our Lord in pure sincerity;
   And wider yet and wider shall the circling
   glory glow,
   As more and more are taught of God that
   mighty love to know.

APPENDIX.

5 Oh, let our adoration for all that He hath done,
Peal out beyond the stars of God, while voice and life are one;
And let our consecration be real, deep, and true:
Oh, even now our hearts shall bow, and joyful vows renew.

6 Now onward, ever onward, from strength to strength we go,
While grace for grace abundantly shall from His fullness flow,
To glory's full fruition, from glory's foretaste here,
Until His very presence crown our happiest New Year.

C. M.

1 Oh, for a thousand tongues to sing
My blest Redeemer's praise,
The glories of my God and King,
The triumphs of His grace!

2 Jesus, the Name that charms our fears,
That bids our sorrows cease;
'Tis music in the sinner's ears,
'Tis life, and health, and peace.

3 He speaks; and listening to His voice,
New life the dead receive,
The mournful, broken hearts rejoice,
The humble poor believe.

4 Hear Him, ye deaf; His praise, ye dumb,
Your loosened tongues employ;
Ye blind, behold your Saviour come:
And leap, ye lame, for joy!

5 My gracious Master and my God,
Assist me to proclaim
And spread through all the earth abroad
The honors of Thy Name.

C. M.

1 Lord, it belongs not to my care
Whether I die or live;
To love and serve Thee is my share,
And this Thy grace must give.

2 If life be long, oh, make me glad
The longer to obey;
If short, no laborer is sad
To end his toilsome day.

3 Christ leads me through no darker rooms
Than He went through before;
And he that to God's kingdom comes
Must enter by this door.

4 Come, Lord, when grace hath made me meet
Thy blessèd face to see:
For if Thy work on earth be sweet,
What will Thy glory be?

5 Then I shall end my sad complaints
And weary, sinful days,
And join with the triumphant saints
That sing my Saviour's praise.

6 My knowledge of that life is small,
The eye of faith is dim;
But 'tis enough that Christ knows all,
And I shall be with Him.

10s.

1 Peace, perfect peace, in this dark world of sin?
The blood of Jesus whispers peace within.

2 Peace, perfect peace, by thronging duties pressed?
To do the will of Jesus, this is rest.

3 Peace, perfect peace, with sorrows surging round?
On Jesus' bosom naught but calm is found.

4 Peace, perfect peace, with loved ones far away?
In Jesus' keeping we are safe, and they.

5 Peace, perfect peace, our future all unknown?
Jesus we know, and He is on the Throne.

6 Peace, perfect peace, death shadowing us and ours?
Jesus has vanquished death and all its powers.

7 It is enough: earth's struggles soon shall cease,
And Jesus call us to Heaven's perfect peace.

10s.

1 Thou, who at Thy first Eucharist didst pray,
That all Thy Church might be for ever one,
Grant us at every Eucharist to say
With longing heart and soul, "Thy will be done."

11

APPENDIX.

Oh, may we all one Bread, one Body be,
Through this blest Sacrament of Unity.

2 For all Thy Church, O Lord, we intercede;
Make Thou our sad divisions soon to
cease;
Draw us the nearer each to each, we plead,
By drawing all to Thee, O Prince of Peace;
Thus may we all one Bread, one Body be,
Through this blest Sacrament of Unity.

3 We pray Thee, too, for wanderers from Thy
fold;
Oh, bring them back, good Shepherd of
the sheep,
Back to the faith which saints believed of
old,
Back to the Church which still that faith
doth keep;
Soon may we all one Bread, one Body be,
Through this blest Sacrament of Unity.

4 So, Lord, at length when Sacraments shall
cease,
May we be one with all Thy Church above,
One with Thy saints in one unbroken peace,
One with Thy saints in one unbounded
love;
More blessèd still, in peace and love to be
One with the Trinity in Unity.

7.6.

1 O Father, bless the children
Brought hither to Thy gate;
Lift up their fallen nature,
Restore their lost estate;

Renew Thy image in them,
And own them, by this sign,
Thy very sons and daughters,
New born of birth divine.

2 O Jesus, Lord, receive them;
Thy loving arms of old
Were opened wide to welcome
The children to Thy fold;

Let these, baptised, and dying,
Then rising from the dead,
Henceforth be living members
Of Thee, their living Head.

3 O Holy Spirit, keep them;
Dwell with them to the last,
Till all the fight is ended,
And all the storms are past.

Renew the gift baptismal,
From strength to strength, till each,
The troublous waves o'ercoming,
The land of life shall reach.

4 O Father, Son, and Spirit,
O Wisdom, Love, and Power,
We wait the promised blessing
In this accepted hour!

We name upon the children
The Threefold Name divine;
Receive them, cleanse them, own them,
And keep them ever Thine.

10.10.7.

1 Lord of the harvest! it is right and meet
That we should lay our first-fruits at Thy
feet
With joyful Alleluia!

2 Sweet is the soul's thanksgiving after
prayer;
Sweet is the worship that with heaven we
share,
Who sing the Alleluia!

3 Lowly we prayed, and Thou didst hear on
high;
Didst lift our hearts and change our suppliant cry
To festal Alleluia!

4 So sing we now in tune with that great
song,
That all the age of ages shall prolong,
The endless Alleluia!

5 To Thee, O Lord of harvest, Who hast
heard
And to Thy white-robed reapers given the
word,
We sing our Alleluia!

6 O Christ, Who in the wide world's ghostly
sea
Hast bid the net be cast anew, to Thee
We sing our Alleluia!

APPENDIX.

7 To Thee, eternal Spirit, Who again
  Hast moved with life upon the slumbrous
    main,
      We sing our Alleluia!

8 Yea, West and East the companies go
    forth:
  "We come!" is sounding to the South
    and North:
      To God sing Alleluia!

9 The fishermen of Jesus far away
  Seek in new waters an immortal prey:
    To Christ sing Alleluia!

10 The holy Dove is brooding o'er the deep,
   And careless hearts are waking out of
    sleep;
      To Him sing Alleluia!

11 Yea, for sweet hope new-born, blest work
    begun,
   Sing Alleluia to the Three in One,
      Adoring Alleluia!

12 Glory to God! the Church in patience
    cries;
   Glory to God! the Church at rest replies,
      With endless Alleluia!

7.6.

1 O Thou before Whose presence
  Naught evil may come in,
  Yet Who dost look in mercy
  Down on this world of sin:
  Oh, give us noble purpose
  To set the sin-bound free,
  And Christ-like, tender pity
  To seek the lost for Thee.

2 Fierce is our subtle foeman:
  The forces at his hand,
  With woes that none can number,
  Despoil the pleasant land;
  All they who war against them,
  In strife so keen and long,
  Must in their Saviour's armor
  Be stronger than the strong.

3 So hast Thou wrought among us
  The great things that we see!
  For things that are we thank Thee,
  And for the things to be:

  For bright Hope is uplifting
  Faint hands and feeble knees,
  To strive beneath Thy blessing
  For greater things than these.

4 Lead on, O Love and Mercy,
  O Purity and Power!
  Lead on till peace eternal
  Shall close this battle-hour:
  Till all who prayed and struggled
  To set their brethren free,
  In triumph, meet to praise Thee,
  Most Holy Trinity.

8.7.8.8.7.

1 Oh, the bitter shame and sorrow,
   That a time could ever be
  When I let the Saviour's pity
  Plead in vain, and proudly answered,
   'All of self, and none of Thee.'

2 Yet He found me: I beheld Him
   Bleeding on th' accursèd tree;
  Heard Him pray, "Forgive them, Father;"
  And my wistful heart said faintly,
   'Some of self, and some of Thee.'

3 Day by day His tender mercy,
   Healing, helping, full and free,
  Sweet and strong, and ah! so patient,
  Brought me lower, while I whispered,
   'Less of self, and more of Thee.'

4 Higher than the highest heavens,
   Deeper than the deepest sea.
  Lord, Thy love at last has conquered;
  Grant me now my soul's desire,
   'None of self, and all of Thee.'

S.M.

1 Far down the ages now,
  Her journey well-nigh done,
  The pilgrim Church pursues her way,
  And longs to reach her crown.

2 No wider is the gate,
  No broader is the way,
  No smoother is the ancient path,
  That leads to light and day.

3 No feebler is the foe,
  No slacker grows the fight,
  Nor less the need of armor tried,
  Of shield and helmet bright.

APPENDIX.

4 Thus onward still we press,
   Through evil and through good,
  Through pain, or poverty, or want,
   Through peril, or through blood.

5 Still faithful to our God,
   And to our Captain true,
  We follow where He leads the way,
   The kingdom still in view.

7.6.

1 Praise to the heavenly Wisdom
  Who knows the hearts of all,
  The saintly life's beginnings,
   The traitor's secret fall:

  Our own ascended Master,
   Who heard His Church's cry,
  Made known His guiding presence,
   And ruled her from on high.

2 Elect in His foreknowledge
   To fill the lost one's place,
  He formed His chosen vessel
   By hidden gifts of grace:

  Then, by the lots disposing,
   He lifted up the poor,
  And set him with the Princes
   On high for evermore.

3 For on the golden breastplate
   Of our great Priest above,
  Twelve are the stones that glisten
   As throbs that heart of love;

  And twelve the fair foundations
   Of Salem's jasper wall;
  And twelve the thrones predestined
   Within her judgment-hall.

4 No mystic gem is lacking
   In that divine array;
  No empty throne shall darken
   The glory of that day;

  For lo! on Twelve the Spirit,
   The Father's promise, came;
  And Twelve went forth together
   To preach the saving Name.

5 Still guide Thy Church, chief Shepherd;
   Her losses still renew;
  Be Thy dread keys entrusted
   To faithful hands and true;

  Apostles of Thy choosing
   May all her rulers be,
  That each with joy may render
   His last account to Thee!

7s.

1 Winter reigneth o'er the land,
   Freezing with its icy breath:
  Dead and bare the tall trees stand;
   All is chill and drear as death.

2 Yet it seemeth but a day
   Since the summer flowers were here,
  Since they stacked the balmy hay,
   Since they reaped the golden ear.

3 Sunny days are past and gone:
   So the years go speeding fast,
  Onward ever, each new one
   Swifter speeding than the last.

4 Life is waning; life is brief;
   Death, like winter, standeth nigh:
  Each one, like the falling leaf,
   Soon shall fade, and fall, and die.

5 But the sleeping earth shall wake,
   And the flowers shall burst in bloom,
  And all nature, rising, break
   Glorious from its wintry tomb.

6 So, Lord, after slumber blest,
   Comes a bright awakening,
  And our flesh in hope shall rest,
   Of a never-fading Spring.

C.M.

1 Lord Jesus, on the holy mount
   We would abide with Thee,
  Still drinking from the blessed fount
   Of grace, so rich and free.

2 There prophets praise Thy glorious Name,
   And deeds which Thou hast done,
  And there the Father's words proclaim
   His own beloved Son.

3 The rays of Thy transfigured face
   Beam with such golden light,
  That we would never leave the place
   Nor lose the heavenly sight.

4 But there is work on earth to do,
   The suffering soul to heal;
  The harvest great, the laborers few
   Thy Kingdom to reveal.

THE HYMNAL, Revised and Enlarged. Being t. Preliminary Report of the Committee on the Hymnal, Appointed by the General Convention of 1886. [New York: James Pott & Co.]

We have great pleasure in acknowledging the receipt of this important volume. The committee are to be congratulated on having reached the end of their two and a half years labor, and we shall look forward with interest to their final and full report, which they do not now present.

We are struck first by the size of this hymn book. It is larger than the one now in use, but not than later English hymnals. The lines of revision and enlargement are plain to be seen. The work of the committee has been especially directed toward making a distinction in classification between hymns for special and common use. Larger provision has been made for holy days and special events, and a greater variety is furnished for the larger festival seasons.

The appendix made by the committee contains hymns particularly suited for country parishes and mission stations. There are also selections adapted for personal use and times of affliction. A generous space has been given to the requirements of Sunday-schools and parochial missions, so as to obviate the necessity for special hymnals.

The care and toil spent on this volume, the definite aims which the committee have had in view, the deliberation with which they have accomplished one of the most difficult of tasks, entitle them to the thanks of the Church. We have only had time, so far, to glance over their goodly volume, and we feel that it is best to defer to future notices the results of a detailed examination of its contents; such an examination is due to the committee, whose work will be best helped by candid and conscientious criticism.

Alleluia ! Alleluia !
For He hath closed hell's yawning door,
Heaven is open evermore:
Hence with sadness;
Sing with gladness
Alleluia !

Alleluia ! Alleluia !
{ Lord, by Thy wounds we call on Thee,
   So from death to set us free,
owly. { That our living
   Be thanksgiving !
Alleluia !

foundly interested listeners are not tightl[y] curbed in ritualistic leading strings, an[d] actually have the hardihood to "enjoy thei[r] selves" at a "solemn music" in the Lord['s] house. The Champion conveniently ignore[s] the lusty mirth of his early prototypes, som[e] of whom even " danced mightily before th[e] Lord," amid the shrill clamor and strepitatio[n] of all manner of orchestral accompaniment.

These "St. John services" have been vigo[r]ously taken up by Mr. George Edward Stubb[s] whose thoroughly trained choir and richl[y] elaborated monthly festival " Evensongs[,] have transplanted much of the popular enth[u]siasm once glowing at St. John's to S[t.] James's church, Madison Avenue.

They have developed an almost embarras[s]ing popular success which has threatened [to] suffocate the regular congregation of that n[ot] very large church with literally a crush [of] attendance, choking up aisles, all standi[ng] room, the great vestibule and all the a[p]proaches to such an extent that the choir w[as] unable to "proceed" and " recede" in liturg[ic] order, and were driven to find way to t[he] chancel furtively as best they could. But t[his] very crush proves among other good thin[gs]

APPENDIX.

5 We may not linger on the mount,
  Where bright Thy glories shine;
  We may not taste the sacred fount
  Of blessedness divine:

6 But let some beams of heavenly light
  Make bright our earthly way;
  Then grant the beatific sight
  Of heaven and endless day.

P. M.

1 I heard a sound of voices
  Around the great white throne,
  With harpers harping on their harps
  To Him that sat thereon;
  "Salvation, glory, honor!"
  I heard the song arise,
  As through the courts of heaven it rolled
  In wondrous harmonies.

2 From every clime and kindred,
  And nations from afar,
  As serried ranks returning home
  In triumph from a war,
  I heard the saints upraising,
  The myriad hosts among,
  In praise of Him Who died and lives,
  Their one glad triumph-song.

3 I saw the holy city,
  The New Jerusalem,
  Come down from heaven a bride adorned
  With jewelled diadem;
  The flood of crystal waters
  Flowed down the golden street;
  And nations brought their honors there,
  And laid them at her feet.

4 And there no sun was needed,
  Nor moon to shine by night,
  God's glory did enlighten all,
  The Lamb Himself the light;
  And there His servants serve Him,
  And, life's long battle o'er,
  Enthroned with Him, their Saviour, King,
  They reign for evermore.

5 O great and glorious vision!
  The Lamb upon His throne;
  O wondrous sight for man to see!
  The Saviour with His own:
  To drink the living waters
  And stand upon the shore,
  Where neither sorrow, sin, nor death
  Shall ever enter more.

6 O Lamb of God Who reignest!
  Thou Bright and Morning Star,
  Whose glory lightens that new earth
  Which now we see from far.
  O worthy Judge eternal!
  When Thou dost bid us come,
  Then open wide the gates of pearl,
  And call Thy servants home.

L. M.

1 Thy Temple is not made with hands,
  'Tis lit by many a golden star;
  The purple heights of mountain lands
  Its everlasting pillars are.

2 Thee, highest heaven cannot contain,
  Great Lord of earth, and sky, and sea!
  Yet enter in, and bless the fane
  Adoring hands have reared for Thee.

3 [*Unworthy gift and touched with fears,
  And memories of our loved at rest;
  Draw nigh, O Lord, and dry our tears,
  And be Thy presence here confest.]

4 For welcome to the babe new born,
  For strengthening hands on bended head,
  For blessings on the marriage morn,
  And sweet words whispered o'er the dead;

5 For food divine to souls sufficed,
  For words that warn, for prayers that press,
  Arise and enter in, O Christ!
  And with Thy presence all things bless.

6 So praise to Thy great Name shall rise
  Up from these walls, this sacred floor,
  Who made, Who saves, Who sanctifies,
  For ever and for evermore.

7s.

1 Jesus, cast a look on me,
  Give me sweet simplicity;
  Make me poor and keep me low,
  Seeking only Thee to know:

2 Weanèd from my lordly self,
  Weanèd from the miser's pelf,
  Weanèd from the scorner's ways,
  Weanèd from the lust of praise.

* To be used of a memorial church.

APPENDIX.

3 All that feeds my busy pride,
Cast it evermore aside;
Bid my will to Thine submit,
Lay me humbly at Thy feet.

4 Make me like a little child,
Of my strength and wisdom spoiled;
Seeing only in Thy light,
Walking only in Thy might:

5 Leaning on Thy loving breast,
Where a weary soul may rest;
Feeling well the peace of God,
Flowing from Thy precious blood.

6.6.4.

1 When the bright morn I see,
My soul I lift to Thee,
Jesus, my King,
E'er in my heart abide,
Each day till eventide,
With comforting.

2 So in night's lonely hour,
Be my protecting power:
On Thee I lean.
Turn Thou my heart to praise,
E'en through life's troubled ways,
And sorrows keen.

3 Thus by no ill beguiled,
O Father! keep Thy child:
Thy spirit pour;
That to some weary heart
Thy love I may impart,
Thine aid implore.

4 Lift me with soaring wings,
Musing on holy things,
Earth's cares above.
Grant me Thy grace, to win
If but one soul, from sin
To Jesus' love.

(c) By the following changes, viz.:

No. 16, vs. 1, line 1, "ere" and "was" for "when" and "did."
No. 20, vs. 4, substitute:
 "Be Thou nigh, should death o'ertake us;
 Jesus then our refuge be,
 And in Paradise awake us,
 There to rest in peace with Thee."
No. 23, vs. 2, line 3, "call" for "trump."
No. 35, vs. 1, line 1, "now that" for "and now."
After 64. Add to first-line references the following:
"No. 443. All praise to Thee, eternal Lord."
No. 64, vs. 4, line 2, "who've" for "who have."
No. 97, vs. 2, line 2, "cross" for "death."
No. 104, by omission of vss. 5, 6, 7, 8, 9.
No. 118, vs. 1,
 "thy terrors now
 Can no longer, death, appal us."
No. 158, by omission of vs. 3.
No. 191, vs. 1, line 1, and vs. 2, line 1, read:
 "For all Thy saints, O Lord."
No. 198, vs. 1. line 2, "his" for "your."
No. 235, D.L.M. for 8s, and omit vs. 5.
No. 236, omit vss. 5, 6, 7.

No. 241, substitute plain type for italics.
No. 249, omit vs. 3.
No. 316, vs. 1, line 2, "sins" for "crimes."
No. 367, omit vs. 3.
No. 386, vs. 2, line 2, "passing" for "pressing."
No. 400, vs. 3, substitute:
 "The sacred, sevenfold grace is Thine,
 Dread Finger of the Hand divine!
 The promise of the Father Thou!
 Who dost the tongue with power endow."
No. 424, reverse order of vss. 3 and 4, and transfer vs. 5 to end of Hy. 426.
No. 447, vs. 2, substitute plural pronouns.
No. 459, vs. 4, line 6, "We praise Thee" for "Thee we praise."
No. 483, vs. 1, line 4, "sky" for "blue;" vs. 2, line 1, "wakes" for "makes."
No. 583, vs. 3, line 4, read "Make us, take us, keep us Thine."
No. 630, vs. 3, lines 2 and 3, "Thou hast."
No. 640, vs. 2, line 7, "let" for "your."
No. 657, vs. 4, line 4, omit "is" after "heaven."
No. 670, vs. 1, line 2, read "Hear us ere the hour of rest."

By striking out the heading "Christian Life" and distributing the hymns under it elsewhere, according to subject.

By transferring Hymn 350 to "Children's Services and Sunday-Schools." and Hymn 253 to "Home and Personal Use." By omitting all Amens.

APPENDIX.

The following is the arrangement, in the final report, of hymns restored from the present Hymnal; and of additional hymns adopted from other sources:

Present Hymnal					Preliminary Report			
8		to go after	42	319				
22	" "	" "	160	320	" "			
26	" "	" "	61	321	" "			
32	" "	" "	148	322	" "			
36	" "	" "	504	323	" "	} in their order	after 374
49	" "	" "	82	324	" "		
57	" "	"	378	325	" "		
70	" "	" "	619	326	" "		
128	" "	" "	617	327	" "		
149	" "	" "	28	328	" "		
158	" "	before	31	329	" "	before 617
218	" "	" "	622	380	" "	" 375
226	" "	after	584	331	" "	after 653
271	" "	" "	257	382	" "	} before 374
277	" "	in place of	489	333	" "
347	" "	to go after	670	334	" "	after 433
383	" "	" "	619	335	" "	" 434
401	" "	" "	672	336	" "	" 436
435	" "	" "	676	337	" "	" 447
402	" "	" "	471	338	" "	" 463
502	" "	" "	530	339	" "	{ " 670
336 Ancient and Modern	" "	" "	647	340	" "
485	" "	" "	307	341	" "	" 437
522	" "	" "	470	342	" "	{
504	" "	" "	504	343	" "	" 522
535	" "	" "	655	344	" "	}
537	" "	" "	522	345	" "	before 412
558	" "	" "	212	346	" "	" 524
563	" "	" "	280	347	" "	{
587	" "	" "	281	348	" "	after 411
607	" "	before	524	349	" "	}
613	" "	after	157	350	" "	" 593
631	" "	" "	618	351	" "	" 517
64 Church Hymns	" "	" "	533	352	" "	" 637
"Lord Jesus, on the holy Mount"	" "	171	353	" "	} " 674
"I heard a sound of voices"	" "	544	354	" "
"Thy Temple is not made with hands"	" "	270	355	" "
"Jesus cast a look on me"	" "	078	356	" "	" 686
"When the bright morn I see"	" "	664	357	" "
				378	" "	" 616

253 Preliminary Report		to go after	687
316	" "	" "	86
317	" "	" "	619
318	" "	" "	672

N. B.—There are three Hymns to go after 619. They go in the following order: No. 70 from Present Hymnal; 317, Preliminary Report; and 383, Present Hymnal. There are also three to go after 670. These go in the following order: 347, Present Hymnal; 339 and 340, Preliminary Report.

A number of verbal corrections and some changes in order were also made, which, it is hoped, may be incorporated in a perfect copy of this Report, to be issued in readiness for the assembling of the General Convention in October next.

H. W. NELSON, JR.,

Secretary.

www.ingramcontent.com/pod-product-compliance
Lightning Source LLC
Chambersburg PA
CBHW020755230426
43666CB00007B/706